Y0-BYZ-124

THE HANDBOOK OF FIRST MORTGAGE UNDERWRITING

THE HANDBOOK OF FIRST MORTGAGE UNDERWRITING

A STANDARDIZED METHOD FOR THE COMMERCIAL REAL ESTATE INDUSTRY

PRECEPT CORPORATION

McGRAW-HILL

New York Chicago San Francisco Lisbon London Madrid Mexico City
Milan New Delhi San Juan Seoul Singapore Sydney Toronto

McGraw-Hill

A Division of The ***McGraw-Hill*** *Companies*

1 2 3 4 5 6 7 8 9 0 DOC/DOC 0 7 6 5 4 3 2 1

ISBN 0-07-138887-7

Printed and bound by R. R. Donnelley & Sons Company.

To contact Precept Corporation, call or write: Precept Corporation, 5375 Mira Sorrento Place, Suite 540, San Diego, CA 92121, (858) 404-6100; fax (858) 404-6101.

McGraw-Hill books are available at special quantity discounts to use as premiums and sales promotions, or for use in corporate training programs. For more information, please write to the Director of Special Sales, Professional Publishing, McGraw-Hill, Two Penn Plaza, New York, NY 10121-2298. Or contact your local bookstore.

This book is printed on recycled, acid-free paper containing a minimum of 50% recycled deinked fiber.

This book is dedicated to two groups of people who are, in many ways, alike.

The first group includes those who sat patiently through our presentations over the past three years, challenged our business model, and, once satisfied, went on to champion Precept within their firms. These firms have invested their precious time and resources to become our investors, strategic partners, lenders, mortgage bankers, brokers, and borrowers. Each has been crucial to Precept's development. While Precept is proud to be affiliated with such prestigious companies, it is the "corporately courageous" and progressive innovators who stood up, summoned their firms to action, and made Precept a reality. Not surprisingly, these are the same people who have directed the evolution of this industry in the past, and I expect they will continue to do so in the future.

The second group of people includes Precept employees, consultants, and board members, who have tirelessly served Precept through equity market volatility, capitalization uncertainty, and the natural frustrations of developing a new way of transacting business.

Tony Adams
Dana Allen
Tanya Anderson
Heather Archer
Erika Baldwin
Michelle Bava
Justin Bert
Scott Bois
Bruce Bradshaw
Cary Carpenter
Diane Conniff
Kathy Corton
Julie de Bourbon
Marc de Bourbon
Sepp Dobler
Pamela 11
John Faraola
Tony Fineman
Lauren FitzGerald
Ryan Gilbert
Carolyn Goldman
Keith Harrison
Nathan Hart
Joseph Heil
Aminah Jeffrey
Niels Johnson
Angie Kim
Michael Klein
Svetlana Kuk
John McGlynn
Daniel Meeks
David O'Connor
Kurt Pollem
Emma Ramos
Steven Rivers
Raymond Schalk
Bruce Skogen
Camilla Solomon
Angela Strauss
Norris Thompson
Chris Tokarski
Richard Turney
Michael Van Konynenburg
Jennifer Vetrovec
Stewart Ward
Terry Wellman
Kahlil Yearwood
Emily Zacharias

Each of these individuals has contributed to what Precept is as an operating platform, as an environment for innovative thought, and as the collective assembly of working relationships dedicated to the redefinition of an industry. The thousands of decisions involved in everything from designing our financing auctions to determining the subject matter covered in this book have been based on their input; their efforts have served as a vital source of personal reinspiration when my own energy levels have waned.

Frank Scavone
Chief Executive Officer
Precept Corporation

CONTENTS

FOREWORD

"Necessity, who is the mother of invention."

Plato

PRELUDE TO CHANGE

As Plato's famous observation suggests, much noteworthy progress is driven by unsatisfactory circumstances. This certainly seemed to be the case in the commercial real estate finance industry during the late 1980s and early 1990s. The culmination of several severe factors, including a real estate recession and a sudden absence of capital, ignited the effort to finally develop a more liquid marketplace for commercial real estate debt.

The foundation for liquidity in any asset class results from the existence of certain universal standards on which all transaction participants can rely. Prior to the start of the Resolution Trust Corporation (RTC)'s takeover and dismantling of the savings and loan industry in 1989, no one lender or other industry participant was driving standard underwriting or origination methodologies.

The RTC, with the help of the investment banks and statistical rating agencies, developed standards for the massive undertaking of pooling and selling the savings and loan assets. The combined effect of this dismantling and the prevailing state of the real estate market was a shortage of commercial real estate debt providers, exacerbating the decline of real estate values.

Into this void stepped Wall Street's investment banks. They began using the newly developed financing structures and marketplace to make loans directly to the real estate community. Unlike the RTC-controlled assets, Wall Street dealt with new loan originations. Rating agency–driven underwriting standards influenced the methodologies Wall Street employed. By the end of the 1990s, about 25% of all outstanding commercial mortgages had been underwritten to rating agency–defined transaction standards, thus initiating standard underwriting practices for new originations.

Through the mid-1990s, the commercial lending market continued to develop underwriting and loan origination standards. As securitized lending market share increased, traditional portfolio lending practices began to migrate toward these standards. However, the transition was again disrupted. Capital market lenders, risking operating margins in the face of industry competition, were caught off guard by outside economic factors that dramatically wrenched the market. As early as the spring of 1998, it became apparent that the capital markets were in a new squeeze. Gross profit margins of securitization were under pressure, while at the same time the costs of maintaining a commercial loan origination platform were escalating. The combination of these two factors seriously eroded profits in the capital markets lending arena. By the arrival of autumn that year, a flight to more secure investments established the outer bounds for the volatility of commercial real estate debt structures. The global debt crunch was a day of reckoning for the existing securitization market. It proved that potential profits could easily be overwhelmed by the risk of holding loans for eventual securitization. The investment banks retracted as commercial mortgage-backed securities spreads widened. This resulted in serious damage to securitization infrastructure as jobs were lost and lending groups disbanded. Perhaps of greater importance was the severely strained relationship with the precious product-delivery channels—the mortgage bankers—that had been created during the prior six years. Not unlike the beginning of the decade, market dynamics had once again accentuated the need for enhanced liquidity.

CURRENT ISSUES

Both commercial mortgage-backed securities (CMBS) originators, chastened by the events of the late 1990s, and other lenders are now very focused on finding ways to operate more efficiently and at reduced expense. Of necessity, they are now scrutinizing the costs associated with sourcing and originating because lending profit margins have been compressed too low. Eventually, as part of this evaluation, CMBS originators will have to face the question of outsourcing. It is most ironic that most Wall Street firms are wringing their hands over the outsourcing. After all, it was these same firms that argued so passionately during the development of the CMBS market that the life companies should be willing to part with their own origination teams and simply buy CMBS. Irony aside, a solution is needed for all participants that will relieve the high costs, including particularly dead-deal risks associated with originating and processing loans, while at the same time facilitating high-quality capital commitment decisions. The wider effect of such a solution will be enhanced market liquidity and acceleration of the evolution of lenders to investors. As investors, lenders can be relieved of validating and processing the instruments (mortgages) in which they invest. In addition, CMBS lenders can turn their balance sheets at significantly greater velocity.

STANDARD & POOR'S VISION

Standard & Poor's (S&P) became involved with Precept Corporation because S&P had worked with many of Precept's principals over the years, from its days at companies such as Nomura, Dechert, and the Capital Company of America. Precept has developed a loan origination platform that combines such high-quality outsourcing with a very sophisticated auction. Unlike the revolutionary advent of securitization, Precept's solution is far more subtle. However, the work required to implement the solution was enormous and could only have been performed by industry experts. What Precept proposed was novel, interesting, and made rational sense. The premise, and the result, is a reversed transaction sequence, whereby complete underwriting of the loan occurs prior to pricing. In theory, this should result in the most efficient origination process for lenders and the most competitive deal terms for borrowers. The notion of participating in such a revolutionary industry solution is consistent with S&P's historic role as an industry innovator.

Outsourcing of the origination process can have an impact on the rating agencies. What S&P likes about the outsourcing concept is that the work of the agency is incorporated early in the origination process. Currently, lenders do not typically price loans based on an actual rating agency evaluation, but rather on the expectations of rating agency conclusions at the later time of securitization. Inherent in the traditional process was that the lender incorporate a "buffer" to cope with the possibility that subordination level expectations will prove wrong. This historic methodology is flawed, and, for that and other reasons, the mortgage originator is not able to make an informed pricing decision on a loan-by-loan basis. This weakness undoubtedly increases the cost of financing to the true customer in the scenario: the borrower.

S&P's perspective is that rating agency services have become commoditized and industry participants want something more than a credit rating. S&P's mission is to add value in a different way by reapplying its analytical expertise and market knowledge. The Precept process provides S&P with a means to add value for originators; drive down the cost of capital for borrowers; and, for the first time in the history of the industry, embrace the primary distribution channel, which is the mortgage banking community.

With Precept, S&P evaluates each loan that is going up for auction to provide a *second independent opinion* of underwritten net cash flow. The resultant benefit is that these issuers, or lenders, have this information prior to making a capital commitment and pricing decision. Thus, they can originate and aggregate in anticipation of securitizing, fully confident of S&P's conclusions about the cash flows that will drive subordination levels. This is particularly useful because, as you know, it takes time to attain a critical mass of loans. An evaluation from S&P, as part of the Precept process, is good for six months. If the loan is brought to market for securitization within that six-month period, it does not have to be reevaluated. In addition, S&P has agreed to credit the cost of each preorigination evaluation to the cost of pool securitization. Therefore, this new process saves CMBS originators time and money and reduces the risk of conducting business.

THE PRACTICAL REALITY OF NECESSARY CHANGE

While consumers of all sorts have a natural affinity for reverse auctions, the implementation of outsourcing will undoubtedly take a while to catch on—in our view, probably as much as a year or two. In general, the real estate finance industry is not quick to embrace technology. The industry is slow moving and the Precept business premise, while apparently simple, involves the support of a new infrastructure that not everyone will immediately understand, however compelling. Adding to the challenge, outsourcing certain lender activities naturally requires that certain lender staff be shifted into different roles—a characteristic in the Precept concept that, because it is threatening to some, might hinder its near-term adoption rate. This necessitates that the Precept message be understood by, and then spread among, the most senior and forward-thinking members of the community. Mortgage bankers, critical participants in the Precept process, have been highly resistant to technology-driven enhancements. This is no small wonder as the tech finance companies that have come and gone, admittedly or not, sought disintermediation.

Regardless of the obstacles, the industry still needs a solution. The real estate debt market is still highly inefficient compared with other asset classes. Many venture-capital-enabled firms recognized the opportunity existent in this market, but failed to capitalize on it—in some respects, actually delaying the in-house development of solutions. While this served to elevate general disillusionment with the notion of technology-driven advancement in some instances, it merely whetted appetites in others. The process of originating a commercial mortgage loan is as complex as the unique nature of the underlying collateral, and it is unlikely with the technology sector in its current state of chaos that any new entrants will be afforded the opportunity to simplify it.

Precept has developed a well-coordinated, standardized process for sourcing, originating, underwriting, closing, and placing a loan. Benefiting from diversified endorsement and investment from some of the most respected names in the industry, Precept has maintained an objective and independent position, essential to the existence of the type of business model Precept represents: a business-to-business exchange with a credible collateral evaluation mechanism. Another critical characteristic is that the *baseline* of information delivered through the system provides ample data for making capital commitment decisions, without diminishing the lenders' ability to draw their own conclusions. Employing a simple reversal of the transaction sequence, lender efficiency is dramatically increased. Given Wall Street's current-day employment game of musical chairs, origination efforts are not as tight as firms would like them to be, and the Precept process will likely offer a welcome, more consistent origination product. Finally, the misappropriated fear of disintermediation by the mortgage banking community should be mitigated by Precept's effort to identify and actively court this group as its indirect sales force.

The benefits of the Precept process are tangible, indeed compelling, and all ultimately flow to the consumer of capital: the borrower. As in all businesses, it is the customer that drives change. In periods of limited capital supply, change can be hampered by those participants that benefit from the existence of inefficiencies, fragmentation, and lack of transparency. The additional "friction" created by these negative market characteristics reduces liquidity and hinders real estate real and relative values. Gradually, faster information delivery systems will decrease the duration of such periodic capital supply limitations, and those participants who have embraced the tools of efficient execution will prevail in the long term. To the lending community, Precept has the potential to be one of the most important of these tools.

Precept's next and greatest challenge is to process adequate product volume. Pricing transparency, and a more practical method of complete market coverage, is finally possible as a result of the recent progress made by the mortgage industry, furthered by the operating platform created by Precept. Thus, it is very important to the mortgage banking community and its clients that Precept succeed.

Gale Scott
Managing Director
Standard & Poor's

INTRODUCTION

This manual articulates a single set of standards for the collection, validation, and analysis of the information necessary to underwrite commercial real estate debt. Specifically, this manual covers first mortgage origination for stabilized hospitality, mobile home community, multifamily, office and industrial, and retail properties.

This manual was originally written as part of the Precept Corporation business platform, because a set of methodologies like it did not already exist within the community. This platform is built around the core idea that commercial real estate underwriting can be performed in a dramatically more efficient and standardized way than the way that it is performed today. Essentially, the Precept model is that underwriting should be performed before lenders make pricing decisions and that it should be done in a way that is universally comprehensible. These standards also must be universally used. Toward this end, Precept has provided its standards to the entire community so that every real estate participant can use them and enjoy all of the efficiencies that result from their existence.

The concept of "standardization" is often misunderstood and loosely applied. Some clarity is needed on this subject. Standardization is much more than a standard set of underwriting definitions. For the purposes of this manual, *standardization* means that the author has developed a single set of rules that dictate every aspect of data collection, validation, analysis, and presentation. Let's consider each topic separately:

- *Data collection.* When a lender underwrites a loan, the lender typically collects thousands of different pieces of information. This information could be collected during any of the various phases of an underwriting, whether it's the site inspection, appraisal, environmental report, engineering report, review of financial statements, review of credit information, lease review, or a variety of other phases. This manual dictates specifically what information should be collected and where that information should be recorded. Let's look at an example:

Site inspection. When an underwriter visits a property and performs a site inspection, he or she might visit the property for hours or even days. The thoroughness of the inspection can vary greatly. Similarly, even where a thorough inspection is completed, the inspecting underwriter might record the information in any number of ways, from a written narration of notes, to a short checklist, to an exhaustive list. This manual sets forth exactly what information must be gathered and provides a specific form to record this information. The net result of this is that the site inspection report can be a predictable and consistent deliverable. All subsequent readers of the report will know exactly what they are getting, what they are not getting, and how to interpret and use the information it contains.

There are dozens of other examples contained in this manual.

- *Data validation.* When a lender collects all of the information necessary to underwrite a loan, steps need to be taken to make sure that the information is accurate. Different lenders may use different methods to validate the information; some may use a higher standard than others. The consequence of this is that borrowers are required to provide varying degrees of supplemental information, thus preventing rating agencies and potential loan investors from being sure of the quality of the information that they are receiving. This manual sets forth standard guidelines as to which data should be validated and how it should be validated. For example, this manual discusses reconciliation of operating expenses to federal tax returns, operating statements to bank statements, operating statements and rent rolls to leases, annual occupancy numbers to point-in-time occupancy numbers in the rent rolls, management fees in operating statements to the management contract, utilities in operating expenses to actual utility bills, real property expenses in the operating statements to real property tax bills, and a variety of other data validation techniques.
- *Data analysis.* Two lenders who collect the exact same data and validate the data in the exact same way can, nevertheless, analyze that data differently and come up with two significantly different cash flow numbers. For example, if a property has not been assessed for real estate taxes in the last 20 years, one lender might rely on the actual tax bill when underwriting, while another

might impute the taxes that would be paid if the property were reassessed. A third party looking at the numbers may not understand how the two lenders' approaches differ. This manual lays out a specific underwriting methodology that would dictate how the lender should look at the problem, clarifying for third parties what they are looking at. Also, if the lender does not choose to follow the approach set forth in this manual, the lender can simply follow its own approach and note any exceptions to the procedure. Thus, lenders will have required flexibility and third parties will have a useful benchmark to work from.

- *Data presentation.* When a lender collects the thousands of different pieces of data necessary to underwrite a loan, the lender needs a single, reliable, comprehensive, and consistent "container" and display or interface for the information. If no such container exists, the lender will not have a useful data repository from which to make analytical and credit decisions. Further, if a third party such as a servicer or rating agency needs access to the information, the third party will want access to the data in a consistent, coherent form. The third party will also want the information presented in a model or display interface that can be modified, manipulated, and updated with future information. If all lenders summarize the information differently, each subsequent reader is subject to the vagaries of each underwriter's summary protocol. This manual sets forth a summary template—the underwriting summary, which breaks down the information into logical categories that are easily reviewed. The template is set forth in a model that can be manipulated, modified, and updated. The model is also prepared in a way that enables the user to easily trace the underwriting conclusions back to the underlying data. The user no longer has to spend hours trying to reconcile underwriting conclusions to source documents.

This manual contains three different forms of underwriting summary: (1) multifamily and mobile home parks; (2) retail, office, and industrial (commercial); and (3) hospitality. Each underwriting summary consists of standard sections with varying content and additional supporting schedules depending on the land use. The standard sections are:

1. Executive Summary
2. Cash Flow Summary

3. Operating Statement Reconciliation
4. Property Description
5. Appraisal Report Summary
6. Property Condition Assessment Summary
7. Environmental Site Assessment Summary
8. Borrower Credit Summary
9. Underwriting Exceptions

Let's consider an example of how the underwriting summary is used. When a lender evaluates a borrower's credit history, the lender might collect a myriad of potential pieces of information: personal credit reports, business credit reports, bank references, credit records, bankruptcy records, litigation records (including judgments as well as pending litigation), tax lien records, and Uniform Commercial Code (UCC) filings. Furthermore, the lender might collect this information on any one of a number of entities or individuals who comprise the borrower. This information is typically obtained from third parties in a variety of different formats and could easily fill an entire file. The Borrower Credit section of the underwriting summary provides an easily readable, logical, well-organized place where this information can be stored on a single page. Any reader will know in advance what has been searched, where it has been searched, what type of information is being flagged, and what people are being researched.

USING THE MANUAL

This manual is not a textbook that can be used to teach someone how to underwrite commercial real estate loans; instead it provides real estate professionals, who have a working knowledge of lending issues, with a framework that can be consistently applied to any lending situation. Following a rigid underwriting process with a clear procedure for documenting exceptions ultimately provides those who receive the underwriting results with work products that can be compared and analyzed on equal terms. Standardization of underwriting cannot replace customized analysis; however, customized analysis should be issue specific. This manual does create a comprehensive uniform process to collect and organize the available information into a consistent starting point from which to begin the analysis and decide which issues require particular attention or might be outside the scope of a standardized underwriting.

The standards set forth in this manual have been developed by Precept Corporation. However, these standards could be used by any lender. As a result, this manual describes how Precept underwrites loans, but readers should assume that these procedures could easily be adopted by them. In various places throughout this manual, capitalized terms are used and then later defined. When you see a capitalized term, please refer to the definition later in the chapter.

THE HANDBOOK OF FIRST MORTGAGE UNDERWRITING

CHAPTER 1

Site Inspection Report

Inspecting the physical real estate and its market are fundamental to a mortgage lender's determination of whether to make a financial commitment and to what extent.

However, there is currently little consistency in the commercial real estate lending industry with respect to site inspections and related reporting. While the industry has developed uniform standards for the completion of other key components of real estate underwriting, including valuation, environmental, and engineering analysis, nothing similar exists for site inspections. (The Mortgage Bankers Association has recently developed a standard inspection form, but it has yet to receive widespread adoption.) This fact is particularly ironic given the significance of the site inspection to prudent lending decisions.

For some industry participants, the site inspection consists of a two-hour exercise which includes a drive-by review of the property and its surroundings. For others, it means a comprehensive market economic analysis, including the inspections of comparable properties. Some lenders rely on the site inspection performed by the appraiser in conjunction with the preparation of the appraisal report to fulfill their site visit requirements. Other lenders conduct a separate site inspection but do not document the results in a material way. Even where lenders have documented site inspection scope requirements, the content, organization, and presentation are unique to each lender. In some cases, the results are even unique to individual banking groups within a lender. The magnitude of the variances in the data elements, including their organization and presentation, make it difficult for rating agencies, bond buyers, and servicers to efficiently evaluate details in a meaningful manner.

The site inspection is the essential link between financial and property analysis. The importance of the site inspection, on the most basic level, is to make sure the property actually exists. Beyond that, the site inspection process plays a key role in determining to what extent the property possesses the physical characteristics and management to compete within its market, based on its ability to meet the needs of current and future tenants. It is the underwriter's opportunity to assess the manager's experience and competency, while obtaining answers to detailed questions pertaining to the property's operating history, physical condition, and tenancy; the manager's history with the property; etc. Given the critical nature of its content, the site inspection should be performed early in the underwriting process so that the underwriter can conduct the bulk of its due diligence with the benefit of the site inspection results.

Of equal importance is the site inspection report itself. This is due to the need of the underwriter and loan funding decision makers to repeatedly reference the results of the site inspection throughout the loan origination process. The site inspection report should act as a repository for all information collected during the inspection. It should be organized in such a way that its contents are meaningful and easily accessed. The site inspection should be performed in accordance with a documented scope in order to ensure complete and efficient capture and dissemination of the related data elements. The need for a documented scope is highlighted by the simple realities of inspecting commercial real estate for loan origination.

The site inspection often represents the only time that the underwriter will see the property and have face-to-face contact with the manager, maintenance personnel, tenant, leasing personnel, area brokers, competitive property personnel, local planning department staff, etc. Moreover, given that the average length of a site inspection is between one and two days, the underwriter's interview of these individuals will likely be brief. Therefore, it is critical to the success of the site inspection that the inspector prepare scripted questions in advance of the site visit and then document the results in an organized manner.

Frequently, the site inspection is not performed by the underwriter directly, or at least not by the individuals responsible for making loan commitment decisions. In this case, the data obtained during the site visit has to be passed from the inspector to the decision makers. The potential for miscommunication is exacerbated given how a great deal of the information the site inspector obtains is verbally communicated during the interview process. As such, certain data elements are being passed from one individual to another at least two or three times before the party making the financial commitment is even involved. This highlights the necessity for a documented scope from which the inspector can conduct the site investigation. With a documented scope, the inspector is required to treat the site inspection report like any other third-party report, given that it is to be self-contained, complete, and coherent. Sufficiently detailed, it prevents the site inspector from passing on conclusions that are derived from anecdotal or unsubstantiated information, often provided by interviewees.

Of course, the existence of a documented scope neither eliminates inaccuracies and miscommunication nor ensures completeness. Furthermore, the existence of a documented scope does not minimize the importance of the inspector's qualifications. However, it does provide a framework from which to evaluate the site inspection performed and from which to identify errors or omissions in the site inspection and reporting processes. For example, most underwriters have experienced the frustration of reading an appraisal report that draws a market rent conclusion for the subject property without providing a clear reconciliation of the conclusion to rental comparables outlined within the same report. The existence of an appraisal scope which requires clear reconciliation of rental comparables to market rent conclusions makes the appraiser's shortfalls easy to identify for correction.

Ultimately, certain components of the site inspection report, such as the property description itself, will need to be extracted for inclusion into the overall underwriting summary. For example, rental comparables identified by the inspector will need to be presented with those identified by the appraiser, and all other relevant sources, in order for the underwriter to draw market rental rate conclusions. Whether this process is automated or not, it is abundantly more efficient if the report from which the information is being extracted is standardized into data fields that contain individual elements of the analysis. This further demonstrates the need for standardized reporting of site inspection information. Along with the conclusions of the appraisal, environmental, and engineering reports, the salient results of the site inspection, summarized in the context of all other due diligence, will place the underwriter in the best position to make an overall assessment of the collateral, its management, and its sponsorship.

CONDUCTING THE SITE INSPECTION

The first step of the site inspection is to prepare questions for the property's on-site and off-site management personnel. Many of the questions are scripted by the site inspection form itself, but others need to be developed through a review of the property's physical and operating histories, as well as available market information. Reviewing as much information as possible prior to the site visit itself results in abundantly more accurate and meaningful analysis.

Site Visit Preparation

Fundamental to this preparation is a review of the property's current rent roll and most recent three-year operating statements. A working knowledge of these documents will allow the inspector to reconcile the tenancy observed during the site inspection and to clarify any operating abnormalities during interviews of management personnel. For example, a review of the subject operating statements might reveal that a large capital expense was incurred recently. Knowing this ahead of time would allow the inspector to ask questions specifically about the expenditure, view the actual capital improvement, and verify that the expense was consistent with the physical improvement made. This type of review is abundantly more accurate than if the inspector simply asks whether any capital improvements were made in the recent past. Likewise, visual observation is more meaningful for the inspector than oral and written explanations alone. Accordingly, as much as possible of the site inspection report should be completed in preparation for the site visit and then revised as conclusions are developed.

Other important areas of preparation are as follows:

- *Existing third-party reports.* To the extent that the appraisal, environmental, and/or property condition reports have been prepared prior to the site inspection, each should be reviewed in its entirety prior to the site visit. This will allow the inspector to visually confirm the salient findings of each report and assess the relevance of each report's conclusion to the overall underwriting.
- *Competition.* The inspector should attempt to understand how the property compares to the other competitive properties in the submarket. This is a critical first step in defining the property's *competitive set,* on which market rental rates and occupancy levels are based. Property management is often a primary resource in

helping to define a subject's competitive set. Furthermore, having both the initial list of competitive properties and the results of the property manager interview regarding those and other properties, the inspector is best prepared to venture into the submarket to complete the review and develop conclusions regarding market competition.

- *Demand generators.* Developing some working knowledge of the property's reported demand generators prior to the site inspection will allow the inspector to ask pointed questions of area brokers and leasing and marketing personnel with respect to the subject's primary sources of demand. The ease of obtaining such information has been extended greatly by the proliferation of the Internet.
- *New supply.* It is often very difficult for an underwriter to access a potential new supply and its relevant impact on a subject property over the course of months, let alone a two-day site inspection. Perceptions of the potential impact of new supply often vary greatly. As a result, it is essential that the underwriter actually view the location and current progress of as much new supply as possible. Making phone calls to local building and planning departments to determine development status makes much more sense prior to the site visit than afterward.

Interviewing Management

The site visit itself should really begin with an interview of management personnel. Scheduling the site inspection so that the right people are able to attend will likely save the inspector hours in follow-up calls. In addition, it is important that this interview take place early in the site visit so that the inspector can frame the issues expected to require special attention prior to actually inspecting the property.

PRECEPT'S SITE INSPECTION

Precept organizes the site inspection into the following categories, and each is addressed in the Precept Site Inspection Report:

A. *Identification.* Basic information used to determine if the property is the one specified to be underwritten. Individual components of the identification section are property name and address, contact information, and affiliation.

B. *Property description.* In-depth categorization of the building's physical characteristics, including description of units and unit mix, size, construction details, parking, and operating system. Additional information required includes comprehensive listing of property amenities, location qualities, management information, and demographic and tenant concentrations.
C. *Exterior condition.* Checklist and ratings guide concerning key exterior factors (e.g., landscaping, paving, façade, signage, etc.).
D. *Interior condition.* Checklist and ratings guide concerning key interior factors (e.g., overall quality of interior, flooring, lighting, etc.).
E. *Property rental data.* Depending on type of property, a concise breakdown of information about renters, tenants, or guests, and the units required to house them. Among the many pieces of information needed here are items such as asking rents, occupancy, number of employees, deposits, leasing activity, etc.
F. *Neighborhood.* A more descriptive section of the report used to ascertain the nature of the geography and developments surrounding the building to be underwritten. Information to be gathered includes, among other items, major off-site demand generators, neighborhood description, and other relevant facts.
G. *New construction.* A listing and compilation of standard information about competitive buildings that are in the planning or development stage. Key data include such items as location, distance from building to be underwritten, number of units, and estimated completion date.
H. *Comparable properties.* An in-depth listing and compilation of data pertaining to existing, competitive buildings within the market area of the building to be underwritten. This information can be separated into two sections: property description (e.g., address, number of units, unit mix, etc.) and rental information (e.g., rates, historical turnover percentage, and concessions).
I. *General summary of property.* Descriptive summation of the general market, the competitiveness of the building to be underwritten, and other relevant comments.

USING THE SITE INSPECTION REPORTS

The site inspection reports are customized for three land categories of land use: (1) multifamily and mobile home; (2) commercial (industrial, office, and retail); and (3) hospitality. As a result, generalized headings also require information specific to the asset classes. For example, the interior condition section in multifamily asks for ratings on kitchen cabinets, carpet, vinyl, etc. For the commercial section, ratings are needed for restaurants or food courts, service areas, elevators, etc. And, for hospitality, ratings are needed for items such as heating and cooling units, restaurant-lounge-bar equipment, exercise equipment, etc.

In addition to the standardized forms for each property type, a number of attachments are also included in the manual:

- For multifamily land uses, attachments are included for service contracts and historical and planned capital expenditures.
- For commercial land uses, attachments are included for service contracts, historical and planned capital expenditures, tenant rollover history, tenant status, and unusual lease provisions.
- For hospitality land uses, attachments are included for service contracts and historical and planned capital expenditures.

For the purpose of providing an example, the commercial site inspection form and attachments have been completed here with sample data. The site inspection form and corresponding attachments for hospitality and multifamily land uses are included in blank form.

SITE INSPECTION REPORT
Commercial

Property Name: Village Square Center

Financing Number: 0128
Property Number: 0238

Property Type: Retail
Property Class (A,B,C): B

Date Performed: 01/08/2001

A. IDENTIFICATION

1. Property:

Property Name	Village Square Center						
Address	1330 Pacific Street						
City	Bellingham	County	Whatcom	State	Washington	Zip	98225
Cross Street	Lakeway						

2. Property Contact Information:

Contact/ Title	Ms. Greta Sustain	How long has contact been affiliated with the Property?	5 years
Company Name	Northwest Management	Address	250 30th Street
Phone	360-676-6025	City	Bellingham
Fax	360-676-6001	State	Washington
Email	gsustain@nmco.com	Zip	98225

B. PROPERTY DESCRIPTION

Property Type Use Category (Check One):

[ ]	Office		CBD or suburban...(high rise, mid rise, low rise) Multitenant, Single Tenant, Professional/Medical, etc.
[X]	Retail	Neighborhood Center	Anchored...(Neighborhood Center, Community Center, Power Center, Factory Outlet, Mall) or Unanchored...(Single Tenant, Strip, Specialty)
[ ]	Industrial		Bulk Distribution/Warehouse, Flex/R&D, Light Manufacturing, Heavy Manufacturing

1. **Property Attributes:**

			Source
a.	Year built	1969	Manager
b.	Year last renovated	1991	

c. Scope of renovation:

New roof, new HVAC, new exterior/interior paint, parking lot resurfaced, new lighting in some spaces.

d. Size

		Source
Gross SF	128,451	Manager
Net rentable SF	128,451	
Total land area (acres)	9.24	
Excess land area (acres)	4.12	
Number of buildings	3	
Number of floors	1	
Number of elevators	0	
Number of entrances	3	
Average floorplate SF		

e. Buildout

		Source
Office (%)		Manager
Retail (%)	100.0%	
Warehouse (%)		
Specify other (%)		

f. Construction Details

		Source
Exterior facade (brick, wood, etc.)	Concrete and wood	Manager
Roof type (pitched, flat, mixed)	Flat	
Roof material (shingle, gravel, tile)	Gravel	
Structure (conc. tilt-up, metal, etc.)	Concrete and metal	
Sprinklered (yes / no) and type	Yes	

g. Parking

		Source
Type (e.g., surface, garage, offsite, etc.)	Surface	Manager
Total parking spaces	948	
Open parking	948	
Covered parking spaces	0	
Parking ratio (parking/1,000 NRSF)	7.38	
Parking charge (hrly, dly, mnthly, etc.)	N/A	

h. Other (Industrial space only)

		Source
Ceiling clear height		
Typical bay size		
Distance between columns		
Total number of doors		
- *number on grade*		
- *number of dock high*		
Number of dock levelers		
Rail access (yes / no)		
Truck court radius		
Tenant electricity sub-metered?		

SITE INSPECTION REPORT
Commercial

Property Name: Village Square Center

Financing Number: 0128
Property Number: 0238

Property Description:

A 128,451 sf retail neighborhood anchored strip center located in Bellingham, Washington. It is anchored by a 56,314 sf Haggens Grocery Store and a 36,060 sf Payless discount/drug store. The Haggens Grocery owns their own store and pad and is not part of the collateral. The total property sf is 184,765 (including Haggens) and was constructed in 1969 on 13.36 acres along Interstate 5 in Bellingham. The Borrowers purchased the property in 1991 for $5 million which did not have the grocery store at the time. By August, 1992 the Borrowers completed a total renovation and the Haggens grocery store was developed by Haggens. In 1995 an A&W fast food outparcel building was added under a ground lease.

2. Property Amenities:

a. Restaurant: Yes
b. Health club: No
c. Security: No
d. On-site manager: No
e. After hours entry system: No

Comments on Amenities (e.g., the general condition of the amenities, description of other amenities, etc.):

The property does not contain any special amenities besides landscaping, park benches, etc. The landscaping appears to be in good condition with a few of the planters needing a minor repair and some touch-up paint on the park benches.

3. Location:

a.	Corner	Yes	(yes, no)
b.	Traffic volume	Medium	(high, medium, low)
c.	Type of front street	Arterial	(arterial, collector, subdivision)
d.	Overall neighborhood appearance	Excellent	(excellent, good, average, poor)
e.	Access to major arteries	Good	(excellent, good, average, poor)
f.	Access to local amenities	Good	(excellent, good, average, poor)
g.	Street appeal	Good	(excellent, good, average, poor)
h	Ingress / Egress	Good	(excellent, good, average, poor)
i.	Ease of left hand turn into Property	Average	(excellent, good, average, poor)
j.	Visibility	Good	(excellent, good, average, poor)
k.	Signage	Excellent	(excellent, good, average, poor)
l.	Signage visibility at intersection	Excellent	(excellent, good, average, poor)
m.	Overall quality of the location	Good	(excellent, good, average, poor)
n.	Location's impact on the Property's ability to secure and retain tenants:	Positive	(positive, not distinguishable, negative)

Comments on Location:

The property is well located on the corner of Pacific and Lakeway. The surroundings are primarily residential and a few other smaller strip retail centers. The subject is a neighborhood center and serves a localized area at the south end of town. Notable neighborhood landmarks include Interstate 5, which is adjacent to the subject, and Western Washington University and its on-campus housing, within 1/4 mile.

4. Management Information:

Manager's Name	Ms. Greta Sustain	Address	250 30th Street
Title	Property Manager	City	Bellingham
Management Co.	Management Northwest	State	Washington
Phone	360-676-6025	Zip	98225
Fax	360-676-6001	Email/ Web Site	gsustain@nmco.com

a.	Management type (owner / outside contractor)	Outside
b.	Property Manager on site daily? (yes / no)	No
c.	If no, how often is site visited by Property Manager?	Once a week
d.	If yes, number of hours daily	
e.	Hours of operation open to tenants	Average 10 am to 8 pm
f.	Years Mgmt. Co. has been associated with Property?	5 years
g.	Does a related party of Mgmt. Co. own any portion of the Property? (if yes, please explain below)	No.
h.	Does the Mgmt. Co. manage other properties for the owner? (yes / no)	Yes
i.	Does the Mgmt. Co. manage other properties for other owner? (yes / no)	Yes
j.	Property Management fee	4.00%
k.	OBTAIN MANAGEMENT COMPANY RESUME	Yes

SITE INSPECTION REPORT
Commercial

Property Name: Village Square Center

Financing Number: 0128
Property Number: 0238

l. Property Management Company's history / experience:

Northwest Management has been active in property management since 1978. The company is owned by Mr. Ronald Oro. Managed properties are in Washington, Montana, and Idaho. Current actual management fee is 4% for nonanchor tenants and 1% for anchored tenants.

m. **PLEASE SEE ATTACHMENT 'A' FOR LIST OF CURRENT SERVICE CONTRACTS:**

5. Leasing Information:

Leasing Agent's Name	John Hegumund	Address	546 Luket Place, Suite 787
Title	Vice President	City	Bellevue
Leasing Company	Retail Leasing Inc.	State	Washington
Phone	206-566-8777	Zip	89745
Fax	206-566-8778	Email/ Web Site	jhegumund@retailleasing.com

a. Leasing Agent type (owner / outside contractor) — Outside
b. Leasing Agent on site daily? (yes / no) — No
c. If yes, number of hours daily — N/A
d. Years leasing Agent has been affiliated with Property? — 4 years
e. Does a related party of leasing agent own any portion of the Property? (if yes, please explain below)

No.

f. Does the Leasing Co. lease other properties for the owner? (yes / no) — Yes
g. Does the Leasing Co. lease other properties for <u>other</u> owner? (yes / no) — No
h. Total actual leasing commission for a new tenant — 5.50%
i. Total actual leasing commission for a renewal tenant — 2.75%
j. Are any of these fees split with other brokers? (if yes, please explain below):

Property manager typically handles renewals, and tenants represented by brokers split the commissions with Retail Leasing Inc.

k. Leasing Company history / experience:

Retail Leasing Inc., is an 18 year old company based in Bellevue, Washington. They lease and manage approximately 2.37 million square feet of retail and office in the greater Seattle area. John Hegumund has been with the firm for 11 years and handles several other shopping centers in the Bellingham area.

6. Other:

a. Comments on ADA compliance:

It appears a sufficient number of handicapped parking spaces (13), ramps, and door sizes sufficient for access to all tenant spaces are provided.

b. **PLEASE SEE ATTACHMENT 'B' FOR EXPLANATION OF HISTORICAL AND PLANNED CAPITAL EXPENDITURES**

SITE INSPECTION REPORT
Commercial

Property Name:	Village Square Center	Financing Number:	0128
		Property Number:	0238

C. EXTERIOR CONDITION

1.	Overall quality of the exterior:	Good	(excellent, good, average, poor)
2.	Landscaping:	Average	(excellent, good, average, poor)
3.	Adequacy of interior roads / parking:	Excellent	(excellent, good, average, poor)
4.	Roads:	Good	(excellent, good, average, poor)
5.	Paving:	Good	(excellent, good, average, poor)
6.	Adequacy of lighting:	Good	(excellent, good, average, poor)
7.	Paint:	Average	(excellent, good, average, poor)
8.	Windows:	Good	(excellent, good, average, poor)
9.	Roof:	Good	(excellent, good, average, poor)
10.	Walls:	Good	(excellent, good, average, poor)
11.	Façade:	Average	(excellent, good, average, poor)
12.	Signage:	Excellent	(excellent, good, average, poor)
13.	Store fronts (retail only):	Good	(excellent, good, average, poor)
14.	Amenities:	Good	(excellent, good, average, poor)
15.	Other (e.g., fountains, sculptures, etc.):	Average	(excellent, good, average, poor)
16.	Loading dock (industrial only):	Average	(excellent, good, average, poor)

Exterior Condition Comments:

Overall, exterior condition is good, but it is apparent that no renovation has occurred for 10 years. There is existing deferred maintenance.

D. INTERIOR CONDITION

1.	Overall quality of the interior:	Good	(excellent, good, average, poor)
2.	Restrooms:	N/A	(excellent, good, average, poor)
3.	Walls (paint / wall coverings):	Good	(excellent, good, average, poor)
4.	Flooring / Carpeting:	Good	(excellent, good, average, poor)
5.	Lobby / Common areas:	N/A	(excellent, good, average, poor)
6.	Elevators:	N/A	(excellent, good, average, poor)
7.	Lighting:	Excellent	(excellent, good, average, poor)
8.	Tenant area (typical office space / store space / or unit):	Good	(excellent, good, average, poor)
9.	Restaurant / Food court area:	Excellent	(excellent, good, average, poor)
10.	Mechanical areas:	Good	(excellent, good, average, poor)
11.	Ceilings:	Good	(excellent, good, average, poor)
12.	Doors:	Good	(excellent, good, average, poor)
13.	Service area (loading dock doors - industrial only):	Good	(excellent, good, average, poor)

Interior Condition Comments:

Average interior condition is good, but will need of renovation/modernization in the near future.

Describe deferred maintenance and Property Management's estimate cost to cure (exterior and interior):

1) Driveway/Parking - Repair, Slurry Seal, Restripe - $20,460
2) Truck Well Repair - Replace damaged concrete (space 400) - $4,300
3) Concrete Paving, Curb and Gutter Repair - Replace where needed - $3,300
4) Trash Dumpster Enclosure Repair - Repair - $200
5) Building Exterior - Repair T-111 siding, caulk and paint - $2,500
6) Roofing and Parapet - Repair roof drains and waterproof parapet - $2,500
7) Preventive Maintenance - Seal cap sheet metals at roof - $5,000
8) Drywall Soffit - Repair from roof leak (space 226) - $100
9)Ceiling Tiles - Replace water damaged tiles - $150

SITE INSPECTION REPORT
Commercial

Property Name: Village Square Center

Financing Number: 0128
Property Number: 0238

E. PROPERTY RENTAL DATA

Name of information source: Greta Sustain
How long has source been affiliated with the Property? 5 years
Company Name for source: Management Northwest
Phone: 360-676-6025
Email: gsustain@nmco.com

1. Current overall average effective rent (existing tenants): 13.80 $/SF
2. Vacancy as of (date): 01/12/2001 — 8,585 SF — 6.7 %
3. % of space rolling over in:
   12 months 7,171 | 6% — 24 months 4,000 | 3% — 36 months 0 | 0%
4. **PLEASE SEE ATTACHMENT 'C' AND 'D' FOR EXPLANATION OF PAST TENANT ROLLOVERS AND TENANT STATUS**
5. Asking rent ($/SF Monthly): Primary space: $12.72 Secondary space: $5.54
6. Rent structure (e.g., NNN, FSG, IG, Mod. Gross, etc.): NNN
   Comments on rent structure:
   Standard retail provisions
7. Concessions currently being offered: Minimal concessions and TIs are being offered: 1-2 mos. free rent for 3-5 yr lease
8. Average down time between leases: 1-2 months
9. New tenant improvement allowance: Range from zero to $2.50/sf depending upon the rental rate
10. Expense stop: Only one tenant has an expense stop in place
11. Lease terms offered: 3 - 10 years
12. Commissions: 5 - 10%
13. Percentage rent explained (if applicable):
    No percentage rent.
14. Pad space available for sale / lease / development: Yes — If so, approximate acres: 4.12 acres
15. **PLEASE SEE ATTACHMENT 'E' FOR EXPLANATION OF UNUSUAL LEASE PROVISIONS**

Property Rental Data Additional Comments:

Round Table Pizza and the A&W outparcel (Norrie & Assoc.) are at higher rents due to recovery of high tenant improvement costs related to restaurant construction. The Children's Co., Payless Drug Store, and JoAnn Fabrics have a lower rental rate due to larger space rented. The subject, as well as the market, are offering minimal rental concessions and tenant improvements. Rental concessions are typically 1 to 2 free months rent on a 3 to 5 year lease. TIs can range from zero to $2.50/sf depending upon the rental rate the tenant pays.

F. TENANT SUMMARY

1. Request Tenant Business resumes/financials: Yes (yes/no)
2. Tenant Summary Comments:
   Subject has 3 tenants with rents in the $18-$19 range. The rent range without these tenants is $12-$15.76. Rental rate range is for non-anchor space.

SITE INSPECTION REPORT
Commercial

Property Name:	Village Square Center	Financing Number: 0128 Property Number: 0238

G. NEIGHBORHOOD

1. Area: Suburban (urban, suburban, rural)
2. Development: 75% (fully developed, over 75%, 25% - 75%, under 25%)
3. Growth rate: Rapid (rapid, steady, slow)
4. Present use %: (should total 100%)

Single family	30%	Multi-family	25%	Commercial	15%
Industrial	15%	Vacant land	15%	Specify other	

5. Change in current use: Unlikely (unlikely / likely)
6. Major off-site demand generators:

Bellingham Demographics: Population: 1990 was 52,179; 1992 was 54,270; and 1999 was 57,830. As of 1999 this represented 39% of the total population of Whatcom County. Estimated median income in Whatcom County in 1999 was $37,082. -The county economy is diversified with 29% employed in wholesale and retail trade; 24% in services; 17% in government; 15% in manufacturing; and the remaining 15% in mining, construction, transportation, and finance/insurance/real estate. -Major employers in Bellingham include Western Washington University (1,429), St. Joseph Hospital (1,175), Bellingham School District (1,002),Georgia Pacific (857), and City & County government (1,300). -Demand generators include the surrounding residential population (adjacent), Western Washington University (1/2 mi. west), the Bellingham CBD (2 mi. north), and the port of Bellingham (1.5 mi. west).

7. Neighborhood Description (Describe immediate surrounding land uses, e.g., Apartment, Office, Industrial, Retail, Undeveloped Land, etc.):

The surrounding neighborhood consists of commercial development to the north (retail, office, hotel, etc.), and multifamily and single family residential development to the east, south, and west. Notable neighborhood landmarks include Interstate 5 which is adjacent to the subject, and Western Washington University and its on-campus housing, within 1/4 mile.

8. Other facts about the neighborhood that may affect, or potentially affect, the Property (e.g., thoroughfares, military base closings, etc.):

See "Property's competitiveness in the market" below.

H. NEW CONSTRUCTION (SUPPLY)

1. New Construction

Source	Project name	Location	Distance from	Est. SqFt	Est. Completion	Asking Rents	Lease Type	Status
Property Manager	Barkley Village	Bellingham	10 miles	150,000	12/1/00	$18-$19	NNN	Near completion

2. Comments on new supply and impact on the Property:

There are no new retail developments planned in the area per the Bellingham Planning Department. The only new project, which is not considered competitive, is Barkley Village.

H. COMPARABLE PROPERTIES

1. Property Description

	COMPARABLE 1	COMPARABLE 2	COMPAF
a. Identification:			
1. Name	Koll Cordata Center	Meridian Village	Sunset Square
2. Street address	1210 11th St.	240 36th St.	1307 E. Sunset Dr.
3. City, State	Bellingham, WA	Bellingham, WA	Bellingham, WA
4. Est. distance from Property	4.5 miles	4.25 miles	3 miles
b. Attributes:			
1. Estimated year built	1991	1979	1990
2. Estimated gross SF			
3. Estimated net SF	324,550	181,594	379,547
c. Major tenants:	Haggen	Brown & Cole Stores	Silver Beach Grocery
	Office Max	Griggs Stationers, Inc.	Linda B's
	Gary's Men's Wear	Vienna Cleaners	Plush Pooch
d. Key amenities:	Major Tenants	Restaurant	New construction

SITE INSPECTION REPORT
Commercial

Property Name: Village Square Center

Financing Number: 0128
Property Number: 0238

Comments on any of the Comparable Properties:

Comp #1: New w/mostly national tenants. Near Regional mall.
Comp #2: Excluding a vacant small anchor outparcel, occ. is 96%.
Comp #3: Condition is superior due to newer construction.

2. Rental Information

		COMPARABLE 1	COMPARABLE 2	COMPARABLE 3
a.	Asking rental rates ($/SF Monthly):			
	1. Prime space	$18 - $19	$12 - $13	$18 - $19
	2. Secondary space	$12 - $15.75	$11 - $11.50	$12 - $15.75
b.	Range of recently executed leases ($/SF Monthly):			
	1. Prime space	$18 - $19	$11 - $12.50	$16 - $17
	2. Secondary space	$12 - $17	$11 - $12.50	$10 - $15
c.	Lease type (gross / net):	NNN	NNN	NNN
d.	Rent concessions (free rent, etc.)	None	1-2 months	1-2 months
e.	Effective net rent (in place)	N/Av	N/Av	N/Av
f.	TI allowance ($/SF):	0 - $2.00	0 - $2.50	0 - $2.00
g.	Expense stop ($/SF):	$0.40 - 1.90	N/A	$0.63 - 1.41
h.	Lease terms offered (in years):	3-10 years	1-10 years	3-10 years
i.	Commissions:	5%	6%	5%
j.	Percentage rent:	$4.00 - 6.00	$4.00 - 7.00	$3.80 - 6.50
k.	Historical annual absorption /SF:	N/Av	N/Av	N/Av
l.	Current occupancy %:	100%	96%	98%

3.	**Rank relative to Property** (inferior, similar, superior)	Superior	Similar	Superior

4. Explain Ranking/ Comments:

Rental comps #1 & #2 are next to a regional mall at the north end of town, serve a different market, and have a higher concentration of national tenants. Comp #3 is considered most competitive due to proximity to the subject. Comps #2 and #3 have a similar number of inline tenant vacancies as the subject (1% to 3%). Comp #1 is fully leased.

I. GENERAL SUMMARY OF PROPERTY

1. Overall comments on the market:

Bellingham is the largest metropolitan area within Whatcom County, comprising 39% of the total population. The economy has shifted from one based on logging and fishing to a more service and retail oriented base. The signing of a 1989 Free Trade Agreement with Canada had a strong impact on the County, enhancing cross-border investment and employment. Due to a lower labor cost and relatively inexpensive land, there has been a considerable amount of Canadian investment in the County. While the trade agreement has encouraged investment by larger companies, the trend of Canadians doing all of their retail shopping in the area has been greatly diminished since the early 1990s due to a closer parity on the exchange rate and incentives in Canadian retailers. While this affects overall retail sales, it will not impact a neighborhood retail center to the extent it would a regional mall.

2. Property's competitiveness in the market:

The subject is well located next to Western Washington University, a residential growth area, and other supporting commercial uses. The property was totally renovated and expanded within the past five years, the tenant mix is well suited for the area, and the strong grocery and drug store anchor tenants make the subject very competitive. The location next to the University is considered superior by other shopping center owners in the market.

3. Other Relevant Comments:

None.

SITE INSPECTION REPORT
Commercial

Property Name:	Village Square Center	Financing Number: 0128 Property Number: 0238

ATTACHMENT A - SERVICE CONTRACTS

Type	Vendor Name	Related Party (Yes/ No) *	Monthly Amount	Expiration	Length of Service	Comments
Elevator Service	N/A					
Landscaping	Olive Landscape	No	$1,800	Dec-00	2 years	
Parking Lot Maintenance	N/A					
Laundry Service	N/A					
Janitorial Service	Porter's Plus	No	$2,700	30 day	2 years	
Trash Removal	Waste Management	No	$2,700	May-01	5 years	
Roof Maintenance	Roof Techs	No			5 years	
HVAC Maintenance	Maintenance Group	No	$1,150	30 day	3 years	
Snow Removal	N/A					
Other						
Other						
Other						
Other						
Other						

* Related Party shall mean Borrower's or Applicant's spouse (if Borrower or Applicant is an individual) and management officials of the Borrower and/or Applicant and their spouses, and/or any individual or entity that controls or is controlled by or is under common control with the Borrower or the Applicant. An individual or entity shall be presumed to have 'control' of entity if it owns more than 20% of the equity interests or otherwise controls its management or policies.

SITE INSPECTION REPORT
Commercial

Property Name:	Village Square Center	Financing Number: 0128 Property Number: 0238

ATTACHMENT B - HISTORICAL AND PLANNED CAPITAL EXPENDITURES

HISTORICAL CAPITAL EXPENDITURES FOR THE PAST THREE YEARS:

#	Description	$ Spent	Date Completed	Comments
1	Parking Lot - Slurry Seal	$9,700	12/1996	In need of repair
2	Parking Lot - Striping	$1,200	12/1999	
3	Exterior Walls - Paint/Finish	$22,000	12/1998	
4	Roof - Repairs	$10,000	05/1998	
5	Water Heaters - Replace	$800	12/1997	
6	HVAC - Refurbish	$12,500	08/1996	
	Total	**$56,200**		

PLANNED CAPITAL EXPENDITURES IN THE NEXT THREE YEARS:

#	Description	Est. Cost	Est. Completion	Comments
1	Driveway/Parking - repair, slurry seal, restripe	$20,460	01/2001	
2	Truck Well Repair	$4,300	03/2001	
3	Concrete Paving, Curb and Gutter Repair	$3,300	12/2001	
4	Trash Dumpster Enclosure Repair	$200	12/2001	
5	Building Exterior	$2,500	01/2002	
6	Roofing and Parapet	$2,500	02/2002	
7	Preventive Maintenance	$5,000	Ongoing	
8	Drywall Soffit	$100	12/2000	
9	Ceiling Tiles	$150	08/2000	
	Total	**$38,510**		

Property Name:	Village Square Center	Financing Number: 0128 Property Number: 0238

ATTACHMENT C - TENANT ROLLOVER HISTORY

HISTORICAL TENANT ROLLOVERS FOR THE PAST FIVE YEARS:

Tenant	Type (Exp, Term, Re, NL)	Date	Square Feet	Rent per SF	Term (Yrs.)	TI per SF	Commissions Paid	Free Rent (Months)	Down Time (Months)
Vitamin Head	Re	07/1997	2,467	$12.30	3.0	$2.25	2.50%		
Consignment	Re	12/1998	1,943	$14.00	5.0	$1.50	2.50%		
Stires	Re	05/1998	2,534	$12.00	5.0	$2.00	2.75%		
Merle Norman	Re	03/2000	2,348	$14.70	5.0		2.75%		
The Children's Co	Re	04/2000	20,000	$3.30	5.0	$2.00	2.50%		
Shoe Repair	Exp	01/1996	1,373	$14.00	5.0				
Sub Shop	NL	03/1996	1,373	$15.50	5.0	$2.00	5.00%		2
Pet Shop	NL	02/2000	1,440	$18.35	5.0	$2.00	5.50%		

Year	Exp	Term	Re	NL	**Net Absorption**
1997			2,467		2,467
1998			4,477		4,477
1999					
2000			22,348	1,440	23,788
2001					
Total			**29,292**	**1,440**	**30,732**
Avg. Annual			**5,858**	**288**	**6,146**

Renewal % **100**

Comments on the above:

Subject property has an outstanding track record of retaining good tenants, as demonstrated by its high renewal rate.

Exp = Expired, Term = Termination, Re = Renewal, NL = New Lease, TI = Tenant Improvements

SITE INSPECTION REPORT
Commercial

Property Name:	Village Square Center	Financing Number: 0128
		Property Number: 0238

ATTACHMENT D - TENANT STATUS

TENANT STATUS EXPECTED IN THE NEXT TWELVE MONTHS:

Tenant/Type	Square Feet	Exp. Date	Status
Vitamin Head	2,467	10/2001	In discussions to renew
Quilt Basket	1,540	08/2001	In discussions to renew
The Bagel Factory	1,791	07/2001	Signed new lease
Frazier Chiropractic	1,373	11/2001	In discussions to renew
Total	7,171		

Comments on the above:

Subject has good track record in retaining tenants, and the leasing broker is confident with its ability to retain rollovers.

SITE INSPECTION REPORT
Commercial

Property Name:	Village Square Center	Financing Number:	0128
		Property Number:	0238

ATTACHMENT E - UNUSUAL LEASE PROVISIONS

Instructions *- For each Property in connection with the requested financing that is subject to any lease agreement, sublease agreement, licensing agreement, or other form of occupancy arrangement which accounts for, in the aggregate, 5% or more of the square footage or total rental income for the Property, Borrower and/ or Applicant must identify and provide a detailed explanation of the terms of any provision in any lease which are uncommon, unusual or atypical.*

1. Purchase, Expansion, Termination and Renewal Options

   a. Describe the terms of tenant's right of first refusal for additional space in the Property:

   Payless Drugs has Right of First Refusal terms.

   b. Describe any termination or cancellation rights:

   Landlord rights

   Landlord has right to terminate in case of Event of Default by Tenant, which generally means failure to pay Rent and various other CAM charges.
   Storage lease can be terminated at anytime by Landlord based on determination that a better use exists.

   Tenant rights

   Tenants' rights to terminate are limited to Casualty and Condemnation terms.

   c. Describe the terms, if any, of tenant's option to purchase the Property:

   There are no options to purchase property.

   d. Describe the terms, if any, of tenant's right to expand the Premises (including effective date(s) of such expansion(s), notice requirements, total square footage of expansion space, basic rent for expansion space, additional rent and charges to be paid by tenant for such space and the party performing the build-out for such space, if applicable):

   Haggens has right to additional space subject to a deadline and terms outlined in the Lease Agreement. Landlord is obligated to provide additional space by offering existing vacant land.

2. Additional Lease Provisions

   a. Assignment/ Subletting restrictions:

   Is allowed, but Tenant must still assume liability for subtenant.

   b. Additional Comments regarding leases (please explain any other unusual lease provisions):

   None.

SITE INSPECTION REPORT
Hospitality

Property Name: ______ Financing Number: ______ Property Number: ______

Property Type ______ Date Performed ______
Property Class (A,B,C) ______
Property Style ______ Full Service...(Resort, Luxury, 1st Class, Mid-Tier), Limited Service, Extended Stay

A. IDENTIFICATION

1. Property:
Property Name ______
Address ______
City ______ County ______ State ______ Zip ______
Cross Street ______

2. Property Contact Information:
Contact/ Title ______
Company Name ______
Phone ______
Fax ______
Email ______

How long has contact been affiliated with the Property? ______
Address ______
City ______
State ______
Zip ______

B. PROPERTY DESCRIPTION

1. Property Attributes: Source
a. Year built ______
b. Year last renovated ______
c. Scope of renovation:

Source

d. Product Mix As of (date): ______

Type of rooms	# of Rooms	% of Total
2 doubles		
Queens		
Kings		
1BD Suite		
2BD Suite		
Other		
Total		

e. Size
Number of rooms ______
Gross SF ______
Largest meeting space SF ______
Retail SF ______
Total land area (acres) ______
Excess land area (acres) ______
Number of floors ______
Number of buildings ______

Source

f. Parking
Total parking spaces ______
Parking ratio (per room) ______
Uncovered parking ______
Covered parking ______
Parking charge (hrly, dly, mnthly, etc.) ______

g. Construction Details
Exterior façade (stucco, brick, vinyl, etc.) ______
Roof type (pitched, flat, mixed, etc.) ______
Roof material (shingle, gravel, tile, etc.) ______
Structure (concrete, wood, steel, etc.) ______

h. Operating Systems
Type of heat ______
Type of air conditioning ______
Number of elevators ______
Fire and life safety system ______
Building(s) sprinklered (yes / no) ______

Property Description:

PRECEPT

SITE INSPECTION REPORT
Hospitality

Property Name: ____________
Financing Number: ____
Property Number: ____

2. Property Amenities/ Guest Services:

Security service	____	Room service	____
Valet parking	____	Business center	____
Laundry service	____	Golf course	____
Indoor pool(s)	____	Tennis court	____
Outdoor pools(s)	____	Game room	____
Health club	____	Cable TV	____
Vending machines	____	Kitchen in room	____
Meeting space	____	Jacuzzi tubs	____
Restaurant / Lounge / Bar	____	Patio / Balcony	____
Concierge	____	Bar	____

Comments on Amenities:

3. Location:

a.	Corner	____	(yes, no)
b.	Traffic volume	____	(high, medium, low)
c.	Type of front street	____	(arterial, collector, subdivision)
d.	Overall neighborhood appearance	____	(excellent, good, average, poor)
e.	Access to major arteries	____	(excellent, good, average, poor)
f.	Access to local amenities	____	(excellent, good, average, poor)
g.	Access to public transportation	____	(excellent, good, average, poor)
h.	Access to shopping	____	(excellent, good, average, poor)
i.	Access to entertainment	____	(excellent, good, average, poor)
j.	Street appeal	____	(excellent, good, average, poor)
k.	Ingress / Egress	____	(excellent, good, average, poor)
l.	Ease of left hand turn into Property	____	(excellent, good, average, poor)
m.	Visibility	____	(excellent, good, average, poor)
n.	Signage	____	(excellent, good, average, poor)
o.	Signage visibility at intersection	____	(excellent, good, average, poor)
p.	Overall quality of the location	____	(excellent, good, average, poor)
q.	Location's impact on the Property's ability to secure and retain guests:	____	(positive, not distinguishable, negative)

Comments on Location:

4. Occupancy Mix:

Group:		Individuals:	
Corporate	____	Business	____
Associations / Conventions	____	Leisure	____
Government	____	Preferred	____
Tour	____	Travel Packages	____
Airline	____	Hotel Packages	____
SMERF (Social, Military, Educational, Religious, Fraternal)	____	Discounts	____
Total		**Total**	

Comments on occupancy mix (e.g., primary demand generator, special contracts, advance bookings, etc.):

SITE INSPECTION REPORT
Hospitality

Property Name: ____________ Financing Number: ______ Property Number: ______

5. **Franchise and Management Information:**

a. Hotel/Motel Franchise
Operator
Contact

Early termination penalty/cost to terminate
Contract expiration date
Annual fee amount
Describe annual fee formula:

b. Restaurant lease
Operator
Contact

Early termination penalty/cost to terminate
Contract expiration date
Annual fee amount
Describe annual fee formula:

c. Manager / Operator
Contact

Early termination penalty/cost to terminate
Contract expiration date
Annual fee amount
Describe annual fee formula:

Years Management Co. has been associated with Property?
Does a related party of Management Co. own any portion of the Property? (if yes, please explain below):

Does the Mgmt. Co. manage other properties for the owner? (yes / no)
Does the Mgmt. Co. manage other properties for <u>other</u> owner? (yes / no)
OBTAIN MANAGEMENT COMPANY RESUME
Management Company's history / experience:

Does Mgmt. Co. conduct or subscribe to a market rental survey? (e.g., Smith or PKF, etc.) ______ if yes, please obtain a copy

d. Reservation system
Operator
Contact

Early termination penalty/cost to terminate
Contract expiration date
Annual fee amount
Describe annual fee formula:

SITE INSPECTION REPORT
Hospitality

Property Name:	Financing Number: Property Number:

e. **PLEASE SEE ATTACHMENT 'A' FOR LIST OF CURRENT SERVICE CONTRACTS:**

6. Other:

a. Comments on ADA compliance:

b. **PLEASE SEE ATTACHMENT 'B' FOR EXPLANATION OF HISTORICAL AND PLANNED CAPITAL EXPENDITURES**

C. EXTERIOR CONDITION

1. Overall quality of the exterior: ______ (excellent, good, average, poor)
2. Landscaping: ______ (excellent, good, average, poor)
3. Adequacy of interior roads / parking: ______ (excellent, good, average, poor)
4. Paving: ______ (excellent, good, average, poor)
5. Adequacy of lighting: ______ (excellent, good, average, poor)
6. Pool(s) / Spa(s): ______ (excellent, good, average, poor)
7. Paint: ______ (excellent, good, average, poor)
8. Windows: ______ (excellent, good, average, poor)
9. Roof: ______ (excellent, good, average, poor)
10. Façade: ______ (excellent, good, average, poor)
11. Signage: ______ (excellent, good, average, poor)
12. Entrance: ______ (excellent, good, average, poor)
13. Other (e.g., fountains, sculptures, etc.): ______ (excellent, good, average, poor)

Exterior Condition Comments:

D. INTERIOR CONDITION

Lobby / Foyer / Common Area

1. Overall quality of the interior: ______ (excellent, good, average, poor)
2. Carpet: ______ (excellent, good, average, poor)
3. Furniture: ______ (excellent, good, average, poor)
4. Convention / meeting space: ______ (excellent, good, average, poor)
5. Elevators: ______ (excellent, good, average, poor)
6. Lighting: ______ (excellent, good, average, poor)
7. Restaurant / Lounge / Bar: ______ (excellent, good, average, poor)
8. Exercise equipment: ______ (excellent, good, average, poor)
9. Service areas: ______ (excellent, good, average, poor)

Rooms

10. Bathrooms: ______ (excellent, good, average, poor)
11. Kitchens: ______ (excellent, good, average, poor)
12. Walls (paint / wall coverings): ______ (excellent, good, average, poor)
13. Carpet: ______ (excellent, good, average, poor)
14. Lighting: ______ (excellent, good, average, poor)
15. Heating / Cooling units: ______ (excellent, good, average, poor)
16 Furniture: ______ (excellent, good, average, poor)
17. Tile / Vinyl: ______ (excellent, good, average, poor)
18. Ceilings: ______ (excellent, good, average, poor)
19. Windows: ______ (excellent, good, average, poor)
20. Doors: ______ (excellent, good, average, poor)

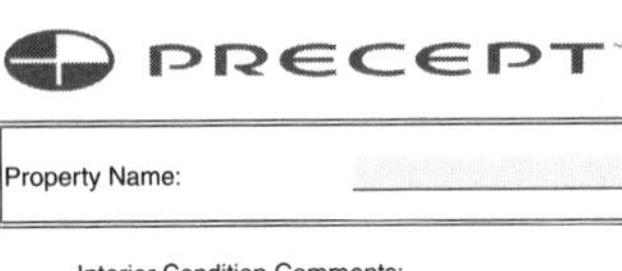

SITE INSPECTION REPORT
Hospitality

Property Name: ____________ Financing Number: ______
Property Number: ______

Interior Condition Comments:

Describe deferred maintenance and Property Management's estimate cost to cure (exterior and interior):

E. PROPERTY RENTAL DATA

Name of information source ____________ How long has source been affiliated with the Property? ______
Company Name for source ____________ Phone ____________ Email ______

1. Room Mix

Type of rooms	# of Rooms	% of Total	ADR	Occupancy	REVPAR
2 doubles					
Queens					
Kings					
1BD Suite					
2BD Suite					
Other					
Total					

2. Discuss room premiums (e.g., view, floor, location, etc.):

3. Discuss recent historical ADR and average occupancy performance:

4. Property Rental Data Additional Comments:

SITE INSPECTION REPORT
Hospitality

Property Name: ____________
Financing Number: ____________
Property Number: ____________

F. NEIGHBORHOOD

1. Area: ____________ (urban, suburban, rural)
2. Development: ____________ (fully developed, over 75%, 25% - 75%, under 25%)
3. Growth rate: ____________ (rapid, steady, slow)
4. Present use %: (should total 100%) Single family ______ Multi-family ______ Commercial ______ Industrial ______ Vacant land ______ Specify other ______
5. Change in current use: ______ (unlikely / likely)
6. Major off-site demand generators:

   Such as largest companies/ employers for the area including non-profit employers such as hospital and university.

7. Neighborhood Description (Describe immediate surrounding land uses, e.g., Apartment, Office, Industrial, Retail, Undeveloped Land, etc.):

   North of the Subject:
   South of the Subject:
   East of the Subject:
   West of the Subject:

8. Other facts about the neighborhood that may affect, or potentially affect, the Property (e.g., nearby thoroughfares, airports, etc.):

G. NEW CONSTRUCTION (SUPPLY)

1. New Construction

Source	Name of project	Location	Distance from	# of Rooms	completion	space SqFt	Est. ADR	Type

SITE INSPECTION REPORT
Hospitality

Property Name: ________ Financing Number: ________ Property Number: ________

2. Comments on new supply and impact on the Property:

H. COMPARABLE PROPERTIES

1. Property Description

	COMPARABLE 1	COMPARABLE 2	COMPARABLE 3
a. Identification:			
1. Name			
2. Street address			
3. City			
4. State			
5. Estimated distance from Property			
b. Attributes:			
1. Number of rooms			
2. Franchise			
3. Manager			
4. Reservation system			
5. Year built/ renovated			
6. Service (Full, Limited, Extended)			
7. Meeting space SF			
8. Number of stories			
9. Number of Restaurant / Lounges			
10. Construction type			
11. Amenities			
12. General condition			
13. Access			
14. Visibility			
15. Guest room quality			
16. Deferred maintenance			
17. Amenities			
18. Overall perception			

Comments on any of the Comparable Properties:

2. Rental Information

	COMPARABLE 1	COMPARABLE 2	COMPARABLE 3
a. ADR			
b. Current occupancy %			
c. REVPAR (ADR X Occupancy)			

3. Rank relative to Property (inferior, similar, superior)			

4. Explain Ranking/ Comments:

SITE INSPECTION REPORT
Hospitality

Property Name:	____________	Financing Number: ____ Property Number: ____

I. **GENERAL SUMMARY OF PROPERTY**

1. Overall comments on the market:
(i.e. does the market appear to be expanding or shrinking, estimated occupancy level for the market, is new construction an indication of reposition of the market or expansion of the existing market)

2. Property's competitiveness in the market:
(describe subject's relative position in the market)

3. Other relevant comments:

SITE INSPECTION REPORT

Hospitality

Property Name: ____________

Financing Number: ____
Property Number: ____

ATTACHMENT A - SERVICE CONTRACTS

Type	Vendor Name	Related Party (Yes/ No) *	Monthly Amount	Expiration	Length of Service	Comments
Elevator Service						
Landscaping						
Cable						
Telephone						
Credit						
Trash Removal						
Advertising						
Laundry						
Snow Removal						
Other						
Other						
Other						
Other						
Other						

SITE INSPECTION REPORT

Hospitality

Property Name: ____________________ Financing Number: ______ Property Number: ______

ATTACHMENT B - HISTORICAL AND PLANNED CAPITAL EXPENDITURES

HISTORICAL CAPITAL EXPENDITURES FOR THE PAST THREE YEARS:

#	Description	$ Spent	Date Completed	Comments
	Total			

PLANNED CAPITAL EXPENDITURES IN THE NEXT THREE YEARS:

#	Description	Est. Cost	Est. Completion	Comments
	Total			

SITE INSPECTION REPORT
Multifamily

Property Name: ____ Financing Number: ____
Property Number: ____

Property Type ____ Date Performed ____
Property Class (A,B,C) ____
Property Style ____ Garden, Mid Rise, High Rise

A. IDENTIFICATION

1. Property:

Property Name ____
Address ____
City ____ County ____ State ____ Zip ____
Cross Street ____

2. Property Contact Information:

Contact/ Title ____
Company Name ____
Phone ____
Fax ____
Email ____

How long has contact been affiliated with the Property? ____
Address ____
City ____
State ____
Zip ____

B. PROPERTY DESCRIPTION

1. **Property Attributes:** Source ____

a. Year built ____
b. Year last renovated ____
c. Scope of renovation:

d. Unit Mix As of (date): ____ Source ____

Unit type	# of Units	Avg. SqFt
Studio/Efficncy		
1 BD/ 1 BA		
2 BD/ 1 BA		
2 BD/ 2 BA		
3 BD/ 2 BA		
Other		
Total/Wtd. Avg.		

e. Size

Number of units ____
Net rentable SF ____
Total land area (acres) ____
Density per acre ____
Excess land area (acres) ____
Number of buildings ____
Number of floors ____
Number of entrances ____

f. Construction Details Source ____

Exterior facade (stucco, brick, vinyl, etc.) ____
Roof type (pitched, flat, mixed, etc.) ____
Roof material (shingle, gravel, tile, etc.) ____
Structure (concrete, wood, steel, etc.) ____
Building(s) sprinklered (yes / no) ____
Gutters / Downspouts (yes / no) ____

g. Parking

Total parking spaces ____
Parking ratio (per unit) ____
Uncovered parking ____ Mnthly Chrg ____
Detached garage spaces ____ Mnthly Chrg ____
Attached garage spaces ____ Mnthly Chrg ____
Carport spaces ____ Mnthly Chrg ____

h. Operating Systems

Type of heat ____ (electric, gas, baseboard)
Type of air conditioning ____ (central, wall unit)
Individual/ type of water heater ____ (gas, electric, oil)
Number of elevators ____
Water/Sewer submeter ____ (yes / no)
Electric submeter ____ (yes / no)
Gas submeter ____ (yes / no)
Appliances ____ (gas, electric)

Property Description:

SITE INSPECTION REPORT
Multifamily

Property Name: ________ Financing Number: ________ Property Number: ________

2. Property Amenities:

Common Area Features		Unit Features	
Clubhouse	____	Washer/Dryer	____ (hookups or)
Gated	____	Dishwasher	____
Pool(s)	____	Microwave	____
Spa(s) / Jacuzzi(s)	____	Fireplace	____
Exercise facility	____	Patio / Balcony	____
Sport court(s) / Tennis court(s)	____	Central HVAC	____
Racquetball court(s)	____	Ceiling fans	____
Playground	____	Ceiling height	____
Business center	____	Vaulted ceilings	____
Laundry room(s)	____	Disposal	____
Storage	____	Intrusion alarms	____
Game room(s)	____	Carpet/ Vinyl	____
Trash Compactor or Dumpsters	____	Cable ready	____

Comments on Amenities (e.g., the general condition of the amenities, description of other amenities, etc.):

3. Location:

a. Corner ____ (yes, no)
b. Traffic volume ____ (high, medium, low)
c. Type of front street ____ (arterial, collector, subdivision)
d. Overall neighborhood appearance ____ (excellent, good, average, poor)
e. Access to major arteries ____ (excellent, good, average, poor)
f. Access to local amenities ____ (excellent, good, average, poor)
g. Access to public transportation ____ (excellent, good, average, poor)
h. Access to schools ____ (excellent, good, average, poor)
i. Access to shopping ____ (excellent, good, average, poor)
j. Street appeal ____ (excellent, good, average, poor)
k. Ingress / Egress ____ (excellent, good, average, poor)
l. Ease of left hand turn into Property ____ (excellent, good, average, poor)
m. Visibility ____ (excellent, good, average, poor)
n. Signage ____ (excellent, good, average, poor)
o. Signage visibility at intersection ____ (excellent, good, average, poor)
p. Overall quality of the location ____ (excellent, good, average, poor)
q. Location's impact on the Property's ability to secure and retain tenants: ____ (positive, not distinguishable, negative)

Comments on Location:

4. Estimated Demographics and Tenant Concentrations:

Estimated Demographics		Tenant Concentrations	
Singles	____	Students	____
Married couples	____	Military	____
Families	____	Corporate	____
Total		Seniors	____
		Other (specify)	____

Current concentration vs. market profile / other comments:

PRECEPT

SITE INSPECTION REPORT
Multifamily

Property Name: ______ Financing Number: ______ Property Number: ______

5. **Management Information:**

Manager's Name		Address	
Title		City	
Management Co.		State	
Phone		Zip	
Fax		Email/ Web Site	

a. Management type (owner/ outside contractor) ______
b. Property Manager on site daily? (Yes / No) ______
c. If no, how often is site visited by Property Manager? ______
d. Is Mgmt./Leasing office on site? ______
e. Hours of operation open to tenants ______
f. Years Mgmt. Co. has been associated with Property? ______
g. Does a related party of Mgmt. Co. own any portion of the Property? (if yes, please explain below)

h. Does the Mgmt. Co. manage other properties for the owner? (Yes/No) ______
i. Does the Mgmt. Co. manage other properties for other owner? (Yes/No) ______
j. Property Management fee ______
k. OBTAIN MANAGEMENT COMPANY RESUME ______
l. Property Management Company's history / experience:

m. Does Mgmt. Co. conduct a market rental survey? ______ if yes, please obtain a copy

n. **PLEASE SEE ATTACHMENT 'A' FOR LIST OF CURRENT SERVICE CONTRACTS:**

6. **Other:**

a. Comments on ADA compliance:

b. **PLEASE SEE ATTACHMENT 'B' FOR EXPLANATION OF HISTORICAL AND PLANNED CAPITAL EXPENDITURES**

C. **EXTERIOR CONDITION**
1. Overall quality of the exterior: ______ (excellent, good, average, poor)
2. Landscaping: ______ (excellent, good, average, poor)
3. Adequacy of interior roads / parking: ______ (excellent, good, average, poor)
4. Paving: ______ (excellent, good, average, poor)
5. Adequacy of lighting: ______ (excellent, good, average, poor)
6. Pool(s) / Spa(s): ______ (excellent, good, average, poor)
7. Paint: ______ (excellent, good, average, poor)
8. Windows: ______ (excellent, good, average, poor)
9. Roof: ______ (excellent, good, average, poor)
10. Façade: ______ (excellent, good, average, poor)
11. Signage: ______ (excellent, good, average, poor)
12. Entrance: ______ (excellent, good, average, poor)
13. Gutters/ Downspouts: ______ (excellent, good, average, poor)
14. Other (fountains, sculptures): ______ (excellent, good, average, poor)
15. Condition of HVAC units: ______ (excellent, good, average, poor)

Exterior Condition Comments:

SITE INSPECTION REPORT
Multifamily

Property Name: ____________

Financing Number: ______
Property Number: ______

D. INTERIOR CONDITION

Common Area

1. Overall quality of the interior: ______ (excellent, good, average, poor)
2. Carpet: ______ (excellent, good, average, poor)
3. Furniture: ______ (excellent, good, average, poor)
4. Exercise equipment: ______ (excellent, good, average, poor)
5. Other amenities: ______ (excellent, good, average, poor)
6. Elevators: ______ (excellent, good, average, poor)
7. Adequacy of lighting: ______ (excellent, good, average, poor)

Units

8. Kitchen cabinets: ______ (excellent, good, average, poor)
9. Kitchen appliances: ______ (excellent, good, average, poor)
10. Carpet: ______ (excellent, good, average, poor)
11. Vinyl: ______ (excellent, good, average, poor)
12. Lighting: ______ (excellent, good, average, poor)
13. Ceilings: ______ (excellent, good, average, poor)
14. Windows: ______ (excellent, good, average, poor)
15. Walls (paint / wall coverings): ______ (excellent, good, average, poor)
16. Doors: ______ (excellent, good, average, poor)
17. Bathrooms: ______ (excellent, good, average, poor)
18. Bathroom cabinets: ______ (excellent, good, average, poor)

Interior Condition Comments:

Describe deferred maintenance and Property Management's estimate cost to cure (exterior and interior):

E. PROPERTY RENTAL DATA

Name of information source ______ How long has source been affiliated with the Property? ______
Company Name for source ______ Phone ______ Email ______

1. Asking rents as of (date): ______

Unit type	# of Units	% of Total	# Vacant	% Vacant	Total SqFt	Avg. SqFt	Avg. Rent	Per SqFt
Studio/Efficncy								
1 BD/ 1 BA								
2 BD/ 1 BA								
2 BD/ 2 BA								
3 BD/ 2 BA								
Other								
Total/ Weighted Avg.								

Discuss unit premiums (e.g., view, floor, location, etc.):

PRECEPT

SITE INSPECTION REPORT
Multifamily

Property Name:
Financing Number:
Property Number:

2. Occupancy: 100.0%
3. Historical turnover:
4. Owner paid expenses:
5. Tenant paid expenses:
6. Concessions currently being offered:
7. Number of employee units and subsidy:
8. Number of models and type:
9. Deposits:
10. Lease terms offered:

11. Discuss recent leasing activity and renewal probabilities:

12. Property Rental Data Additional Comments:

F. NEIGHBORHOOD

1. Area: (urban, suburban, rural)
2. Development: (fully developed, over 75%, 25% - 75%, under 25%)
3. Growth rate: (rapid, steady, slow)
4. Present use %: (should total 100%) Single family ___ Multi-family ___ Commercial ___ Industrial ___ Vacant land ___ Specify other ___

5. Change in current use: (unlikely / likely)
6. Major off-site demand generators:

Such as largest companies/ employers for the area including non-profit employers such as hospital and university.

7. Neighborhood Description (Describe immediate surrounding land uses, e.g., Apartment, Office, Industrial, Retail, Undeveloped Land, etc.):

North of the Subject:
South of the Subject:
East of the Subject:
West of the Subject:

8. Other facts about the neighborhood that may affect, or potentially affect, the Property (e.g., thoroughfares, military base closings, etc.):

PRECEPT

SITE INSPECTION REPORT
Multifamily

Property Name: ____________

Financing Number: ____
Property Number: ____

G. NEW CONSTRUCTION (SUPPLY)

1. New Construction

Source	Name of project	Location	Distance from	# of Units	Completion	Avg SqFt	Asking Rent	Per SqFt

2. Comments on new supply and impact on the Property:

H. COMPARABLE PROPERTIES

1. Property Description

	COMPARABLE 1	COMPARABLE 2	COMPARABLE 3
a. Identification:			
1. Name			
2. Street address			
3. City, State			
4. Est. distance from Property			
b. Attributes:			
1. Number of units			
2. Owner/ Manager			
3. Year built/ renovated			
4. Land area (acres):			
Density per acre			
c. Major amenities:			

d. Unit Mix

Unit type	# of Units	# of Units	# of Units
Studio/Efficncy			
1 BD/ 1 BA			
2 BD/ 1 BA			
2 BD/ 2 BA			
3 BD/ 2 BA			
Other			

Comments on any of the Comparable Properties:

PRECEPT

SITE INSPECTION REPORT
Multifamily

Property Name:		Financing Number:
		Property Number:

2. **Rental Information**

	COMPARABLE 1		COMPARABLE 2		COMPARABLE 3	
a. Asking rental rates:	Price	SqFt	Price	SqFt	Price	SqFt
Studio/ Efficiency						
1 BD/ 1 BA						
2 BD/ 1 BA						
2 BD/ 2 BA						
3 BD/ 2 BA						
Other						
b. Rent concessions						
c. Effective net rent (in place)						
d. Lease terms offered (months)						
e. Historical turnover %						
f. Current occupancy %						
g. Deposits						
h. Tenant pays for...						
3. **Rank relative to Property** (inferior, similar, superior)						

4. **Explain Ranking/ Comments:**

I. **GENERAL SUMMARY OF PROPERTY**

1. Overall comments on the market:
(i.e. does the market appear to be expanding or shrinking, estimated occupancy level for the market, is new construction an indication of reposition of the market or expansion of the existing market)

2. Property's competitiveness in the market:
(describe subject's relative position in the market)

3. Other relevant comments:

SITE INSPECTION REPORT
Multifamily

Property Name:	Financing Number:
	Property Number:

ATTACHMENT A - SERVICE CONTRACTS

Type	Vendor Name	Related Party (Yes/ No) *	Monthly Amount	Expiration	Length of Service	Comments
Elevator Service						
Landscaping						
Cable						
Telephone						
Credit						
Trash Removal						
Advertising						
Laundry						
Snow Removal						
Other						
Other						
Other						
Other						
Other						

* Related Party shall mean Borrower's or Applicant's spouse (if Borrower or Applicant is an individual) and management officials of the Borrower and/or Applicant and their spouses, and/or any individual or entity that controls or is controlled by or is under common control with the Borrower or the Applicant. An individual or entity shall be presumed to have 'control' of entity if it owns more than 20% of the equity interests or otherwise controls its management or policies.

SITE INSPECTION REPORT
Multifamily

Property Name:	Financing Number:
	Property Number:

ATTACHMENT B - HISTORICAL AND PLANNED CAPITAL EXPENDITURES

HISTORICAL CAPITAL EXPENDITURES FOR THE PAST THREE YEARS:

#	Description	Amount Spent	Date Completed	Comments
	Total			

PLANNED CAPITAL EXPENDITURES IN THE NEXT THREE YEARS:

#	Description	Est. Cost	Est. Completion	Comments
	Total			

CHAPTER 2

Overview of the Cash Flow Underwriting Process

The elevation of cash flow analysis to a key role in the underwriting process can be traced back to the early 1990s, when the focus of commercial underwriting shifted from loan-to-value analysis to debt service coverage analysis. This significant change occurred, in part, because of a decline in the perceived credibility of valuation methodologies employed in the late 1980s, but perhaps more notably because the capital market's delivery of capital to the real estate community had relied on the use of structured finance instruments.

The challenge of underwriting commercial real estate cash flow is that each asset is unique and contains distinctive characteristics with respect to cash flow stability. This means that the individual property's historical cash flow is critical to the underwriting process. Complicating this process, however, is the fact that individual property owner and property managers' accounting practices are almost as unique as the properties themselves. Even in the hotel sector, where a uniform chart of accounts has existed for decades, inconsistencies are widespread.

As a result, lenders typically perform various types of procedures in order to understand and develop a sense of comfort with figures provided in historical operating statements. These procedures can range from comparing operating statements to income tax returns to reconstructing income and expense line items from general ledgers. The nature of these will also dictate what information the borrower is required to submit to a lender for consideration. Two different lenders might take very different approaches to determining historical cash flow. Lender A, for example, might reallocate what a borrower represented as an "undistributed repairs and maintenance" expense to a "rooms expense" for a hotel property. Lender B's more simplistic approach might leave the same "repairs and maintenance" expense to be categorized as "undistributed." The result could be a material difference in each lender's representation of departmental profit. As such, the varying nature of each lender's requirements for the collection and confirmation of operating data can yield materially different results.

These inconsistencies can be compounded by the differences in how lenders draw conclusions from historical data. Using the same example noted previously, assume that Lender B makes an adjustment to "rooms revenue" from the historical cash flow for purposes of drawing an underwriting conclusion, and correspondingly adjusts "rooms expense" on a percentage basis under the assumption that rooms expenses are completely variable. Lender B's original nonreallocation of the undistributed repairs and maintenance expense now has net cash flow implications. Lender B may make a similar occupancy adjustment but adjust the same undistributed expenses for its perceived variability. Thus, the original difference in the lender's allocations of the repairs and maintenance expense now has potentially larger implications than misstating departmental profit.

The problem here is not that lenders have different opinions in how to conclude underwritten net cash flow—differences in perceived risk and corresponding adjustments are inevitable. The problem in the example above is that each of the lenders was working with two different versions of the same historical cash flow. Due to the inconsistency in the compilation of the historical cash flow, the difference in the two lenders' opinions of how to conclude underwritten cash flow was exacerbated.

Precept believes that the success of the cash flow underwriting process is rooted in the consistent collection, normalization, and confirmation of historical operating data. Just as a long list of historical stock prices is more meaningfully evaluated in the form of a graph, the organized, consistent, concise presentation of a property's operating history empowers an underwriter to efficiently draw accurate conclusions. The conclusion of the Precept cash flow underwriting process is to estimate the stabilized annual cash flow that a property will generate over the property's remaining useful life (this process is referred to herein as the *cash flow underwriting process*). Cash flow is estimated primarily on the basis of the property's actual operating history, taking into account current market conditions and foreseeable future events that may impact the property's operating performance. To determine this cash flow, Precept will consider various factors, including, but not limited to, tenant credit quality, lease terms, vacancy rates, credit loss, expense levels, potential tax increases, capital expenditures, and the costs associated with retenanting space.

The following five chapters contain Precept's systematic approach for determining cash flow analysis for six different land uses: multifamily, mobile home park, retail, office, industrial, and hotel properties. Each property-specific chapter outlines the four steps that Precept will take to determine cash flows, including: (1) *property statement collection,* (2) *operating statement normalization,* (3) *data confirmation,* and (4) *estimation of stabilized property cash flow.* Each line item within Precept's estimated future stabilized cash flow is discussed in terms of Precept's *standard definition, method of derivation,* and *additional considerations.* Precept's approach to cash flow analysis is intentionally rigid. The value of the rigidity is that the ultimate user of its results will know exactly what it is being provided. This does not imply that all properties should be underwritten in strict accordance to the specific income and expense line-item derivations outlined herein. Rather, this method provides a framework from which to evaluate cash flows on a consistent basis, with clear documentation of exceptions to the systematic method of derivations for each component of operating cash flow.

STEP 1: PROPERTY STATEMENT COLLECTION

Complete current and historical cash flow statements, rent rolls, delinquency/aging reports, sales reports, occupancy reports, etc. for each property (collectively, the *property statements*) are vital to the accuracy and reliability of the cash flow underwriting process. Cash flow statements outlining the revenue generated and the expenses incurred by a property over time (the *operating statements*) are of primary importance. Precept will discuss with each potential borrower the status of operating statements in order to determine whether the existing operating statements are sufficient for Precept to perform its cash flow analysis, or whether Precept will require more detailed or updated information. Incomplete or dated operating information may be unreliable and therefore will not be utilized.

At a minimum, each borrower shall submit to Precept (1) certified operating statements for the three most recent complete calendar or fiscal years, (2) certified statements sufficient to allow Precept to assemble a trailing-12-month cash flow, and (3) a certified pro forma cash flow statement or budget for a property, if available. Three years of historical operating statements are required, as trends and anomalies in the operating history are difficult to identify with shorter periods of time. Trailing-12-month operating statements can be compiled using either (1) the actual monthly operating statements for the most recent 12 months or (2) a combination of monthly, quarterly, or semiannual operating statements.

STEP 2: OPERATING STATEMENT NORMALIZATION

Presentation of the operating statements from different periods of time in an organized and consistent manner is critical to meaningful comparison analysis for underwriting purposes. The underwriting process begins by entering the operating statements into the section of the underwriting summary labeled "Operating Statement Reconciliation." In this section, Precept will make all adjustments necessary to "normalize" the three sources (the *cash flow data sources*) of information generally used in determining underwritten cash flow: (1) the historical operating statements, (2) the appraiser's projection of a property's cash flow for the first year of the loan (the *first-year cash flow*), and (3) a property's pro forma cash flow statement or budget provided by the potential borrower. By normalizing the cash flows from each of these sources and from different periods of time, each cash flow can be more accurately compared to the others.

The process of "normalizing" the cash flow data involves three steps. The first step is to allocate individual cash flow statement line items from the sources noted above into Precept's standard cash flow line items, which vary by land use. The second step is to adjust individual cash flow statement income and expense line items for one-time nonoperating, nonrecurring, and non-property-related items (e.g., interest income, capital improvement expense, depreciation and mortgage interest expense, etc.). The last step is to adjust individual cash flow statement income and expense line items for payment or receivable timing that distorts revenue or expenses for a given period (for example, a tax bill for the current year that was paid in December of the previous year). The normalization process is not intended to be a complete reaccounting of the property's detailed income and expenses in accordance with a standard system of accounting. Precept will only reorganize the income and expense figures at the level presented within the property's operating statements.

Operating Statement Reconciliation Section of the Underwriting Summary

In the first column of the Operating Statement Reconciliation section of the underwriting summary, Precept transcribes the revenue and expense line-item headings found on a property's operating statements to the standard revenue and expense heading templates found in the underwriting summary. The standard revenue and expense heading templates will vary based on land use. Precept will transcribe the various line items of a property's operating statements to the most closely corresponding Precept category headings. The line-item names from the operating statements will be noted in this column (beneath the Precept category headings) so that a Precept lender can refer between the source documents and the underwriting summary at any time.

The remaining columns of the operating statement reconciliation are divided into groups of four columns (each a *group of four*) that correspond with the cash flow data sources as follows: (1) depending on the number of periods of collected historical operating statements, one group of four for each period; (2) a property's pro forma operating statement or budget; and (3) the appraiser's projected first-year cash flow statement. Each group of four is divided as follows:

Statement Column	Adjustment Column	Operating Column	Notes Column
Actual historical revenue and expense data for each item in the heading list based on the operating statements, pro forma, and appraisal report.	The adjustments made by Precept (all will be footnoted) to "normalize" the data.	The sum of Column 1 and Column 2. This calculation is handled automatically by the spreadsheet	Notes regarding any adjustments made by Precept.

With respect to historical operating statements, if a trailing-12-month operating statement for a property is not available, and the property is not a hotel, Precept will annualize the most recent operating statements, provided these operating statements include at least the prior six months and Precept does not believe a particular property experiences seasonal fluctuations in revenues or expenses. Precept may annualize revenues or expenses separately if either is seasonal. If a property experiences seasonal fluctuations in revenues or expenses and the operating statements for a trailing-12-month period are not available, Precept will rely on the prior full calendar year operating history of a property, if available, as the basis for its trailing-12-month analysis. In all cases, Precept will identify the data collection period which is the basis for any underwriting in the underwriting summary.

When inputting information from the historical operating statements into the Statement column, Precept will note significant revenue items (e.g., insurance settlements, lease cancellation payments, collection of legal settlements) and expense items (e.g., renovations to a property, legal settlements, major purchases) that appear to be nonrecurring or that have a significant fluctuation in any particular period. For income and/or expense lines determined to be nonrecurring, Precept will make a deduction in the Adjustment column and footnote the logic behind the adjustment. Precept will also include these footnotes in the Cash Flow Summary page of the underwriting summary where appropriate. Precept will also make a deduction from line items for items such as interest expense, loan amortization, and depreciation.

For properties located in jurisdictions that bill utility charges such as water and sewer through property tax bills, Precept will make every effort to separate the total tax bills into the appropriate categories, utilizing the operating statement reconciliation. If this separation cannot be accomplished with reasonable accuracy, Precept will present the total expense as real property taxes, but will clearly note the inclusion of nontax charges.

In making income and expense determinations, Precept will rely on various sources, including operating statements, a property budget or a pro forma cash flow statement, a summary of occupancy, a summary of capital expenditures, a summary of delinquencies, and the appraisal report. Precept may also rely on other written documentation provided by the borrower, or on conversations with the borrower or accounting personnel, which will be noted as such.

STEP 3: DATA CONFIRMATION

Given Precept's strong reliance on property statements for underwriting purposes, Precept will conduct various procedures to confirm the property's operating history, including, but not limited to, a reconciliation of operating statements to federal income tax returns and various other source documents (e.g., bank statements, utility bills, tax bills, etc.). Precept will also review leases and estoppel certificates, and confirm that their terms correspond to those represented in the rent roll.

It is important to note that these procedures will not verify each piece of data outlined in the property statements. This review is intended as a representative sampling confirming Precept's understanding of the operating history as presented in the property statements.

In the event that these procedures identify inaccuracies or misrepresentations within the normalized operating history, corresponding adjustments will be made and footnoted within the appropriate section of the underwriting summary, and/or the borrower may be asked to resubmit one or more property statements.

Loans Greater than $15 Million

For loans greater than $15 million, Precept will require that an independent Certified Public Accountant (CPA) perform certain agreed-upon procedures. The CPA agreed-upon procedures may be modified by Precept in order to fit a given property's historical operating characteristics. The results of the CPA's report will be reviewed by Precept in lieu of Precept conducting various internal data confirmation procedures.

STEP 4: ESTIMATION OF STABILIZED PROPERTY CASH FLOW

For all land uses except hotels, Precept will employ two cash flow underwriting methodologies. Both methodologies produce similar estimates for future operating expenses but differ in their approach to estimating future property revenues. The first method, referred to as *trailing 12 months* (TTM), uses the most recent trailing-12-month operating revenues as the basis for determining underwritten property revenue. The second method, referred to as *leases in place* (LIP), used for all property types except hotels, uses a current property rent roll as the basis for determining a property's underwritten revenue. For hotel properties, Precept will make only one estimate of stabilized cash flow utilizing the TTM methodology.

The LIP and TTM underwritten cash flows will be outlined separately and will include the same level of revenue and expense detail as dictated by Precept's standard cash flow line items discussed previously. Each line item will be derived using Precept's standard methods of derivation for each land use. The source of each individual line-item figure included in the underwritten cash flows will be clearly noted with comments immediately adjacent to each figure or with footnotes. Moreover, material exceptions to Precept's standard underwriting methodology will be outlined in a separate section of the underwriting summary entitled "Underwriting Exceptions."

All references to "market" statistics and analysis are meant to be inclusive of relevant submarkets. Precept will always evaluate the Property's submarket in light of the larger market and will, in most cases, place greater emphasis on submarket statistics given their closer proximity to the Property.

CHAPTER 3

Retail Shopping Centers—Cash Flow Analysis

The complexity of underwriting cash flows for retail properties is due to a number of factors. Unlike other commercial land uses, retail tenants rely on a collective consumer traffic flow. In certain retail configurations, such as malls, the traffic flow is partly attributed to the strength of anchor tenants. Further complicating a cash flow analysis, retail property owners often structure percentage rent leases and/or create highly complex expense reimbursement structures. Careful evaluation of mark-to-market issues and retenanting costs are also required.

A retail property's cash flow and corresponding value are subject to the terms provided for in the tenant lease agreements. As a result, an in-depth review of tenant lease provisions is critical to accurate cash flow analysis. What makes this especially difficult is the fact that retail lease agreements, particularly those for anchors, are often customized to represent complicated negotiations between the tenant and the landlord.

The custom nature of tenant lease agreements makes it difficult to compare rental rates to one another for purposes of evaluating their relationship to market levels. The length of lease terms can render current contractual rents irrelevant for purposes of establishing market rent for the subject property. Unless the property has recent leasing activity, the underwriter is required to rely on lease comparables from other properties and/or perform occupancy cost analysis in order to determine market rental rates.

The accrual nature of most retail reimbursement collections, combined with complicated reimbursement calculations, makes it difficult to reconcile actual reimbursement collections with actual expenses for the same period of time. The complicated nature of reimbursements often leads to errors in landlord billings to tenants, which can either understate or overstate actual collections when compared to contractual entitlements. At times, landlords will not actively bill tenants for certain reimbursable expenses in light of market conditions or pending lease negotiations. Thus, reimbursements require careful consideration from the underwriter.

Another factor requiring careful attention is the codependency of tenants and the relative strength of anchors. This requires an evaluation of anchor sales activity, material lease provisions such as continuous operation and go-dark clauses, and changes in retail concepts that may correspondingly require space configurations.

Finally, retail cash flow analysis requires an evaluation of costs associated with re-leasing vacant space and renegotiating new leases for existing tenants upon expiration. The components of these costs include tenant improvement allowances, brokerage commissions, and free rent. Tenant improvements and free rent are negotiated in conjunction with numerous other lease provisions—most notably, rent and term. This requires that the underwriter evaluate these costs on an effective basis.

The following is Precept's systematic approach to cash flow analysis for retail shopping centers. Overall, it is intentionally rigid. The value of the rigidity is that the ultimate user of its results will know exactly what it is being provided. This does not imply that all retail properties should be underwritten in strict accordance to the specific income and expense line-item derivations outlined herein. In fact, there are several areas of the following methodology that require subjective judgments by the user. However, Precept's approach does provide a framework from which to evaluate retail cash flows on a consistent basis, with clear documentation of exceptions to the systematic method of derivations for each component of operating cash flow.

For your reference, following are the relevant sections of the Precept Underwriting Summary pertaining to the concepts and methodologies contained in this chapter and specific to retail shopping centers. This underwriting summary has been populated in order to provide an example of how it should be utilized for the capture, analysis, and maintenance of due diligence data. It is anticipated that the underwriter will complete the underwriting summary while conducting the underwriting analysis.

STEP 1: PROPERTY STATEMENT COLLECTION

Operating Statements

Precept will require the borrower to submit certified cash flow statements for (1) the past three full years (calendar or fiscal), (2) the current partial year (year to date), and (3) the prior partial year (for the same months relative to the current partial year). The borrower may substitute a complete trailing-12-month cash flow statement for the partial-year statements. In addition to the historical cash flow statements, Precept will require the borrower to submit a certified budget or pro forma for the current full year.

Additional Considerations. Precept will make every effort to obtain partial-year or trailing-12-month statements for periods that end within 3 months (partial months excluded) of the effective underwriting date.

Rent Rolls

Precept will require the borrower to provide a certified current list of tenants and their monthly financial rental obligations. Information on each tenant space will include at a minimum the following information or other information sufficient to allow Precept to derive the following:

1. Tenant name
2. Space identifier
3. Square footage
4. Lease start and end dates
5. Lease options
6. Financial rental obligations (base rent, reimbursements, percentage rent, etc.)

In addition to the information just listed, Precept will also request a rent roll as of the end of each operating statement period.

CASH FLOW SUMMARY

Village Square Center

Property Number: 0238
Financing Number: 0128
Square Feet: 128,451

	1998 /SF	1998	1998 %	NOTE	1999 /SF	1999	1999 %	NOTE	2000 /SF	2000	2000 %	NOTE
	Through: 12/31/1998 Income				Through: 12/31/1999 Income				Through: 12/31/2000 Income			
REVENUES												
Gross Potential Rent	-	-	-		-	-	-		-	-	-	
Collected Rent	8.73	1,121,277	87.0%		8.36	1,073,945	88.6%		8.43	1,083,086	89.5%	
Percentage Rent	-	-	-		-	-	-		-	-	-	
Recoveries												
Common Area Maintenance (CAM)	1.16	148,484	11.5%		0.99	127,654	10.5%		0.92	117,639	9.7%	
Real Estate Taxes	0.08	10,410	0.8%		0.08	10,513	0.9%		0.07	9,181	0.8%	
Insurance	0.03	3,307	0.3%		0.00	550	0.0%		0.01	759	0.1%	
Other Expense Recoveries	-	-	-		(0.00)	(89)	-0.0%		(0.01)	(1,051)	-0.1%	
Total Recoveries	1.26	**162,201**	12.6%		1.08	**138,628**	11.4%		0.99	**126,528**	10.5%	
Other Income - 1	0.04	4,639	0.4%	1	0.00	73	0.0%		0.01	924	0.1%	
Other Income - 2	-	-	-		-	-	-		-	-	-	
Total Gross Income	10.03	**1,288,117**	**100.0%**		9.44	**1,212,646**	**100.0%**		9.42	**1,210,538**	**100.0%**	
Mark-to-Market	-	-	-		-	-	-		-	-	-	
Vacancy and Credit Loss	-	-	-		-	-	-		-	-	-	
Effective Gross Income	**10.03**	**1,288,117**	**100.0%**		**9.44**	**1,212,646**	**100.0%**		**9.42**	**1,210,538**	**100.0%**	
EXPENSES												
Variable												
Management Fee	0.28	36,484	2.8%		0.27	34,297	2.8%		0.27	34,144	2.8%	
Payroll & Benefits	-	-	-		-	-	-		-	-	-	
Utilities	0.18	22,726	1.8%		0.18	23,693	2.0%		0.19	24,658	2.0%	
Repairs & Maintenance	0.24	30,228	2.3%		0.22	28,118	2.3%		0.19	24,540	2.0%	
Common Area Maintenance (CAM)	-	-	-		-	-	-		-	-	-	
Administrative	0.05	6,433	0.5%		0.02	2,888	0.2%		0.05	6,550	0.5%	
Other Variable Expense - 1	0.04	5,541	0.4%		0.02	2,782	0.2%		0.04	4,900	0.4%	
Other Variable Expense - 2	-	-	-		-	-	-		-	-	-	
Other Variable Expense - 3	-	-	-		-	-	-		-	-	-	
Total Variable Expenses	0.79	**101,413**	**7.9%**		0.71	**91,778**	**7.6%**		0.74	**94,792**	**7.8%**	
Fixed												
Real Property Taxes	0.54	69,375	5.4%		0.55	70,034	5.8%		0.55	70,212	5.8%	
Insurance	0.10	12,821	1.0%	2	0.14	17,966	1.5%		0.12	15,971	1.3%	
Other Fixed Expense -1	-	-	-		-	-	-		-	-	-	
Other Fixed Expense - 2	-	-	-		-	-	-		-	-	-	
Other Fixed Expense - 3	-	-	-		-	-	-		-	-	-	
Total Fixed Expenses	0.64	**82,196**	**6.4%**		0.69	**88,000**	**7.3%**		0.67	**86,183**	**7.1%**	
Total Expenses	**1.43**	**183,609**	**14.3%**		**1.40**	**179,778**	**14.8%**		**1.41**	**180,975**	**14.9%**	
CASH FLOWS												
Net Operating Income	**8.60**	**1,104,508**	**85.7%**		**8.04**	**1,032,868**	**85.2%**		**8.02**	**1,029,563**	**85.1%**	
Capital Expenditures												
Reserves for Replacements	0.14	17,983	1.4%		0.15	18,625	1.5%		0.15	19,268	1.6%	
Re-Tenanting Costs	0.13	16,418	1.3%		0.15	19,016	1.6%		0.17	22,222	1.8%	
Other Capital Expenses -1	0.19	24,523	1.9%		0.23	28,910	2.4%		0.24	31,399	2.6%	
Other Capital Expenses - 2	-	-	-		-	-	-		-	-	-	
Total Capital Expenditures	0.46	**58,924**	**4.6%**		0.52	**66,551**	**5.5%**		0.57	**72,889**	**6.0%**	
Net Cash Flow	**$8.14**	**$1,045,584**	**81.2%**		**$7.52**	**$966,317**	**79.7%**		**$7.45**	**$956,674**	**79.0%**	

Notes:

1. The parking lot was leased during off hours to a local event planner.
2. The insurance cost was artfiically low as the property received a volume discount from being insured together with other properties owned by the borrower.
3. This reflects the actual fee required in the management agreement.

/SF	TTM 12/31/2000 Income	%	NOTE	/SF	Precept TTM	%	NOTE	/SF	Precept LIP	%	NOTE	Comments
-	-	-		-	-	-		$9.63	$1,237,536	90.1%		Base Rent per 1/12/01 Rent Roll.
8.43	1,083,086	89.5%		8.43	1,083,086	89.5%		-	-	-		Actual 2000 Collections.
-	-	-		-	-	-		-	-	-		
0.92	117,639	9.7%		0.92	117,639	9.7%		0.98	126,153	9.2%		Incremental reimbursement for increased expenses
0.07	9,181	0.8%		0.07	9,181	0.8%		0.07	9,181	0.7%		based on actual leases. The full reimb.
0.01	759	0.1%		0.01	759	0.1%		0.01	759	0.1%		of management expense has been common in this
(0.01)	(1,051)	-0.1%										market for several years. (see reimb. schedule)
0.99	126,528	10.5%		0.99	127,579	10.5%		1.06	136,093	9.9%		
0.01	924	0.1%		-	-	-		-	-	-		
-	-	-		-	-	-		-	-	-		
9.42	1,210,538	100.0%		9.43	1,210,665	100.0%		10.69	1,373,629	100.0%		
-	-	-		-	-	-		-	-	-		
-	-	-		-	-	-		(0.92)	(118,473)	-8.6%		Actual vacancy of 8.8%
9.42	1,210,538	100.0%		9.43	1,210,665	100.0%		9.77	1,255,156	91.4%		

/SF	TTM	%	NOTE	/SF	Precept TTM	%	NOTE	/SF	Precept LIP	%	NOTE	Comments
0.27	34,144	2.8%	3	0.47	60,533	5.0%		0.49	62,758	5.0%		Precept's standard min. mgmt. fee of 5% of EGI.
-	-	-		-	-	-		-	-	-		
0.19	24,658	2.0%		0.19	24,658	2.0%		0.19	24,658	2.0%		TTM
0.19	24,540	2.0%		0.22	27,654	2.3%		0.22	27,654	2.2%		Average of 1998, 1999, and 2000.
-	-	-		-	-	-		-	-	-		
0.05	6,550	0.5%		0.05	6,551	0.5%		0.05	6,551	0.5%		TTM
0.04	4,900	0.4%		0.04	4,900	0.4%		0.04	4,900	0.4%		TTM
-	-	-		-	-	-						
-	-	-		-	-	-		-	-	-		
0.74	94,792	7.8%		0.97	124,296	10.3%		0.98	126,521	10.1%		
0.55	70,212	5.8%		0.56	72,166	6.0%		0.56	72,166	5.7%		Actual 2000/2001 assessment per tax collector
0.12	15,971	1.3%		0.14	17,845	1.5%		0.14	17,845	1.4%		Actual 2001 premium
-	-	-		-	-	-		-	-	-		
-	-	-		-	-	-		-	-	-		
-	-	-		-	-	-		-	-	-		
0.67	86,183	7.1%		0.70	90,011	7.4%		0.70	90,011	7.2%		
1.41	180,975	14.9%		1.67	214,307	17.7%		1.69	216,532	17.3%		

/SF	TTM	%	NOTE	/SF	Precept TTM	%	NOTE	/SF	Precept LIP	%	NOTE	Comments
8.02	1,029,563	85.1%		7.76	996,358	82.3%		8.09	1,038,624	82.7%		
0.15	19,268	1.6%		0.15	19,268	1.6%		0.15	19,268	1.5%		$.15/sf (Engineer's estimate is $.04 PSF)
0.54	70,000	5.8%		0.56	71,986	5.9%		0.56	71,986	5.7%		See rollover analysis
0.24	31,399	2.6%		0.05	7,000	0.6%		0.05	7,000	0.6%		Biannual monitoring well testing
-	-	-		-	-	-		-	-	-		
0.94	120,667	10.0%		0.76	98,254	8.1%		0.76	98,254	7.8%		
$7.08	$908,896	75.1%		$6.99	$898,104	74.2%		$7.32	$940,370	74.9%		

CASH FLOW SUMMARY (Cont...)

Village Square Center

Property Number: 0238 Financing Number: 0128 Square Feet: 128,451	/SF	Precept TTM	%	/SF	Precept LIP	%	/SF	S & P	%
REVENUES									
Gross Potential Rent	-	-	-	$9.63	$1,237,536	90.1%	$9.63	$1,237,536	90.7%
OR Collected Rent	$8.43	$1,083,086	89.5%	-	-	-	-	-	-
Percentage Rent	-	-	-	-	-	-	-	-	-
Recoveries									
Common Area Maintenance (CAM)	0.92	117,639	9.7%	0.98	126,153	9.2%	0.92	117,639	8.6%
Real Estate Taxes	0.07	9,181	0.8%	0.07	9,181	0.7%	0.07	9,181	0.7%
Insurance	0.01	759	0.1%	0.01	759	0.1%	0.01	759	0.1%
Other Expense Recoveries	-	-	-	-	-	-	-	-	-
Total Recoveries	0.99	**127,579**	10.5%	1.06	**136,093**	9.9%	0.99	**127,579**	9.3%
Other Income - 1	-	-	-	-	-	-	-	-	-
Other Income - 2	-	-	-	-	-	-	-	-	-
Total Gross Income	9.43	**1,210,665**	**100.0%**	10.69	**1,373,629**	**100.0%**	10.63	**1,365,115**	**100.0%**
Mark-to-Market	-	-	-	-	-	-	-	-	-
Vacancy and Credit Loss	-	-	-	(0.92)	(118,473)	-8.6%	(1.06)	(136,512)	-10.0%
Effective Gross Income	**9.43**	**1,210,665**	**100.0%**	**9.77**	**1,255,156**	**91.4%**	**9.56**	**1,228,604**	**90.0%**
EXPENSES									
Variable									
Management Fee	0.47	60,533	5.0%	0.49	62,758	5.0%	0.48	61,430	5.0%
Payroll & Benefits	-	-	-	-	-	-	-	-	-
Utilities	0.19	24,658	2.0%	0.19	24,658	2.0%	0.19	24,658	2.0%
Repairs & Maintenance	0.22	27,654	2.3%	0.22	27,654	2.2%	0.22	27,654	2.3%
Common Area Maintenance (CAM)	-	-	-	-	-	-	-	-	-
Administrative	0.05	6,551	0.5%	0.05	6,551	0.5%	0.05	6,551	0.5%
Other Variable Expense - 1	0.04	4,900	0.4%	0.04	4,900	0.4%	0.04	4,900	0.4%
Other Variable Expense - 2	-	-	-	-	-	-	-	-	-
Other Variable Expense - 3	-	-	-	-	-	-	-	-	-
Total Variable Expenses	0.97	**124,296**	**10.3%**	0.98	**126,521**	**10.1%**	0.97	**125,193**	**10.2%**
Fixed									
Real Property Taxes	0.56	72,166	6.0%	0.56	72,166	5.7%	0.56	72,166	5.9%
Insurance	0.14	17,845	1.5%	0.14	17,845	1.4%	0.14	17,845	1.5%
Other Fixed Expense -1	-	-	-	-	-	-	-	-	-
Other Fixed Expense - 2	-	-	-	-	-	-	-	-	-
Other Fixed Expense - 3	-	-	-	-	-	-	-	-	-
Total Fixed Expenses	0.70	**90,011**	**7.4%**	0.70	**90,011**	**7.2%**	0.70	**90,011**	**7.3%**
Total Expenses	**1.67**	**214,307**	**17.7%**	**1.69**	**216,532**	**17.3%**	**1.68**	**215,204**	**17.5%**
CASH FLOWS									
Net Operating Income	**7.76**	**996,358**	**82.3%**	**8.09**	**1,038,624**	**82.7%**	**7.89**	**1,013,399**	**82.5%**
Capital Expenditures									
Reserves for Replacements	0.15	19,268	1.6%	0.15	19,268	1.5%	0.20	25,690	2.1%
Re-Tenanting Costs	0.56	71,986	5.9%	0.56	71,986	5.7%	0.62	79,747	6.5%
Other Capital Expenses -1	0.05	7,000	0.6%	0.05	7,000	0.6%	0.05	7,000	0.6%
Other Capital Expenses - 2	-	-	-	-	-	-	-	-	-
Total Capital Expenditures	0.76	**98,254**	**8.1%**	0.76	**98,254**	**7.8%**	0.88	**112,437**	**9.2%**
Net Cash Flow	**6.99**	**$898,104**	**74.2%**	**7.32**	**$940,370**	**74.9%**	**7.01**	**$900,962**	**73.3%**

Notes:

Comments	/SF	Bidder	%	NOTE	Comments
Leases in Place	-	-	-		
TTM	-	-	-		
	-	-	-		
TTM	-	-	-		
TTM	-	-	-		
TTM	-	-	-		
	-	-	-		
	-	-	-		
	-	-	-		
	-	-	-		
	-	-	-		
	-	-	-		
Current vacancy of 8.6% + U/W additional 1.4%.	-	-	-		
	-	-	-		
5% of EGI	-	-	-		
	-	-	-		
TTM	-	-	-		
1999 due to recent decreases.	-	-	-		
	-	-	-		
TTM	-	-	-		
TTM	-	-	-		
	-	-	-		
	-	-	-		
	-	-	-		
2000/2001 Assessment.	-	-	-		
2001 Premium	-	-	-		
	-	-	-		
	-	-	-		
	-	-	-		
	-	-	-		
	-	-	-		
	-	-	-		
$.20 PSF	-	-	-		
$4/$2 new/ren. TIs, 5%/2.5% new/ren. comm.	-	-	-		
Current annual monitoring well expense.	-	-	-		
	-	-	-		
	-	-	-		
	-	-	-		

CASH FLOW SUMMARY (Cont...)

Village Square Center

Property Number: 0238
Financing Number: 0128
Square Feet: 128,451

	/SF	1998	%	/SF	TTM	%	/SF	Appraisal	%
		Through: 12/31/1998 Income			12/31/2000 Income			1/20/2001	
REVENUES									
Gross Potential Rent	-	-	-	-	-	-	$9.32	$1,196,631	84.4%
Collected Rent	8.73	1,121,277	87.0%	8.43	1,083,086	89.5%	-	-	-
Percentage Rent	-	-	-	-	-	-	-	-	-
Recoveries									
Common Area Maintenance (CAM)	1.16	148,484	11.5%	0.92	117,639	9.7%	1.04	133,535	9.4%
Real Estate Taxes	0.08	10,410	0.8%	0.07	9,181	0.8%	0.54	69,072	4.9%
Insurance	0.03	3,307	0.3%	0.01	759	0.1%	0.14	18,274	1.3%
Other Expense Recoveries	-	-	-	(0.01)	(1,051)	-0.1%	-	-	-
Total Recoveries	1.26	**162,201**	12.6%	0.99	**126,528**	10.5%	1.72	**220,881**	15.6%
Other Income - 1	0.04	4,639	0.4%	0.01	924	0.1%	-	-	-
Other Income - 2	-	-	-	-	-	-	-	-	-
Total Gross Income	10.03	**1,288,117**	**100.0%**	9.42	**1,210,538**	**100.0%**	11.04	**1,417,512**	**100.0%**
Mark-to-Market	-	-	-	-	-	-	-	-	-
Vacancy and Credit Loss	-	-	-	-	-	-	(0.64)	(82,733)	-5.8%
Effective Gross Income	**10.03**	**1,288,117**	**100.0%**	**9.42**	**1,210,538**	**100.0%**	**10.39**	**1,334,779**	**94.2%**
EXPENSES									
Variable									
Management Fee	0.28	36,484	2.8%	0.27	34,144	2.8%	0.29	37,374	2.8%
Payroll & Benefits	-	-	-	-	-	-	-	-	-
Utilities	0.18	22,726	1.8%	0.19	24,658	2.0%	0.18	23,245	1.7%
Repairs & Maintenance	0.24	30,228	2.3%	0.19	24,540	2.0%	0.27	34,956	2.6%
Common Area Maintenance (CAM)	-	-	-	-	-	-	-	-	-
Administrative	0.05	6,433	0.5%	0.05	6,550	0.5%	0.06	7,544	0.6%
Other Variable Expense - 1	0.04	5,541	0.4%	0.04	4,900	0.4%	0.02	2,019	0.2%
Other Variable Expense - 2	-	-	-	-	-	-	-	-	-
Other Variable Expense - 3	-	-	-	-	-	-	-	-	-
Total Variable Expenses	0.79	**101,413**	**7.9%**	0.74	**94,792**	**7.8%**	0.82	**105,138**	**7.9%**
Fixed									
Real Property Taxes	0.54	69,375	5.4%	0.55	70,212	5.8%	0.55	70,524	5.3%
Insurance	0.10	12,821	1.0%	0.12	15,971	1.3%	0.15	18,703	1.4%
Other Fixed Expense -1	-	-	-	-	-	-	-	-	-
Other Fixed Expense - 2	-	-	-	-	-	-	-	-	-
Other Fixed Expense - 3	-	-	-	-	-	-	-	-	-
Total Fixed Expenses	0.64	**82,196**	**6.4%**	0.67	**86,183**	**7.1%**	0.69	**89,227**	**6.7%**
Total Expenses	**1.43**	**183,609**	**14.3%**	**1.41**	**180,975**	**14.9%**	**1.51**	**194,365**	**14.6%**
CASH FLOWS									
Net Operating Income	**8.60**	**1,104,508**	**85.7%**	**8.02**	**1,029,563**	**85.1%**	**8.88**	**1,140,414**	**85.4%**
Capital Expenditures									
Reserves for Replacements	0.14	17,983	1.4%	0.15	19,268	1.6%	0.15	18,928	1.4%
Re-Tenanting Costs	0.13	16,418	1.3%	0.54	70,000	5.8%	0.52	66,268	5.0%
Other Capital Expenses -1	0.19	24,523	1.9%	0.24	31,399	2.6%	-	-	-
Other Capital Expenses - 2	-	-	-	-	-	-	-	-	-
Total Capital Expenditures	0.46	**58,924**	**4.6%**	0.94	**120,667**	**10.0%**	0.66	**85,196**	**6.4%**
Net Cash Flow	**$8.14**	**$1,045,584**	**81.2%**	**$7.08**	**$908,896**	**75.1%**	**$8.21**	**$1,055,218**	**79.1%**

Notes:

Comments	/SF	Budget	%	NOTE	Comments	Borrower Comments
	$9.66	$1,240,720	84.9%			
	-	-	-			
	-	-	-			
	1.05	135,000	9.2%			
	0.56	72,500	5.0%			
	0.11	13,500	0.9%			
	-	-	-			
	1.72	**221,000**	15.1%			
	-	-	-			
	-	-	-			
	11.38	**1,461,720**	**100.0%**			
	-	-	-			
	(0.80)	(103,370)	-7.1%			
	10.57	**1,358,350**	**92.9%**			
	0.43	54,934	4.0%			
	-	-	-			
	0.18	23,250	1.7%			
	0.25	31,500	2.3%			
	-	-	-			
	0.03	4,000	0.3%			
	0.03	3,500	0.3%			
	-	-	-			
	-	-	-			
	0.91	**117,184**	**8.6%**			
	0.56	72,500	5.3%			
	0.11	13,500	1.0%			
	-	-	-			
	-	-	-			
	-	-	-			
	0.67	**86,000**	**6.3%**			
	1.58	**203,184**	**15.0%**			
	8.99	**1,155,166**	**85.0%**			
	-	-	-			
	0.35	45,280	3.3%			
	0.10	12,845	0.9%			
	-	-	-			
	0.45	**58,125**	**4.3%**			
	$8.54	**$1,097,041**	**80.8%**			

OP STMT RECONCILIATION

Village Square Center

Property Number: 0238
Financing Number: 0128
Square Feet: 128,451

	1998			N O T E
	Statement	**Adjustment**	**Operating**	
	Through:	**12/31/1998**		
	Stmt. Type:	Income		
REVENUES				
Gross Potential Rent				
-	-	-	-	
-	-	-	-	
-	-	-	-	
Gross Potential Rent	-	-	-	
Collected Rent				
-	1,121,277	-	1,121,277	
-	-	-	-	
-	-	-	-	
Collected Rent	1,121,277	-	1,121,277	
Percentage Rent				
-	-	-	-	
-	-	-	-	
-	-	-	-	
Percentage Rent	-	-	-	
Recoveries				
Common Area Maintenance (CAM)	148,484	-	148,484	
Real Estate Taxes	10,410	-	10,410	
Insurance	3,307	-	3,307	
Other Expense Recoveries	-	-	-	
Total Recoveries	162,201	-	162,201	
Other Income - 1				
Late Charges & NSF	1,784	(1,784)	0	1
Other Re-occurring Charges	4,639	-	4,639	
Miscellaneous	14,000	(14,000)	-	2
Deposits to Tenant A/C	-	-	-	
Personal Property Tax Recov.	-	-	-	
Electricity	-	-	-	
-	-	-	-	
Other Income - 1	20,423	(15,784)	4,639	
Other Income - 2				
-	-	-	-	
-	-	-	-	
-	-	-	-	
-	-	-	-	
-	-	-	-	
Other Income - 2	-	-	-	
Total Gross Income	**1,303,901**	**(15,784)**	**1,288,117**	

1999			N	2000			N
Statement	Adjustment	Operating	O	Statement	Adjustment	Operating	O
Through:	12/31/99		T	Through:	12/31/00		T
Stmt. Type:	Income		E	Stmt. Type:	Income		E
-	-	-		-	-	-	
-	-	-		-	-	-	
-	-	-		-	-	-	
-	-	-		-	-	-	
1,073,945	-	1,073,945		1,083,086	-	1,083,086	
-	-	-		-	-	-	
-	-	-		-	-	-	
1,073,945	-	1,073,945		1,083,086	-	1,083,086	
-	-	-		-	-	-	
-	-	-		-	-	-	
-	-	-		-	-	-	
-	-	-		-	-	-	
127,654	-	127,654		117,639	-	117,639	
10,513	-	10,513		9,181	-	9,181	
550	-	550		759	-	759	
(89)	-	(89)		(1,051)	-	(1,051)	
138,628	-	138,628		126,528	-	126,528	
4,913	(4,913)	-	3	1,423	(1,423)	-	
-	-	-		784	-	784	
-	-	-		40	-	40	
-	-	-		-	-	-	
73	-	73		100	-	100	
-	-	-		-	-	-	
-	-	-		-	-	-	
4,986	(4,913)	73		2,347	(1,423)	924	
-	-	-		-	-	-	
-	-	-		-	-	-	
-	-	-		-	-	-	
-	-	-		-	-	-	
-	-	-		-	-	-	
-	-	-		-	-	-	
1,217,559	**(4,913)**	**1,212,646**		**1,211,961**	**(1,423)**	**1,210,538**	

OP STMT RECONCILIATION

Village Square Center

Property Number: 0238
Financing Number: 0128
Square Feet: 128,451

	1998		
	Statement	Adjustment	Operating
	Through:	12/31/1998	
	Stmt. Type:	Income	
Mark-to-Market			
-	-	-	-
-	-	-	-
-	-	-	-
Mark-to-Market	-	-	-
Vacancy and Credit Loss			
-	-	-	-
-	-	-	-
-	-	-	-
Vacancy and Credit Loss	-	-	-
Effective Gross Income	1,303,901	(15,784)	1,288,117

EXPENSES (Variable)	CAM Pools #1	#2	#3	Statement	Adjustment	Operating
Management Fee						
Management Fee	x	x		36,484	-	36,484
-				-	-	-
Management Fee				36,484	-	36,484
Payroll & Benefits						
					-	-
					-	-
					-	-
					-	-
					-	-
Payroll & Benefits				-	-	-
Utilities						
Electricity	x	x		5,616	-	5,616
Water/Sewer		x		16,295	-	16,295
Owner Utilities		x		814	-	814
Water Irrigation	x	x		-	-	-
Recoverable Utilities	x	x		-	-	-
Utilities				22,726	-	22,726
Repairs & Maintenance						
HVAC Maint.	x	x		4,282	-	4,282
Repair & Maint.-C/A		x		7,929	-	7,929
Owner HVAC		x		838	-	838
Owner R&M		x		549	-	549
Sidewalk Powerwash	x	x		-	-	-
Exterminating	x	x		175	-	175
Snow Removal	x	x		-	-	-
Landscape Maint/Lot Sweep	x	x		16,455	-	16,455
-				-	-	-
Repairs & Maintenance				30,228	-	30,228
Common Area Maintenance (CAM)						
-				-	-	-
-				-	-	-
-				-	-	-
-				-	-	-
Common Area Maintenance (CAM)				-	-	-

1999			N	2000			N
Statement	Adjustment	Operating	O	Statement	Adjustment	Operating	O
Through:	12/31/99		T	Through:	12/31/00		T
Stmt. Type:	Income		E	Stmt. Type:	Income		E
-	-	-		-	-	-	
-	-	-		-	-	-	
-	-	-		-	-	-	
-	-	-		-	-	-	
-	-	-		-	-	-	
-	-	-		-	-	-	
-	-	-		-	-	-	
-	-	-		-	-	-	
1,217,559	**(4,913)**	**1,212,646**		**1,211,961**	**(1,423)**	**1,210,538**	
34,297	-	34,297		34,144	-	34,144	
-	-	-		-	-	-	
34,297	-	34,297		34,144	-	34,144	
-	-	-		-	-	-	
-	-	-		-	-	-	
-	-	-		-	-	-	
-	-	-		-	-	-	
-	-	-		-	-	-	
-	-	-		-	-	-	
5,595	-	5,595		6,101	-	6,101	
16,733	-	16,733		17,373	-	17,373	
1,101	-	1,101		1,074	-	1,074	
176	-	176		-	-	-	
88	-	88		110	-	110	
23,693	-	23,693		24,658	-	24,658	
3,126	-	3,126		3,109	-	3,109	
15,679	(4,000)	11,679	4	10,522	-	10,522	
-	-	-		56	-	56	
181	-	181		662	-	662	
747	-	747		-	-	-	
-	-	-		857	-	857	
-	-	-		354	-	354	
12,385	-	12,385		8,980	-	8,980	
-	-	-		-	-	-	
32,118	(4,000)	28,118		24,540	-	24,540	
-	-	-		-	-	-	
-	-	-		-	-	-	
-	-	-		-	-	-	
-	-	-		-	-	-	
-	-	-		-	-	-	

OP STMT RECONCILIATION

Village Square Center

Property Number: 0238
Financing Number: 0128
Square Feet: 128,451

				1998			
				Statement	**Adjustment**	**Operating**	**NOTE**
				Through:	**12/31/1998**		
				Stmt. Type:	Income		
Administrative							
Accounting Fees	x	x		1,450	-	1,450	
Appraisal	x	x		8,500	(8,500)	-	5
Architect	x	x		3,232	(3,232)	(1)	6
Development Svcs.	x	x		-	-	-	
Bank Charges	x	x		75	-	75	
Commissions (see below)	x	x		-	-	-	
Mail & Delivery	x	x		332	-	332	
Legal Fees	x	x		3,840	-	3,840	
Rent/Lease Payments	x	x		737	-	737	
-				-	-	-	
Administrative				18,165	(11,732)	6,433	
Other Variable Expense - 1							
Alarm Monitoring	x	x		1,839	-	1,839	
Owner Misc	x	x		3,702	-	3,702	
-				-	-	-	
-				-	-	-	
-				-	-	-	
-				-	-	-	
Other Variable Expense - 1				5,541	-	5,541	
Other Variable Expense - 2							
-				-	-	-	
-				-	-	-	
-				-	-	-	
Other Variable Expense - 2				-	-	-	
Other Variable Expense - 3							
-				-	-	-	
-				-	-	-	
-				-	-	-	
Other Variable Expense - 3				-	-	-	
Total Variable Expenses				**113,145**	**(11,732)**	**101,413**	

EXPENSES (Fixed)

				Statement	Adjustment	Operating	Note
Real Property Taxes							
Real Property Taxes		x		69,234	-	69,234	
Personal Property Taxes	x	x		141	-	141	
-				-	-	-	
Real Property Taxes				69,375	-	69,375	
Insurance							
Insurance		x		12,821	-	12,821	
-				-	-	-	
-				-	-	-	
Insurance				12,821	-	12,821	
Other Fixed Expense -1							
-				-	-	-	
-				-	-	-	
-				-	-	-	
Other Fixed Expense -1				-	-	-	

1999			N	2000			N
Statement	Adjustment	Operating	O	Statement	Adjustment	Operating	O
Through:	12/31/99		T	Through:	12/31/00		T
Stmt. Type:	Income		E	Stmt. Type:	Income		E
1,800	-	1,800		1,800	-	1,800	
-	-	-		-	-	-	
-	-	-		-	-	-	
-	-	-		-	-	-	
-	-	-		-	-	-	
-	-	-		-	-	-	
26	-	26		182	-	182	
611	-	611		4,117	-	4,117	
451	-	451		451	-	451	
-	-	-		-	-	-	
2,888	-	2,888		6,550	-	6,550	
1,940	-	1,940		2,727	-	2,727	
842	-	842		2,173	-	2,173	
-	-	-		-	-	-	
-	-	-		-	-	-	
-	-	-		-	-	-	
-	-	-		-	-	-	
2,782	-	2,782		4,900	-	4,900	
-	-	-		-	-	-	
-	-	-		-	-	-	
-	-	-		-	-	-	
-	-	-		-	-	-	
-	-	-		-	-	-	
-	-	-		-	-	-	
-	-	-		-	-	-	
-	-	-		-	-	-	
95,778	**(4,000)**	**91,778**		**94,792**	**-**	**94,792**	

Statement	Adjustment	Operating	Note	Statement	Adjustment	Operating	Note
69,915	-	69,915		70,115	-	70,115	
119	-	119		97	-	97	
-	-	-		-	-	-	
70,034	-	70,034		70,212	-	70,212	
17,966	-	17,966		15,971	-	15,971	
-	-	-		-	-	-	
-	-	-		-	-	-	
17,966	-	17,966		15,971	-	15,971	
-	-	-		-	-	-	
-	-	-		-	-	-	
-	-	-		-	-	-	
-	-	-		-	-	-	

OP STMT RECONCILIATION

Village Square Center

Property Number: 0238
Financing Number: 0128
Square Feet: 128,451

	1998		
	Statement	**Adjustment**	**Operating**
	Through:	**12/31/1998**	
	Stmt. Type:	Income	
Other Fixed Expense - 2			
-	-	-	-
-	-	-	-
-	-	-	-
Other Fixed Expense - 2	-	-	-
Other Fixed Expense - 3			
-	-	-	-
-	-	-	-
-	-	-	-
Other Fixed Expense - 3	-	-	-
Total Fixed Expenses	**82,196**	**-**	**82,196**
Total Expenses	**195,341**	**(11,732)**	**183,609**
Net Operating Income	**1,108,560**	**(4,052)**	**1,104,508**

CAPITAL EXPENDITURES

	Statement	Adjustment	Operating
Reserves for Replacements			
Imputed Reserves	17,983	-	17,983
-	-	-	-
-	-	-	-
Reserves for Replacements	17,983	-	17,983
Re-Tenanting Costs			
Leasing Commissions	16,418	-	16,418
TI's	-	-	-
-	-	-	-
Re-Tenanting Costs	16,418	-	16,418
Other Capital Expenses -1			
Survey & Review Fees	-	-	-
Capital Expenditures	24,523	-	24,523
-	-	-	-
-	-	-	-
-	-	-	-
-	-	-	-
Other Capital Expenses -1	24,523	-	24,523
Other Capital Expenses - 2			
-	-	-	-
-	-	-	-
-	-	-	-
-	-	-	-
-	-	-	-
-	-	-	-
Other Capital Expenses - 2	-	-	-
Total Capital Expenditures	**58,924**	**-**	**58,924**
Net Cash Flow	**$1,049,636**	**($4,052)**	**$1,045,584**

1999			N	2000			N
Statement	Adjustment	Operating	O	Statement	Adjustment	Operating	O
Through:	12/31/99		T	Through:	12/31/00		T
Stmt. Type:	Income		E	Stmt. Type:	Income		E
-	-	-		-	-	-	
-	-	-		-	-	-	
-	-	-		-	-	-	
-	-	-		-	-	-	
-	-	-		-	-	-	
-	-	-		-	-	-	
-	-	-		-	-	-	
-	-	-		-	-	-	
88,000	-	88,000		86,183	-	86,183	
183,778	(4,000)	179,778		180,975	-	180,975	
1,033,781	(913)	1,032,868		1,030,986	(1,423)	1,029,563	
18,625	-	18,625		19,268	-	19,268	
-	-	-		-	-	-	
-	-	-		-	-	-	
18,625	-	18,625		19,268	-	19,268	
19,016	-	19,016		22,222	-	22,222	
-	-	-		-	-	-	
-	-	-		-	-	-	
19,016	-	19,016		22,222	-	22,222	
-	-	-		18,198	-	18,198	
28,910	-	28,910		13,201	-	13,201	
-	-	-		-	-	-	
-	-	-		-	-	-	
-	-	-		-	-	-	
-	-	-		-	-	-	
28,910	-	28,910		31,399	-	31,399	
-	-	-		-	-	-	
-	-	-		-	-	-	
-	-	-		-	-	-	
-	-	-		-	-	-	
-	-	-		-	-	-	
-	-	-		-	-	-	
-	-	-		-	-	-	
66,551	-	66,551		72,889	-	72,889	
$967,230	($913)	$966,317		$958,097	($1,423)	$956,674	

OP STMT RECONCILIATION

Village Square Center

Property Number: 0238
Financing Number: 0128
Square Feet: 128,451

	1998		N
Statement	**Adjustment**	**Operating**	O
Through:	**12/31/1998**		T
Stmt. Type:	Income		E

OCCUPANCY	**Physical**	**Economic**	**Conclusion**
January			
February			
March			
April			
May			
June			
July			
August			
September			
October			
November			
December			
Calculated Average			
Override	93.10%		93.10%
Concluded Average	93.10%		93.10%

1999			N	2000			N
Statement	Adjustment	Operating	O	Statement	Adjustment	Operating	O
Through:	12/31/99		T	Through:	12/31/00		T
Stmt. Type:	Income		E	Stmt. Type:	Income		E

Physical	Economic	Conclusion		Physical	Economic	Conclusion	
90.50%		90.50%		91.00%		91.00%	
90.50%		90.50%		91.00%		91.00%	

OP STMT RECONCILIATION

Village Square Center

Property Number: 0238
Financing Number: 0128
Square Feet: 128,451

	TTM		
Statement	Adjustment	Operating	
Through:	12/31/2000		
Stmt. Type:	Income		

REVENUES

	Statement	Adjustment	Operating
Gross Potential Rent			
-	-	-	-
-	-	-	-
-	-	-	-
Gross Potential Rent	-	-	-
Collected Rent			
-	1,083,086	-	1,083,086
-	-	-	-
-	-	-	-
Collected Rent	1,083,086	-	1,083,086
Percentage Rent			
-	-	-	-
-	-	-	-
-	-	-	-
Percentage Rent	-	-	-
Recoveries			
Common Area Maintenance (CAM)	117,639	-	117,639
Real Estate Taxes	9,181	-	9,181
Insurance	759	-	759
Other Expense Recoveries	(1,051)	-	(1,051)
Total Recoveries	126,528	-	126,528
Other Income - 1			
Late Charges & NSF	-	-	-
Other Re-occurring Charges	784	-	784
Miscellaneous	40	-	40
Deposits to Tenant A/C	-	-	-
Personal Property Tax Recov.	100	-	100
Electricity	-	-	-
-	-	-	-
Other Income - 1	924	-	924
Other Income - 2			
-	-	-	-
-	-	-	-
-	-	-	-
-	-	-	-
-	-	-	-
Other Income - 2	-	-	-
Total Gross Income	**1,210,538**	**-**	**1,210,538**

YTD			N	YTD Prior			N
Statement	Adjustment	Operating	O	Statement	Adjustment	Operating	O
Through:	12/31/2000		T	Through:			T
Stmt. Type:	Income		E	Stmt. Type:	Income		E
-	-	-		-	-	-	
-	-	-		-	-	-	
-	-	-		-	-	-	
-	-	-		-	-	-	
1,083,086	-	1,083,086		-	-	-	
-	-	-		-	-	-	
-	-	-		-	-	-	
1,083,086	-	1,083,086		-	-	-	
-	-	-		-	-	-	
-	-	-		-	-	-	
-	-	-		-	-	-	
-	-	-		-	-	-	
117,639	-	117,639		-	-	-	
9,181	-	9,181		-	-	-	
759	-	759		-	-	-	
(1,051)	-	(1,051)		-	-	-	
126,528	-	126,528		-	-	-	
-	-	-		-	-	-	
784	-	784		-	-	-	
40	-	40		-	-	-	
-	-	-		-	-	-	
100	-	100		-	-	-	
-	-	-		-	-	-	
-	-	-		-	-	-	
924	-	924		-	-	-	
-	-	-		-	-	-	
-	-	-		-	-	-	
-	-	-		-	-	-	
-	-	-		-	-	-	
-	-	-		-	-	-	
-	-	-		-	-	-	
1,210,538	**-**	**1,210,538**		-	-	-	

OP STMT RECONCILIATION

Village Square Center

				Statement	Adjustment	Operating
Property Number: 0238						
Financing Number: 0128					**TTM**	
Square Feet: 128,451						
				Through:	**12/31/2000**	
				Stmt. Type:	Income	
Mark-to-Market						
-				-	-	-
-				-	-	-
-				-	-	-
Mark-to-Market				-	-	-
Vacancy and Credit Loss						
-				-	-	-
-				-	-	-
-				-	-	-
Vacancy and Credit Loss				-	-	-
Effective Gross Income				**1,210,538**	**-**	**1,210,538**
EXPENSES (Variable)	**CAM Pools**					
	#1	**#2**	**#3**			
Management Fee						
Management Fee	x	x		34,144	-	34,144
-				-	-	-
Management Fee				34,144	-	34,144
Payroll & Benefits						
				-	-	-
				-	-	-
				-	-	-
				-	-	-
				-	-	-
Payroll & Benefits				-	-	-
Utilities						
Electricity	x	x		6,101	-	6,101
Water/Sewer		x		17,373	-	17,373
Owner Utilities		x		1,074	-	1,074
Water Irrigation	x	x		-	-	-
Recoverable Utilities	x	x		110	-	110
Utilities				24,658	-	24,658
Repairs & Maintenance						
HVAC Maint.	x	x		3,109	-	3,109
Repair & Maint.-C/A		x		10,522	-	10,522
Owner HVAC		x		56	-	56
Owner R&M		x		662	-	662
Sidewalk Powerwash	x	x		-	-	-
Exterminating	x	x		857	-	857
Snow Removal	x	x		354	-	354
Landscape Maint/Lot Sweep	x	x		8,980	-	8,980
-				-	-	-
Repairs & Maintenance				24,540	-	24,540
Common Area Maintenance (CAM)						
-				-	-	-
-				-	-	-
-				-	-	-
-				-	-	-
Common Area Maintenance (CAM)				-	-	-

YTD			N	YTD Prior			N
Statement	Adjustment	Operating	O	Statement	Adjustment	Operating	O
Through:	12/31/2000		T	Through:			T
Stmt. Type:	Income		E	Stmt. Type:	Income		E
-	-	-		-	-	-	
-	-	-		-	-	-	
-	-	-		-	-	-	
-	-	-		-	-	-	
-	-	-		-	-	-	
-	-	-		-	-	-	
-	-	-		-	-	-	
-	-	-		-	-	-	
1,210,538	**-**	**1,210,538**		**-**	**-**	**-**	

Statement	Adjustment	Operating	NOTE	Statement	Adjustment	Operating	NOTE
34,144	-	34,144		-	-	-	
-	-	-		-	-	-	
34,144	-	34,144		-	-	-	
-	-	-		-	-	-	
-	-	-		-	-	-	
-	-	-		-	-	-	
-	-	-		-	-	-	
-	-	-		-	-	-	
-	-	-		-	-	-	
6,101	-	6,101		-	-	-	
17,373	-	17,373		-	-	-	
1,074	-	1,074		-	-	-	
-	-	-		-	-	-	
110	-	110		-	-	-	
24,658	-	24,658		-	-	-	
3,109	-	3,109		-	-	-	
10,522	-	10,522		-	-	-	
56	-	56		-	-	-	
662	-	662		-	-	-	
-	-	-		-	-	-	
857	-	857		-	-	-	
354	-	354		-	-	-	
8,980	-	8,980		-	-	-	
-	-	-		-	-	-	
24,540	-	24,540		-	-	-	
-	-	-		-	-	-	
-	-	-		-	-	-	
-	-	-		-	-	-	
-	-	-		-	-	-	
-	-	-		-	-	-	

OP STMT RECONCILIATION

Village Square Center

Property Number: 0238
Financing Number: 0128
Square Feet: 128,451

				TTM Statement	Adjustment	Operating
				Through:	**12/31/2000**	
				Stmt. Type:	Income	
Administrative						
Accounting Fees	x	x		1,800	-	1,800
Appraisal	x	x		-	-	-
Architect	x	x		-	-	-
Development Svcs.	x	x		-	-	-
Bank Charges	x	x		-	-	-
Commissions (see below)	x	x		-	-	-
Mail & Delivery	x	x		182	-	182
Legal Fees	x	x		4,117	-	4,117
Rent/Lease Payments	x	x		451	-	451
-				-	-	-
Administrative				6,550	-	6,550
Other Variable Expense - 1						
Alarm Monitoring	x	x		2,727	-	2,727
Owner Misc	x	x		2,173	-	2,173
-				-	-	-
-				-	-	-
-				-	-	-
-				-	-	-
Other Variable Expense - 1				4,900	-	4,900
Other Variable Expense - 2						
-				-	-	-
-				-	-	-
-				-	-	-
Other Variable Expense - 2				-	-	-
Other Variable Expense - 3						
-				-	-	-
-				-	-	-
-				-	-	-
Other Variable Expense - 3				-	-	-
Total Variable Expenses				**94,792**	**-**	**94,792**
EXPENSES (Fixed)						
Real Property Taxes						
Real Property Taxes		x		70,115	-	70,115
Personal Property Taxes	x	x		97	-	97
-				-	-	-
Real Property Taxes				70,212	-	70,212
Insurance						
Insurance		x		15,971	-	15,971
-				-	-	-
-				-	-	-
Insurance				15,971	-	15,971
Other Fixed Expense -1						
-				-	-	-
-				-	-	-
-				-	-	-
Other Fixed Expense -1				-	-	-

YTD			N	YTD Prior			N
Statement	Adjustment	Operating	O	Statement	Adjustment	Operating	O
Through:	12/31/2000		T	Through:			T
Stmt. Type:	Income		E	Stmt. Type:	Income		E
1,800	-	1,800		-	-	-	
-	-	-		-	-	-	
-	-	-		-	-	-	
-	-	-		-	-	-	
-	-	-		-	-	-	
-	-	-		-	-	-	
182	-	182		-	-	-	
4,117	-	4,117		-	-	-	
451	-	451		-	-	-	
-	-	-		-	-	-	
6,550	-	6,550		-	-	-	
2,727	-	2,727		-	-	-	
2,173	-	2,173		-	-	-	
-	-	-		-	-	-	
-	-	-		-	-	-	
-	-	-		-	-	-	
-	-	-		-	-	-	
4,900	-	4,900		-	-	-	
-	-	-		-	-	-	
-	-	-		-	-	-	
-	-	-		-	-	-	
-	-	-		-	-	-	
-	-	-		-	-	-	
-	-	-		-	-	-	
-	-	-		-	-	-	
-	-	-		-	-	z -	
94,792	**-**	**94,792**		**-**	**-**	**-**	

70,115	-	70,115		-	-	-	
97	-	97		-	-	-	
-	-	-		-	-	-	
70,212	-	70,212		-	-	-	
15,971	-	15,971		-	-	-	
-	-	-		-	-	-	
-	-	-		-	-	-	
15,971	-	15,971		-	-	-	
-	-	-		-	-	-	
-	-	-		-	-	-	
-	-	-		-	-	-	
-	-	-		-	-	-	

OP STMT RECONCILIATION

Village Square Center

Property Number: 0238
Financing Number: 0128
Square Feet: 128,451

	TTM Statement	TTM Adjustment	TTM Operating
Through:		12/31/2000	
Stmt. Type:		Income	
Other Fixed Expense - 2			
-	-	-	-
-	-	-	-
-	-	-	-
Other Fixed Expense - 2	-	-	-
Other Fixed Expense - 3			
-	-	-	-
-	-	-	-
-	-	-	-
Other Fixed Expense - 3	-	-	-
Total Fixed Expenses	**86,183**	**-**	**86,183**
Total Expenses	**180,975**	**-**	**180,975**
Net Operating Income	**1,029,563**	**-**	**1,029,563**
CAPITAL EXPENDITURES			
Reserves for Replacements			
Imputed Reserves	19,268	-	19,268
-	-	-	-
-	-	-	-
Reserves for Replacements	19,268	-	19,268
Re-Tenanting Costs			
Leasing Commissions	20,000	-	20,000
TI's	50,000	-	50,000
-	-	-	-
Re-Tenanting Costs	70,000	-	70,000
Other Capital Expenses -1			
Survey & Review Fees	18,198	-	18,198
Capital Expenditures	13,201	-	13,201
-	-	-	-
-	-	-	-
-	-	-	-
-	-	-	-
Other Capital Expenses -1	31,399	-	31,399
Other Capital Expenses - 2			
-	-	-	-
-	-	-	-
-	-	-	-
-	-	-	-
-	-	-	-
-	-	-	-
Other Capital Expenses - 2	-	-	-
Total Capital Expenditures	**120,667**	**-**	**120,667**
Net Cash Flow	**$908,896**	**-**	**$908,896**

YTD			NOTE	YTD Prior			NOTE
Statement	Adjustment	Operating		Statement	Adjustment	Operating	
Through:	12/31/2000			Through:			
Stmt. Type:	Income			Stmt. Type:	Income		
-	-	-		-	-	-	
-	-	-		-	-	-	
-	-	-		-	-	-	
-	-	-		-	-	-	
-	-	-		-	-	-	
-	-	-		-	-	-	
-	-	-		-	-	-	
-	-	-		-	-	-	
86,183	**-**	**86,183**		**-**	**-**	**-**	
180,975	**-**	**180,975**		**-**	**-**	**-**	
1,029,563	**-**	**1,029,563**		**-**	**-**	**-**	
-	-	-		-	-	-	
-	-	-		-	-	-	
-	-	-		-	-	-	
-	-	-		-	-	-	
22,222	-	22,222		-	-	-	
-	-	-		-	-	-	
-	-	-		-	-	-	
22,222	-	22,222		-	-	-	
18,198	-	18,198		-	-	-	
-	-	-		-	-	-	
-	-	-		-	-	-	
-	-	-		-	-	-	
-	-	-		-	-	-	
-	-	-		-	-	-	
18,198	-	18,198		-	-	-	
-	-	-		-	-	-	
-	-	-		-	-	-	
-	-	-		-	-	-	
-	-	-		-	-	-	
-	-	-		-	-	-	
-	-	-		-	-	-	
-	-	-		-	-	-	
40,420	**-**	**40,420**		**-**	**-**	**-**	
$989,143	**-**	**$989,143**		**-**	**-**	**-**	

OP STMT RECONCILIATION

Village Square Center

Property Number: 0238
Financing Number: 0128
Square Feet: 128,451

TTM			NOTE
Statement	**Adjustment**	**Operating**	
Through:	**12/31/2000**		
Stmt. Type:	Income		

OCCUPANCY

	Physical	Economic	Conclusion
January			
February			
March			
April			
May			
June			
July			
August			
September			
October			
November			
December			
Calculated Average			
Override	92.50%		92.50%
Concluded Average	92.50%		92.50%

YTD			NOTE	YTD Prior			NOTE
Statement	Adjustment	Operating		Statement	Adjustment	Operating	
Through:	12/31/2000			Through:			
Stmt. Type:	Income			Stmt. Type:	Income		

Physical	Economic	Conclusion		Physical	Economic	Conclusion	
91.00%		91.00%					
91.00%		91.00%					

OP STMT RECONCILIATION

Village Square Center

Property Number: 0238
Financing Number: 0128
Square Feet: 128,451

	Statement	Appraisal Adjustment	Operating
	Through:	1/20/2001	
	Stmt. Type:		
REVENUES			
Gross Potential Rent			
-	-	1,196,631	1,196,631
-	-	-	-
-	-	-	-
Gross Potential Rent	-	1,196,631	1,196,631
Collected Rent			
-	-	-	-
-	-	-	-
-	-	-	-
Collected Rent	-	-	-
Percentage Rent			
-	-	-	-
-	-	-	-
-	-	-	-
Percentage Rent	-	-	-
Recoveries			
Common Area Maintenance (CAM)	-	133,535	133,535
Real Estate Taxes	-	69,072	69,072
Insurance	-	18,274	18,274
Other Expense Recoveries	-	-	-
Total Recoveries	-	220,881	220,881
Other Income - 1			
Late Charges & NSF	-	-	-
Other Re-occurring Charges	-	-	-
Miscellaneous	-	-	-
Deposits to Tenant A/C	-	-	-
Personal Property Tax Recov.	-	-	-
Electricity	-	-	-
-	-	-	-
Other Income - 1	-	-	-
Other Income - 2			
-	-	-	-
-	-	-	-
-	-	-	-
-	-	-	-
-	-	-	-
Other Income - 2	-	-	-
Total Gross Income	**-**	**1,417,512**	**1,417,512**

N O T E	Budget Statement	Budget Adjustment	Operating	N O T E
	Through:	12/31/2001		
	Stmt. Type:	Income		
	1,240,720	-	1,240,720	
	-	-	-	
	-	-	-	
	1,240,720	-	1,240,720	
	-	-	-	
	-	-	-	
	-	-	-	
	-	-	-	
	-	-	-	
	-	-	-	
	-	-	-	
	-	-	-	
	135,000	-	135,000	
	72,500	-	72,500	
	13,500	-	13,500	
	-	-	-	
	221,000	-	221,000	
	5,000	(5,000)	-	
	-	-	-	
	10,000	(10,000)	-	
	-	-	-	
	-	-	-	
	-	-	-	
	-	-	-	
	15,000	(15,000)	-	
	-	-	-	
	-	-	-	
	-	-	-	
	-	-	-	
	-	-	-	
	-	-	-	
	1,476,720	**(15,000)**	**1,461,720**	

OP STMT RECONCILIATION

Village Square Center

Property Number: 0238
Financing Number: 0128
Square Feet: 128.451

	Appraisal			NOTE	Budget			NOTE
	Statement	Adjustment	Operating		Statement	Adjustment	Operating	
	Through:	1/20/2001			Through:	12/31/2001		
	Stmt. Type:				Stmt. Type:	Income		
Mark-to-Market								
-	-	-	-		-	-	-	
-	-	-	-		-	-	-	
-	-	-	-		-	-	-	
Mark-to-Market	-	-	-		-	-	-	
Vacancy and Credit Loss								
-	(82,733)	-	(82,733)		(103,370)	-	(103,370)	
-	-	-	-		-	-	-	
-	-	-	-		-	-	-	
Vacancy and Credit Loss	(82,733)	-	(82,733)		(103,370)	-	(103,370)	
Effective Gross Income	**(82,733)**	**1,417,512**	**1,334,779**		**1,373,350**	**(15,000)**	**1,358,350**	

EXPENSES (Variable)	CAM Pools #1	#2	#3	Appraisal Statement	Adjustment	Operating	NOTE	Budget Statement	Adjustment	Operating	NOTE
Management Fee											
Management Fee	x	x		37,374		37,374		54,934	-	54,934	
-				-	-	-		-	-	-	
Management Fee				37,374	-	37,374		54,934	-	54,934	
Payroll & Benefits											
				-	-	-		-	-	-	
				-	-	-		-	-	-	
				-	-	-		-	-	-	
				-	-	-		-	-	-	
				-	-	-		-	-	-	
Payroll & Benefits				-	-	-		-	-	-	
Utilities											
Electricity	x	x		-	23,245	23,245		5,500	-	5,500	
Water/Sewer		x		-	-	-		16,750	-	16,750	
Owner Utilities		x		-	-	-		1,000	-	1,000	
Water Irrigation	x	x		-	-	-		-	-	-	
Recoverable Utilities	x	x		-	-	-		-	-	-	
Utilities				-	23,245	23,245		23,250	-	23,250	
Repairs & Maintenance											
HVAC Maint.	x	x		-	34,956	34,956		3,500	-	3,500	
Repair & Maint.-C/A		x		-	-	-		12,000	-	12,000	
Owner HVAC		x		-	-	-		-	-	-	
Owner R&M		x		-	-	-		1,000	-	1,000	
Sidewalk Powerwash	x	x		-	-	-		1,000	-	1,000	
Exterminating	x	x		-	-	-		-	-	-	
Snow Removal	x	x		-	-	-		-	-	-	
Landscape Maint/Lot Sweep	x	x		-	-	-		14,000	-	14,000	
-				-	-	-		-	-	-	
Repairs & Maintenance				-	34,956	34,956		31,500	-	31,500	
Common Area Maintenance (CAM)											
-				-	-	-		-	-	-	
-				-	-	-		-	-	-	
-				-	-	-		-	-	-	
-				-	-	-		-	-	-	
Common Area Maintenance (CAM)				-	-	-		-	-	-	

OP STMT RECONCILIATION

Village Square Center

Property Number: 0238
Financing Number: 0128
Square Feet: 128,451

				Appraisal			NOTE	Budget			NOTE
				Statement	Adjustment	Operating		Statement	Adjustment	Operating	
				Through:	1/20/2001			Through:	12/31/2001		
				Stmt. Type:				Stmt. Type:	Income		
Administrative											
Accounting Fees	x	x		-	7,544	7,544		2,200	-	2,200	
Appraisal	x	x		-	-	-		-	-	-	
Architect	x	x		-	-	-		-	-	-	
Development Svcs.	x	x		-	-	-		-	-	-	
Bank Charges	x	x		-	-	-		250	-	250	
Commissions (see below)	x	x		-	-	-		-	-	-	
Mail & Delivery	x	x		-	-	-		100	-	100	
Legal Fees	x	x		-	-	-		1,000	-	1,000	
Rent/Lease Payments	x	x		-	-	-		450	-	450	
-				-	-	-		-	-	-	
Administrative				-	7,544	7,544		4,000	-	4,000	
Other Variable Expense - 1											
Alarm Monitoring	x	x		-	2,019	2,019		2,500	-	2,500	
Owner Misc	x	x		-	-	-		1,000	-	1,000	
-				-	-	-		-	-	-	
-				-	-	-		-	-	-	
-				-	-	-		-	-	-	
-				-	-	-		-	-	-	
Other Variable Expense - 1				-	2,019	2,019		3,500	-	3,500	
Other Variable Expense - 2											
-				-	-	-		-	-	-	
-				-	-	-		-	-	-	
-				-	-	-		-	-	-	
Other Variable Expense - 2				-	-	-		-	-	-	
Other Variable Expense - 3											
-				-	-	-		-	-	-	
-				-	-	-		-	-	-	
-				-	-	-		-	-	-	
Other Variable Expense - 3				-	-	-		-	-	-	
Total Variable Expenses				**37,374**	**67,764**	**105,138**		**117,184**	**-**	**117,184**	

EXPENSES (Fixed)

				Statement	Adjustment	Operating	NOTE	Statement	Adjustment	Operating	NOTE
Real Property Taxes											
Real Property Taxes		x		-	70,524	70,524		71,000	-	71,000	
Personal Property Taxes	x	x		-	-	-		1,500	-	1,500	
-				-	-	-		-	-	-	
Real Property Taxes				-	70,524	70,524		72,500	-	72,500	
Insurance											
Insurance		x		-	18,703	18,703		13,500	-	13,500	
-				-	-	-		-	-	-	
-				-	-	-		-	-	-	
Insurance				-	18,703	18,703		13,500	-	13,500	
Other Fixed Expense -1											
-				-	-	-		-	-	-	
-				-	-	-		-	-	-	
-				-	-	-		-	-	-	
Other Fixed Expense -1				-	-	-		-	-	-	

OP STMT RECONCILIATION

Village Square Center

Property Number: 0238
Financing Number: 0128
Square Feet: 128,451

	Statement	Appraisal Adjustment	Operating
	Through:	1/20/2001	
	Stmt. Type:		
Other Fixed Expense - 2			
-	-	-	-
-	-	-	-
-	-	-	-
Other Fixed Expense - 2	-	-	-
Other Fixed Expense - 3			
-	-	-	-
-	-	-	-
-	-	-	-
Other Fixed Expense - 3	-	-	-
Total Fixed Expenses	**-**	**89,227**	**89,227**
Total Expenses	**37,374**	**156,991**	**194,365**
Net Operating Income	**(120,107)**	**1,260,521**	**1,140,414**
CAPITAL EXPENDITURES			
Reserves for Replacements			
Imputed Reserves	-	18,928	18,928
-	-	-	-
-	-	-	-
Reserves for Replacements	-	18,928	18,928
Re-Tenanting Costs			
Leasing Commissions	-	66,268	66,268
TI's	-	-	-
-	-	-	-
Re-Tenanting Costs	-	66,268	66,268
Other Capital Expenses -1			
Survey & Review Fees	-	-	-
Capital Expenditures	-	-	-
-	-	-	-
-	-	-	-
-	-	-	-
-	-	-	-
Other Capital Expenses -1	-	-	-
Other Capital Expenses - 2			
-	-	-	-
-	-	-	-
-	-	-	-
-	-	-	-
-	-	-	-
-	-	-	-
Other Capital Expenses - 2	-	-	-
Total Capital Expenditures	**-**	**85,196**	**85,196**
Net Cash Flow	**($120,107)**	**$1,175,325**	**$1,055,218**

N O T E	Budget Statement	Adjustment	Operating	N O T E
	Through:	12/31/2001		
	Stmt. Type:	Income		
	-	-	-	
	-	-	-	
	-	-	-	
	-	-	-	
	-	-	-	
	-	-	-	
	-	-	-	
	-	-	-	
	86,000	**-**	**86,000**	
	203,184	**-**	**203,184**	
	1,170,166	**(15,000)**	**1,155,166**	
	-	-	-	
	-	-	-	
	-	-	-	
	-	-	-	
	45,280	-	45,280	
	-	-	-	
	-	-	-	
	45,280	-	45,280	
	-	-	-	
	12,845	-	12,845	
	-	-	-	
	-	-	-	
	-	-	-	
	-	-	-	
	12,845	-	12,845	
	-	-	-	
	-	-	-	
	-	-	-	
	-	-	-	
	-	-	-	
	-	-	-	
	-	-	-	
	58,125	**-**	**58,125**	
	$1,112,041	**($15,000)**	**$1,097,041**	

OP STMT RECONCILIATION

Village Square Center

Property Number: 0238
Financing Number: 0128
Square Feet: 128,451

Statement
Through:
Stmt. Type:

OCCUPANCY

	Physical
January	
February	
March	
April	
May	
June	
July	
August	
September	
October	
November	
December	
Calculated Average	
Override	
Concluded Average	

Appraisal		N	Budget			N
Adjustment	Operating	O	Statement	Adjustment	Operating	O
1/20/2001		T	Through:	12/31/2001		T
		E	Stmt. Type:	t		E

Economic	Conclusion		Physical	Economic	Conclusion	
			95.00%		95.00%	
			95.00%		95.00%	

OP STMT RECONCILIATION

Village Square Center

	January Statement	February Statement	March Statement	April Statement	May Statement	June Statement
Property Number: 0238						
Financing Number: 0128						
Square Feet: 128,451	0	0	0	0	0	0
REVENUES						
Gross Potential Rent						
-	-	-	-	-	-	-
-	-	-	-	-	-	-
-	-	-	-	-	-	-
Gross Potential Rent	-	-	-	-	-	-
Collected Rent						
-	-	-	-	-	-	-
-	-	-	-	-	-	-
-	-	-	-	-	-	-
Collected Rent	-	-	-	-	-	-
Percentage Rent						
-	-	-	-	-	-	-
-	-	-	-	-	-	-
-	-	-	-	-	-	-
Percentage Rent	-	-	-	-	-	-
Recoveries						
Common Area Maintenance (CAM)	-	-	-	-	-	-
Real Estate Taxes	-	-	-	-	-	-
Insurance	-	-	-	-	-	-
Other Expense Recoveries	-	-	-	-	-	-
Total Recoveries	-	-	-	-	-	-
Other Income - 1						
Late Charges & NSF	-	-	-	-	-	-
Other Re-occurring Charges	-	-	-	-	-	-
Miscellaneous	-	-	-	-	-	-
Deposits to Tenant A/C	-	-	-	-	-	-
Personal Property Tax Recov.	-	-	-	-	-	-
Electricity	-	-	-	-	-	-
-	-	-	-	-	-	-
Other Income - 1	-	-	-	-	-	-
Other Income - 2						
-	-	-	-	-	-	-
-	-	-	-	-	-	-
-	-	-	-	-	-	-
-	-	-	-	-	-	-
-	-	-	-	-	-	-
Other Income - 2	-	-	-	-	-	-
Total Gross Income	-	-	-	-	-	-

July	August	September	October	November	December	N	1	1 Months Annualized	
Statement	Statement	Statement	Statement	Statement	Statement	O	Statement	Adjustment	Operating
0	0	0	0	0	0	T	Through:		
						E	Stmt. Type:		
-	-	-	-	-	-		-	-	-
-	-	-	-	-	-		-	-	-
-	-	-	-	-	-		-	-	-
-	-	-	-	-	-		-	-	-
-	-	-	-	-	-		-	-	-
-	-	-	-	-	-		-	-	-
-	-	-	-	-	-		-	-	-
-	-	-	-	-	-		-	-	-
-	-	-	-	-	-		-	-	-
-	-	-	-	-	-		-	-	-
-	-	-	-	-	-		-	-	-
-	-	-	-	-	-		-	-	-
-	-	-	-	-	-		-	-	-
-	-	-	-	-	-		-	-	-
-	-	-	-	-	-		-	-	-
-	-	-	-	-	-		-	-	-
-	-	-	-	-	-		-	-	-
-	-	-	-	-	-		-	-	-
-	-	-	-	-	-		-	-	-
-	-	-	-	-	-		-	-	-
-	-	-	-	-	-		-	-	-
-	-	-	-	-	-		-	-	-
-	-	-	-	-	-		-	-	-
-	-	-	-	-	-		-	-	-
-	-	-	-	-	-		-	-	-
-	-	-	-	-	-		-	-	-
-	-	-	-	-	-		-	-	-
-	-	-	-	-	-		-	-	-
-	-	-	-	-	-		-	-	-
-	-	-	-	-	-		-	-	-
-	-	-	-	-	-		-	-	-
-	-	-	-	-	-		-	-	-

OP STMT RECONCILIATION

Village Square Center

Property Number: 0238 Financing Number: 0128 Square Feet: 128,451				January Statement	February Statement	March Statement	April Statement	May Statement	June Statement
				0	0	0	0	0	0
Mark-to-Market									
-				-	-	-	-	-	-
-				-	-	-	-	-	-
-				-	-	-	-	-	-
Mark-to-Market				-	-	-	-	-	-
Vacancy and Credit Loss									
-				-	-	-	-	-	-
-				-	-	-	-	-	-
-				-	-	-	-	-	-
Vacancy and Credit Loss				-	-	-	-	-	-
Effective Gross Income				-	-	-	-	-	-
EXPENSES (Variable)	**CAM Pools**								
	#1	**#2**	**#3**						
Management Fee									
Management Fee	x	x		-	-	-	-	-	-
-				-	-	-	-	-	-
Management Fee				-	-	-	-	-	-
Payroll & Benefits									
				-	-	-	-	-	-
				-	-	-	-	-	-
				-	-	-	-	-	-
				-	-	-	-	-	-
				-	-	-	-	-	-
Payroll & Benefits				-	-	-	-	-	-
Utilities									
Electricity	x	x		-	-	-	-	-	-
Water/Sewer		x		-	-	-	-	-	-
Owner Utilities		x		-	-	-	-	-	-
Water Irrigation	x	x		-	-	-	-	-	-
Recoverable Utilities	x	x		-	-	-	-	-	-
Utilities				-	-	-	-	-	-
Repairs & Maintenance									
HVAC Maint.	x	x		-	-	-	-	-	-
Repair & Maint.-C/A		x		-	-	-	-	-	-
Owner HVAC		x		-	-	-	-	-	-
Owner R&M		x		-	-	-	-	-	-
Sidewalk Powerwash	x	x		-	-	-	-	-	-
Exterminating	x	x		-	-	-	-	-	-
Snow Removal	x	x		-	-	-	-	-	-
Landscape Maint/Lot Sweep	x	x		-	-	-	-	-	-
-				-	-	-	-	-	-
Repairs & Maintenance				-	-	-	-	-	-
Common Area Maintenance (CAM)									
-				-	-	-	-	-	-
-				-	-	-	-	-	-
-				-	-	-	-	-	-
-				-	-	-	-	-	-
Common Area Maintenance (CAM)				-	-	-	-	-	-

July	August	September	October	November	December	N	1	1 Months Annualized	
Statement	Statement	Statement	Statement	Statement	Statement	O	Statement	Adjustment	Operating
0	0	0	0	0	0	T	Through:		
						E	Stmt. Type:		
-	-	-	-	-	-		-	-	-
-	-	-	-	-	-		-	-	-
-	-	-	-	-	-		-	-	-
-	-	-	-	-	-		-	-	-
-	-	-	-	-	-		-	-	-
-	-	-	-	-	-		-	-	-
-	-	-	-	-	-		-	-	-
-	-	-	-	-	-		-	-	-
-	-	-	-	-	-		-	-	-
-	-	-	-	-	-		-	-	-
-	-	-	-	-	-		-	-	-
-	-	-	-	-	-		-	-	-
-	-	-	-	-	-		-	-	-
-	-	-	-	-	-		-	-	-
-	-	-	-	-	-		-	-	-
-	-	-	-	-	-		-	-	-
-	-	-	-	-	-		-	-	-
-	-	-	-	-	-		-	-	-
-	-	-	-	-	-		-	-	-
-	-	-	-	-	-		-	-	-
-	-	-	-	-	-		-	-	-
-	-	-	-	-	-		-	-	-
-	-	-	-	-	-		-	-	-
-	-	-	-	-	-		-	-	-
-	-	-	-	-	-		-	-	-
-	-	-	-	-	-		-	-	-
-	-	-	-	-	-		-	-	-
-	-	-	-	-	-		-	-	-
-	-	-	-	-	-		-	-	-
-	-	-	-	-	-		-	-	-
-	-	-	-	-	-		-	-	-
-	-	-	-	-	-		-	-	-
-	-	-	-	-	-		-	-	-
-	-	-	-	-	-		-	-	-
-	-	-	-	-	-		-	-	-
-	-	-	-	-	-		-	-	-
-	-	-	-	-	-		-	-	-
-	-	-	-	-	-		-	-	-
-	-	-	-	-	-		-	-	-

OP STMT RECONCILIATION

Village Square Center

Property Number: 0238
Financing Number: 0128
Square Feet: 128,451

				January Statement	February Statement	March Statement	April Statement	May Statement	June Statement
				0	0	0	0	0	0
Administrative									
Accounting Fees	x	x		-	-	-	-	-	-
Appraisal	x	x		-	-	-	-	-	-
Architect	x	x		-	-	-	-	-	-
Development Svcs.	x	x		-	-	-	-	-	-
Bank Charges	x	x		-	-	-	-	-	-
Commissions (see below)	x	x		-	-	-	-	-	-
Mail & Delivery	x	x		-	-	-	-	-	-
Legal Fees	x	x		-	-	-	-	-	-
Rent/Lease Payments	x	x		-	-	-	-	-	-
-				-	-	-	-	-	-
Administrative				-	-	-	-	-	-
Other Variable Expense - 1									
Alarm Monitoring	x	x		-	-	-	-	-	-
Owner Misc	x	x		-	-	-	-	-	-
-				-	-	-	-	-	-
-				-	-	-	-	-	-
-				-	-	-	-	-	-
-				-	-	-	-	-	-
Other Variable Expense - 1				-	-	-	-	-	-
Other Variable Expense - 2									
-				-	-	-	-	-	-
-				-	-	-	-	-	-
-				-	-	-	-	-	-
Other Variable Expense - 2				-	-	-	-	-	-
Other Variable Expense - 3									
-				-	-	-	-	-	-
-				-	-	-	-	-	-
-				-	-	-	-	-	-
Other Variable Expense - 3				-	-	-	-	-	-
Total Variable Expenses				-	-	-	-	-	-
EXPENSES (Fixed)									
Real Property Taxes									
Real Property Taxes		x		-	-	-	-	-	-
Personal Property Taxes	x	x		-	-	-	-	-	-
-				-	-	-	-	-	-
Real Property Taxes				-	-	-	-	-	-
Insurance									
Insurance		x		-	-	-	-	-	-
-				-	-	-	-	-	-
-				-	-	-	-	-	-
Insurance				-	-	-	-	-	-
Other Fixed Expense -1									
-				-	-	-	-	-	-
-				-	-	-	-	-	-
-				-	-	-	-	-	-
Other Fixed Expense -1				-	-	-	-	-	-

July	August	September	October	November	December	N	1	1 Months Annualized	
Statement	Statement	Statement	Statement	Statement	Statement	O	Statement	Adjustment	Operating
0	0	0	0	0	0	T	Through:		
						E	Stmt. Type:		
-	-	-	-	-	-		-	-	-
-	-	-	-	-	-		-	-	-
-	-	-	-	-	-		-	-	-
-	-	-	-	-	-		-	-	-
-	-	-	-	-	-		-	-	-
-	-	-	-	-	-		-	-	-
-	-	-	-	-	-		-	-	-
-	-	-	-	-	-		-	-	-
-	-	-	-	-	-		-	-	-
-	-	-	-	-	-		-	-	-
-	-	-	-	-	-		-	-	-
-	-	-	-	-	-		-	-	-
-	-	-	-	-	-		-	-	-
-	-	-	-	-	-		-	-	-
-	-	-	-	-	-		-	-	-
-	-	-	-	-	-		-	-	-
-	-	-	-	-	-		-	-	-
-	-	-	-	-	-		-	-	-
-	-	-	-	-	-		-	-	-
-	-	-	-	-	-		-	-	-
-	-	-	-	-	-		-	-	-
-	-	-	-	-	-		-	-	-
-	-	-	-	-	-		-	-	-
-	-	-	-	-	-		-	-	-
-	-	-	-	-	-		-	-	-
-	-	-	-	-	-		-	-	-
-	-	-	-	-	-		-	-	-

-	-	-	-	-	-		-	-	-
-	-	-	-	-	-		-	-	-
-	-	-	-	-	-		-	-	-
-	-	-	-	-	-		-	-	-
-	-	-	-	-	-		-	-	-
-	-	-	-	-	-		-	-	-
-	-	-	-	-	-		-	-	-
-	-	-	-	-	-		-	-	-
-	-	-	-	-	-		-	-	-
-	-	-	-	-	-		-	-	-
-	-	-	-	-	-		-	-	-
-	-	-	-	-	-		-	-	-

OP STMT RECONCILIATION

Village Square Center

Property Number: 0238
Financing Number: 0128
Square Feet: 128,451

	January Statement	February Statement	March Statement	April Statement	May Statement	June Statement
	0	0	0	0	0	0
Other Fixed Expense - 2						
-	-	-	-	-	-	-
-	-	-	-	-	-	-
-	-	-	-	-	-	-
Other Fixed Expense - 2	-	-	-	-	-	-
Other Fixed Expense - 3						
-	-	-	-	-	-	-
-	-	-	-	-	-	-
-	-	-	-	-	-	-
Other Fixed Expense - 3	-	-	-	-	-	-
Total Fixed Expenses	-	-	-	-	-	-
Total Expenses	-	-	-	-	-	-
Net Operating Income	-	-	-	-	-	-
CAPITAL EXPENDITURES						
Reserves for Replacements						
Imputed Reserves	-	-	-	-	-	-
-	-	-	-	-	-	-
-	-	-	-	-	-	-
Reserves for Replacements	-	-	-	-	-	-
Re-Tenanting Costs						
Leasing Commissions	-	-	-	-	-	-
TI's	-	-	-	-	-	-
-	-	-	-	-	-	-
Re-Tenanting Costs	-	-	-	-	-	-
Other Capital Expenses -1						
Survey & Review Fees	-	-	-	-	-	-
Capital Expenditures	-	-	-	-	-	-
-	-	-	-	-	-	-
-	-	-	-	-	-	-
-	-	-	-	-	-	-
-	-	-	-	-	-	-
Other Capital Expenses -1	-	-	-	-	-	-
Other Capital Expenses - 2						
-	-	-	-	-	-	-
-	-	-	-	-	-	-
-	-	-	-	-	-	-
-	-	-	-	-	-	-
-	-	-	-	-	-	-
-	-	-	-	-	-	-
Other Capital Expenses - 2	-	-	-	-	-	-
Total Capital Expenditures	-	-	-	-	-	-
Net Cash Flow	-	-	-	-	-	-

July	August	September	October	November	December	N	1	1 Months Annualized	
Statement	Statement	Statement	Statement	Statement	Statement	O	Statement	Adjustment	Operating
0	0	0	0	0	0	T	Through:		
						E	Stmt. Type:		
-	-	-	-	-	-		-	-	-
-	-	-	-	-	-		-	-	-
-	-	-	-	-	-		-	-	-
-	-	-	-	-	-		-	-	-
-	-	-	-	-	-		-	-	-
-	-	-	-	-	-		-	-	-
-	-	-	-	-	-		-	-	-
-	-	-	-	-	-		-	-	-
-	-	-	-	-	-		-	-	-
-	-	-	-	-	-		-	-	-
-	-	-	-	-	-		-	-	-

July	August	September	October	November	December	NOTE	Statement	Adjustment	Operating
-	-	-	-	-	-		-	-	-
-	-	-	-	-	-		-	-	-
-	-	-	-	-	-		-	-	-
-	-	-	-	-	-		-	-	-
-	-	-	-	-	-		-	-	-
-	-	-	-	-	-		-	-	-
-	-	-	-	-	-		-	-	-
-	-	-	-	-	-		-	-	-
-	-	-	-	-	-		-	-	-
-	-	-	-	-	-		-	-	-
-	-	-	-	-	-		-	-	-
-	-	-	-	-	-		-	-	-
-	-	-	-	-	-		-	-	-
-	-	-	-	-	-		-	-	-
-	-	-	-	-	-		-	-	-
-	-	-	-	-	-		-	-	-
-	-	-	-	-	-		-	-	-
-	-	-	-	-	-		-	-	-
-	-	-	-	-	-		-	-	-
-	-	-	-	-	-		-	-	-
-	-	-	-	-	-		-	-	-
-	-	-	-	-	-		-	-	-
-	-	-	-	-	-		-	-	-
-	-	-	-	-	-		-	-	-

OP STMT RECONCILIATION

Village Square Center

Property Number: 0238
Financing Number: 0128
Square Feet: 128,451

January Statement	February Statement	March Statement	April Statement	May Statement	June Statement
0	0	0	0	0	0

OCCUPANCY

January
February
March
April
May
June
July
August
September
October
November
December
Calculated Average
Override
Concluded Average

Notes and Comments:

1. Late charges were excluded from operating income.
2. The adjustment reflects the one time sale of a maintenance truck previously used at the property.
3. Late charges were excluded from operating income.

July	August	September	October	November	December	N	1	1 Months Annualized	
Statement	Statement	Statement	Statement	Statement	Statement	O	Statement	Adjustment	Operating
0	0	0	0	0	0	T	Through:		
						E	Stmt. Type:		

Notes and Comments:

RENT ROLL RECONCILIATION

Village Square Center

Rent Roll Date: 1/12/01

A	**Anchor Retail**
S	**Shop Retail**
O	**Office**
L	**Indust**

Space #	Tenant Name	Credit, National, Regional, Local, Other	Rollover Characterization	
OCCUPIED				
1	The Children's Co	Local	A	Anchor Retail
2	Payless Drug	Local	A	Anchor Retail
3	A&W (Groundleased Outparcel)	Local	S	Shop Retail
4	Vitamin Head	Local	S	Shop Retail
5	Merle Norman (beauty/tanning)	Local	S	Shop Retail
6	Sehome Cleaners	Local	S	Shop Retail
7	Sehome Cleaners	Local	S	Shop Retail
8	Quarterback Sports (sports bar)	Local	S	Shop Retail
9	Stires (Books)	Local	S	Shop Retail
10	Haircrafters	Local	S	Shop Retail
11	Consignment	Local	S	Shop Retail
12	Quilt Basket	Local	S	Shop Retail
13	Round Table Pizza	Local	S	Shop Retail
14	Corkrum	Local	S	Shop Retail
15	Pet Shop	Local	S	Shop Retail
16	Thai One	Local	S	Shop Retail
17	JoAnn Fabrics	Local	S	Shop Retail
18	B'ham Therapy	Local	S	Shop Retail
19	Pack N Mail	Local	S	Shop Retail
20	The Bagel Factory	Local	S	Shop Retail
21	Frazier Chiropractic	Local	S	Shop Retail
22	Sub Shop	Local	S	Shop Retail
23	Encore Entertainment (Video)	Local	S	Shop Retail
24	Storage (Various)	Local	S	Shop Retail
25	Ranney Moss (Dark: tenant trying to sublease)		S	Shop Retail
TOTAL OCCUPIED				
% Of Gross Potential				
VACANT				
26	Vacant Space	Local	S	Shop Retail
TOTAL VACANT				
% Of Gross Potential				
TOTAL OCCUPIED AND VACANT (GROSS POTENTIAL)				

Property Number: 0238
Deal Number: 0128

Lease Type	Rent Roll (SF)	Lease (SF)	Estoppel (SF)	Conclusion (SF)
Retail		20,000		20,000
Retail		36,060		36,060
Retail		3,000		3,000
Retail		2,467		2,467
Retail		2,348		2,348
Retail		1,811		1,811
Retail		1,578		1,578
Retail		5,156		5,156
Retail		2,534		2,534
Retail		1,200		1,200
Retail		1,943		1,943
Retail		1,540		1,540
Retail		3,500		3,500
Retail		1,440		1,440
Retail		1,440		1,440
Retail		1,440		1,440
Retail		14,515		14,515
Retail		2,673		2,673
Retail		1,339		1,339
Retail		1,791		1,791
Retail		1,373		1,373
Retail		1,373		1,373
Retail		5,739		5,739
Retail		2,123		2,123
Retail		1,483		1,483
	0	**119,866**	**0**	**119,866**
				93.32%
	8,585			8,585
	8,585			8,585
				6.68%
	8,585	**119,866**	**0**	**128,451**

RENT ROLL RECONCILIATION

Village Square Center

Rent Roll Date: 1/12/01

Space #	Tenant Name	Lease Start/ Possession Date	Move-In/ Occupancy Date	Rent Start Date	Expiration Date
		ORIGINAL LEASE			
OCCUPIED					
1	The Children's Co			4/1/88	4/1/01
2	Payless Drug			9/1/93	9/1/14
3	A&W (Groundleased Outparcel)			7/1/97	7/1/17
4	Vitamin Head			10/1/97	10/1/01
5	Merle Norman (beauty/tanning)			3/1/95	3/1/01
6	Sehome Cleaners			6/1/94	6/1/04
7	Sehome Cleaners			4/1/96	4/1/01
8	Quarterback Sports (sports bar)			3/1/94	3/1/04
9	Stires (Books)			5/1/98	5/1/03
10	Haircrafters			1/1/94	1/1/04
11	Consignment			12/1/98	12/1/03
12	Quilt Basket			8/1/95	8/1/01
13	Round Table Pizza			6/1/93	6/1/03
14	Corkrum			9/1/98	9/1/03
15	Pet Shop			2/1/00	2/1/05
16	Thai One			8/1/98	8/1/03
17	JoAnn Fabrics			10/1/93	10/1/04
18	B'ham Therapy			4/1/94	4/1/99
19	Pack N Mail			4/1/94	4/1/04
20	The Bagel Factory			7/1/95	7/1/01
21	Frazier Chiropractic			11/1/95	11/1/00
22	Sub Shop			3/1/96	3/1/01
23	Encore Entertainment (Video)			5/1/93	5/1/00
24	Storage (Various)				
25	Ranney Moss (Dark: tenant trying to sublease)			10/15/95	10/31/02
TOTAL OCCUPIED					
% Of Gross Potential					
VACANT					
26	Vacant Space				
TOTAL VACANT					
% Of Gross Potential					
TOTAL OCCUPIED AND VACANT (GROSS POTENTIAL)					

Property Number: 0238
Financing Number: 0128

Term Occ. to Exp.	Options (e.g., 2(5yr))	CURRENT LEASE Current Lease Same (Y/N)	Option Y/N	Current Begin Date	Expiration Date	Term Beg. to Exp.
101.3	2 @ 5 yr ;1 @ 4 yr	Y	N	4/1/88	4/1/01	13.0
114.7	5 @ 5 years	Y	N	9/1/93	9/1/14	21.0
117.6	1 @ 10 years	Y	N	7/1/97	7/1/17	20.0
101.8	No options	Y	N	10/1/97	10/1/01	4.0
101.2	1 @ 5 years	Y	N	3/1/95	3/1/01	6.0
104.5	1 @ 10 years	Y	N	6/1/94	6/1/04	10.0
101.3	1 @ 5 years	Y	N	4/1/96	4/1/01	5.0
104.2	1 @ 5 years	Y	N	3/1/94	3/1/04	10.0
103.4	1 @ 5 years	Y	N	5/1/98	5/1/03	5.0
104.1	1 @ 5 years	Y	N	1/1/94	1/1/04	10.0
104.0	1 @ 5 years	Y	N	12/1/98	12/1/03	5.0
101.7	1 @ 5 years	Y	N	8/1/95	8/1/01	6.0
103.5	1 @ 10 years	Y	N	6/1/93	6/1/03	10.0
103.7	1 @ 5 years	Y	N	9/1/98	9/1/03	5.0
105.2	1 @ 5 years	Y	N	2/1/00	2/1/05	5.0
103.7	1 @ 5 years	Y	N	8/1/98	8/1/03	5.0
104.8	2 @ 5 years	Y	N	10/1/93	10/1/04	11.0
99.3	1 @ 5 years	Y	Y	4/1/99	4/1/02	3.0
104.3	1 @ 5 years	Y	N	4/1/94	4/1/04	10.0
101.6	1 @ 5 years	Y	N	7/1/95	7/1/01	6.0
100.9	1 @ 5 years	Y	N	11/1/95	11/1/00	5.0
101.2	1 @ 5 years	Y	N	3/1/96	3/1/01	5.0
100.4	1 @ 5 years	Y	N	5/1/00	5/1/05	5.0
102.9	No options	Y	N	10/15/95	10/31/02	7.0

RENT ROLL RECONCILIATION

Village Square Center

Rent Roll Date: 1/12/01

Space #	Tenant Name	Rent Roll	Lease	Estoppel	Appraisal
	OCCUPIED				
1	The Children's Co		$5,500		
2	Payless Drug		$20,383		
3	A&W (Groundleased Outparcel)		$4,833		
4	Vitamin Head		$2,537		
5	Merle Norman (beauty/tanning)		$2,886		
6	Sehome Cleaners		$2,075		
7	Sehome Cleaners		$1,644		
8	Quarterback Sports (sports bar)		$6,445		
9	Stires (Books)		$2,534		
10	Haircrafters		$1,500		
11	Consignment		$2,267		
12	Quilt Basket		$2,021		
13	Round Table Pizza		$5,250		
14	Corkrum		$1,680		
15	Pet Shop		$2,202		
16	Thai One		$1,320		
17	JoAnn Fabrics		$10,019		
18	B'ham Therapy		$3,007		
19	Pack N Mail		$1,620		
20	The Bagel Factory		$2,150		
21	Frazier Chiropractic		$1,487		
22	Sub Shop		$1,773		
23	Encore Entertainment (Video)		$7,413		
24	Storage (Various)		$708		
25	Ranney Moss (Dark: tenant trying to sublease)		$0		
	TOTAL OCCUPIED	$ -	$ 93,255	$ -	$ -
	% Of Gross Potential				
	VACANT				
26	Vacant Space	$9,873			
	TOTAL VACANT	9,873			
	% Of Gross Potential				
	TOTAL OCCUPIED AND VACANT (GROSS POTENTIAL)				

Property Number: 0238
Financing Number: 0128

BASE RENT				
	Conclusion			
	>>Mthly("M")/Yrly("Y")			
Market	M	Annual	PSF/YR	PSF/MTH
$5,500	$5,500	$66,000	$3.30	$0.28
$20,383	$20,383	$244,600	$6.78	$0.57
$4,500	$4,833	$57,996	$19.33	$1.61
$2,537	$2,537	$30,444	$12.34	$1.03
$2,886	$2,886	$34,632	$14.75	$1.23
$2,075	$2,075	$24,900	$13.75	$1.15
$1,644	$1,644	$19,728	$12.50	$1.04
$6,445	$6,445	$77,340	$15.00	$1.25
$2,534	$2,534	$30,408	$12.00	$1.00
$1,500	$1,500	$17,997	$15.00	$1.25
$2,267	$2,267	$27,202	$14.00	$1.17
$2,021	$2,021	$24,257	$15.75	$1.31
$4,375	$5,250	$63,000	$18.00	$1.50
$1,680	$1,680	$20,160	$14.00	$1.17
$1,800	$2,202	$26,429	$18.35	$1.53
$1,320	$1,320	$15,840	$11.00	$0.92
$10,019	$10,019	$120,229	$8.28	$0.69
$3,007	$3,007	$36,084	$13.50	$1.12
$1,620	$1,620	$19,443	$14.52	$1.21
$2,150	$2,150	$25,801	$14.41	$1.20
$1,487	$1,487	$17,849	$13.00	$1.08
$1,773	$1,773	$21,276	$15.50	$1.29
$7,413	$7,413	$88,956	$15.50	$1.29
$708	$708	$8,492	$4.00	$0.33
$1,671	$0	$0	$0.00	$0.00
$ 93,316	**$ 93,255**	**$ 1,119,063**		
	90.43%			
	$9,873	$118,473	$13.80	$1.15
	$ 9,873	**$ 118,473**		
	9.57%			
	$103,128	**1,237,536**		

RENT ROLL RECONCILIATION

Village Square Center

Rent Roll Date: 1/12/01

Space #	Tenant Name	REIMBURSEMENTS (from Reimb Reconciliation)						
		CAM		Property Tax		Insurance		Total Reimb.
		Conclusion	Per SF	Conclusion	Per SF	Conclusion	Per SF	
OCCUPIED								
1	The Children's Co	0	$0.00	$0	$0.00	$0	$0.00	
2	Payless Drug	0	$0.00	$0	$0.00	$0	$0.00	
3	A&W (Groundleased Outparcel)	0	$0.00	$0	$0.00	$0	$0.00	
4	Vitamin Head	0	$0.00	$0	$0.00	$0	$0.00	
5	Merle Norman (beauty/tanning)	0	$0.00	$0	$0.00	$0	$0.00	
6	Sehome Cleaners	0	$0.00	$0	$0.00	$0	$0.00	
7	Sehome Cleaners	0	$0.00	$0	$0.00	$0	$0.00	
8	Quarterback Sports (sports bar)	0	$0.00	$0	$0.00	$0	$0.00	
9	Stires (Books)	0	$0.00	$0	$0.00	$0	$0.00	
10	Haircrafters	0	$0.00	$0	$0.00	$0	$0.00	
11	Consignment	0	$0.00	$0	$0.00	$0	$0.00	
12	Quilt Basket	0	$0.00	$0	$0.00	$0	$0.00	
13	Round Table Pizza	0	$0.00	$0	$0.00	$0	$0.00	
14	Corkrum	0	$0.00	$0	$0.00	$0	$0.00	
15	Pet Shop	0	$0.00	$0	$0.00	$0	$0.00	
16	Thai One	0	$0.00	$0	$0.00	$0	$0.00	
17	JoAnn Fabrics	0	$0.00	$0	$0.00	$0	$0.00	
18	B'ham Therapy	0	$0.00	$0	$0.00	$0	$0.00	
19	Pack N Mail	0	$0.00	$0	$0.00	$0	$0.00	
20	The Bagel Factory	0	$0.00	$0	$0.00	$0	$0.00	
21	Frazier Chiropractic	0	$0.00	$0	$0.00	$0	$0.00	
22	Sub Shop	0	$0.00	$0	$0.00	$0	$0.00	
23	Encore Entertainment (Video)	0	$0.00	$0	$0.00	$0	$0.00	
24	Storage (Various)	0	$0.00	$0	$0.00	$0	$0.00	
25	Ranney Moss (Dark: tenant trying to sublease)	0	$0.00	$0	$0.00	$0	$0.00	
		0		$0		$0		
		0		$0		$0		
TOTAL OCCUPIED		**0**	**0**	**0**	**0**	**0**	**0**	
% Of Gross Potential								
VACANT								
26	Vacant Space							
TOTAL VACANT								
% Of Gross Potential								
TOTAL OCCUPIED AND VACANT (GROSS POTENTIAL)		**0**		**0**		**0**		

Property Number: 0238
Financing Number: 0128

PERCENTAGE RENT					
Gross Sales					
1997		1998		1999	
$'s	Per SF	$'s	Per SF	$'s	Per SF
0		0		0	
0		0		0	

RENT ROLL RECONCILIATION

Village Square Center

Rent Roll Date: 1/12/01

Space #	Tenant Name	Rent %	Sales Breakpoint	Offsets $'s	Offsets Description	Calculated 1999 Sales	Percentage Rent Conclusion
		PERCENTAGE RENT (Cont...) — Rent Calculation					
OCCUPIED							
1	The Children's Co						
2	Payless Drug						
3	A&W (Groundleased Outparcel)						
4	Vitamin Head						
5	Merle Norman (beauty/tanning)						
6	Sehome Cleaners						
7	Sehome Cleaners						
8	Quarterback Sports (sports bar)						
9	Stires (Books)						
10	Haircrafters						
11	Consignment						
12	Quilt Basket						
13	Round Table Pizza						
14	Corkrum						
15	Pet Shop						
16	Thai One						
17	JoAnn Fabrics						
18	B'ham Therapy						
19	Pack N Mail						
20	The Bagel Factory						
21	Frazier Chiropractic						
22	Sub Shop						
23	Encore Entertainment (Video)						
24	Storage (Various)						
25	Ranney Moss (Dark: tenant trying to sublease)						
TOTAL OCCUPIED							0
% Of Gross Potential							
VACANT							
26	Vacant Space						
TOTAL VACANT							
% Of Gross Potential							
TOTAL OCCUPIED AND VACANT (GROSS POTENTIAL)							0

Property Number: 0238
Financing Number: 0128

	OTHER		
Gross Rent	Occupancy Cost as % of 1999 Sales	Market Gross Rent	Additional Rent Adjustment
$66,000			
$244,600			
$57,996			
$30,444			
$34,632			
$24,900			
$19,728			
$77,340			
$30,408			
$17,997			
$27,202			
$24,257			
$63,000			
$20,160			
$26,429			
$15,840			
$120,229			
$36,084			
$19,443			
$25,801			
$17,849			
$21,276			
$88,956			
$8,492			
1,119,063		**0**	**0**
1,119,063		**0**	**0**

Village Square Center
TENANT ROLLOVER ANALYSIS

#	Tenants	Tenant Type	SF	Monthly Rent	Annual Rent/SF	Start Date	Exp. Date
1	The Children's Co (Local)	Anchor Retail	20,000	$5,500	$3.3	1/0/00	4/1/01
2	Payless Drug (Local)	Anchor Retail	36,060	$20,383	$6.8	1/0/00	9/1/14
3	A&W (Groundleased Outparcel) (Local)	Shop Retail	3,000	$4,833	$19.3	1/0/00	7/1/17
4	Vitamin Head (Local)	Shop Retail	2,467	$2,537	$12.3	1/0/00	10/1/01
5	Merle Norman (beauty/tanning) (Local)	Shop Retail	2,348	$2,886	$14.7	1/0/00	3/1/01
6	Sehome Cleaners (Local)	Shop Retail	1,811	$2,075	$13.7	1/0/00	6/1/04
7	Sehome Cleaners (Local)	Shop Retail	1,578	$1,644	$12.5	1/0/00	4/1/01
8	Quarterback Sports (sports bar) (Local)	Shop Retail	5,156	$6,445	$15.0	1/0/00	3/1/04
9	Stires (Books) (Local)	Shop Retail	2,534	$2,534	$12.0	1/0/00	5/1/03
10	Haircrafters (Local)	Shop Retail	1,200	$1,500	$15.0	1/0/00	1/1/04
11	Consignment (Local)	Shop Retail	1,943	$2,267	$14.0	1/0/00	12/1/03
12	Quilt Basket (Local)	Shop Retail	1,540	$2,021	$15.8	1/0/00	8/1/01
13	Round Table Pizza (Local)	Shop Retail	3,500	$5,250	$18.0	1/0/00	6/1/03
14	Corkrum (Local)	Shop Retail	1,440	$1,680	$14.0	1/0/00	9/1/03
15	Pet Shop (Local)	Shop Retail	1,440	$2,202	$18.4	1/0/00	2/1/05
16	Thai One (Local)	Shop Retail	1,440	$1,320	$11.0	1/0/00	8/1/03
17	JoAnn Fabrics (Local)	Shop Retail	14,515	$10,019	$8.3	1/0/00	10/1/04
18	B'ham Therapy (Local)	Shop Retail	2,673	$3,007	$13.5	1/0/00	4/1/99
19	Pack N Mail (Local)	Shop Retail	1,339	$1,620	$14.5	1/0/00	4/1/04
20	The Bagel Factory (Local)	Shop Retail	1,791	$2,150	$14.4	1/0/00	7/1/01
21	Frazier Chiropractic (Local)	Shop Retail	1,373	$1,487	$13.0	1/0/00	11/1/00
22	Sub Shop (Local)	Shop Retail	1,373	$1,773	$15.5	1/0/00	3/1/01
23	Encore Entertainment (Video) (Local)	Shop Retail	5,739	$7,413	$15.5	1/0/00	5/1/00
24	Storage (Various) (Local)	Shop Retail	2,123	$708	$4.0	1/0/00	1/0/00
25	Ranney Moss (Dark: tenant trying to sublease) ()	Shop Retail	1,483	$0	$0.0	1/0/00	10/31/02

	SF	Monthly Rent
Total Anchor Retail	56,060	25,883
Total Shop Retail	63,806	67,372
Total Office	0	0
Total Indust	0	0
Total Combined Anchor & Shop	119,866	93,255
% of Square Footage Expiring		
Cumulative Square Footage Expirations		
Cumulative % of Square Footage Expiring		

	Anchor Retail	Shop Retail	Office	Indust
Average Lease Term	107.50	98.43		
Average Rent/SF/Year	$5.54	$12.67		

Rollover Cost Assumptions:	Anchor Retail	Shop Retail	Office	Indust
New Tenant Improvements ($/SF)	$4.00	$3.00		
Renewal Tenant Improvements ($/SF)	$2.00	$1.00		
New Commissions (% of Lease Value)	5.00%	5.50%		
Renewal Commissions (% of Lease Value)	2.50%	2.50%		
Months of Downtime	0	0		
Months of Free Rent	0	0		
Average Term (Years)	10	5		
Retention Ratio (%)	100.00%	60.00%		
Renewal Rental Rate ($/SF/Year)	$5.54	$12.72		

COMMENTS:

Estimated Rollover Costs:	Average Term Full Roll	Actual Leases (10yr Avg.)
Tenant Improvements	$34,182	$25,890
Commissions (New and Renewal)	$37,804	$31,397
Downtime	$0	$0
Free Rent	$0	$0
Total Rollover Costs/Year	**$71,986**	**$57,287**

Square Feet Expiring (in thousands)									
2001	**2002**	**2003**	**2004**	**2005**	**2006**	**2007**	**2008**	**2009**	**2010**
20.0									
2.5					2.5				
2.3					2.3				
			1.8					1.8	
1.6					1.6				
			5.2					5.2	
		2.5					2.5		
			1.2					1.2	
		1.9					1.9		
1.5					1.5				
		3.5					3.5		
		1.4					1.4		
				1.4					1.4
		1.4					1.4		
			14.5					14.5	
			2.7					2.7	
			1.3					1.3	
1.8					1.8				
				1.4					1.4
1.4					1.4				
				5.7					5.7
				2.1					2.1
	1.5					1.5			

2001	2002	2003	2004	2005	2006	2007	2008	2009	2010
20	**0**	**0**	**0**	**0**	**0**	**0**	**0**	**0**	**0**
11	**1**	**11**	**27**	**11**	**11**	**1**	**11**	**27**	**11**
0	**0**	**0**	**0**	**0**	**0**	**0**	**0**	**0**	**0**
0	**0**	**0**	**0**	**0**	**0**	**0**	**0**	**0**	**0**
31	**1**	**11**	**27**	**11**	**11**	**1**	**11**	**27**	**11**
26%	**1%**	**9%**	**22%**	**9%**	**9%**	**1%**	**9%**	**22%**	**9%**
31	**33**	**43**	**70**	**81**	**92**	**93**	**104**	**131**	**142**
26%	**27%**	**36%**	**59%**	**67%**	**77%**	**78%**	**87%**	**109%**	**118%**

Round Table Pizza and the A&W outparcel (Norrie & Assoc.) are at higher rents due to recovery of high tenant improvement costs related to restaurant construction. The Children's Co., Payless Drug Store, and JoAnn Fabrics have a lower rental rate due to larger space rented. The subject, as well as the market, are offering minimal rental concessions and tenant improvements. Rental concessions are typically 1 to 2 free months rent on a 3 to 5 year lease. TIs can range from zero to $2.50/sf depending upon the rental rate the tenant pays.

2001	2002	2003	2004	2005	2006	2007	2008	2009	2010
$60	$3	$20	$48	$19	$20	$3	$20	$48	$19
$54	$3	$26	$63	$25	$26	$3	$26	$63	$25
$0	$0	$0	$0	$0	$0	$0	$0	$0	$0
$0	$0	$0	$0	$0	$0	$0	$0	$0	$0
$114	**$6**	**$45**	**$111**	**$44**	**$46**	**$6**	**$45**	**$111**	**$44**

REIMBURSEMENT RECONCILIATION

Village Square Center

		Pro Rata = 1	Stop/Fixed = 3	Fixed Cap = 5
Property Number:	**0238**	Stop/S.F. = 2	Base Year = 4	
Financing Number:	**0128**			

		Common Area Maintenance		
Tenant	**SF**	**Reimb. Calc. Type**	**CAM Factor**	**% Admin. Mark-up**
The Children's Co	20,000	1		15%
Payless Drug	36,060	2	0.5	10%
A&W (Groundleased Outparcel)	3,000	3	1500	15%
Vitamin Head	2,467	4	1999	15%
Merle Norman (beauty/tanning)	2,348	5	2000	15%
Sehome Cleaners	1,811	1		15%
Sehome Cleaners	1,578	1		15%
Quarterback Sports (sports bar)	5,156	1		15%
Stires (Books)	2,534	1		15%
Haircrafters	1,200	1		15%
Consignment	1,943	1		15%
Quilt Basket	1,540	1		15%
Round Table Pizza	3,500	1		15%
Corkrum	1,440	1		15%
Pet Shop	1,440	1		15%
Thai One	1,440	1		15%
JoAnn Fabrics	14,515	1		15%
B'ham Therapy	2,673	1		15%
Pack N Mail	1,339	1		15%
The Bagel Factory	1,791	1		15%
Frazier Chiropractic	1,373	1		15%
Sub Shop	1,373	1		15%
Encore Entertainment (Video)	5,739	1		15%
Storage (Various)	2,123	1		15%
Ranney Moss (Dark: tenant trying to sublease)	1,483	1		15%
TOTAL	**119,866**			

Occupancy

Occupancy Override

Occupancy Adjusted Reimbursement Total

Actual Reimbursement (from Op Stmt Reconciliation)

Comments:

	Calculated							
Incl. in Avg.>>				U/W				CAM Reimb.
CAM Pool					Rent Roll	Lease	Estoppel	Conclusion
2	$32,876	$32,190	$32,405	$38,771				
1	$5,170	$1,178	$2,105	$48,836				
2	$3,431	$3,329	$3,361	$4,316				
1	$285	$0	$66	$3,409				
1	$1,579	$1,308	$1,371	$2,000				
1	$1,218	$1,009	$1,057	$3,511				
1	$1,061	$879	$921	$3,059				
1	$3,468	$2,871	$3,010	$9,995				
1	$1,704	$1,411	$1,479	$4,912				
1	$807	$668	$700	$2,326				
1	$1,307	$1,082	$1,134	$3,767				
1	$1,036	$858	$899	$2,985				
1	$2,354	$1,949	$2,043	$6,785				
1	$969	$802	$841	$2,792				
1	$969	$802	$841	$2,792				
1	$969	$802	$841	$2,792				
1	$9,763	$8,083	$8,473	$28,138				
1	$1,798	$1,489	$1,560	$5,182				
1	$901	$746	$782	$2,596				
1	$1,205	$997	$1,045	$3,472				
1	$923	$765	$801	$2,662				
1	$923	$765	$801	$2,662				
1	$3,860	$3,196	$3,350	$11,125				
1	$1,428	$1,182	$1,239	$4,116				
1	$997	$826	$866	$2,875				
	81,002	**69,186**	**71,991**	**205,874**	-	-	-	-

93.1%	90.5%	91.0%
$80,814	$67,098	$70,204

$148,484	**$127,654**	**$117,639**

REIMBURSEMENT RECONCILIATION

Village Square Center

	Pro Rata = 1	Stop/Fixed = 3	Fixed Cap = 5
Property Number: 0238	Stop/S.F. = 2	Base Year = 4	
Financing Number: 0128			

Property Taxes

Tenant	SF	Reimb. Calc. Type	CAM Factor	% Admin. Mark-up
The Children's Co	20,000	1		
Payless Drug	36,060	2		
A&W (Groundleased Outparcel)	3,000	1		
Vitamin Head	2,467	1		
Merle Norman (beauty/tanning)	2,348	1		
Sehome Cleaners	1,811	1		
Sehome Cleaners	1,578	1		
Quarterback Sports (sports bar)	5,156	1		
Stires (Books)	2,534	1		
Haircrafters	1,200	1		
Consignment	1,943	1		
Quilt Basket	1,540	1		
Round Table Pizza	3,500	1		
Corkrum	1,440	1		
Pet Shop	1,440	1		
Thai One	1,440	1		
JoAnn Fabrics	14,515	1		
B'ham Therapy	2,673	1		
Pack N Mail	1,339	1		
The Bagel Factory	1,791	1		
Frazier Chiropractic	1,373	1		
Sub Shop	1,373	1		
Encore Entertainment (Video)	5,739	1		
Storage (Various)	2,123	1		
Ranney Moss (Dark: tenant trying to sublease)	1,483	1		
TOTAL	**119,866**			

Occupancy

Occupancy Override

Occupancy Adjusted Reimbursement Total

Actual Reimbursement (from Op Stmt Reconciliation)

Comments:

Are property tax reimb. included in CAM (Y/N)?

Rent Roll	Lease	Estoppel	Calculated 1998	1999	2000	U/W	PT Reimb. Conclusion
			$10,802	$10,904	$10,932	$11,236	
			$19,476	$19,661	$19,711	$20,259	
			$1,620	$1,636	$1,640	$1,685	
			$1,332	$1,345	$1,348	$1,386	
			$1,268	$1,280	$1,283	$1,319	
			$978	$987	$990	$1,017	
			$852	$860	$863	$887	
			$2,785	$2,811	$2,818	$2,897	
			$1,369	$1,382	$1,385	$1,424	
			$648	$654	$656	$674	
			$1,049	$1,059	$1,062	$1,092	
			$832	$840	$842	$865	
			$1,890	$1,908	$1,913	$1,966	
			$778	$785	$787	$809	
			$778	$785	$787	$809	
			$778	$785	$787	$809	
			$7,839	$7,914	$7,934	$8,155	
			$1,444	$1,457	$1,461	$1,502	
			$723	$730	$732	$752	
			$967	$976	$979	$1,006	
			$742	$749	$750	$771	
			$742	$749	$750	$771	
			$3,100	$3,129	$3,137	$3,224	
			$1,147	$1,158	$1,160	$1,193	
			$801	$809	$811	$833	
-	-	-	**64,738**	**65,353**	**65,519**	**67,343**	-

1998	1999	2000
93.1%	90.5%	91.0%
90.0%	90.0%	90.0%
$62,438	$63,031	$63,191

1998	1999	2000
$10,410	**$10,513**	**$9,181**

REIMBURSEMENT RECONCILIATION

Village Square Center

		Pro Rata = 1	Stop/Fixed = 3	Fixed Cap = 5
Property Number:	**0238**	Stop/S.F. = 2	Base Year = 4	
Financing Number:	**0128**			
		Insurance		
Tenant	**SF**	**Reimb. Calc. Type**	**CAM Factor**	**% Admin. Mark-up**
The Children's Co	20,000	1		
Payless Drug	36,060	1		
A&W (Groundleased Outparcel)	3,000	1		
Vitamin Head	2,467	1		
Merle Norman (beauty/tanning)	2,348	1		
Sehome Cleaners	1,811	1		
Sehome Cleaners	1,578	1		
Quarterback Sports (sports bar)	5,156	1		
Stires (Books)	2,534	1		
Haircrafters	1,200	1		
Consignment	1,943	1		
Quilt Basket	1,540	1		
Round Table Pizza	3,500	1		
Corkrum	1,440	1		
Pet Shop	1,440	1		
Thai One	1,440	1		
JoAnn Fabrics	14,515	1		
B'ham Therapy	2,673	1		
Pack N Mail	1,339	1		
The Bagel Factory	1,791	1		
Frazier Chiropractic	1,373	1		
Sub Shop	1,373	1		
Encore Entertainment (Video)	5,739	1		
Storage (Various)	2,123	1		
Ranney Moss (Dark: tenant trying to sublease)	1,483	1		
TOTAL	**119,866**			

Occupancy

Occupancy Override

Occupancy Adjusted Reimbursement Total

Actual Reimbursement (from Op Stmt Reconciliation)

Comments:

Are insurance reimb. included in CAM (Y/N)?

Rent Roll	Lease	Estoppel	Calculated 1998	1999	2000	U/W	Ins. Reimb. Conclusion
			$1,996	$2,797	$2,487	$2,778	
			$3,599	$5,044	$4,484	$5,010	
			$299	$420	$373	$417	
			$246	$345	$307	$343	
			$234	$328	$292	$326	
			$181	$253	$225	$252	
			$158	$221	$196	$219	
			$515	$721	$641	$716	
			$253	$354	$315	$352	
			$120	$168	$149	$167	
			$194	$272	$242	$270	
			$154	$215	$191	$214	
			$349	$490	$435	$486	
			$144	$201	$179	$200	
			$144	$201	$179	$200	
			$144	$201	$179	$200	
			$1,449	$2,030	$1,805	$2,016	
			$267	$374	$332	$371	
			$134	$187	$166	$186	
			$179	$251	$223	$249	
			$137	$192	$171	$191	
			$137	$192	$171	$191	
			$573	$803	$714	$797	
			$212	$297	$264	$295	
			$148	$207	$184	$206	
-	-	-	**11,964**	**16,765**	**14,904**	**16,652**	-

1998	1999	2000
93.1%	90.5%	91.0%
90.0%	90.0%	90.0%
$11,539	$16,169	$14,374
$3,307	**$550**	**$759**

LEASE COMPARABLES

Village Square Center

#	Property	Tenant	Location	Date	Square Feet	Base Rent PSF	Lease Term
	Subject-New						
1	Subject	Corkrum	Subject	Jun-00	1,440	$ 14.00	20
2	Subject	Shires Books	Subject	Jun-00	2,534	$ 12.00	20
3	Subject	Thai One	Subject	Jun-00	1,440	$ 11.00	20
4							
5							
6							
7							
8							
9							
10							
11							
12							
13							
		Sub Total/Average			**5,414**	**$ 12.27**	**20.00**
	Subject-Renewal						
14	Sunset Square	Pacific Linen	Bellingham	Jun-00	19,842	$ 7.70	10
15	Lake Meridian	Bartell Drug	King County	Jun-00	14,892	$ 7.00	15
16	Koll Cordata Center	Koll Cordata Center	Bellingham	Jun-00	2,200	$ 13.00	5
17	Ground Lease Food Comp.	Jack-In-The Box	Federal Way	Jun-00	3,100	$ 18.71	20
18							
19							
20							
21							
22							
		Sub Total/Average			**40,034**	**$ 8.58**	**10.81**

#	Property	Tenant	Location	Date	Square Feet	Base Rent PSF	Lease Term
	Competitive-New						
23							
24							
25							
26							
27							
		Sub Total/Average			-		
	Competitive-Renewal						
28							
29							
30							
31							
32							
		Sub Total/Average			-		

Property Number: 0238
Financing Number: 0128

Months Free Rent	Free Rent Per Year	Tenant Imp.	Tenant Imp. PSF	Tenant Imp. PSF/YR	Net Effect Rent PSF/YR	Leasing Commission	Comm. %	Location (+,-,=)	Condition (+,-,=)	Source
0	$ -		$ -	$ -	$ 14.00			=	=	Lease
0	$ -		$ -	$ -	$ 12.00			=	=	Lease
0	$ -		$ -	$ -	$ 11.00			=	=	Lease
0	**$ -**	**$ -**	**$ -**	**$ -**	**$ 12.27**	**$ -**	**0.0%**			
0	$ -		$ -	$ -	$ 7.70			=	+	Appraisal
0	$ -		$ -	$ -	$ 7.00			=	=	Appraisal
0	$ -		$ -	$ -	$ 13.00			=	+	Appraisal
0	$ -		$ -	$ -	$ 18.71			=	=	Underwriter
0	**$ -**	**$ -**	**$ -**	**$ -**	**$ 8.58**	**$ -**	**0.0%**			
		$ -				**$ -**				
		$ -				**$ -**				

Current TTM Occupancy		Physical	Economic
Based on Rent Roll Dated	1/12/01	93.3%	90.4%

		Physical (P) Economic (E)	As of Date U/W	Appraisal
Market		Physical (P)	01/11/01	N/A
Submarket		Physical (P)	01/11/01	01/05/01
Current	(Property)	P	1/12/01	01/05/01
TTM	(Property)	P	12/31/2000	12/31/00
2000	(Property)	P	12/31/00	12/31/00
1999	(Property)	P	12/31/99	12/31/99
1998	(Property)	P	12/31/98	12/31/98

Comments:

Occupancy has been stable in the low 90s for the past several years.

Rental Comparables Summary

#	Name/Location	Distance from Subject	SF	Physical Occupancy
S	**Village Square Center, Bellingham**		128,451	93.3%
1	Koll Cordata Center	4.5 Miles N.	324,550	92.30%
2	Meridian Village	4.25 Miles N.	181,594	96.50%
3	Sunset Square	3 Miles N.	379,547	96.40%
4	Lakeway Center	1 Mile N.	86,200	100.00%
5				

Comments:

Subject has 3 tenants with rents in the $18-$19 range. The rent range without
Rental rate range is for nonanchor space. The subject is a neighborhood center
different market and have a higher concentration of national tenants. Comparables
subject (1 to 3) except comp 1, which is fully leased.

Sale Comparables Summary

#	Name/Location	SF	Year Built
1	Inglewood Village	63,261	1965
2	Lake Meridian Marketplace	143,786	1990
3	Coal Creek Marketplace	52,177	1991
4	Evergreen Village	104,801	1972
5	Blaine International Center	128,073	1992
6			

Comments:

These sales comps were the most recent sales with available information.
Sale comps 1 - 4 are all located in the Seattle area 90 miles south of the subject.
downward by the appraiser from $16,800,000 to $16,360,000 to eliminate the
subject loan. All of the sales comps are considered to have a superior location

Village Square Center

OCCUPANCY, RENTAL RATES AND SALES DATA

Property Number: 0238
Financing Number: 0128

Is property stabilized?	Yes
If "No," est. stabilization date:	N/A

Occupancy		
U/W	**Appraisal**	**Comments**
92.5%	92.0%	The underwriters market consists of 6 comparable properties within 4.5 miles of the subject.
92.5%	90.0%	Appraisers estimate is for in-line space only
93.3%	92.0%	Differing dates of evaluation
92.5%	91.0%	
91.0%	91.0%	
90.5%	90.0%	
93.1%	N/A	Not provided

Year Built	**Avg Rent/ Rent Range per SF**	**Compare to subject (+, - , =) Location**	**Condition**	**Source**	**Comments**
1969	$12-$19			Rent Roll	Anchor rents are $3.30 & $6.80 sf (2 anchors)
1991	$12-$14	=	+	Appraisal	New w/mostly national tenants. Near regional mall.
1979	$11-$12.50	=	=	Appraisal	Excluding a vacant small anchor outparcel, occ. is 96%.
1990	$10-$17	=	+	Appraisal	Condition is superior due to newer construction.
1990	$12-$18	=	+	Appraisal	This is direct competition due to proximity to the subject.

these tenants is $12-$15.76. See mark-to-mark schedule.
and serves a localized area at the south end of town. Rental comps 1 & 2 are next to a regional mall at the north end of town, serve a
3 & 4 are considered most competitive due to proximity to the subject. Most comps have a similar number of in-line tenant vacancies as the

Date Sold	**Sale Price**	**Value Per SF**	**Seller**	**Buyer**	**Cap Rate**	**Source**
10/95	$6,297,000	$100	CBB Assoc.	Harriette Raab	9.15%	Appraisal
03/94	$16,360,000	$114	PWC Equities-I	Spieker Properties L.P.	10.47%	Appraisal
10/92	$6,590,000	$126	First Western Dev.	Joshua Green Corp.	9.52%	Appraisal
08/94	$9,250,000	$88	Robert Steinberg	Gateway Buena Park	9.68%	Appraisal
12/92	$14,635,000	$114	SRV Developments	Sylvan S. Shulman Trust	9.00%	Appraisal

Comp #5 is located in Blaine, WA, 20 miles north of the subject near the Canadian border. The sale price of comp #2 has been adjusted
value of excess land for future development included in the sale. Sale comp #3 was developed by the principals of the borrowing entity for the
to the subject. With the exception of sales comp #4, rated as inferior in condition, all are considered to be in superior condition to the subject.

General Property Characteristics:

Property Type / Description	Office			Retail	Anchor
Property Class (A, B, C)	B		Total land area (acres)		
Gross SF	128,451		Excess land area (acres)		
Net rentable SF	128,451		Number of floors		
Year built	1969		Number of buildings		
Year last renovated	1991		Number of elevators		

Property Description Comments (e.g., space, usage, etc.):

A 128,451 sf retail neighborhood anchored strip center located in Bellingham, Washington. It is anchored by a 56,314 sf Haggens owns their own store and pad and is not part of the collateral. The total property sf is 184,765 (including Haggens) and was Borrowers purchased the property in 1991 for $5 million which did not have the grocery store at the time. By August, 1992 the developed by Haggens. In 1995 an A&W fast food outparcel building was added under a ground lease.

Exterior Condition ("Ex/Good/Avg/Poor/NA"):

Overall quality of the exterior	Good
Landscaping	Average
Adequacy of roads / parking	Excellent
Paving	Good to Avg.
Adequacy of lighting	Good
Paint	Average
Windows	Good
Roof	Good
Walls	Good
Façade	Average

Interior Condition ("Ex/Good/Avg/Poor/NA"):

Overall quality of the interior	Good
Restrooms	N/A
Walls (paint / wall coverings)	Good
Flooring / Carpeting	Good
Lobby / Common areas	N/A
Elevators	N/A
Lighting	Excellent
Tenant area (typical space)	Good
Restaurant / Food court area	Excellent
Mechanical areas	Good

Neighborhood Description:

The subject is a 184,765 sf neighborhood strip center constructed in 1969 on 13.36 acres along Interstate 5 in Bellingham, Payless discount/drug store. The Haggens store site and improvements are owned by Haggens and are not part of the collateral.

Amenities:

Restaurant / Food court	Yes	Security	No
Health club	No	On-site manager	No

Major off-site demand generators:

Bellingham Demographics: Population: 1990 was 52,179; 1992 was 54,270; and 1999 was 57,830. As of 1999 this represented Whatcom County in 1999 was $37,082. -The county economy is diversified with 29% employed in wholesale and retail trade; 24% mining, construction, transportation, and finance/insurance/real estate. -Major employers in Bellingham include Western Washington (1,002),Georgia Pacific (857), and City & County government (1,300). -Demand generators include the surrounding residential CBD (2 mi. north), and the port of Bellingham (1.5 mi. west).

Property Number:	**0238**	
Financing Number:	**0128**	

Non Owned)	Industrial		
9.24		Type of parking	Surface
4.12		Total parking spaces	948
1		Exterior facade	Concrete and Wood
3		Roof type	Flat
0		Sprinklered (yes / no)	Yes

Grocery Store and a 36,060 sf Payless discount/drug store. The Haggens Grocery constructed in 1969 on 13.36 acres along Interstate 5 in Bellingham. The Borrowers completed a total renovation and the Haggens grocery store was

Location Characteristics:

Corner (Yes / No)	Yes
Traffic volume (low, medium, high)	Medium
Access to major arteries	Good
Access to local amenities	Good
Street appeal	Good
Ingress / Egress	Good
Ease of left hand turn into Property	Average
Visibility	Good
Signage	Excellent
Overall quality of the location	Good

Washington. It is anchored by a 56,314 sf Haggens Grocery Store and a 36,060 sf

After hours entry system	No

39% of the total population of Whatcom County. Estimated median income in in services; 17% in government; 15% in manufacturing; and the remaining 15% in University (1,429), St. Joseph Hospital (1,175), Bellingham School District population (adjacent), Western Washington University (1/2 mi. west), the Bellingham

Village Square Center
PROPERTY DESCRIPTION

Comments on location:

The property is well located on the corner of 36th and Burnham. The surroundings are primarily residential

Property Management Information:

Property Management Company	Northwest Management
Property Manager's Name	Greta Sustain
Company's web site	N/A
Property Manager on site daily? (yes / no)	no
Years Mgmt. Co. associated with the Property	5 years
Mgmt. type (outside contractor / owner)	outside contractor
Property management fee	4%
Manages properties for other owner	yes

Property Management Company's History/Experience:

Northwest Management has been active in property management since 1978. The company is owned by Mr. Ronald Oro. Managed properties are in Washington, Montana, and Idaho. Current actual management fee is 4% for nonanchor tenants and 1% for anchored tenants.

REAL ESTATE TAX SUMMARY

General Tax Information:

Tax Identification	See Comments
Assessor's Phone Number	360-676-6774
Tax Abatements? (Yes/No)	No
Tax Abatement Expiration Date(s)	N/A

Real Estate Tax Assessment History:

Fiscal Year Ending	Market Value	Conversion Factor	Assessed Value	Millage Rate
2000	$5,946,410	1.00000	$5,946,410	0.0121
1999	$5,703,250	1.00000	$5,703,250	0.0123
1998	$5,550,850	1.00000	$5,550,850	0.0126

Comments On Real Estate Taxes (Status of tax appeals and description of other assessments):

Millage can only go up 6% per year by law. When millage goes up assessments usually decrease to avoid and a few other smaller strip retail centers.

Leasing Agent Information:

Leasing Company	Retail Leasing Inc.
Leasing Agent's Name	John Hegumund
Company's Web Site	jhegumund@retailleasing.com
Leasing agent on site daily (yes / no)	No
Years Leasing Agent associated with the Property	4 years
Leasing type (outside contractor / owner)	Outside
Total actual leasing commissions new	5.50%
Total actual leasing commissions renewal	2.75%

Leasing Company's History/Experience:

Retail Leasing Inc., is an 18 year old company based in Bellevue, Washington. They lease and manage approximately 2.37 million square feet of retail and office in the greater Seattle area. John Hegumund has been with the firm for 11 years and handles several other shopping centers in the Bellingham area.

Last Re-assessment Date (month/year)	1999
Assessment currently under appeal?	No
Next assessment date (month/year)	2003

Total Property Tax	Other Assessments	Total Tax Liability	Comments
$72,142	$0	$72,142	Commercial property is reassessed every 4 years
$70,115	$0	$70,115	
$69,915	$0	$69,915	

unreasonable increases. Tax Acct No's. 370306-390535-0002 & 370306-405540-0000.

Additional Considerations. In the event that rent rolls are not available as of the end of the operating statement periods, Precept will obtain rent rolls for historical points-in-time that are available.

Summary of Annual Occupancy

Precept will request that the borrower provide corresponding physical and/or economic occupancy figures for the operating statement periods. Precept may request monthly occupancy statistics where severe income fluctuations exist. This is not a required item given that economic occupancy during historical periods can at least be estimated by comparing actual rent collections from the operating statements to estimated Gross Potential Rent for the same periods. Precept may request monthly occupancy statistics where severe income fluctuations exist.

Additional Considerations. Precept will compare the summary of annual occupancy numbers with point-in-time occupancy indicated by historical rent rolls (explained later).

Summary of Delinquencies (or Aging Report)

Precept will require the borrower to provide a current summary of tenants that are delinquent in their financial rental obligations, including the length of time each tenant has been delinquent and the dollar amount of the delinquency. Precept will also request a summary of delinquencies as of the end of each operating statement period.

Additional Considerations. In the event that a summary of delinquencies is not available as of the end of each operating statement period, Precept will request that the borrower provide the summary for historical points-in-time that are available.

Summary of Historical Capital Expenditures

Precept will request that the borrower provide a brief description of capital expenditures made to the property within the operating statement periods (past three years), including the timing and cost of such improvements.

Additional Considerations. In addition to providing relevant detail regarding the property's physical improvements, this summary will be utilized to make any necessary adjustments for nonrecurring expenditures in the Operating Statement Reconciliation section of the underwriting summary.

STEP 2: OPERATING STATEMENT NORMALIZATION

Standard Cash Flow Line Items

Precept will use the Operating Statement Reconciliation section of the underwriting summary to normalize the operating statements as set forth herein. For retail land uses, Precept's standard cash flow line items are indicated in bold typeface in the following table:

Revenues

Gross Potential Rent
  Or Collected Rent
Percentage Rent
Expense Reimbursements
  Common Area Maintenance (CAM)
  Real Estate Taxes
  Insurance
  Other Expense Recoveries
  Total Expense Reimbursements
Other Income—1
Other Income—2
  Total Gross Income
Mark-to-Market
Vacancy
Credit Loss
  Total Effective Gross Income

Expenses

Variable
  Management Fee
  Payroll and Benefits
  Utilities
  Repairs and Maintenance
  Common Area Maintenance (CAM)
  Administrative
  Other Variable Expense—1
  Other Variable Expense—2
  Other Variable Expense—3
    Total Variable Expense

Fixed

Real Property Taxes
Insurance
Other Fixed Expense—1
Other Fixed Expense—2
Other Fixed Expense—3

Total Fixed Expense

Total Expenses

Net Operating Income

Capital Expenditures

Reserves for Replacement
Retenanting Costs
Other Capital Expense—1
Other Capital Expense—2

Total Capital Expenditures

Net Cash Flow

The headings in the preceding table are group descriptions, and the line items in bold italics are calculated fields. The generic line items (e.g., Other Income—1, Other Fixed Expense—1, etc.) are reserved for income and/or expenditures from the operating statements that either do not clearly fit within Precept's standard line items or that Precept determines to be more meaningful as separate line items (e.g., ground rent, etc.). In these cases, the generic Precept line-item title in the table will be replaced with the actual operating statement line-item title.

Precept anticipates that a portion of borrower-provided historical operating statements will reflect Collected Rent in lieu of Gross Potential Rent and corresponding Vacancy. Therefore, Precept's standard cash flow line items allow for one or the other, but not both.

Compiling a Trailing-12-Month or Annualized Operating Statement

In some cases the borrower will not have provided Precept with a current trailing-12-month operating statement that can be directly entered into the Operating Statement Reconciliation section of the underwriting summary. In this event, Precept will compile a trailing-12-month statement or create an annualized statement, provided that the operating statements obtained from the borrower allow Precept to do so in a meaningful manner. For example, if the borrower is able to provide operating statements for the past full calendar year *A*, the current partial year *B* (year to date), and the prior partial year *C* (for the same months relative to the current partial year), the trailing-12-month cash flow would be compiled by subtracting *C*, the prior partial year, from *A*, the past full calendar year, and adding *B*, the current partial year, to the result. This compilation would be completed on a line-by-line basis, and results would appear in the Operating Statement Reconciliation section of the model, with a "trailing-12" or "TTM" designation. Whenever possible this method of compiling the trailing-12-month cash flow will be used.

This calculation will not always be possible, given, for example, the absence of prior partial-year statements that correspond to the same number of months as the statements for the current partial year. In this event, the trailing-12-month cash flow may be calculated using the partial-year formula, or the trailing-12 may be replaced with annualized figures.

Partial-Year Formula

$$\text{TTM} = \text{current partial year} + \left[\frac{\text{most recent full year}}{12} \times (12 - x)\right]$$

where x = the number of months of operating statements used for the current partial year.

Precept will determine whether to calculate the trailing-12-month cash flow using the partial-year formula or to simply annualize the current partial year on the following basis:

Current Partial-Year Operating Statements	Prior Full-Year Operating Statements	Action
Less than 6 months	None	Do not calculate TTM
Less than 6 months	Yes	Use the partial-year formula
6 months or greater	None	Annualize the period available
6 months or greater	Yes	Use the partial-year formula

Rent Roll Reconciliation

Precept anticipates that most borrower rent rolls will not (1) provide sufficient individual lease details and/or (2) be organized in a manner such that Precept can efficiently summarize and analyze individual lease terms for underwriting purposes. Therefore, Precept will reconstruct the rent roll provided by the borrower within the underwriting summary. This process requires transposing the rent roll to Precept's standard rent roll summary within the underwriting summary. Precept will add to this information any relevant leasing details provided in documents separate from the rent roll (e.g., a summary of tenant improvement costs, lease termination provisions, etc.) and will show lease details on a varying basis (e.g., rent per square foot per year vs. rent per square foot per month, etc.). In addition, Precept will add market rental data to the rent roll summary and conduct analysis for such items as occupancy cost and average rental rate calculations.

STEP 3: DATA CONFIRMATION

In addition to the collection and normalization of property operating statements, Precept will conduct other various procedures confirming the property's operating history. If these procedures identify inaccuracies or misrepresentations within the normalized operating history, corresponding adjustments will be made and footnoted within the appropriate section of the underwriting summary, and/or the borrower may be asked to resubmit one or more property statements. Moreover, if individual income and expense line items presented in the property operating statements are volatile from year to year, Precept may increase the sample size (length of the operating period) for data confirmation purposes.

Federal Income Tax Return Review

Precept will reconcile the property's operating statements to the borrower or current owner's most recent available federal income tax returns. Precept expects that total income reported in the tax return will be within 5% of Total Effective Gross Income reported in the operating statements. If this expectation is not met, Precept will require an explanation from the borrower, which will be noted within the Income Tax Reconciliation section of the underwriting summary.

While individual expense line-item titles often differ between tax returns and operating statements (making line-item comparisons difficult), overall expenses are expected to be consistent. To the greatest extent possible, Precept will group individual expense line items from the tax returns so that they are consistent with the expense line items of operating statements. For example, Precept may total all expense line items except Real Property Taxes and Insurance, and compare the result to the same from the operating statements. At a minimum, Precept will compare overall expenses from the tax returns, with obvious adjustments for interest and depreciation, to overall expenses from the corresponding operating statement. If comparable line items, line-item groupings, and/or Total Expenses differ between the two sources by more than 10%, Precept will require borrower explanations that will be noted within the Income Tax Reconciliation section of the underwriting summary.

Additional Considerations. Federal income tax returns may not always be available, given that some borrowers may be using the contemplated financing as purchase money. If this is the case, Precept will continue the data confirmation procedures outlined here in lieu of the income tax reconciliation.

Bank Statement Review

Precept will reconcile Total Effective Gross Income from the operating statements for the most recent 12-month period to actual bank statements reflecting property income. This reconciliation will not be conducted if the federal income tax return review is completed and yields no discrepancies with respect to property income.

Lease Reviews

In order to confirm lease terms outlined within the current rent roll and identify special lease provisions that may materially impact the property's future operations, Precept will review tenant lease agreements. This procedure requires sorting the tenants by the amount of base rent payable by each tenant. Precept will then conduct a "flip" review of each lease to determine the various types of lease forms, followed by a full lease review for each tenant that represents at least 5% of the total base rental revenue and for each tenant that has a lease agreement form that was not previously reviewed, up to a cumulative total of 75% of the total base rental revenue. The results of the lease reviews will be documented in Precept's lease review form.

Estoppel Certificate Review

Precept will review all estoppel certificates provided by the borrower. Precept will reconcile the terms outlined in the estoppel certificates to the current rent roll and lease agreements. Precept will also investigate all tenant notes on the estoppel certificates that indicate potential problems with the physical improvements, disputes between the borrower and the tenant, etc. Precept will pay particular attention to estoppel certificates from tenants that have past-due balances reflected in the summary of delinquencies.

Occupancy Review

Precept will compare the summary of annual occupancy numbers with point-in-time occupancy indicated by historical rent rolls and estimated economic occupancy derived by comparing actual rent collections from the operating statements to Gross Potential Rent for the same periods. If the operating statements do not provide a Gross Potential Rent figure, Precept will estimate it based on the historical rent rolls.

Expense Reimbursements Review

Utilizing the indicative expense reimbursement formulas from the rent rolls and the lease reviews, Precept will recalculate total Expense Reimbursements for historical periods and compare these estimates to actual collections outlined within the operating statements.

Management Fee Review

Precept will reconcile historical Management Fee expenses from the operating statements to the current management contract.

Payroll and Benefits Expense Review

Precept will reconcile historical Payroll and Benefits expenses to the borrower's summary of property employees and payroll.

Utilities Expense Review

Precept will reconcile Utilities expenses from the operating statements to actual utility bills for the most recent 12-month period.

Real Property Tax Expense Review

Precept will reconcile Real Property Taxes from the operating statements to actual tax bills for the most recent 12-month period.

Capital Expenditures Review

Precept will reconcile capital expenditures from the operating statements to the summary of historical capital expenditures provided by the borrower.

Other

Depending on (1) the results of the procedures outlined previously, (2) the sophistication of the borrower's accounting system, and (3) the volatility of individual operating statement figures, Precept may conduct additional procedures, including, but not limited to, a detailed income and expense ledger review for certain periods of time in order to better understand the components of the property's operations.

STEP 4: ESTIMATION OF STABILIZED PROPERTY CASH FLOW

As previously described, Precept will conclude an underwritten Net Cash Flow on a trailing-12-month (TTM) basis and on a leases-in-place (LIP) basis. While the process of deriving underwritten operating expenses is the same for each of these methodologies, the derivation of underwritten revenues is different between TTM and LIP.

Revenues

Gross Potential Rent

Standard Definition. *Gross Potential Rent* is an estimate of the annual fixed base rent that would be collected if the property were 100% occupied for one year.

Method of Derivation

LIP. Gross Potential Rent is calculated by annualizing the sum of (1) the total monthly rent in place for occupied space (based on the most current rent roll) and (2) the monthly Market Rent for each vacant space:

Gross Potential Rent (LIP) = (total monthly base rent for current tenants + monthly Market Rent for each vacant space) × 12 months

To be considered in occupancy for purposes of the foregoing calculation, existing noncredit tenants must have paid full rent for at least one month and credit tenants must be in occupancy pursuant to an executed lease (collectively, a *qualifying lease*). Precept will review the most recent three months of rent collections to determine which tenants meet these criteria. Precept will request explanations of any discrepancies between the rent roll and actual collections, and will adjust underwritten current rent accordingly.

MARKET RENT. *Market Rent* is determined by comparing property-level rental rate data from the rent roll with market data from the site inspection report and appraisal report. Upon reviewing the site inspection report and appraisal report, Precept may also conduct direct interviews of leasing brokers in order to clarify market conditions. The primary source of the Market Rent conclusion will be actual leasing at the property within the past two years as determined from the most current rent roll.

First, Precept will average the rental rates from the most recent leases for each of the property's comparable spaces (shop, anchor, end-cap, outparcels, 0 to 1000 square feet, 1000 to 3000 square feet etc.). Second, the average comparable rental rate within the property will be compared to the market rent conclusions in the site inspection report and appraisal report to confirm that the three sources are supportive of each other. Third, provided that the site inspection report and appraisal report conclusions do not deviate from the property's comparable rental rate average by more than 5%, the Market Rent conclusion will be equal to the property's comparable rental rate average. If either the site inspection report or appraisal report market rent conclusions deviate by more than 5% from the property's comparable rental rate average, the Market Rent conclusion will be between the high and low of the three indicators. The exact Market Rent conclusion will depend on the particular reason(s) for the deviations. The exact source of the Market Rent conclusion will be noted in the underwriting summary.

For purposes of the preceding analysis, rental rates will be compared on an effective basis to account for offsets or additions in the form of free rent, abnormal expense reimbursements, and tenant improvement costs that deviate dramatically from underwritten levels (discussed later). *Effective Rental Rates* will be calculated as follows:

Effective Rental Rate, \$ per square foot
= (base rent for the full term of the lease, \$
– deviation from underwritten Expense Reimbursements
and underwritten tenant improvement allowances, \$
+ total value of free rent for the lease term, \$) / lease term, years

ADDITIONAL CONSIDERATIONS. Market Rent is often difficult to determine for retail space. Rates may vary dramatically across competing retail centers as well as within a particular center depending on the location, size of the space, and preexisting build-outs or use permits. Tenants adjacent to an anchor or with large frontage generally pay higher lease rates. Smaller tenants also tend to pay higher lease rates per square foot ("per square footage"). Precept expects that the largest deviations from current Market Rent will be found for older leases. Precept will review the most recently executed leases and calculate Effective Rental Rates for a large enough sample (as determined by Precept) of tenants to determine the Effective Rental Rate levels the property is currently achieving. Precept will also calculate effective market rental rates for competitive space when possible. Overall, Precept will use its analysis of market leasing conditions to determine the relative attractiveness of the financial terms under which a tenant occupies its space and determine the leasing packages a property can expect to achieve for new leases.

Regardless of whether existing rent is below market or management has been successful in implementing rent increases upon tenant rollover (e.g., anticipated increase in future revenue), Precept will not give credit for future rental rate increases beyond the inclusion of Market Rent for vacant square footage in the Gross Potential Rent calculation.

TTM. Gross Potential Rent will equal the Gross Potential Rent figure provided in the trailing-12-month operating statement. Precept will not conclude Gross Potential Rent if the trailing-12-month operating statement does not provide such a figure.

Collected Rent

Standard Definition—TTM Only. *Collected Rent* is an estimate of the annual fixed base rent that will be collected over the first year of the loan term net of actual Vacancy and Credit Loss. Collected Rent is reserved for the TTM methodology and will not be included if Gross Potential Rent is concluded.

Method of Derivation. Collected Rent is concluded based on actual rent received in the trailing-12-month period.

Percentage Rent

Standard Definition. *Percentage Rent* is an estimate of the annual rent that the property will generate based on retail sales of tenants' businesses. In most cases, Percentage Rent is calculated based on gross sales revenue that exceeds a specified minimum sales level referred to as a *breakpoint.*

Method of Derivation—LIP and TTM. Precept will verify the historical Percentage Rent collections for each tenant paying Percentage Rent. Precept will review Percentage Rent using each tenant's historical sales figures, applicable breakpoints, and the borrower's sales revenue participation percentages. Once verified, Precept will use these historical Percentage Rent payments as the basis for underwriting Percentage Rent.

Precept will then adjust the historical Percentage Rent level as follows:

1. Precept will eliminate any Percentage Rent for tenants no longer leasing space at the property.
2. Precept will make downward adjustments of 10% or more to the sales of any tenant with declining or nonstable sales, and recalculate the Percentage Rent that the tenant would pay at the lower sales level.
3. Precept will decrease sales by 20 to 30% for any tenant facing significant new competition or other factors that are likely to cause a decline in sales.

Precept will compare the sum of the tenant's base rent and Percentage Rent to current Market Rent, paying particular attention to the tenant's remaining lease term and location alternatives. Precept will adjust the Percentage Rent downward in situations where the tenant's all-in rent is above market and the borrower's ability to collect Percentage Rent may soon be compromised. This particular adjustment differs from the mark-to-market adjustment discussed later in that it will only be made to Percentage Rent, while the mark-to-market focuses on adjusting base rent.

Based on the adjustment results of the previously described analysis, Precept will calculate Percentage Rent as follows:

$$\text{Percentage Rent amount, \$} = (\text{tenant annual sales, \$} - \text{breakpoint, \$}) \times \text{borrower's participation percentage, \%}$$

Additional Considerations. When verifying historic Percentage Rent collections, Precept will pay particular attention to timing of Percentage Rent payments (quarterly, semiannually, annually, etc.), Expense Reimbursement offsets to Percentage Rent, and/or year-end true-ups that cause annual operating statements to misrepresent true annualized collections. The preceding derivation for Percentage Rent will also apply to tenants who pay only Percentage Rent with no minimum or base rent (sometimes referred to as *Percentage Rent in lieu*). Tenants paying only Percentage Rent will be clearly noted within the underwriting summary.

Expense Reimbursements.

Standard Definition. *Expense Reimbursements* are estimates of the annual amount of income the property will receive from tenants to offset variable and fixed operating expenses. Precept organizes reimbursements into four categories: (1) real property taxes, (2) insurance premiums, (3) common area maintenance (CAM), and (4) other.

Method of Derivation—LIP and TTM. Precept first concludes the actual expense levels for each of the four Expense Reimbursement categories (see the Expenses subsection of this chapter). Precept then calculates historical recovery percentages for each of the four Expense Reimbursement categories by analyzing the historical recovery percentages for trends and general stability. If the data randomly fluctuates between historical periods, Precept will use the average recovery percentage for the three-year historical period. If the recovery percentage is declining over time, Precept will use a figure at or below the most recent recovery percentage level, depending on the cause of the decline. Under the TTM methodology, Precept calculates underwritten Expense Reimbursements by multiplying the underwriting reimbursement percentage by the underwritten expense for each Expense Reimbursement category, subject to a cap at the lower of the following:

- Contractual expense recovery obligations of the tenants
- Underwritten expenses

Under the LIP methodology, the preceding derivation will include justifiable reimbursements associated with new qualifying leases.

Additional Considerations. Precept will verify tenant reimbursement obligations by performing lease reviews. Of particular importance will be reimbursement provisions for expense categories (e.g., real property taxes) that Precept underwrites at a level materially in excess of the historical expense. In this case, Precept will verify that a commensurate increase in reimbursement based on the preceding methodology is supportable based on the tenant's lease obligations and overall Market Rent. Moreover, Precept will reconcile historical reimbursements to the borrower's billing summary (or actual bills if a summary is not available) to confirm collections.

Other Income–1 and 2

Standard Definition. *Other Income* is an estimate of the annual recurring income generated from sources that are ancillary or incidental to the property's base rental revenue. Examples include parking fees, storage rentals, resale of utilities, and signage and antenna fees.

Method of Derivation—LIP and TTM. Precept will include as underwritten revenue only those items individually or in aggregate having consistent history and strong expectations for future collections. If such amounts comprise more than 5.0% of Total Effective Gross Income, Precept will request documentation confirming and explaining the sources of revenue. Precept will base the underwritten amount of Other Income on the most recent 12-month collections or an average of historical collections for which Precept has operating statements. Underwritten Other Income in excess of 5.0% of Total Effective Gross Income will be noted as to source in either the Cash Flow Summary section or the Operating Statement Reconciliation page of the underwriting summary. The underwriting summary allows Other Income to be categorized into three separate line items.

Additional Considerations. Precept will exclude interest income from Other Income provided that operating statements give sufficient detail from which to do so.

Mark-to-Market

Standard Definition. *Mark-to-Market* is a downward adjustment made to Gross Potential Rent or Collected Rent to reflect the overall amount that the property's current rental rates exceed market rates.

Method of Derivation. First, the current base rent for each comparable type of space within the property will be subtracted from the corresponding Market Rent conclusion (explained previously under Gross Potential Rent). The comparable type of space within the property will depend on the property's individual characteristics but may include shop, anchor, endcap, outparcels, 0 to 1000 square feet, 1000 to 3000 square feet, etc. Next, Precept will determine the Mark-to-Market adjustment by taking the lesser of zero or the sum of the following two subtotals:

- The sum of Market Rent less current base rent for each tenant space that is currently leased with a remaining term less than or equal to three years.
- The sum of Market Rent less current base rent for each tenant space that is currently leased at a base rent that exceeds Market Rent by more than 10% and has a remaining lease term greater than three years.

For purposes of the preceding calculation, Precept will perform an additional step in deriving Mark-to-Market when sales data for one or more tenants is available—a total occupancy cost evaluation. *Occupancy Costs* are defined as the sum of annual base rent, Percentage Rent, and Expense Reimbursements, and are evaluated as a percentage of a tenant's annual gross sales. Precept uses the occupancy cost percentage to identify tenants whose occupancy costs are above the levels merited by their sales. Precept will pay particular attention to unstable anchor tenants. If the overall performance of the property is strong, Precept will not make adjustments for small individual tenants with high occupancy costs because these tenants are likely to be replaced upon termination. Precept will use the following guidelines for adjusting rental revenue based on an analysis of occupancy costs upon lease termination:

Maximum Levels for the Occupancy Cost Ratio	
In-line tenant	16.0%
Mall or grocery anchor	6.0%
Other anchor tenant (quasi-anchor)	10.0%
Food court and restaurants	22.0%

For all unstable anchor tenants (as defined later) and if *Occupancy Cost Ratios* exceed maximum levels for more than 10% of the tenants (measured using each tenant's contribution to total base rent revenue), Precept will calculate an *Occupancy Cost Cap Deduction* for tenants with Occupancy Cost Ratios that exceed the maximum levels by more than 3% as follows:

Occupancy Cost Cap Deduction, \$ = annual tenant sales revenue, \$
× (tenant's occupancy ratio, % – appropriate maximum
Occupancy Cost Ratio, %

Additional Considerations. When making the foregoing calculation, Precept may rely on recent leasing information at the property and competing properties if obtained from the borrower, the appraisal firm, local property and leasing brokers, or market research from local and national property brokerage and real estate consulting firms.

Vacancy

Standard Definition. *Vacancy* is an estimate of the annual economic loss that the property will experience from Gross Potential Rent, or the annual additional economic loss that the property will experience from Collected Rent, due to a portion of the property being unoccupied and/or not leased.

Method of Derivation

LIP. Vacancy is calculated by taking the product of (1) Gross Potential Rent and (2) the greater of Retail Minimum Vacancy Percentage, Actual Vacancy Percentage, and Market Vacancy Percentage.

TTM. If Gross Potential Rent is concluded, Vacancy will equal the corresponding vacancy figure from the normalized trailing-12-month operating statements. Otherwise, if Collected Rent is concluded, Vacancy will be calculated as follows:

Vacancy = the greater of zero and {[(the greater of Retail Minimum
Vacancy Percentage, Actual Vacancy Percentage,
or Market Vacancy Percentage) – Actual Vacancy Percentage]
× [the sum of Collected Rent/(1 – Actual Vacancy Percentage)]}

Retail Minimum Vacancy Percentage is the economic weighted average of concluded Minimum Vacancy for each type of space. Concluded *Minimum Vacancy* will be 0 to 5% for anchor space, and 5 to 10% for nonanchor space.

In the event that Collected Rent is concluded in lieu of Gross Potential Rent, underwritten Vacancy represents the difference between Actual Vacancy Percentage and the greater of Retail Minimum Vacancy Percentage and Market Vacancy Percentage.

Anchor Space. In order to estimate stabilized vacancy for anchor tenants, Precept will take into account the remaining lease term, lease cancellation options, tenant credit quality, tenant sales revenues, overall occupancy cost, functionality of the space for the current and future user, market rent levels, and market vacancy rates for similar space. Precept will pay particular attention to the Property's historical anchor occupancy and corresponding changes in relevant market dynamics, including supply and demand of space in the Property's submarket. Precept will use the following guidelines for underwriting the Retail Minimum Vacancy Percentage for anchor space vacancy:

STABLE ANCHOR TENANTS. The typical range for underwriting anchor vacancy for stable anchor tenants is 0 to 5% of anchor base rent and Expense Reimbursements.

UNSTABLE ANCHOR TENANTS. If Precept considers the anchor tenant unstable, Precept will use a larger vacancy deduction. The size of the Vacancy deduction will depend on the reasons for the instability and the prevailing market conditions for the space. The following is a list of typical reasons for anchor instability and the approaches Precept uses in underwriting such instability:

- *Corporate credit issues.* If Precept determines that the parent corporation is experiencing financial or operational difficulty, Precept will calculate a vacancy deduction for the space assuming 6 to 18 months of downtime over a lease term commensurate with market lease terms for comparable space, but generally not longer than 10 to 15 years. Precept will also include such space in the Tenant Rollover Analysis section of the underwriting summary.
- *Tenant expected to move.* If Precept determines that a tenant is rumored, known, or expected to move to a different space in the market, Precept will determine if the floor plate layout and size would be satisfactory for the newest stores in the chain. For example, both Store A and Store B leased stores of 75,000 to 85,000 square feet 10 years ago. They now prefer stores of over 110,000 square feet for their newer Super-Store A and Store B

Super Center formats. Both tenants have been known to vacate the smaller spaces for retail centers with larger floor plates, leaving the old centers without an anchor. If the tenant has done well in the space but is leaving, or could leave, for better or larger space, Precept will underwrite downtime of 12 to 24 months over a lease term commensurate with market lease terms for comparable space, but generally not longer than 10 to 15 years, and will include the space in the Tenant Rollover Analysis section of the underwriting summary.

- *Strong center/weak tenant.* If Precept believes a tenant is the wrong tenant for the space or the tenant's concept is flawed, but the center is otherwise strong and the space is desirable for other anchors, as long as the center is well located and otherwise performing very well for other tenants, Precept will underwrite 6 to 18 months of downtime over a lease term commensurate with market lease terms for comparable space, but generally not longer than 10 to 15 years, as vacancy for the tenant and will include the space in the Tenant Rollover Analysis section of the underwriting summary.
- *Weak center/strong tenant.* If Precept believes the retail center itself is the problem rather than the anchor tenant, Precept will determine whether the space is obsolete and may never be re-leased or whether the space can be re-leased at a lower rent with some downtime assumed to re-lease the space. If the space would be very difficult to re-lease, Precept will underwrite the space as vacant. If the space can be re-leased at a lower rate, Precept will underwrite downtime of 24 to 36 months over a lease term commensurate with market lease terms for comparable space, but generally not longer than 10 to 15 years, and will include the space in the Tenant Rollover Analysis section of the underwriting summary.

Based on the preceding, Precept will calculate downtime as Vacancy as follows:

$$\text{Initial Vacancy deduction, \$} = \frac{\text{downtime, months}}{\text{lease term, months}} \times (\text{base rent, \$} + \text{recoveries, \$})$$

Nonanchor Space. Precept will estimate stabilized vacancy for nonanchor space by evaluating the quality of a property, tenant credit quality, tenant-specific and overall center sales revenues, location of the center, historical vacancy, and historical credit losses. Precept will pay particular attention to the property's historical nonanchor occupancy and corresponding changes in relevant market dynamics, including supply and demand of space in the property's submarket. Precept uses the following guidelines for underwriting the Retail Minimum Vacancy Percentage for nonanchor space:

MODERATE TO STRONG PROPERTIES. For moderate to strong properties (e.g., properties at which greater than 50% of the nonanchor rent roll, as determined by the number of tenants, is comprised of national and regional tenants), Precept will adjust the nonanchor space vacancy rate to equal the greater of the Actual Vacancy Percentage, market vacancy percentage, and 5%.

WEAK PROPERTIES. Precept will use a Retail Minimum Vacancy Percentage of 7.5% for weak properties. Precept considers a property weak if (1) 75% of the in-line tenants are local or small regional companies, (2) the anchor tenants are local or small regional companies, (3) the center has no anchor, or (4) the average annual nonanchor sales are less than $250 per square foot.

PROPERTIES IN WEAK MARKETS. Precept will use a Retail Minimum Vacancy Percentage of 7.5% for properties in weak markets. Precept considers a market weak if (1) market vacancy is in excess of 12%, (2) the market's economy is stagnant or is suffering declining regional economic growth, or (3) annual nonanchor tenant rental rates are below $12 per square foot.

Precept will not underwrite ground-floor vacancy for nonanchor space at less than the market vacancy rate unless a property is clearly superior and has demonstrated the ability to outperform its competition. Precept will never assume a vacancy of less than 5%.

For non-ground-level floors (e.g., subterranean or second and third floor) Precept will not underwrite vacancy for nonanchor space at less than the Market Vacancy Percentage plus 5% unless a property is clearly superior and has demonstrated the ability to outperform its competition. Precept will never assume nonanchor vacancy for ground-floor space of less than 10%.

Additional Considerations. When making the foregoing calculation, Precept may rely on recent leasing information at the property and competing properties if obtained from a borrower, the appraisal firm, local property and leasing brokers, and market research from local and national property brokerage and real estate consulting firms.

Actual Vacancy Percentage

LIP. *Actual Vacancy Percentage* is derived by dividing the sum of annual Market Rent for all unoccupied and/or unleased units by Gross Potential Rent.

TTM. *Actual Vacancy Percentage* is equal to the reported vacancy figure for the trailing-12-month period. If a vacancy figure is not reported for the trailing-12-month period, Actual Vacancy Percentage will be derived as follows:

$$\text{Actual Vacancy Percentage} = 1 - \frac{\text{Collected Rent}}{\text{LIP Gross Potential Rent}}$$

Market Vacancy Percentage. *Market Vacancy Percentage* shall be determined by Precept after conducting a reconciliation analysis of the appraisal report's concluded market vacancy (or one minus the appraiser's concluded market occupancy) and the site inspection report's concluded market vacancy. When reviewing the appraisal report and site inspection report, Precept will pay particular attention to demand growth versus anticipated new supply and how these factors relate to stabilized occupancy for the property. The Market Vacancy Percentage will be a number between the appraiser's concluded market vacancy (or one minus the appraiser's concluded market occupancy) and the site inspection report's concluded market vacancy.

Credit Loss

Standard Definition. *Credit Loss* is an estimate of the annual economic loss that the property will experience due to the inability to collect scheduled rent from various tenants.

Method of Derivation

LIP. Credit Loss is concluded based on a comparison of historical Credit Loss at the property to market data from the site inspection report and appraisal report. The primary basis for the Credit Loss conclusion will be the property's actual three-year historical Credit Loss, with emphasis placed on the most recent 12-month period and most recent tenant arrearage report. If Credit Loss over the three-year history is volatile or declining, Precept will use an average of Credit Loss for the collected three-year history. If historical Credit Loss is systematically increasing, Precept's conclusion will be consistent with the most recent

12-month period. The Credit Loss conclusion will be compared to similar data in the site inspection and appraisal reports to ensure that these sources are supportive of historical levels.

TTM. Credit Loss will be concluded on the same basis as LIP, except in cases where Collected Rent is used in lieu of Gross Potential Rent. In this case, the underwritten Credit Loss will represent the difference, if any, between the actual Credit Loss reflected in Collected Rent and the total stabilized Credit Loss concluded using the LIP methodology.

Additional Considerations. Many times operating statements do not separately identify Credit Loss. Precept will endeavor to determine Credit loss history in these cases through conversations with the borrower and, if necessary, by reconciling historical rent rolls to the appropriate operating statements. In many cases the Credit Loss adjustment to Gross Potential Rent will be incorporated in the Vacancy adjustment because property-level data and market-level data are not discerning enough for Precept to draw individual conclusions.

Expenses

Management Fee

Standard Definition. *Management Fee* is an estimate of the annual amount an independent management company would charge to comprehensively oversee the property's operations.

Method of Derivation. Precept will underwrite the Management Fees to equal the greater of the following:

- The management fees set forth in the current management contract
- The market Management Fee Precept determines would be required to engage a competent third-party property management firm
- 5% of Total Effective Gross Income (e.g., Gross Potential Rent + Percentage Rent + Expense Reimbursements + Other Income − Mark-to-Market − Vacancy and Credit Loss) except as noted here:
  Regional and superregional shopping malls: greater of 5.0% of base rent and Percentage Rent or 4.0% of Total Effective Gross Income

Single-tenant property: 3.0 to 4.0% of Total Effective Gross Income
Nonmall property larger than 350,000 square feet: 4.0 to 4.5% of Total Effective Gross Income

Additional Considerations. Precept will determine the market Management Fee based on its review of the Site Inspection Report and Appraisal Report. In the event that the property is borrower-managed, the borrower's fee or related payroll and benefits will be evaluated in lieu of the Management Fee for purposes of the preceding analysis.

Payroll and Benefits

Standard Definition. *Payroll and Benefits* are the total annual amount of wages paid to all personnel, including payroll taxes, workman's compensation insurance, health insurance, and other employee benefits that have not been allocated directly to other expense categories.

Method of Derivation. Payroll and Benefits are determined based on a comparison of historical Payroll and Benefits at the property to market and industry data. The primary basis for the Payroll and Benefits conclusion will be the property's actual three-year historical Payroll and Benefits, with emphasis placed on the most recent 12-month period for which Precept has sufficient data. If Payroll and Benefits over the three-year history are volatile or declining, Precept will use an average of Payroll and Benefits for the collected three-year history. If historical Payroll and Benefits are systematically increasing, Precept's conclusion will be consistent with the most recent 12-month period. The Payroll and Benefits conclusion will be compared to market data from one or more of the following sources: Institute of Real Estate Management (IREM), Urban Land Institute (ULI), and appraisal reports.

Additional Considerations. The first step in concluding underwritten Payroll and Benefits is to determine how the borrower has accounted for such expenses. In cases where the borrower accounts for personnel costs in functional categories (e.g., maintenance personnel under Repairs and Maintenance expenses and leasing staff under administration) as opposed to aggregating labor costs in one line item, Precept will conduct its analysis on the functional category level. In doing so, Precept will seek assurances that the level of staffing and staff compensation levels are adequate to operate the property in a commercially reasonable and prudent manner. When comparing the property's historical figures to market data, Precept will ensure that comparisons are meaningful in terms of accounting methodology. Precept will pay particular attention to Payroll and Benefits expenses in situations involving an owner-operated property because of the increased likelihood that reported expenses are not true indications of the Payroll and Benefits expenses necessary to operate a property with third-party management. Precept will reconcile Payroll and Benefits expenses from either the trailing-12-month or most recent year-end operating statements to the borrower's written summary of all property-related labor expenses.

Utilities

Standard Definition. *Utilities* are the total annual amount of water, sewer, electricity, gas, and other applicable utility expenses.

Method of Derivation. Utilities expenses are concluded based on a historical Utilities expense. The primary basis for the Utilities conclusion will be the property's actual three-year historical Utilities expenses, with emphasis placed on the most recent 12-month period. If Utilities expenses over the three-year history are volatile or declining, Precept will utilize an average of Utilities expenses for the collected three-year history. If historical Utilities expenses are systematically increasing, Precept's conclusion will be consistent with the most recent 12-month period.

Additional Considerations. Utilities expenses are often seasonal in nature and are sometimes billed less frequently than on a monthly basis. Therefore, Precept will underwrite Utilities expenses based on a full year of operating history (if available) rather than annualizing a partial year's operating statements. Precept will include an inflation factor if the information on which the Utilities expenses are calculated is older than one year. Precept will reconcile Utilities expenses from either the trailing-12-month or most recent year-end operating statements to actual utility bills for that same period, or portion thereof if a full 12 months is not available.

Repairs and Maintenance

Standard Definition. *Repairs and Maintenance* expenses are estimates of the total annual costs of general interior and exterior repairs and maintenance exclusive of capital expenditures. Repairs and Maintenance costs include gardening; landscaping; exterior spot painting; elevator maintenance contracts; boiler inspection and repair contracts; heating, ventilating, and air-conditioning (HVAC) service contracts; plumbing, electrical, and window repairs; plastering; carpentry; masonry; street sweeping; light maintenance; and tenant turnover cleaning and painting. Payroll and Benefits of the maintenance personnel may or may not be included in this category, depending on the accounting system of a borrower. *Note:* All or a portion of Repairs and Maintenance expenses may be classified as CAM for underwriting purposes (see Common Area Maintenance expense category.)

Method of Derivation. Repairs and Maintenance expenses are concluded based on a comparison of historical Repairs and Maintenance expenses at the property to market and industry data. The primary basis for the Repairs and Maintenance conclusion will be the property's actual three-year historical Repairs and Maintenance costs, with emphasis placed on the most recent 12-month period. If Repairs and Maintenance expenses over the three-year history are volatile or declining, Precept will use an average of Repairs and Maintenance expenses for the collected three-year history. If historical Repairs and Maintenance expenses are systematically increasing, Precept's conclusion will be consistent with the most recent 12-month period. The Repairs and Maintenance conclusion will be compared to market data from one or more of the following sources: Institute of Real Estate Management (IREM), Urban Land Institute (ULI), and appraisal reports.

Additional Considerations. Capital expenses that add significant longevity to the remaining life of the property (e.g., new roof, new boiler, or parking lot resurfacing) should not be included in this line item. Repairs to such items, however, should be included in Repairs and Maintenance.

Common Area Maintenance

Standard Definition. *Common Area Maintenance* (CAM) is an estimate of Repairs and Maintenance expenses that are necessary to maintain property components common to all tenants. For underwriting purposes, this category is reserved for expenses that are contractually reimbursed by tenants in whole or in part. The CAM line item will be underwritten only if the property's operating statements provide sufficient detail to differentiate CAM expenses from overall Repairs and

Maintenance. Absent this detail, all CAM expenses will be grouped with overall Repairs and Maintenance expenses under the heading Repairs and Maintenance as previously noted, and the CAM line item will be left blank.

Method of Derivation. CAM is concluded based on a comparison of historical CAM at the property to market and industry data. The primary basis for the CAM conclusion will be the property's actual three-year historical CAM, with emphasis placed on the most recent 12-month period. If CAM over the three-year history is volatile or declining, Precept will use an average of CAM for the collected three-year history. If historical CAM is systematically increasing, Precept's conclusion will be consistent with the most recent 12-month period. The sum of the CAM and Repairs and Maintenance conclusions will be compared to overall repairs and maintenance market data from one or more of the following sources: Institute of Real Estate Management (IREM), Urban Land Institute (ULI), and appraisal reports.

Administrative

Standard Definition. *Administrative* expenses are an estimate of the annual total of all administrative costs necessary to operate the property, exclusive of Management Fees. Administrative expenses include legal and accounting fees, marketing and advertising, dues to professional organizations, and all on-site telephone and building office expenses. Depending on the borrower's method of accounting, this category may also include Payroll and Benefits for related staff.

Method of Derivation. Administrative expenses are concluded based on a comparison of historical Administrative expenses at the property to apartment market and industry data. The primary basis for the Administrative expense conclusion will be the property's actual three-year historical Administrative expenses, with emphasis placed on the most recent 12-month period. If Administrative expenses over the three-year history are volatile or declining, Precept will use an average of Administrative expenses for the collected three-year history. If historical Administrative expenses are systematically increasing, Precept's conclusion will be consistent with the most recent 12-month period. The Administrative expense conclusion will be compared to market data from one or more of the following sources: Institute of Real Estate Management (IREM), Urban Land Institute (ULI), and appraisal reports.

Additional Considerations. Administrative expenses include the annual cost to advertise and market the property to prospective tenants in order to maintain occupancy and rental rates at the level underwritten. To the extent that marketing and advertising expenses represent more than 25% of total Administrative costs, Precept will separate Marketing and Advertising from Administrative expenses by utilizing one of the Other Variable Expense line items noted in the next subsection. The Marketing and Advertising expense line item may include, among other things, costs associated with advertising, marketing administration, property promotions, and merchant association contributions. To the extent that the property's space is not leased with third-party broker representation, Precept will attempt to recategorize in-house and on-site leasing expenses from Administration to Retenanting Costs (described later).

Other Variable Expense—1, 2, and 3

Standard Definition. *Other Variable Expense—1, 2, and 3* includes generic line items that are reserved for variable expenditures from the operating statements that either do not clearly fit within Precept's standard line items or that Precept determines to be more meaningful as separate line items.

In these cases, the generic Precept line-item title will be replaced with the actual operating statement line-item title. In the event that Other Variable Expenses account for more than 3.0% of the Total Expenses, Precept will require explanations of such expenses and will summarize such information in either the Cash Flow Summary or Operating Statement Reconciliation section of the underwriting summary.

Real Property Taxes

Standard Definition. *Real Property Taxes* are all taxes assessed against the real property of the property by a state or political subdivision of the state, such as a county or city, including assessments for public improvements.

Method of Derivation. Precept will conclude Real Property Taxes based on the greater of the following:

- The most recent tax bill adjusted for known increases in tax rates and/or impending upward reassessments, and any tax abatements that expire in less than 22.5 years.
- The *Market Real Property Tax* determined by the property's potential Real Property Tax liability assuming a current (near-term) reassessment or a periodic reassessment. For purposes of this

estimation, Precept will attempt to follow the appropriate jurisdiction's reassessment methodology in conjunction with the following guidelines:

Near-term reassessment. For jurisdictions where Real Property Taxes are recalculated upon transfer as a percentage of the transfer price or are generally not subject to systematic reassessments, Precept will estimate Market Real Property Tax by multiplying the appropriate local taxation rate by a proposed first mortgage amount. The proposed first mortgage amount will be an estimate of what Precept believes the loan amount will be based on its underwriting. If no information about the potential loan amount is available, Precept generally will use a first mortgage amount equal to 75% of the estimated current property value.

Periodic reassessment. For jurisdictions where reassessments take place on a periodic basis, Precept will estimate Market Real Property Tax, taking into account the following factors:

- Real property taxes at competing properties (on a per-square-foot basis, sales price basis, etc.)
- Trends in local commercial property values and taxation rates
- The assumptions made by the appraisers regarding their estimate of the Real Property Tax

Additional Considerations. Precept will not underwrite Real Property Taxes below the most recent tax bill without written correspondence from the local taxation authorities confirming the lower assessment and/or taxation rate. If Precept determines it is warranted (if unique taxation structures are identified by Precept), Precept will discuss taxation frameworks with the local tax assessor to understand and clarify these issues.

Insurance

Standard Definition. *Insurance* shall mean all policies of insurance against loss or damage by fire and against loss or damage by other risks or hazards, including, without limitation, liability, riot, civil commotion, vandalism, malicious mischief, burglary, theft, flood, or earthquake.

Method of Derivation. Precept will underwrite Insurance expense at the greater of (1) the most recent insurance bill, or (2) market insurance premiums for Precept standard coverage levels for a single property policy.

Additional Considerations. Precept will adjust the Insurance expense item, described in point (2) of the preceding paragraph, upward in those instances where a property has inadequate coverage levels or below-market insurance rates (which could not be replicated by a new owner or are due to the fact that a property is covered by a blanket insurance policy covering a property and other properties that are not part of the collateral).

Other Fixed Expense–1, 2, and 3

Standard Definition. *Other Fixed Expense—1, 2, and 3* includes generic line items that are reserved for fixed expenditures from the operating statements that either do not clearly fit within Precept's standard line items or that Precept determines to be more meaningful as separate line items.

In these cases, the generic Precept line-item title will be replaced with the actual operating statement line-item title, and Precept will calculate the Other Fixed Expenses as the greater of (1) the fixed expenses for the prior 12-month period or (2) the three-year average for fixed expenses, if available. In the event that Other Fixed Expenses account for more than 3.0% of the Total Expenses, Precept will require explanations of such expenses and will summarize such information in either the Cash Flow Summary or Operating Statement Reconciliation section of the underwriting summary. One of the more common Other Fixed Expense categories is Ground Rent.

Ground Rent (If Applicable). Precept will generally underwrite *Ground Rent* using 75% of the proposed amortization schedule of the loan amount.

Total Expenses

Standard Definition. Upon drawing conclusions for each of the Other Variable and Other Fixed Expenses categories, Precept will compare the Total Expenses on a per-unit and percentage basis to market and industry averages and ranges.

The sources of market and industry data will include the Precept Appraisal Report, the Institute of Real Estate Management, and the Urban Land Institute. In the event that the underwritten level of Total Expenses is not supported by this data, Precept will review its conclusions for each of the expense line items, paying particular attention to those that are closer to the lower end of the market and/or industry range. Precept will adjust these expenses either individually or in the aggregate so that the Total Expenses underwritten are supported by market and industry statistics.

Capital Expenditures

Reserves for Replacement

Standard Definition. *Reserves for Replacement* costs are an estimate of the average annual expenditures required for replacement of building components that have shorter useful lives than the structure itself. Building components that require periodic replacement include roofs, parking lot asphalt, HVAC equipment, and windows.

Method of Derivation. Reserves for Replacement will be concluded based on the greater of (1) $0.15 per square foot of total leasable area per year and (2) the total ongoing physical needs annual average estimated in the Property Condition Assessment Summary section of the underwriting summary.

Additional Considerations. Precept will review the property condition assessment's conclusions for reasonableness, taking into account the property's age, common-area structures, and overall improvement condition required to generate the underwritten Effective Gross Rental Income.

Retenanting Costs

Standard Definition. *Retenanting Costs* are broken into two categories: (1) tenant improvements (TIs) and (2) leasing commissions. TIs include the costs associated with improving space in order to induce tenants to execute leases and take occupancy. Leasing commissions are fees paid to brokers involved in bringing the property and tenant together.

Method of Derivation. Precept will first group each tenant into logical categories similar to the comparable space groupings made during the market monthly rent analysis (shop, anchor, endcap, outparcels, 0 to 1000 square feet, 1000 to 3000 square feet, etc.). For each space grouping, Precept will then make assumptions for renewal probability, average lease term, average lease rental rate, tenant improvement allowances, and leasing commissions. Using the following formula, Precept will calculate the estimated *Average Annual Tenant Improvement*

Amount and *Leasing Commission Amount* for each space grouping, the aggregate sum of which will be used by Precept as the underwritten retenanting Costs:

Average Annual Tenant Improvement Amount, $
= (Retenanting Square Footage per Annum × Renewal Probability, %
× renewal tenant improvement per square foot, $)
+ [Retenanting Square Footage per Annum × (1 – Renewal Probability, %)
× new tenant improvement per square foot, $]

Leasing Commission Amount, $ = (Retenanting Square Footage per Annum
× average rental rate per square foot per year, $ × Renewal Probability, %
× renewal leasing commission, %) + [Retenanting Square Footage
per Annum × average rental rate per square foot per year, $
× (1 – Renewal Probability, %) × new leasing commission, %]

Note: for purposes of the preceding calculation, *retenanting Square Footage per Annum* = total square footage of space for which rental revenue was underwritten / Average Lease Term, years.

Renewal Probability. The *Renewal Probability* value is the estimated probability that a tenant will renew its lease upon expiration. Precept will assume that 60% of the tenants (measured by square footage) will renew their leases upon expiration. Notwithstanding this rule, Precept may assign renewal probabilities of greater than 60% (but in no event higher than 70%) if Precept is provided with evidence proving historical tenant retention in excess of 60% for leases which have expired over the previous five years. This evidence is not required as part of the loan submission package and will need to be obtained specifically for buildings with high retention rates. Furthermore, Precept may assign renewal probabilities of less than 60% when Precept believes that more than 60% of the tenants (by square footage) will vacate upon lease expiration (e.g., tenant base does not appear stable, a property has significantly higher Vacancy than its competitors, or tenant sales are rapidly declining).

Average Lease Term. An *Average Lease Term* assumption is necessary for each space grouping when calculating Retenanting Costs. To estimate the stabilized annual square footage rollover, Precept will divide the total square footage for each tenant space grouping by an assumed Average Lease Term for each space grouping. In making lease term assumptions, Precept will review the following: (1) leases executed within the last two years at the property, (2) the remaining average lease terms for the tenants at the property, and (3) the average lease term for comparable leases in the market, to establish supportable assumptions. Precept will use an Average Lease Term that is consistent with leases being signed in the market unless a property leasing activity supports a deviation from the market term. Nonmarket leases may also have nonmarket TIs, as TIs are correlated with lease terms (e.g., longer lease terms receive higher tenant improvement amounts). Lease terms longer than those being signed at the property should be used in rollover calculations only when tenant improvement amounts are being underwritten at amounts higher than those being given at the property.

Lease Rental Rate. Precept will use the lower of the average rental rate in place at a property or the Market Rent for each space grouping. Precept does not use a higher rental rate in situations where the lease rates for the current tenants are below market because the increased cost for leasing commissions associated with new leases will be offset by the increase in rental revenue from these same leases. Precept's underwritten rental revenue does not include the potentially higher rental revenue associated with retenanting, and, therefore, does not include the associated higher leasing commissions.

Tenant Improvements. For purposes of this analysis, TIs include free rent given by the owner in lieu of, or in addition to, a tenant improvement allowance. Precept evaluates these two components of Retenanting Costs together, given the dependency that improvement allowances and free rent often have on each other during lease negotiations (e.g., free rent during the build-out of space, free rent in lieu of tenant improvements, etc.). The amount of TI required to sign new tenants customarily is two to three times the amount of concessions required to sign renewal tenants. Precept will determine underwritten TI and free rent on a per-square-foot basis for each space grouping. Precept will make two calculations, one for new leases and the other for renewal leases using market data and the Average Lease Term for each space grouping. Precept's assumptions regarding TI and free rent will be similar to those found in comparable leases with the same Average Lease Term. Better than average credit quality tenants, larger tenants, and longer lease terms will generally receive a higher level of concessions.

Leasing Commissions. Leasing commissions are fees paid to brokers that represent the owner of a property (*listing broker*) or that represent a tenant (*procuring broker*). Precept will review the leasing commission schedule for the market in which a property is located and identify the party responsible for paying the leasing commissions. In some instances, space can be leased directly to a tenant without a broker. In most instances, however, the owner and the tenant each have a broker. A property owner almost always pays the listing broker and usually pays the procuring broker. Depending on the market, the brokers will each get paid separate commissions or split a total commission (calculated as a percentage of the total base rent payable over the term of the lease) ranging from 2.5 to 4.0% for renewal leases and 4.0 to 6.0% for new leases. In some markets and more typically for large spaces, leasing commissions are calculated on a square-foot basis rather than as a percentage of total base rent due. Commissions taking this form generally range from $2 to $5 per square foot. Precept will make two calculations for leasing commissions, one for new leases and one for renewal leases. For underwriting purposes, Precept will determine the leasing commission rate for each space grouping and the total commissions paid in the market by landlords assuming all leases are signed using third-party leasing brokers. Precept will not underwrite leasing commissions at less than 4% of total lease term rental revenue for new leases and 2% for renewals (without adequate support).

Unlike other expense categories, underwriting Retenanting Costs is largely independent of the historical cost. Retenanting Costs fluctuate significantly from year to year, depending on the quantity and type of space being leased and whether the leases involve new or renewal tenants. The cost of both TIs and leasing commissions tend to be higher (historically at least double) for new leases than for renewal leases. Precept will underwrite Retenanting Costs on a lease-specific basis by grouping the existing tenants into logical groups and estimating future Retenanting Costs for each group.

Additional Considerations. Precept may look to the following sources of information to determine current market conditions for TIs and leasing commissions, free rent, and lease terms:

- All leases executed over the last three years at a property
- The current leasing package offered at a property for each space grouping, using information from discussions with a borrower and the borrower's leasing representative

- The appraiser's rollover cost assumptions, using the appraisal report
- Leasing packages for comparable space currently available and comparable signed leases in the market during the last two years

Other Capital Expense–1 and 2

Standard Definition. *Other Capital Expense—1 and 2* includes generic line items that are reserved for capital expenditures that were not represented in the property condition assessment's ongoing physical needs analysis or that Precept determines to be more meaningful as separate line items.

Other Capital Expenses, for example, could include an improvement recommended by the environmental engineer. Precept will require explanations of such expenses and will summarize such information in either the Cash Flow Summary or Operating Statement Reconciliation section of the underwriting summary.

CHAPTER 4

Multifamily Properties—Cash Flow Analysis

Multifamily properties is generally one of the more straightforward assets to underwrite. The larger reason for this is that most adults have at some point in their lives rented an apartment and therefore have first-hand knowledge of the operational basics. This is much different from commercial land uses, where a small minority of loan originators have hands-on experience in the operation of such land uses as hotels, retail malls, office buildings, etc. Beyond this basic reality, there are three main reasons why multifamily properties are easier to underwrite on a systematic basis.

First, apartment properties typically encompass short-term leases of one year or less across a diversified tenant base. With the exception of stabilized vacancy, this fact usually means that an underwriter can make a determination regarding stabilized rental revenue by evaluating the property's actual historical performance. This is different from commercial land uses, which are subject to, for example, lease agreements of 5-, 10-, and 15-year lengths in that market rental rate levels are not necessarily reflected by the property's past rental revenue.

Second, lease negotiations between a landlord and tenant are largely limited to the rental rate and length of the lease agreement. There are not material customized components to rental agreements, such as tenant improvement allowances, that require effective rental rate analysis in order to be meaningfully compared to one another. Periodic specials, such as reduced security deposit and/or free rent periods, are fixed and offered on a programmatic basis. These realities of multifamily operation make it easy to compare rental rates within and outside of the subject property.

Third, the expenses associated with operating multifamily properties are generally easier to understand and reconcile to industry averages. The physical characteristics of the property, including the number of apartment units, its amenities, and how utilities are metered, largely frame appropriate expense levels. This is different from a hotel property, for example, where there are many nuances to operating expenses and how they are accounted for on a departmental basis.

As a result of the straightforward nature of apartment properties, income and expense conclusions for purposes of establishing stabilized cash flow conclusions can be drawn on a more systematic basis. Of course, multifamily properties with less traditional uses (single demand generators, shared living arrangements, etc.) create challenges to underwriting within very specific guidelines.

The following is Precept's systematic approach to cash flow analysis for multifamily land uses. As previously stated, it is intentionally rigid. The value of the rigidity is that the ultimate user of its results will know exactly what is being provided. This does not imply that all multifamily properties should be underwritten in strict accordance to the specific income and expense line-item derivations outlined herein. Rather, it provides a framework from which to evaluate multifamily cash flows on a consistent basis, with clear documentation of exceptions to the systematic method of derivations for each component of operating cash flow.

For your reference, following are the relevant sections of the Precept Underwriting Summary pertaining to the concepts and methodologies contained in this chapter and specific to the multifamily land use. The underwriting summary provides the critical framework for the capture, analysis, and maintenance of due diligence data. It is anticipated that the underwriter will complete the underwriting summary while conducting the underwriting analysis.

PRECEPT™

CASH FLOW SUMMARY
Property Name

Property Number: 0000	Occ:			N				N				N				N				N	
Deal Number: 0000	/Unit	1997	%	O T	/Unit	1998	%	O T	/Unit	TTM	%	O T	/Unit	Precept TTM	%	O T	/Unit	Precept LIP	%	O T	Comments
Units: 0	Through: 12/31/1997			E	Through: 12/31/1998			E	Through: 12/31/1999			E				E				E	
REVENUES Financials:	Income			S	Income			S	Income			S				S				S	
Gross Potential Rent		-	-			-	-			-	-			-	-			-	-		
OR Collected Rent		-	-			-	-			-	-			-	-			-	-		
Vacancy		-	-			-	-			-	-			-	-			-	-		
Credit Loss		-	-			-	-			-	-			-	-			-	-		
Concessions		-	-			-	-			-	-			-	-			-	-		
Effective Gross Rental Income		-	-			-	-			-	-			-	-			-	-		
Other Income - 1			-				-				-			-	-			-	-		
Other Income - 2		-	-			-	-			-	-			-	-			-	-		
Other Income - 3		-	-			-	-			-	-			-	-			-	-		
Total Effective Gross Income		-	-			-	-			-	-			-	-			-	-		
EXPENSES																					
Variable																					
Management Fee		-	-			-	-			-	-			-	-			-	-		
Payroll & Benefits		-	-			-	-			-	-			-	-			-	-		
Utilities		-	-			-	-			-	-			-	-			-	-		
Repairs & Maintenance		-	-			-	-			-	-			-	-			-	-		
Marketing and Advertising		-	-			-	-			-	-			-	-			-	-		
General and Administrative		-	-			-	-			-	-			-	-			-	-		
Other Variable Expense - 1		-	-			-	-			-	-			-	-			-	-		
Other Variable Expense - 2		-	-			-	-			-	-			-	-			-	-		
Other Variable Expense - 3		-	-			-	-			-	-			-	-			-	-		
Total Variable Expense		-	-			-	-			-	-			-	-			-	-		
Fixed																					
Real Estate Taxes		-	-			-	-			-	-			-	-			-	-		
Insurance		-	-			-	-			-	-			-	-			-	-		
Other Fixed Expense - 1		-	-			-	-			-	-			-	-			-	-		
Other Fixed Expense - 2		-	-			-	-			-	-			-	-			-	-		
Other Fixed Expense - 3		-	-			-	-			-	-			-	-			-	-		
Total Fixed Expense		-	-			-	-			-	-			-	-			-	-		
Total Expenses		-	-			-	-			-	-			-	-			-	-		
CASH FLOWS																					
Net Operating Income		-	-			-	-			-	-			-	-			-	-		
Capital Expenditures:																					
Reserves for Replacement		-	-			-	-			-	-			-	-			-	-		
Other Capital Expense - 1		-	-			-	-			-	-			-	-			-	-		
Other Capital Expense - 2		-	-			-	-			-	-			-	-			-	-		
Other Capital Expense - 3		-	-			-	-			-	-			-	-			-	-		
Total Capital Expenditures		-	-			-	-			-	-			-	-			-	-		
Net Cash Flow		-	-			-	-			-	-			-	-			-	-		

Notes and Comments:

PRECEPT™

CASH FLOW SUMMARY (Continued)

Property Name

Property Number: 0000
Deal Number: 0000
Units: 0

Financials:	/Unit	Precept TTM	%	NOTES	/Unit	Precept LIP	%	NOTES	/Unit	Rating Agency	%	NOTES	Comments	NOTES	/Unit	Bidder	%	NOTES	Comments
REVENUES																			
Gross Potential Rent		-	-			-	-			-	-					-	-		
OR Collected Rent		-	-			-	-			-	-					-	-		
Vacancy		-	-			-	-			-	-					-	-		
Credit Loss		-	-			-	-			-	-					-	-		
Concessions		-	-			-	-			-	-					-	-		
Effective Gross Rental Income		-	-			-	-			-	-					-	-		
Other Income - 1		-	-			-	-			-	-					-	-		
Other Income - 2		-	-			-	-			-	-					-	-		
Other Income - 3		-	-			-	-			-	-					-	-		
Total Effective Gross Income		-	-			-	-			-	-					-	-		
EXPENSES																			
Variable																			
Management Fee		-	-			-	-			-	-					-	-		
Payroll & Benefits		-	-			-	-			-	-					-	-		
Utilities		-	-			-	-			-	-					-	-		
Repairs & Maintenance		-	-			-	-			-	-					-	-		
Marketing and Advertising		-	-			-	-			-	-					-	-		
General and Administrative		-	-			-	-			-	-					-	-		
Other Variable Expense - 1		-	-			-	-			-	-					-	-		
Other Variable Expense - 2		-	-			-	-			-	-					-	-		
Other Variable Expense - 3		-	-			-	-			-	-					-	-		
Total Variable Expense		-	-			-	-			-	-					-	-		
Fixed																			
Real Estate Taxes		-	-			-	-			-	-					-	-		
Insurance		-	-			-	-			-	-					-	-		
Other Fixed Expense - 1		-	-			-	-			-	-					-	-		
Other Fixed Expense - 2		-	-			-	-			-	-					-	-		
Other Fixed Expense - 3		-	-			-	-			-	-					-	-		
Total Fixed Expense		-	-			-	-			-	-					-	-		
Total Expenses		-	-			-	-			-	-					-	-		
CASH FLOWS																			
Net Operating Income		-	-			-	-			-	-					-	-		
Capital Expenditures:																			
Reserves for Replacement		-	-			-	-			-	-					-	-		
Other Capital Expense - 1		-	-			-	-			-	-					-	-		
Other Capital Expense - 2		-	-			-	-			-	-					-	-		
Other Capital Expense - 3		-	-			-	-			-	-					-	-		
Total Capital Expenditures		-	-			-	-			-	-					-	-		
Net Cash Flow		-	-			-	-			-	-					-	-		

Notes and Comments:

PRECEPT™

CASH FLOW SUMMARY (Continued)
Property Name

Property Number: 0000	Occ:			Occ:										
Deal Number: 0000	/Unit	1999	%	/Unit	TTM	%	Comments	/Unit	Appraisal	%	/Unit	Budget	%	Comments	Borrower's Comments
Units: 0	Through: 12/31/1999			Through: 12/31/1999											
REVENUES Financials:	Income			Income											

	1999 /Unit	1999 %	TTM /Unit	TTM %	Comments	Appraisal /Unit	Appraisal %	Budget /Unit	Budget %	Comments	Borrower's Comments
REVENUES											
Gross Potential Rent	-	-	-	-		-	-	-	-		
OR Collected Rent	-	-	-	-		-	-	-	-		
Vacancy	-	-	-	-		-	-	-	-		
Credit Loss	-	-	-	-		-	-	-	-		
Concessions	-	-	-	-		-	-	-	-		
Effective Gross Rental Income	-	-	-	-		-	-	-	-		
Other Income - 1	-	-	-	-		-	-	-	-		
Other Income - 2	-	-	-	-		-	-	-	-		
Other Income - 3	-	-	-	-		-	-	-	-		
Total Effective Gross Income	-	-	-	-		-	-	-	-		
EXPENSES											
Variable											
Management Fee	-	-	-	-		-	-	-	-		
Payroll & Benefits	-	-	-	-		-	-	-	-		
Utilities	-	-	-	-		-	-	-	-		
Repairs & Maintenance	-	-	-	-		-	-	-	-		
Marketing and Advertising	-	-	-	-		-	-	-	-		
General and Administrative	-	-	-	-		-	-	-	-		
Other Variable Expense - 1	-	-	-	-		-	-	-	-		
Other Variable Expense - 2	-	-	-	-		-	-	-	-		
Other Variable Expense - 3	-	-	-	-		-	-	-	-		
Total Variable Expense	-	-	-	-		-	-	-	-		
Fixed											
Real Estate Taxes	-	-	-	-		-	-	-	-		
Insurance	-	-	-	-		-	-	-	-		
Other Fixed Expense - 1	-	-	-	-		-	-	-	-		
Other Fixed Expense - 2	-	-	-	-		-	-	-	-		
Other Fixed Expense - 3	-	-	-	-		-	-	-	-		
Total Fixed Expense	-	-	-	-		-	-	-	-		
Total Expenses	-	-	-	-		-	-	-	-		
CASH FLOWS											
Net Operating Income	-	-	-	-		-	-	-	-		
Capital Expenditures:											
Reserves for Replacement	-	-	-	-		-	-	-	-		
Other Capital Expense - 1	-	-	-	-		-	-	-	-		
Other Capital Expense - 2	-	-	-	-		-	-	-	-		
Other Capital Expense - 3	-	-	-	-		-	-	-	-		
Total Capital Expenditures	-	-	-	-		-	-	-	-		
Net Cash Flow	-	-	-	-		-	-	-	-		

PRECEPT™

OP STMT RECONCILIATION

Property Name

	1				2				3				4			
	1997			NOTES	1998			NOTES	1999			NOTES	TTM			NOTES
Property Number: 0000	Statement	Adjustment	Operating		Statement	Adjustment	Operating		Statement	Adjustment	Operating		Statement	Adjustment	Operating	
Deal Number: 0000																
Units: 0	Through:	12/31/1997			Through:	12/31/1998			Through:	12/31/1999			Through:	12/31/1999		
	Financials:	Income			Financials:	Income			Financials:	Income			Stmt. Type:	Income		
REVENUES																
Gross Potential Rent																
-	-	-	-		-	-	-		-	-	-		-	-	-	
-	-	-	-		-	-	-		-	-	-		-	-	-	
-	-	-	-		-	-	-		-	-	-		-	-	-	
Gross Potential Rent	-	-	-		-	-	-		-	-	-		-	-	-	
Collected Rent																
-	-	-	-		-	-	-		-	-	-		-	-	-	
-	-	-	-		-	-	-		-	-	-		-	-	-	
-	-	-	-		-	-	-		-	-	-		-	-	-	
Collected Rent	-	-	-		-	-	-		-	-	-		-	-	-	
Vacancy																
-	-	-	-		-	-	-		-	-	-		-	-	-	
-	-	-	-		-	-	-		-	-	-		-	-	-	
-	-	-	-		-	-	-		-	-	-		-	-	-	
Vacancy	-	-	-		-	-	-		-	-	-		-	-	-	
Credit Loss																
-	-	-	-		-	-	-		-	-	-		-	-	-	
-	-	-	-		-	-	-		-	-	-		-	-	-	
-	-	-	-		-	-	-		-	-	-		-	-	-	
Credit Loss	-	-	-		-	-	-		-	-	-		-	-	-	
Concessions																
-	-	-	-		-	-	-		-	-	-		-	-	-	
-	-	-	-		-	-	-		-	-	-		-	-	-	
-	-	-	-		-	-	-		-	-	-		-	-	-	
Concessions	-	-	-		-	-	-		-	-	-		-	-	-	
Effective Gross Rental Income	-	-	-		-	-	-		-	-	-		-	-	-	
Other Income - 1																
-	-	-	-		-	-	-		-	-	-		-	-	-	
-	-	-	-		-	-	-		-	-	-		-	-	-	
-	-	-	-		-	-	-		-	-	-		-	-	-	
-	-	-	-		-	-	-		-	-	-		-	-	-	
-	-	-	-		-	-	-		-	-	-		-	-	-	
-	-	-	-		-	-	-		-	-	-		-	-	-	
-	-	-	-		-	-	-		-	-	-		-	-	-	
Other Income - 1	-	-	-		-	-	-		-	-	-		-	-	-	
Other Income - 2																
-	-	-	-		-	-	-		-	-	-		-	-	-	
-	-	-	-		-	-	-		-	-	-		-	-	-	
-	-	-	-		-	-	-		-	-	-		-	-	-	
Other Income - 2	-	-	-		-	-	-		-	-	-		-	-	-	
Other Income - 3																
-	-	-	-		-	-	-		-	-	-		-	-	-	
-	-	-	-		-	-	-		-	-	-		-	-	-	
-	-	-	-		-	-	-		-	-	-		-	-	-	
Other Income - 3	-	-	-		-	-	-		-	-	-		-	-	-	
Total Effective Gross Income	-	-	-		-	-	-		-	-	-		-	-	-	

PRECEPT™

OP STMT RECONCILIATION

Property Name

	1				2				3				4			
	1997			N O T E S	1998			N O T E S	1999			N O T E S	TTM			N O T E S
Property Number: 0000	Statement	Adjustment	Operating		Statement	Adjustment	Operating		Statement	Adjustment	Operating		Statement	Adjustment	Operating	
Deal Number: 0000																
Units: 0	Through:	12/31/1997			Through:	12/31/1998			Through:	12/31/1999			Through:	12/31/1999		
	Financials:	Income			Financials:	Income			Financials:	Income			Stmt. Type:	Income		
EXPENSES (Variable)																
Management Fee																
-	-	-	-		-	-	-		-	-	-		-	-	-	
-	-	-	-		-	-	-		-	-	-		-	-	-	
Management Fee	-	-	-		-	-	-		-	-	-		-	-	-	
Payroll & Benefits																
-	-	-	-		-	-	-		-	-	-		-	-	-	
-	-	-	-		-	-	-		-	-	-		-	-	-	
-	-	-	-		-	-	-		-	-	-		-	-	-	
-	-	-	-		-	-	-		-	-	-		-	-	-	
-	-	-	-		-	-	-		-	-	-		-	-	-	
-	-	-	-		-	-	-		-	-	-		-	-	-	
Payroll & Benefits	-	-	-		-	-	-		-	-	-		-	-	-	
Utilities																
-	-	-	-		-	-	-		-	-	-		-	-	-	
-	-	-	-		-	-	-		-	-	-		-	-	-	
-	-	-	-		-	-	-		-	-	-		-	-	-	
-	-	-	-		-	-	-		-	-	-		-	-	-	
-	-	-	-		-	-	-		-	-	-		-	-	-	
-	-	-	-		-	-	-		-	-	-		-	-	-	
Utilities	-	-	-		-	-	-		-	-	-		-	-	-	
Repairs & Maintenance																
-	-	-	-		-	-	-		-	-	-		-	-	-	
-	-	-	-		-	-	-		-	-	-		-	-	-	
-	-	-	-		-	-	-		-	-	-		-	-	-	
-	-	-	-		-	-	-		-	-	-		-	-	-	
-	-	-	-		-	-	-		-	-	-		-	-	-	
-	-	-	-		-	-	-		-	-	-		-	-	-	
-	-	-	-		-	-	-		-	-	-		-	-	-	
-	-	-	-		-	-	-		-	-	-		-	-	-	
-	-	-	-		-	-	-		-	-	-		-	-	-	
-	-	-	-		-	-	-		-	-	-		-	-	-	
-	-	-	-		-	-	-		-	-	-		-	-	-	
Repairs & Maintenance	-	-	-		-	-	-		-	-	-		-	-	-	
Marketing and Advertising																
-	-	-	-		-	-	-		-	-	-		-	-	-	
-	-	-	-		-	-	-		-	-	-		-	-	-	
-	-	-	-		-	-	-		-	-	-		-	-	-	
-	-	-	-		-	-	-		-	-	-		-	-	-	
-	-	-	-		-	-	-		-	-	-		-	-	-	
-	-	-	-		-	-	-		-	-	-		-	-	-	
Marketing and Advertising	-	-	-		-	-	-		-	-	-		-	-	-	
General and Administrative																
-	-	-	-		-	-	-		-	-	-		-	-	-	
-	-	-	-		-	-	-		-	-	-		-	-	-	
-	-	-	-		-	-	-		-	-	-		-	-	-	
-	-	-	-		-	-	-		-	-	-		-	-	-	
-	-	-	-		-	-	-		-	-	-		-	-	-	
General and Administrative	-	-	-		-	-	-		-	-	-		-	-	-	
Other Variable Expense - 1																
-	-	-	-		-	-	-		-	-	-		-	-	-	
-	-	-	-		-	-	-		-	-	-		-	-	-	
Other Variable Expense - 1	-	-	-		-	-	-		-	-	-		-	-	-	
Other Variable Expense - 2																
-	-	-	-		-	-	-		-	-	-		-	-	-	
-	-	-	-		-	-	-		-	-	-		-	-	-	
Other Variable Expense - 2	-	-	-		-	-	-		-	-	-		-	-	-	
Other Variable Expense - 3																
-	-	-	-		-	-	-		-	-	-		-	-	-	
-	-	-	-		-	-	-		-	-	-		-	-	-	
Other Variable Expense - 3	-	-	-		-	-	-		-	-	-		-	-	-	
Total Variable Expenses	-	-	-		-	-	-		-	-	-		-	-	-	

PRECEPT

OP STMT RECONCILIATION

Property Name

	1				2				3				4			
	1997			N	1998			N	1999			N	TTM			N
Property Number: 0000	Statement	Adjustment	Operating	O	Statement	Adjustment	Operating	O	Statement	Adjustment	Operating	O	Statement	Adjustment	Operating	O
Deal Number: 0000				T				T				T				T
Units: 0	Through:	12/31/1997		E	Through:	12/31/1998		E	Through:	12/31/1999		E	Through:	12/31/1999		E
	Financials:	Income		S	Financials:	Income		S	Financials:	Income		S	Stmt. Type:	Income		S
EXPENSES (Fixed)																
Real Estate Taxes																
-	-	-	-		-	-	-		-	-	-		-	-	-	
-	-	-	-		-	-	-		-	-	-		-	-	-	
-	-	-	-		-	-	-		-	-	-		-	-	-	
Real Estate Taxes	-	-	-		-	-	-		-	-	-		-	-	-	
Insurance																
-	-	-	-		-	-	-		-	-	-		-	-	-	
-	-	-	-		-	-	-		-	-	-		-	-	-	
-	-	-	-		-	-	-		-	-	-		-	-	-	
Insurance	-	-	-		-	-	-		-	-	-		-	-	-	
Other Fixed Expense - 1																
-	-	-	-		-	-	-		-	-	-		-	-	-	
-	-	-	-		-	-	-		-	-	-		-	-	-	
-	-	-	-		-	-	-		-	-	-		-	-	-	
Other Fixed Expense - 1	-	-	-		-	-	-		-	-	-		-	-	-	
Other Fixed Expense - 2																
-	-	-	-		-	-	-		-	-	-		-	-	-	
-	-	-	-		-	-	-		-	-	-		-	-	-	
-	-	-	-		-	-	-		-	-	-		-	-	-	
Other Fixed Expense - 2	-	-	-		-	-	-		-	-	-		-	-	-	
Other Fixed Expense - 3																
-	-	-	-		-	-	-		-	-	-		-	-	-	
-	-	-	-		-	-	-		-	-	-		-	-	-	
-	-	-	-		-	-	-		-	-	-		-	-	-	
Other Fixed Expense - 3	-	-	-		-	-	-		-	-	-		-	-	-	
Total Fixed Expenses	-	-	-		-	-	-		-	-	-		-	-	-	
Total Expenses	-	-	-		-	-	-		-	-	-		-	-	-	
Net Operating Income	-	-	-		-	-	-		-	-	-		-	-	-	

PRECEPT™

OP STMT RECONCILIATION

Property Name

	1				2				3				4			
	1997			N	1998			N	1999			N	TTM			N
Property Number: 0000	Statement	Adjustment	Operating	O	Statement	Adjustment	Operating	O	Statement	Adjustment	Operating	O	Statement	Adjustment	Operating	O
Deal Number: 0000				T				T				T				T
Units: 0	Through:	12/31/1997		E	Through:	12/31/1998		E	Through:	12/31/1999		E	Through:	12/31/1999		E
	Financials:	Income		S	Financials:	Income		S	Financials:	Income		S	Stmt. Type:	Income		S
CAPITAL EXPENDITURES																
Reserves for Replacement																
-	-	-	-		-	-	-		-	-	-		-	-	-	
-	-	-	-		-	-	-		-	-	-		-	-	-	
-	-	-	-		-	-	-		-	-	-		-	-	-	
Reserves for Replacement	-	-	-		-	-	-		-	-	-		-	-	-	
Other Capital Expense - 1																
-	-	-	-		-	-	-		-	-	-		-	-	-	
-	-	-	-		-	-	-		-	-	-		-	-	-	
-	-	-	-		-	-	-		-	-	-		-	-	-	
-	-	-	-		-	-	-		-	-	-		-	-	-	
-	-	-	-		-	-	-		-	-	-		-	-	-	
-	-	-	-		-	-	-		-	-	-		-	-	-	
Other Capital Expense - 1	-	-	-		-	-	-		-	-	-		-	-	-	
Other Capital Expense - 2																
-	-	-	-		-	-	-		-	-	-		-	-	-	
-	-	-	-		-	-	-		-	-	-		-	-	-	
-	-	-	-		-	-	-		-	-	-		-	-	-	
-	-	-	-		-	-	-		-	-	-		-	-	-	
-	-	-	-		-	-	-		-	-	-		-	-	-	
-	-	-	-		-	-	-		-	-	-		-	-	-	
Other Capital Expense - 2	-	-	-		-	-	-		-	-	-		-	-	-	
Other Capital Expense - 3																
-	-	-	-		-	-	-		-	-	-		-	-	-	
-	-	-	-		-	-	-		-	-	-		-	-	-	
-	-	-	-		-	-	-		-	-	-		-	-	-	
-	-	-	-		-	-	-		-	-	-		-	-	-	
-	-	-	-		-	-	-		-	-	-		-	-	-	
-	-	-	-		-	-	-		-	-	-		-	-	-	
Other Capital Expense - 3	-	-	-		-	-	-		-	-	-		-	-	-	
Total Capital Expenditures	-	-	-		-	-	-		-	-	-		-	-	-	
Net Cash Flow	-	-	-		-	-	-		-	-	-		-	-	-	

PRECEPT™

OP STMT RECONCILIATION
Property Name

	1				2				3				4			
	1997			N	1998			N	1999			N	TTM			N
Property Number: 0000	Statement	Adjustment	Operating	O	Statement	Adjustment	Operating	O	Statement	Adjustment	Operating	O	Statement	Adjustment	Operating	O
Deal Number: 0000				T				T				T				T
Units: 0	Through:	12/31/1997		E	Through:	12/31/1998		E	Through:	12/31/1999		E	Through:	12/31/1999		E
	Financials:	Income		S	Financials:	Income		S	Financials:	Income		S	Stmt. Type:	Income		S

OCCUPANCY	Physical	Economic	Conclusion		Physical	Economic	Conclusion		Physical	Economic	Conclusion		Physical	Economic	Conclusion	
January																
February																
March																
April																
May																
June																
July																
August																
September																
October																
November																
December																
Calculated Average																
Override													0.00%			
Concluded Average																

PRECEPT™

OP STMT RECONCILIATION

Property Name

	5				6				7				8			
	YTD			N	YTD Prior			N	Appraisal			N	Budget			N
Property Number: 0000	Statement	Adjustment	Operating	O	Statement	Adjustment	Operating	O	Statement	Adjustment	Operating	O	Statement	Adjustment	Operating	O
Deal Number: 0000				T				T				T				T
Units: 0	Through:			E	Through:			E	Through:			E	Through:			E
	Stmt. Type:			S	Stmt. Type:			S	Stmt. Type:			S	Stmt. Type:			S
REVENUES																
<u>Gross Potential Rent</u>																
-	-	-	-		-	-	-		-	-	-		-	-	-	
-	-	-	-		-	-	-		-	-	-		-	-	-	
-	-	-	-		-	-	-		-	-	-		-	-	-	
Gross Potential Rent	-	-	-		-	-	-		-	-	-		-	-	-	
<u>Collected Rent</u>																
-	-	-	-		-	-	-		-	-	-		-	-	-	
-	-	-	-		-	-	-		-	-	-		-	-	-	
-	-	-	-		-	-	-		-	-	-		-	-	-	
Collected Rent	-	-	-		-	-	-		-	-	-		-	-	-	
<u>Vacancy</u>																
-	-	-	-		-	-	-		-	-	-		-	-	-	
-	-	-	-		-	-	-		-	-	-		-	-	-	
-	-	-	-		-	-	-		-	-	-		-	-	-	
Vacancy	-	-	-		-	-	-		-	-	-		-	-	-	
<u>Credit Loss</u>																
-	-	-	-		-	-	-		-	-	-		-	-	-	
-	-	-	-		-	-	-		-	-	-		-	-	-	
-	-	-	-		-	-	-		-	-	-		-	-	-	
Credit Loss	-	-	-		-	-	-		-	-	-		-	-	-	
<u>Concessions</u>																
-	-	-	-		-	-	-		-	-	-		-	-	-	
-	-	-	-		-	-	-		-	-	-		-	-	-	
-	-	-	-		-	-	-		-	-	-		-	-	-	
Concessions	-	-	-		-	-	-		-	-	-		-	-	-	
Effective Gross Rental Income	-	-	-		-	-	-		-	-	-		-	-	-	
<u>Other Income - 1</u>																
-	-	-	-		-	-	-		-	-	-		-	-	-	
-	-	-	-		-	-	-		-	-	-		-	-	-	
-	-	-	-		-	-	-		-	-	-		-	-	-	
-	-	-	-		-	-	-		-	-	-		-	-	-	
-	-	-	-		-	-	-		-	-	-		-	-	-	
-	-	-	-		-	-	-		-	-	-		-	-	-	
-	-	-	-		-	-	-		-	-	-		-	-	-	
Other Income - 1	-	-	-		-	-	-		-	-	-		-	-	-	
<u>Other Income - 2</u>																
-	-	-	-		-	-	-		-	-	-		-	-	-	
-	-	-	-		-	-	-		-	-	-		-	-	-	
-	-	-	-		-	-	-		-	-	-		-	-	-	
Other Income - 2	-	-	-		-	-	-		-	-	-		-	-	-	
<u>Other Income - 3</u>																
-	-	-	-		-	-	-		-	-	-		-	-	-	
-	-	-	-		-	-	-		-	-	-		-	-	-	
-	-	-	-		-	-	-		-	-	-		-	-	-	
Other Income - 3	-	-	-		-	-	-		-	-	-		-	-	-	
Total Effective Gross Income	-	-	-		-	-	-		-	-	-		-	-	-	

PRECEPT™

OP STMT RECONCILIATION
Property Name

	5				6				7				8			
	YTD			NOTES	YTD Prior			NOTES	Appraisal			NOTES	Budget			NOTES
Property Number: 0000	Statement	Adjustment	Operating		Statement	Adjustment	Operating		Statement	Adjustment	Operating		Statement	Adjustment	Operating	
Deal Number: 0000																
Units: 0	Through:				Through:				Through:				Through:			
	Stmt. Type:				Stmt. Type:				Stmt. Type:				Stmt. Type:			
EXPENSES (Variable)																
Management Fee																
-	-	-	-		-	-	-		-	-	-		-	-	-	
-	-	-	-		-	-	-		-	-	-		-	-	-	
Management Fee	-	-	-		-	-	-		-	-	-		-	-	-	
Payroll & Benefits																
-	-	-	-		-	-	-		-	-	-		-	-	-	
-	-	-	-		-	-	-		-	-	-		-	-	-	
-	-	-	-		-	-	-		-	-	-		-	-	-	
-	-	-	-		-	-	-		-	-	-		-	-	-	
-	-	-	-		-	-	-		-	-	-		-	-	-	
-	-	-	-		-	-	-		-	-	-		-	-	-	
Payroll & Benefits	-	-	-		-	-	-		-	-	-		-	-	-	
Utilities																
-	-	-	-		-	-	-		-	-	-		-	-	-	
-	-	-	-		-	-	-		-	-	-		-	-	-	
-	-	-	-		-	-	-		-	-	-		-	-	-	
-	-	-	-		-	-	-		-	-	-		-	-	-	
-	-	-	-		-	-	-		-	-	-		-	-	-	
-	-	-	-		-	-	-		-	-	-		-	-	-	
Utilities	-	-	-		-	-	-		-	-	-		-	-	-	
Repairs & Maintenance																
-	-	-	-		-	-	-		-	-	-		-	-	-	
-	-	-	-		-	-	-		-	-	-		-	-	-	
-	-	-	-		-	-	-		-	-	-		-	-	-	
-	-	-	-		-	-	-		-	-	-		-	-	-	
-	-	-	-		-	-	-		-	-	-		-	-	-	
-	-	-	-		-	-	-		-	-	-		-	-	-	
-	-	-	-		-	-	-		-	-	-		-	-	-	
-	-	-	-		-	-	-		-	-	-		-	-	-	
-	-	-	-		-	-	-		-	-	-		-	-	-	
-	-	-	-		-	-	-		-	-	-		-	-	-	
-	-	-	-		-	-	-		-	-	-		-	-	-	
Repairs & Maintenance	-	-	-		-	-	-		-	-	-		-	-	-	
Marketing and Advertising																
-	-	-	-		-	-	-		-	-	-		-	-	-	
-	-	-	-		-	-	-		-	-	-		-	-	-	
-	-	-	-		-	-	-		-	-	-		-	-	-	
-	-	-	-		-	-	-		-	-	-		-	-	-	
-	-	-	-		-	-	-		-	-	-		-	-	-	
-	-	-	-		-	-	-		-	-	-		-	-	-	
Marketing and Advertising	-	-	-		-	-	-		-	-	-		-	-	-	
General and Administrative																
-	-	-	-		-	-	-		-	-	-		-	-	-	
-	-	-	-		-	-	-		-	-	-		-	-	-	
-	-	-	-		-	-	-		-	-	-		-	-	-	
-	-	-	-		-	-	-		-	-	-		-	-	-	
-	-	-	-		-	-	-		-	-	-		-	-	-	
General and Administrative	-	-	-		-	-	-		-	-	-		-	-	-	
Other Variable Expense - 1																
-	-	-	-		-	-	-		-	-	-		-	-	-	
-	-	-	-		-	-	-		-	-	-		-	-	-	
Other Variable Expense - 1	-	-	-		-	-	-		-	-	-		-	-	-	
Other Variable Expense - 2																
-	-	-	-		-	-	-		-	-	-		-	-	-	
-	-	-	-		-	-	-		-	-	-		-	-	-	
Other Variable Expense - 2	-	-	-		-	-	-		-	-	-		-	-	-	
Other Variable Expense - 3																
-	-	-	-		-	-	-		-	-	-		-	-	-	
-	-	-	-		-	-	-		-	-	-		-	-	-	
Other Variable Expense - 3	-	-	-		-	-	-		-	-	-		-	-	-	
Total Variable Expenses	-	-	-		-	-	-		-	-	-		-	-	-	

PRECEPT™

OP STMT RECONCILIATION

Property Name

	5				6				7				8			
	YTD			NOTES	YTD Prior			NOTES	Appraisal			NOTES	Budget			NOTES
Property Number: 0000	Statement	Adjustment	Operating		Statement	Adjustment	Operating		Statement	Adjustment	Operating		Statement	Adjustment	Operating	
Deal Number: 0000																
Units: 0	Through:				Through:				Through:				Through:			
	Stmt. Type:				Stmt. Type:				Stmt. Type:				Stmt. Type:			
EXPENSES (Fixed)																
Real Estate Taxes																
-		-	-	-		-	-	-		-	-	-		-	-	-
-		-	-	-		-	-	-		-	-	-		-	-	-
-		-	-	-		-	-	-		-	-	-		-	-	-
Real Estate Taxes		-	-	-		-	-	-		-	-	-		-	-	-
Insurance																
-		-	-	-		-	-	-		-	-	-		-	-	-
-		-	-	-		-	-	-		-	-	-		-	-	-
-		-	-	-		-	-	-		-	-	-		-	-	-
Insurance		-	-	-		-	-	-		-	-	-		-	-	-
Other Fixed Expense - 1																
-		-	-	-		-	-	-		-	-	-		-	-	-
-		-	-	-		-	-	-		-	-	-		-	-	-
-		-	-	-		-	-	-		-	-	-		-	-	-
Other Fixed Expense - 1		-	-	-		-	-	-		-	-	-		-	-	-
Other Fixed Expense - 2																
-		-	-	-		-	-	-		-	-	-		-	-	-
-		-	-	-		-	-	-		-	-	-		-	-	-
-		-	-	-		-	-	-		-	-	-		-	-	-
Other Fixed Expense - 2		-	-	-		-	-	-		-	-	-		-	-	-
Other Fixed Expense - 3																
-		-	-	-		-	-	-		-	-	-		-	-	-
-		-	-	-		-	-	-		-	-	-		-	-	-
-		-	-	-		-	-	-		-	-	-		-	-	-
Other Fixed Expense - 3		-	-	-		-	-	-		-	-	-		-	-	-
Total Fixed Expenses		-	-	-		-	-	-		-	-	-		-	-	-
Total Expenses		-	-	-		-	-	-		-	-	-		-	-	-
Net Operating Income		-	-	-		-	-	-		-	-	-		-	-	-

PRECEPT

OP STMT RECONCILIATION

Property Name

	5				6				7				8			
	YTD			N	YTD Prior			N	Appraisal			N	Budget			N
Property Number: 0000	Statement	Adjustment	Operating	O	Statement	Adjustment	Operating	O	Statement	Adjustment	Operating	O	Statement	Adjustment	Operating	O
Deal Number: 0000				T				T				T				T
Units: 0	Through:			E	Through:			E	Through:			E	Through:			E
	Stmt. Type:			S	Stmt. Type:			S	Stmt. Type:			S	Stmt. Type:			S
CAPITAL EXPENDITURES																
Reserves for Replacement																
-	-	-	-		-	-	-		-	-	-		-	-	-	
-	-	-	-		-	-	-		-	-	-		-	-	-	
-	-	-	-		-	-	-		-	-	-		-	-	-	
Reserves for Replacement	-	-	-		-	-	-		-	-	-		-	-	-	
Other Capital Expense - 1																
-	-	-	-		-	-	-		-	-	-		-	-	-	
-	-	-	-		-	-	-		-	-	-		-	-	-	
-	-	-	-		-	-	-		-	-	-		-	-	-	
-	-	-	-		-	-	-		-	-	-		-	-	-	
-	-	-	-		-	-	-		-	-	-		-	-	-	
-	-	-	-		-	-	-		-	-	-		-	-	-	
Other Capital Expense - 1	-	-	-		-	-	-		-	-	-		-	-	-	
Other Capital Expense - 2																
-	-	-	-		-	-	-		-	-	-		-	-	-	
-	-	-	-		-	-	-		-	-	-		-	-	-	
-	-	-	-		-	-	-		-	-	-		-	-	-	
-	-	-	-		-	-	-		-	-	-		-	-	-	
-	-	-	-		-	-	-		-	-	-		-	-	-	
-	-	-	-		-	-	-		-	-	-		-	-	-	
Other Capital Expense - 2	-	-	-		-	-	-		-	-	-		-	-	-	
Other Capital Expense - 3																
-	-	-	-		-	-	-		-	-	-		-	-	-	
-	-	-	-		-	-	-		-	-	-		-	-	-	
-	-	-	-		-	-	-		-	-	-		-	-	-	
-	-	-	-		-	-	-		-	-	-		-	-	-	
-	-	-	-		-	-	-		-	-	-		-	-	-	
-	-	-	-		-	-	-		-	-	-		-	-	-	
Other Capital Expense - 3	-	-	-		-	-	-		-	-	-		-	-	-	
Total Capital Expenditures	-	-	-		-	-	-		-	-	-		-	-	-	
Net Cash Flow	-	-	-		-	-	-		-	-	-		-	-	-	

PRECEPT™

OP STMT RECONCILIATION

Property Name

	5				6				7				8			
	YTD			N	YTD Prior			N	Appraisal			N	Budget			N
Property Number: 0000	Statement	Adjustment	Operating	O	Statement	Adjustment	Operating	O	Statement	Adjustment	Operating	O	Statement	Adjustment	Operating	O
Deal Number: 0000				T				T				T				T
Units: 0	Through:			E	Through:			E	Through:			E	Through:			E
	Stmt. Type:			S	Stmt. Type:			S	Stmt. Type:			S	Stmt. Type:			S

OCCUPANCY	Physical	Economic	Conclusion		Physical	Economic	Conclusion		Physical	Economic	Conclusion		Physical	Economic	Conclusion	
January																
February																
March																
April																
May																
June																
July																
August																
September																
October																
November																
December																
Calculated Average																
Override	0.00%				0.00%											
Concluded Average																

PRECEPT™

OP STMT RECONCILIATION

Property Name

Property Number: 0000
Deal Number: 0000
Units: 0

	0	0	0	0	0	0	0	0	0	0	0	0	0 Months			NOTES
	January	February	March	April	May	June	July	August	September	October	November	December	Statement	Adjustment	Operating	
	Statement	Statement	Statement	Statement	Statement	Statement	Statement	Statement	Statement	Statement	Statement	Statement	Through:			
													Stmt. Type:			
REVENUES																
Gross Potential Rent																
-	-	-	-	-	-	-	-	-	-	-	-	-	-	-	-	
-	-	-	-	-	-	-	-	-	-	-	-	-	-	-	-	
-	-	-	-	-	-	-	-	-	-	-	-	-	-	-	-	
Gross Potential Rent	-	-	-	-	-	-	-	-	-	-	-	-	-	-	-	
Collected Rent																
-	-	-	-	-	-	-	-	-	-	-	-	-	-	-	-	
-	-	-	-	-	-	-	-	-	-	-	-	-	-	-	-	
-	-	-	-	-	-	-	-	-	-	-	-	-	-	-	-	
Collected Rent	-	-	-	-	-	-	-	-	-	-	-	-	-	-	-	
Vacancy																
-	-	-	-	-	-	-	-	-	-	-	-	-	-	-	-	
-	-	-	-	-	-	-	-	-	-	-	-	-	-	-	-	
-	-	-	-	-	-	-	-	-	-	-	-	-	-	-	-	
Vacancy	-	-	-	-	-	-	-	-	-	-	-	-	-	-	-	
Credit Loss																
-	-	-	-	-	-	-	-	-	-	-	-	-	-	-	-	
-	-	-	-	-	-	-	-	-	-	-	-	-	-	-	-	
-	-	-	-	-	-	-	-	-	-	-	-	-	-	-	-	
Credit Loss	-	-	-	-	-	-	-	-	-	-	-	-	-	-	-	
Concessions																
-	-	-	-	-	-	-	-	-	-	-	-	-	-	-	-	
-	-	-	-	-	-	-	-	-	-	-	-	-	-	-	-	
-	-	-	-	-	-	-	-	-	-	-	-	-	-	-	-	
Concessions	-	-	-	-	-	-	-	-	-	-	-	-	-	-	-	
Effective Gross Rental Income	-	-	-	-	-	-	-	-	-	-	-	-	-	-	-	
Other Income - 1																
-	-	-	-	-	-	-	-	-	-	-	-	-	-	-	-	
-	-	-	-	-	-	-	-	-	-	-	-	-	-	-	-	
-	-	-	-	-	-	-	-	-	-	-	-	-	-	-	-	
-	-	-	-	-	-	-	-	-	-	-	-	-	-	-	-	
-	-	-	-	-	-	-	-	-	-	-	-	-	-	-	-	
-	-	-	-	-	-	-	-	-	-	-	-	-	-	-	-	
-	-	-	-	-	-	-	-	-	-	-	-	-	-	-	-	
Other Income - 1	-	-	-	-	-	-	-	-	-	-	-	-	-	-	-	
Other Income - 2																
-	-	-	-	-	-	-	-	-	-	-	-	-	-	-	-	
-	-	-	-	-	-	-	-	-	-	-	-	-	-	-	-	
-	-	-	-	-	-	-	-	-	-	-	-	-	-	-	-	
Other Income - 2	-	-	-	-	-	-	-	-	-	-	-	-	-	-	-	
Other Income - 3																
-	-	-	-	-	-	-	-	-	-	-	-	-	-	-	-	
-	-	-	-	-	-	-	-	-	-	-	-	-	-	-	-	
-	-	-	-	-	-	-	-	-	-	-	-	-	-	-	-	
Other Income - 3	-	-	-	-	-	-	-	-	-	-	-	-	-	-	-	
Total Effective Gross Income	-	-	-	-	-	-	-	-	-	-	-	-	-	-	-	

PRECEPT™

OP STMT RECONCILIATION

Property Name

	0	0	0	0	0	0	0	0	0	0	0	0	**0 Months**			**N**
	January	**February**	**March**	**April**	**May**	**June**	**July**	**August**	**September**	**October**	**November**	**December**				
Property Number: 0000	**Statement**	**Statement**	**Statement**	**Statement**	**Statement**	**Statement**	**Statement**	**Statement**	**Statement**	**Statement**	**Statement**	**Statement**	**Statement**	**Adjustment**	**Operating**	**O**
Deal Number: 0000																**T**
Units: 0													**Through:**			**E**
													Stmt. Type:			**S**
EXPENSES (Variable)																
Management Fee																
-	-	-	-	-	-	-	-	-	-	-	-	-	-	-	-	
-	-	-	-	-	-	-	-	-	-	-	-	-	-	-	-	
Management Fee	-	-	-	-	-	-	-	-	-	-	-	-	-	-	-	
Payroll & Benefits																
-	-	-	-	-	-	-	-	-	-	-	-	-	-	-	-	
-	-	-	-	-	-	-	-	-	-	-	-	-	-	-	-	
-	-	-	-	-	-	-	-	-	-	-	-	-	-	-	-	
-	-	-	-	-	-	-	-	-	-	-	-	-	-	-	-	
-	-	-	-	-	-	-	-	-	-	-	-	-	-	-	-	
-	-	-	-	-	-	-	-	-	-	-	-	-	-	-	-	
Payroll & Benefits	-	-	-	-	-	-	-	-	-	-	-	-	-	-	-	
Utilities																
-	-	-	-	-	-	-	-	-	-	-	-	-	-	-	-	
-	-	-	-	-	-	-	-	-	-	-	-	-	-	-	-	
-	-	-	-	-	-	-	-	-	-	-	-	-	-	-	-	
-	-	-	-	-	-	-	-	-	-	-	-	-	-	-	-	
-	-	-	-	-	-	-	-	-	-	-	-	-	-	-	-	
-	-	-	-	-	-	-	-	-	-	-	-	-	-	-	-	
Utilities	-	-	-	-	-	-	-	-	-	-	-	-	-	-	-	
Repairs & Maintenance																
-	-	-	-	-	-	-	-	-	-	-	-	-	-	-	-	
-	-	-	-	-	-	-	-	-	-	-	-	-	-	-	-	
-	-	-	-	-	-	-	-	-	-	-	-	-	-	-	-	
-	-	-	-	-	-	-	-	-	-	-	-	-	-	-	-	
-	-	-	-	-	-	-	-	-	-	-	-	-	-	-	-	
-	-	-	-	-	-	-	-	-	-	-	-	-	-	-	-	
-	-	-	-	-	-	-	-	-	-	-	-	-	-	-	-	
-	-	-	-	-	-	-	-	-	-	-	-	-	-	-	-	
-	-	-	-	-	-	-	-	-	-	-	-	-	-	-	-	
-	-	-	-	-	-	-	-	-	-	-	-	-	-	-	-	
-	-	-	-	-	-	-	-	-	-	-	-	-	-	-	-	
Repairs & Maintenance	-	-	-	-	-	-	-	-	-	-	-	-	-	-	-	
Marketing and Advertising																
-	-	-	-	-	-	-	-	-	-	-	-	-	-	-	-	
-	-	-	-	-	-	-	-	-	-	-	-	-	-	-	-	
-	-	-	-	-	-	-	-	-	-	-	-	-	-	-	-	
-	-	-	-	-	-	-	-	-	-	-	-	-	-	-	-	
-	-	-	-	-	-	-	-	-	-	-	-	-	-	-	-	
-	-	-	-	-	-	-	-	-	-	-	-	-	-	-	-	
Marketing and Advertising	-	-	-	-	-	-	-	-	-	-	-	-	-	-	-	
General and Administrative																
-	-	-	-	-	-	-	-	-	-	-	-	-	-	-	-	
-	-	-	-	-	-	-	-	-	-	-	-	-	-	-	-	
-	-	-	-	-	-	-	-	-	-	-	-	-	-	-	-	
-	-	-	-	-	-	-	-	-	-	-	-	-	-	-	-	
-	-	-	-	-	-	-	-	-	-	-	-	-	-	-	-	
General and Administrative	-	-	-	-	-	-	-	-	-	-	-	-	-	-	-	
Other Variable Expense - 1																
-	-	-	-	-	-	-	-	-	-	-	-	-	-	-	-	
-	-	-	-	-	-	-	-	-	-	-	-	-	-	-	-	
Other Variable Expense - 1	-	-	-	-	-	-	-	-	-	-	-	-	-	-	-	
Other Variable Expense - 2																
-	-	-	-	-	-	-	-	-	-	-	-	-	-	-	-	
-	-	-	-	-	-	-	-	-	-	-	-	-	-	-	-	
Other Variable Expense - 2	-	-	-	-	-	-	-	-	-	-	-	-	-	-	-	
Other Variable Expense - 3																
-	-	-	-	-	-	-	-	-	-	-	-	-	-	-	-	
-	-	-	-	-	-	-	-	-	-	-	-	-	-	-	-	
Other Variable Expense - 3	-	-	-	-	-	-	-	-	-	-	-	-	-	-	-	
Total Variable Expenses	-	-	-	-	-	-	-	-	-	-	-	-	-	-	-	

PRECEPT

OP STMT RECONCILIATION

Property Name

Property Number: 0000
Deal Number: 0000
Units: 0

	0	0	0	0	0	0	0	0	0	0	0	0	0 Months			N O T E S
	January	February	March	April	May	June	July	August	September	October	November	December				
	Statement	Statement	Statement	Statement	Statement	Statement	Statement	Statement	Statement	Statement	Statement	Statement	Statement	Adjustment	Operating	
													Through:			
													Stmt. Type:			
EXPENSES (Fixed)																
Real Estate Taxes																
-	-	-	-	-	-	-	-	-	-	-	-	-	-	-	-	
-	-	-	-	-	-	-	-	-	-	-	-	-	-	-	-	
-	-	-	-	-	-	-	-	-	-	-	-	-	-	-	-	
Real Estate Taxes	-	-	-	-	-	-	-	-	-	-	-	-	-	-	-	
Insurance																
-	-	-	-	-	-	-	-	-	-	-	-	-	-	-	-	
-	-	-	-	-	-	-	-	-	-	-	-	-	-	-	-	
-	-	-	-	-	-	-	-	-	-	-	-	-	-	-	-	
Insurance	-	-	-	-	-	-	-	-	-	-	-	-	-	-	-	
Other Fixed Expense - 1																
-	-	-	-	-	-	-	-	-	-	-	-	-	-	-	-	
-	-	-	-	-	-	-	-	-	-	-	-	-	-	-	-	
-	-	-	-	-	-	-	-	-	-	-	-	-	-	-	-	
Other Fixed Expense - 1	-	-	-	-	-	-	-	-	-	-	-	-	-	-	-	
Other Fixed Expense - 2																
-	-	-	-	-	-	-	-	-	-	-	-	-	-	-	-	
-	-	-	-	-	-	-	-	-	-	-	-	-	-	-	-	
-	-	-	-	-	-	-	-	-	-	-	-	-	-	-	-	
Other Fixed Expense - 2	-	-	-	-	-	-	-	-	-	-	-	-	-	-	-	
Other Fixed Expense - 3																
-	-	-	-	-	-	-	-	-	-	-	-	-	-	-	-	
-	-	-	-	-	-	-	-	-	-	-	-	-	-	-	-	
-	-	-	-	-	-	-	-	-	-	-	-	-	-	-	-	
Other Fixed Expense - 3	-	-	-	-	-	-	-	-	-	-	-	-	-	-	-	
Total Fixed Expenses	-	-	-	-	-	-	-	-	-	-	-	-	-	-	-	
Total Expenses	-	-	-	-	-	-	-	-	-	-	-	-	-	-	-	
Net Operating Income	-	-	-	-	-	-	-	-	-	-	-	-	-	-	-	

PRECEPT™

OP STMT RECONCILIATION
Property Name

Property Number: 0000
Deal Number: 0000
Units: 0

	0	0	0	0	0	0	0	0	0	0	0	0	0 Months			N O T E S
	January	February	March	April	May	June	July	August	September	October	November	December				
	Statement	Statement	Statement	Statement	Statement	Statement	Statement	Statement	Statement	Statement	Statement	Statement	Statement	Adjustment	Operating	
													Through:			
													Stmt. Type:			
CAPITAL EXPENDITURES																
Reserves for Replacement																
-	-	-	-	-	-	-	-	-	-	-	-	-	-	-	-	
-	-	-	-	-	-	-	-	-	-	-	-	-	-	-	-	
-	-	-	-	-	-	-	-	-	-	-	-	-	-	-	-	
Reserves for Replacement	-	-	-	-	-	-	-	-	-	-	-	-	-	-	-	
Other Capital Expense - 1																
-	-	-	-	-	-	-	-	-	-	-	-	-	-	-	-	
-	-	-	-	-	-	-	-	-	-	-	-	-	-	-	-	
-	-	-	-	-	-	-	-	-	-	-	-	-	-	-	-	
-	-	-	-	-	-	-	-	-	-	-	-	-	-	-	-	
-	-	-	-	-	-	-	-	-	-	-	-	-	-	-	-	
-	-	-	-	-	-	-	-	-	-	-	-	-	-	-	-	
Other Capital Expense - 1	-	-	-	-	-	-	-	-	-	-	-	-	-	-	-	
Other Capital Expense - 2																
-	-	-	-	-	-	-	-	-	-	-	-	-	-	-	-	
-	-	-	-	-	-	-	-	-	-	-	-	-	-	-	-	
-	-	-	-	-	-	-	-	-	-	-	-	-	-	-	-	
-	-	-	-	-	-	-	-	-	-	-	-	-	-	-	-	
-	-	-	-	-	-	-	-	-	-	-	-	-	-	-	-	
-	-	-	-	-	-	-	-	-	-	-	-	-	-	-	-	
Other Capital Expense - 2	-	-	-	-	-	-	-	-	-	-	-	-	-	-	-	
Other Capital Expense - 3																
-	-	-	-	-	-	-	-	-	-	-	-	-	-	-	-	
-	-	-	-	-	-	-	-	-	-	-	-	-	-	-	-	
-	-	-	-	-	-	-	-	-	-	-	-	-	-	-	-	
-	-	-	-	-	-	-	-	-	-	-	-	-	-	-	-	
-	-	-	-	-	-	-	-	-	-	-	-	-	-	-	-	
-	-	-	-	-	-	-	-	-	-	-	-	-	-	-	-	
Other Capital Expense - 3	-	-	-	-	-	-	-	-	-	-	-	-	-	-	-	
Total Capital Expenditures	-	-	-	-	-	-	-	-	-	-	-	-	-	-	-	
Net Cash Flow	-	-	-	-	-	-	-	-	-	-	-	-	-	-	-	

PRECEPT™

OP STMT RECONCILIATION

Property Name

Property Number: 0000
Deal Number: 0000
Units: 0

0	0	0	0	0	0	0	0	0	0	0	0
January	**February**	**March**	**April**	**May**	**June**	**July**	**August**	**September**	**October**	**November**	**December**
Statement	**Statement**	**Statement**	**Statement**	**Statement**	**Statement**	**Statement**	**Statement**	**Statement**	**Statement**	**Statement**	**Statement**

0 Months			**NOTES**
Statement	**Adjustment**	**Operating**	
Through:			
Stmt. Type:			

Note and Comments:

OCCUPANCY

January
February
March
April
May
June
July
August
September
October
November
December
Calculated Average
Override
Concluded Average

PRECEPT™

Property Name
OCCUPANCY, RENTAL RATES AND SALES DATA

Property Number: 0000
Deal Number: 0000

Current Occupancy:

		Physical	Economic
Based on Rent Roll Dated			

Is property stabilized?	
If "No," est. stabilization date:	

		Occupancy	As of Date	Physical (P) Economic (E)	Source	Comments
Market						
Sub-market						
Current	(Property)					
TTM	(Property)					
1999	(Property)					
1998	(Property)					
1997	(Property)					

Comments on Current Occupancy:

Rental Comparable Property Summary:

#	Property Name/Location	Distance from Subject	Units	Physical Occupancy	Year Built	Avg Rent or Rent Range per Unit	Compare to subject (+, -, =) Location	Condition	Source	Comments
S	**Property Name, Property City**		0	0.0%	0					
1										
2										
3										
4										
5										

Comments on Comparable Property:

Sales Comparable Summary:

#	Property Name/Location	Units	Year Built	Date Sold	Sale Price	Value Per Unit	Seller	Buyer	Estimated Cap Rate	Estimated NOI/Unit
1										
2										
3										
4										
5										

Comments on Sales Comparable (e.g., source of information and general comments on each property, etc.):

PRECEPT™

Property Name
PROPERTY DESCRIPTION

Property Number: 0000
Deal Number: 0000

General Property Characteristics:

Property Style					
Property Class (A, B, C, D)		Total land area (acres)		Type of parking	
Number of units		Density per acre		Total parking spaces	
Net rentable SF		Excess land area (acres)		Exterior facade	
Year built		Number of floors		Roof type	
Year last renovated		Number of buildings		Sprinklered (yes / no)	

Property Description Comments (e.g., space, usage, etc.):

Exterior Condition ("Ex/Good/Avg/Poor/NA"):

Overall quality of the exterior	
Landscaping	
Adequacy of roads / parking	
Paving	
Adequacy of lighting	
Pool(s) / Spa(s)	
Paint	
Windows	
Roof	
Façade	

Interior Condition ("Ex/Good/Avg/Poor/NA"):

Common Area	
Overall quality of the interior	
Carpet	
Furniture	
Exercise equipment	
Adequacy of lighting	
Units	
Kitchen cabinets	
Kitchen appliances	
Carpet / Vinyl	
Bathrooms	

Location Characteristics:

Corner (yes / no)	
Traffic volume (low, medium, high)	
Access to major arteries	
Access to local amenities	
Street appeal	
Ingress / Egress	
Ease of left hand turn into property	
Visibility	
Signage	
Overall quality of the location	

Neighborhood Description:

North of Site:
South of Site:
East of Site:
West of Site:

Unit Mix:

Unit Type	# of Units	% of Total	Unit Size	Total SF
Other				
Other				
Other				
Total / Wtd. Avg.				

Property Specific Amenities "X":

Clubhouse	
Gated	
Pool(s)	
Spa(s)	
Exercise facility	
Sport court	
Racquetball court	
Playground	
Business center	
Laundry room	
Storage	

Unit Specific Amenities "X":

Washer/Dryer	
Dishwasher	
Microwave	
Fireplace	
Patio/Balcony	
Central HVAC	
Ceiling fans	
Ceiling height	
Vaulted ceilings	
Disposal	
Intrusion alarms	

PRECEPT™

Property Name
PROPERTY DESCRIPTION

Property Number: 0000
Deal Number: 0000

Tenant Concentration:

Students	
Military	
Corporates	
Seniors	

Comments:

Major Off-site Demand Generators:

Property Management Information:

Property Management Company's Name	
Property Manager's Name	
Property Manager on site daily (yes / no)	
Years Co. has managed the Property	
Mgmt. Type (owner / outside contractor)	
Manages properties for other owner	
Property management fee	

Property Management Company's History/Experience:

REAL ESTATE TAX SUMMARY

General Tax Information:

Tax identification		Last re-assessment date (month/year)	
Assessor's phone number		Assessment currently under appeal?	
Tax abatements? (yes / no)		Next assessment date (month/year)	
Tax abatement expiration date(s)			

Real Estate Tax Assessment History:

Fiscal Year Ending	Market Value	Conversion Factor	Assessed Value	Millage Rate	Total Property Tax	Other Assessments	Total Tax Liability	Comments

Comments On Real Estate Taxes (Status of tax appeals and description of other assessments):

STEP 1: PROPERTY STATEMENT COLLECTION

Operating Statements

Precept will require the borrower to submit certified cash flow statements for (1) the past three full years (calendar or fiscal), (2) the current partial year (year to date), and (3) the prior partial year (for the same months relative to the current partial year). The borrower may substitute a complete trailing-12-month cash flow statement for the partial-year statements. In addition to the historical cash flow statements, Precept will require the borrower to submit a certified budget or pro forma for the current full year.

Additional Considerations. Precept will make every effort to obtain partial-year or trailing-12-month statements for periods that end within 3 months (partial months excluded) of the effective underwriting date.

Rent Rolls

Precept will require the borrower to provide a certified current list of tenants and their monthly financial rental obligations. Information on each tenant/apartment will include, at a minimum, the following information or other information sufficient to allow Precept to derive the following:

1. Unit/apartment number
2. Unit/apartment description (if all units are not identical)
3. Lease start date
4. Original and current lease term (month-to-month, one-year, etc.)
5. Security deposit and financial rental obligations (apartment rent, garage rent, etc.)

In addition to the information just listed, Precept will also request a rent roll as of the end of each operating statement period.

Additional Considerations. In the event that rent rolls are not available as of the end of the operating statement periods, Precept will obtain rent rolls for historical points-in-time that are available.

Summary of Annual Occupancy

Precept will request that the borrower provide corresponding physical and/or economic occupancy figures for the operating statement periods. This is not a required item, given that economic occupancy during historical periods can be estimated by comparing actual rent collections from the operating statements to Gross Potential Rent for the same periods. Precept may request monthly occupancy statistics where either seasonality or severe income fluctuations exist.

Additional Considerations. Precept will compare the summary of annual occupancy numbers with point-in-time occupancy indicated by historical rent rolls (explained later).

Summary of Delinquencies (or Aging Report)

Precept will require the borrower to provide a current summary of tenants that are delinquent in their financial rental obligations, including the length of time each tenant has been delinquent and the dollar amount of the delinquency (summary of delinquencies). Precept will also request a summary of delinquencies as of the end of each operating statement period.

Additional Considerations. In the event that a summary of delinquencies is not available as of the end of each operating statement period, Precept will request that the borrower provide the summary for historical points-in-time that are available.

Summary of Historical Capital Expenditures

Precept will request that the borrower provide a brief description of capital expenditures made to the property within the operating statement periods (past three years), including the timing and cost of such capital expenditures.

Additional Considerations. In addition to providing relevant detail regarding the property's physical improvements, this summary will be utilized to make any necessary adjustments for nonrecurring expenditures in the Operating Statement Reconciliation section of the underwriting summary.

STEP 2: OPERATING STATEMENT NORMALIZATION

Standard Cash Flow Line Items

Precept will use the Operating Statement Reconciliation section of the underwriting summary to normalize the operating statements as set forth herein. For multifamily land uses, Precept's standard cash flow line items are indicated in bold typeface in the following table:

Revenues

Gross Potential Rent
  or Collected Rent
Vacancy
Credit Loss
Concessions

Effective Gross Rental Income

Other Income—1
Other Income—2
Other Income—3

Total Effective Gross Income

Expenses

Variable
  Management Fee
  Payroll and Benefits
  Utilities
  Repairs and Maintenance
  Marketing and Advertising
  Administrative
  Other Variable Expense—1
  Other Variable Expense—2
  Other Variable Expense—3

Total Variable Expense

Fixed
  Real Property Taxes
  Insurance
  Other Fixed Expense—1
  Other Fixed Expense—2
  Other Fixed Expense—3

Total Fixed Expense

Total Expenses

Net Operating Income

Capital Expenditures
Reserves for Replacement
Other Capital Expense—1
Other Capital Expense—2
Total Capital Expenditures
Net Cash Flow

The headings in the preceding table are group descriptions and the line items in bold italics are calculated fields. The generic line items (e.g., Other Income—1, Other Fixed Expense—1, etc.) are reserved for income and/or expenditures from the operating statements that either do not clearly fit within Precept's standard line items or that Precept determines to be more meaningful as separate line items (e.g., parking income, ground rent, etc.). In these cases, the generic Precept line-item title in the table will be replaced with the actual operating statement line-item title. For example, an operating statement line item entitled "Unit prep and leasing fee" would be difficult to divide between Precept's standard Repairs and Maintenance and Administrative line items. Therefore, Unit Prep and Leasing Fee would be given its own title, replacing Other Variable Expense—1.

Precept anticipates that a portion of borrower-provided historical operating statements will reflect Collected Rent in lieu of Gross Potential Rent and corresponding rent loss due to Vacancy. Therefore, Precept's standard cash flow line items allow for one or the other, but not both.

Compiling a Trailing-12-Month or Annualized Operating Statement

In some cases the borrower will not have provided Precept with a current trailing-12-month operating statement that can be directly entered into the Operating Statement Reconciliation section of the underwriting summary. In this event, Precept will compile a trailing-12-month statement or create an annualized statement, provided that the operating statements obtained from the borrower allow Precept to do so in a meaningful manner. For example, if the borrower is able to provide operating statements for the past full calendar year *A*, the current partial year *B* (year to date), and the prior partial year *C* (for the same months relative to the current partial year), the trailing-12-month cash flow would be compiled by subtracting *C*, the prior partial year, from *A*, the past full calendar year, and adding *B*, the current partial year, to the result. This compilation would be completed on a line-by-line basis, and results would appear in the Operating Statement Reconciliation section of the model, with a "trailing-12" or "TTM" designation. Whenever possible this method of compiling the trailing-12-month cash flow will be used.

This calculation will not always be possible, given, for example, the absence of prior partial-year statements that correspond to the same number of months as the statements for the current partial year. In this event, the trailing-12-month cash flow may be calculated using the partial-year formula, or the trailing-12 may be replaced with annualized figures.

Partial-Year Formula

$$\text{TTM} = \text{current partial year} + \left[\frac{\text{most recent full year}}{12} \times (12 - x)\right]$$

where x = the number of months of operating statements used for the current partial year

Precept will determine whether to calculate the trailing-12-month cash flow using the partial-year formula or to simply annualize the current partial year on the following basis:

Current Partial-Year Operating Statements	Prior Full-Year Operating Statements	Action
Less than 6 months	None	Do not calculate TTM
Less than 6 months	Yes	Use the partial-year formula
6 months or greater	None	Annualize the period available
6 months or greater	Yes	Use the partial-year formula

STEP 3: DATA CONFIRMATION

In addition to the collection and normalization of the property's operating statements, Precept will conduct other various procedures confirming the property's operating history. If these procedures identify inaccuracies or misrepresentations within the normalized operating history, corresponding adjustments will be made and footnoted within the appropriate section of the underwriting summary, and/or the borrower may be asked to resubmit one or more property statements. Moreover, if individual income and expense line items presented in the property's operating statements are volatile from year to year, Precept may increase the sample size (length of the operating period) for data confirmation purposes.

Federal Income Tax Return Review

Precept will reconcile the operating statements to the borrower or current owner's most recent available federal income tax returns. Precept expects that total income reported in the tax return will be within 5% of Total Effective Gross Income reported in the operating statements. If this expectation is not met, Precept will require an explanation from the borrower, which will be noted within the Income Tax Reconciliation section of the underwriting summary.

While individual expense line-item titles often differ between tax returns and operating statements (making line-item comparisons difficult), overall expenses are expected to be consistent. To the greatest extent possible, Precept will group individual expense line items from the tax returns so that they are consistent with the expense line items of operating statements. For example, Precept may total all expense line items except Real Property Taxes and Insurance, and compare the result to the same from the operating statements. At a minimum, Precept will compare overall expenses from the tax returns, with obvious adjustments for interest and depreciation, to overall expenses from the corresponding operating statement. If comparable line items, line-item groupings, and/or Total Expenses differ between the two sources by more than 10%, Precept will require borrower explanations that will be noted within the Income Tax Reconciliation section of the underwriting summary.

Additional Considerations. Federal income tax returns may not always be available, given that some borrowers may be using the contemplated financing as purchase money. If this is the case, Precept will continue the data confirmation procedures outlined here in lieu of the income tax reconciliation.

Bank Statement Review

Precept will reconcile Total Effective Gross Income from the operating statements for the most recent 12-month period to actual bank statements reflecting property income. This reconciliation will not be conducted if the federal income tax return review is completed and yields no discrepancies with respect to property income.

Lease Reviews

Precept will review the property's standard lease agreement form to confirm basic rental payment terms.

Occupancy Review

Precept will compare the summary of annual occupancy numbers with point-in-time occupancy indicated by historical rent rolls and estimated economic occupancy (derived by comparing actual rent collections from the operating statements to Gross Potential Rent for the same periods). If the operating statements do not provide a Gross Potential Rent figure, Precept will estimate it based on the historical rent rolls.

Management Fee Review

Precept will reconcile historical Management Fee expenses from the operating statements to the current management contract.

Payroll and Benefits Expense Review

Precept will reconcile historical Payroll and Benefits expenses to the borrower's summary of property employees and payroll.

Utilities Expense Review

Precept will reconcile the Utilities expenses from the operating statements to actual utility bills for the most recent 12-month period.

Real Property Tax Expense Review

Precept will reconcile Real Property Taxes from the operating statements to actual tax bills for the most recent 12-month period.

Capital Expenditures Review

Precept will reconcile capital improvement expenses from the operating statements to the summary of historical capital expenditures provided by the borrower.

Other

Depending on (1) the results of the procedures outlined previously, (2) the sophistication of the borrower's accounting system, and (3) the volatility of individual operating statement figures, Precept may conduct additional procedures, including, but not limited to, a detailed income and expense ledger review for certain periods of time in order to better understand the components of the property's operations.

STEP 4: ESTIMATION OF STABILIZED PROPERTY CASH FLOW

As previously described, Precept will conclude an underwritten Net Cash Flow on a trailing-12-month (TTM) basis and on a leases-in-place (LIP) basis. While the process of deriving underwritten operating expenses is the same for each of these methodologies, the derivation of underwritten revenues is different.

Revenues

Gross Potential Rent

Standard Definition. *Gross Potential Rent* is an estimate of the annual fixed base rent that would be collected if the property were 100% occupied for one year.

Method of Derivation

LIP. Gross Potential Rent is calculated by annualizing the sum of (1) the total monthly rent in place for occupied units (based on the most current rent roll) and (2) the monthly Market Rent for each vacant unit:

Gross Potential Rent (LIP) = (total monthly base rent for current tenants + monthly Market Rent for each vacant unit) × 12 months

TTM. Gross Potential Rent will equal the Gross Potential Rent figure provided in the trailing-12-month operating statement. Precept will not conclude Gross Potential Rent if the trailing-12-month operating statement does not provide such a figure.

MARKET RENT. *Market Rent* is derived by comparing property-level rental rate data from the rent roll with apartment market data from the site inspection report and appraisal report. The primary source of the Market Rent conclusion will be actual leasing history provided by the most current rent roll. First, the rental rates from the most recent leases for each property's comparable unit type will be averaged. Second, the average comparable rental rate within the property will be compared to the market rent conclusions in the site inspection report and appraisal report to confirm that the three sources are supportive of each other. Last, provided that the site inspection report and appraisal report conclusions do not deviate from the property's comparable rental rate average by more than 5%, the Market Rent conclusion will be equal to the property's comparable rental rate average. In the event that either the site inspection report or appraisal report market rent conclusions deviate by more than 5% from the property's comparable rental rate average, the Market Rent conclusion will be between the high and low of the three indicators. The exact Market Rent conclusion will depend on the reason(s) for the deviations. In all cases, the exact source of the Market Rent conclusion will be noted in the underwriting summary.

Additional Considerations. Regardless of whether existing rent is below market, or management has been successful in implementing rent increases, Precept will not give credit for future rental rate increases beyond the inclusion of Market Rent for vacant units in the Gross Potential Rent calculation. Rent for furnished units will be evaluated on an unfurnished basis, and expenses directly associated with furnishings will not be reflected in Net Cash Flow. Precept will evaluate the relationship between length of leases (e.g., month-to-month vs. one-year) and rental rates to determine if premiums exist for certain lease terms.

Collected Rent

Standard Definition—TTM Only. *Collected Rent* is an estimate of the annual fixed base rent that will be collected over the first year of the loan term net of actual Vacancy, Credit Loss, and Concessions. Collected Rent is reserved for the TTM methodology and will not be included if Gross Potential Rent is available.

Method of Derivation. Collected Rent is concluded based on actual rent received during the trailing-12-month period.

Vacancy

Standard Definition. *Vacancy* is an estimate of the annual economic loss that the property will experience from Gross Potential Rent due to a portion of the property being unoccupied and/or not leased.

Method of Derivation

LIP. Vacancy is calculated by taking the product of (1) Gross Potential Rent and (2) the greater of Multifamily Minimum Vacancy Percentage, Actual Vacancy Percentage, or Market Vacancy Percentage.

TTM. If gross Potential Rent is concluded, Vacancy will equal the greater of (1) the corresponding vacancy figure from the normalized trailing-12-month operating statement or (2) the product of the Multifamily Minimum Vacancy Percentage and Gross Potential Rent. Otherwise, if Collected Rent is concluded, Vacancy will be calculated as follows:

Vacancy = the greater of zero and {[(the greater of Multifamily Minimum Vacancy Percentage, Actual Vacancy Percentage, or Market Vacancy Percentage) – Actual Vacancy Percentage] × [Collected Rent/(1 – Actual Vacancy Percentage)]}

where Multifamily Minimum Vacancy Percentage = 5%.

Note: In the event that Collected Rent is concluded in lieu of Gross Potential Rent, underwritten Vacancy percentage represents the difference between Actual Vacancy Percentage and the greater of Minimum Vacancy Percentage and Market Vacancy Percentage.

Actual Vacancy Percentage

LIP. *Actual Vacancy Percentage* is derived by dividing the sum of annual Market Rent for all vacant units by Gross Potential Rent.

TTM. *Actual Vacancy Percentage* is equal to the reported vacancy figure for the trailing-12-month period. If a vacancy figure is not reported for the trailing-12-month period, Actual Vacancy Percentage will be derived as follows:

$$\text{Actual Vacancy Percentage} = 1 - \frac{\text{Collected Rent}}{\text{LIP Gross Potential Rent}}$$

Market Vacancy Percentage. *Market Vacancy Percentage* shall be determined by Precept after conducting a reconciliation analysis of the appraisal report's concluded market vacancy (or one minus the appraiser's concluded market occupancy) and the site inspection report's concluded market vacancy for the property. The Market Vacancy Percentage will be a number between the appraiser's concluded market vacancy (or one minus the appraiser's concluded market occupancy) and the site inspection report's concluded market vacancy.

Additional Considerations. When reviewing the appraisal and site inspection reports, Precept will pay particular attention to demand growth versus anticipated new supply and how these factors relate to stabilized occupancy for the property. Precept will also evaluate the potential impact tenant-demand concentrations (e.g., students, military, etc.) may have on stabilized occupancy. Precept will specifically address tenant concentrations that represent more than 20% of occupancy. Precept will not distinguish between lease terms ranging from one month to one year for underwritten Vacancy.

Credit Loss

Standard Definition. *Credit Loss* is an estimate of the annual economic loss that the property will experience due to the inability to collect scheduled rent from various tenants.

Method of Derivation

LIP. Credit Loss is concluded based on a comparison of historical Credit Loss at the property to apartment market data from the site inspection report and appraisal report. The primary basis for the Credit Loss conclusion will be the property's actual three-year historical Credit Loss, with emphasis placed on the most recent 12-month period and most recent tenant arrearage report. If Credit Loss over the three-year history is volatile or declining, Precept will use an average of Credit Loss for the collected three-year history. If historical Credit Loss is systematically increasing, Precept's conclusion will be consistent with the most recent 12-month period. The Credit Loss conclusion will be compared to similar data in the site inspection report and appraisal report to ensure that these sources are supportive of historical levels.

TTM. Credit Loss will be concluded on the same basis as LIP, except in cases where Collected Rent is used in lieu of Gross Potential Rent. In this case, the underwritten Credit Loss will represent the difference, if any, between the actual Credit Loss reflected in Collected Rent and the total stabilized Credit Loss concluded using the LIP methodology.

Additional Considerations. Many times operating statements do not separately identify Credit Loss. Precept will endeavor to determine Credit Loss history in these cases through conversations with the borrower and, if necessary, by reconciling historical rent rolls to the appropriate operating statements. In many cases the Credit Loss adjustment to Gross Potential Rent will be incorporated in the Vacancy adjustment because property-level data and market-level data are not discerning enough for Precept to draw individual conclusions. In cases where Credit Loss is systematically increasing, Precept will investigate the reason(s) for the increases. Depending on the results, Precept's Credit Loss conclusion may reflect an adjustment to the most recent 12-month period; however, such an adjustment will be listed as an exception based on the method of derivation previously detailed. In either case, the basis for the Credit Loss conclusion will be clearly noted within the underwriting summary.

Concessions

Standard Definition. *Concessions* adjustments are an estimate of the annual cost of incentives that the property will offer in order to induce tenants to sign leases and take occupancy.

Method of Derivation

LIP. The Concessions adjustment is concluded based on a comparison of historical Concessions at the property to apartment market data from the site inspection and appraisal reports. The primary basis for the Concessions conclusion will be the property's actual three-year historical Concessions in relation to Gross Potential Rent and Vacancy, with emphasis placed on the most recent 12-month period and current rent roll. The history-based Concessions conclusion will be compared to similar data in the site inspection report and appraisal report to ensure that these sources are supportive of historical levels.

TTM. Concessions will be concluded on the same basis as LIP, except in cases where Collected Rent is used in lieu of Gross Potential Rent. In this case, the underwritten Concessions will represent the difference, if any, between the actual Concessions reflected in Collected Rent and the total stabilized Concessions loss concluded using the LIP methodology.

Additional Considerations. Many times operating statements do not separately account for Concessions. In many cases the Concessions adjustment to Gross Potential Rent will be incorporated in the Vacancy adjustment because property-level data and market-level data are not discerning enough for Precept to draw individual conclusions.

Other Income–1, 2, and 3

Standard Definition. *Other Income* is an estimate of the annual recurring income generated from sources that are ancillary or incidental to the property's base rental revenue. Examples include parking fees, laundry, storage, cable, application fees, nonsufficient funds fees, and late fees.

Method of Derivation—LIP and TTM. Precept will include as underwritten revenue only those items individually or in aggregate having consistent history and strong expectations for future collections. If such amounts comprise more than 5.0% of Total Effective Gross Income, Precept will request documentation confirming and explaining the sources of revenue. Precept will base the underwritten amount of Other Income on the most recent 12-month collections or an average of historical collections for which Precept has operating statements. Underwritten Other Income in excess of 5.0% of Total Effective Gross Income will be noted as to source in either the Cash Flow Summary section or the Operating Statement Reconciliation page of the underwriting summary. The underwriting summary allows for Other Income to be categorized into three separate line items.

Additional Considerations. Precept will exclude interest income from Other Income provided that operating statements give sufficient detail from which to do so.

Expenses

Management Fee

Standard Definition. *Management Fee* is an estimate of the annual amount an independent management company would charge to comprehensively oversee the property's operations. The Management Fee does not include the cost of on-site management personnel or on-site administrative costs.

Method of Derivation. Precept will underwrite the Management Fees to equal the greater of the following:

- The management fees set forth in the current management contract
- The market Management Fee Precept determines would be required to engage a competent third-party property management firm
- 5.0% of Total Effective Gross Income (e.g., base rent plus other income less deductions) for lending situations involving 300 or fewer units; 4.5% of Total Effective Gross Income for lending situations involving 300 to 500 units; and 4.0% for lending situations involving more than 500 units.

Additional Considerations. Precept will determine the market management fee based on its review of the site inspection and appraisal reports. In the event that the property is borrower managed, the borrower's fee or related payroll and benefits will be evaluated in lieu of the Management Fee for purposes of the preceding analysis. The given unit figures are on a per-property basis. However, for single loans collateralized by multiple properties located in close geographical proximity, Precept will consider the aggregate the number of units for purposes of establishing the Management Fee expense.

Payroll and Benefits

Standard Definition. *Payroll and Benefits* are the total annual amount of wages paid to all personnel, including the allowable rental value of apartments given to employees as part of their compensation, payroll taxes, workman's compensation insurance, health insurance, and other employee benefits that have not been allocated directly to other expense categories.

Method of Derivation. Payroll and Benefits are determined based on a comparison of historical Payroll and Benefits at the property to apartment market and industry data. The primary basis for the Payroll and Benefits conclusion will be the property's actual three-year historical Payroll and Benefits, with emphasis placed on the most recent 12-month period for which Precept has sufficient data. If Payroll and Benefits over the three-year history are volatile or declining, Precept will use an average of Payroll and Benefits for the collected three-year history. If historical Payroll and Benefits are systematically increasing, Precept's conclusion will be consistent with the most recent 12-month period. The Payroll and Benefits conclusion will be compared to market data from one or more of the following sources: National Apartment Association (NAA), Institute of Real Estate Management (IREM), Multifamily Housing Institute, Urban Land Institute (ULI), and the appraisal report.

Additional Considerations. The first step in concluding underwritten Payroll and Benefits is to determine how the borrower has accounted for such expenses. In cases where the borrower accounts for personnel costs in functional categories (e.g., maintenance personnel under repairs and maintenance expenses and leasing staff under administration) as opposed to aggregating labor costs in one line item, Precept will conduct its analysis on the functional category level. In doing so, Precept will seek assurances that the level of staffing and staff compensation levels are adequate to operate the property in a commercially reasonable and prudent manner. When comparing the property's historical figures to market data, Precept will ensure that comparisons are meaningful in terms of accounting methodology. Precept will pay particular attention to Payroll and Benefits expenses in situations involving an owner-operated property because of the increased likelihood that reported expenses are not true indications of the Payroll and Benefits expenses necessary to operate a property with third-party management.

Utilities

Standard Definition. *Utilities* are the total annual amount of water, sewer, electricity, gas, and other applicable utility expenses.

Method of Derivation. Utilities expenses are concluded based on historical Utilities expenses. The primary basis for the Utilities conclusion will be the property's actual three-year historical Utilities expenses, with emphasis placed on the most recent 12-month period. If Utilities expenses over the three-year history are volatile or declining, Precept will utilize an average of Utilities expenses for the collected three-year history. If historical Utilities expenses are systematically increasing, Precept's conclusion will be consistent with the most recent 12-month period.

Additional Considerations. Utilities expenses are often seasonal in nature and are sometimes billed less frequently than on a monthly basis. Therefore, Precept will underwrite Utilities expenses based on a full year of operating history (if available) rather than annualizing a partial year's operating statements. Precept will include an inflation factor if the information on which the Utilities costs are calculated is older than one year. Precept will reconcile the Utilities expenses from either the trailing-12-month or most recent year-end operating statements to actual utility bills for that same period, or portion thereof if a full 12 months is not available.

Repairs and Maintenance

Standard Definition. *Repairs and Maintenance* expenses are estimates of the total annual costs of general interior and exterior Repairs and Maintenance exclusive of capital expenditures. Repairs and Maintenance costs include gardening; landscaping; exterior spot painting; elevator maintenance contracts; boiler inspection and repair contracts; heating, ventilating, and air-conditioning (HVAC) service contracts; plumbing, electrical, and window repairs; plastering; carpentry; masonry; street sweeping; light maintenance; and tenant turnover cleaning and painting. Payroll and Benefits of the maintenance personnel may or may not be included in this category, depending on the accounting system of the borrower.

Method of Derivation. Repairs and Maintenance expenses are concluded based on a comparison of historical Repairs and Maintenance expenses at the property to apartment market and industry data. The primary basis for the Repairs and Maintenance conclusion will be the property's actual three-year historical Repairs and Maintenance costs, with emphasis placed on the most recent 12-month period. If Repairs and Maintenance expenses over the three-year history are volatile or declining, Precept will use an average of Repairs and Maintenance expenses for the collected three-year history. If historical Repairs and Maintenance expenses are systematically increasing, Precept's conclusion will be consistent with the most recent 12-month period. The Repairs and Maintenance conclusion will be compared to market data from one or more of the following sources: National Apartment Association (NAA), Institute of Real Estate Management (IREM), Multifamily Housing Institute, Urban Land Institute (ULI), and the appraisal report.

Additional Considerations. Capital expenditures that add significant longevity to the remaining life of the property (e.g., new roof, new boiler, or parking lot resurfacing) should not be included in this line item. Repairs to such items, however, should be included in Repairs and Maintenance.

Marketing and Advertising

Standard Definition. *Marketing and Advertising* expenses are estimates of the annual costs to advertise and market the property to prospective tenants in order to maintain occupancy and rental rates at the level underwritten.

Method of Derivation. Marketing and Advertising expenses are concluded based on a comparison of historical Marketing and Advertising costs at the property to apartment market and industry data. The primary basis for the Marketing and Advertising conclusion will be the property's actual three-year historical Marketing and Advertising costs, with emphasis placed on the most recent 12-month period. If Marketing and Advertising expenses over the three-year history are volatile or declining, Precept will use an average of Marketing and Advertising expenses for the collected three-year history. If historical Marketing and Advertising expenses are systematically increasing, Precept's conclusion will be consistent with the most recent 12-month period. The Marketing and Advertising conclusion will be compared to market data from one or more of the following sources: National Apartment Association (NAA), Institute of Real Estate Management (IREM), Multifamily Housing Institute, Urban Land Institute (ULI), and appraisal reports.

Additional Considerations. The Marketing and Advertising expense line item will include costs associated with advertising, marketing administration, and property promotions.

Administrative

Standard Definition. *Administrative* expenses are an estimate of the annual total of all administrative costs necessary to operate the property, exclusive of Management Fees. Administrative expenses include legal and accounting fees, dues to professional organizations, and all on-site telephone and building office expenses. Depending on the borrower's method of accounting, this category may also include Payroll and Benefits for related staff.

Method of Derivation. Administrative expenses are concluded based on a comparison of historical Administrative expenses at the property to apartment market and industry data. The primary basis for the Administrative conclusion will be the property's actual three-year historical Administrative expenses, with emphasis placed on the most recent 12-month period. If Administrative expenses over the three-year history are volatile or declining, Precept will use an average of Administrative expenses for the collected three-year history. If historical Administrative expenses are systematically increasing, Precept's conclusion will be consistent with the most recent 12-month period. The Administrative expense conclusion will be compared to market data from one or more of the following sources: National Apartment Association (NAA), Institute of Real Estate Management (IREM), Multifamily Housing Institute, Urban Land Institute (ULI), and the appraisal report.

Other Variable Expense–1, 2, and 3

Standard Definition. *Other Variable Expense—1, 2, and 3* includes generic line items that are reserved for variable expenditures from the operating statements that either do not clearly fit within Precept's standard line items or that Precept determines to be more meaningful as separate line items.

In these cases, the generic Precept line-item title will be replaced with the actual operating statement line-item title. For example, an operating statement line item entitled "Unit prep and leasing fee" would be difficult to divide between Precept's standard Repairs and Maintenance and Administrative line items. Therefore, Unit Prep and Leasing Fee would be given its own title, replacing Other Variable Expense—1. In the event that Other Variable Expenses account for more than 5.0% of the Total Expenses, Precept will require explanations of such expenses and will summarize such information in either the Cash Flow Summary or Operating Statement Reconciliation sections of the underwriting summary.

Real Property Taxes

Standard Definition. *Real Property Taxes* are all taxes assessed against the real property of the property by a state or political subdivision of the state, such as a county or city, including assessments for public improvements.

Method of Derivation. Precept will conclude Real Property Taxes based on the greater of the following:

- The most recent tax bill adjusted for known increases in tax rates and/or impending upward reassessments, and any tax abatements that expire in less than 22.5 years.
- The *Market Real Property Tax* determined by the property's potential Real Property Tax liability assuming a current (near-term) reassessment or a periodic reassessment. For purposes of this estimation, Precept will attempt to follow the appropriate jurisdiction's reassessment methodology in conjunction with the following guidelines:

  Near-term reassessment. For jurisdictions where Real Property Taxes are recalculated upon transfer as a percentage of the transfer price or are generally not subject to systematic reassessments, Precept will estimate Market Real Property Tax by multiplying the appropriate local taxation rate by a proposed first mortgage amount. The proposed first mortgage amount will be an estimate of what Precept believes the loan amount will be, based on its underwriting. If no information about the potential loan amount is available, Precept generally will use a first mortgage amount equal to 75% of the estimated current property value.

  Periodic reassessment. For jurisdictions where reassessments take place on a periodic basis, Precept will estimate Market Real Property Tax, taking into account the following factors:
  - Real Property Taxes at competing properties (on a per-square-foot basis, sales price basis, etc.)
  - Trends in local commercial property values and taxation rates
  - The assumptions made by the appraisers regarding their estimate of the Real Property Tax

Additional Considerations. Precept will not underwrite Real Property Taxes below the most recent tax bill without written correspondence from the local taxation authorities confirming the lower assessment and/or taxation rate. If Precept determines it is warranted (if unique taxation structures are identified by Precept), Precept will discuss taxation frameworks with the local tax assessor to understand and clarify these issues.

Insurance

Standard Definition. *Insurance* shall mean all policies of insurance against loss or damage by fire and against loss or damage by other risks or hazards, including, without limitation, liability, riot, civil commotion, vandalism, malicious mischief, burglary, theft, flood, or earthquake.

Method of Derivation. Precept will underwrite Insurance expense at the greater of (1) the most recent insurance bill, or (2) market insurance premiums for Precept standard coverage levels for a single property policy.

Additional Considerations. Precept will adjust the Insurance expense item, described in point (2) of the preceding paragraph, upward in those instances where a property has inadequate coverage levels or below-market insurance rates (which could not be replicated by a new owner or are due to the fact that a property is covered by a blanket insurance policy covering a property and other properties that are not part of the collateral).

Other Fixed Expense–1, 2, and 3

Standard Definition. *Other Fixed Expense—1, 2, and 3* includes generic line items that are reserved for fixed expenditures from the operating statements that either do not clearly fit within Precept's standard line items or that Precept determines to be more meaningful as separate line items.

In these cases, the generic Precept line-item title will be replaced with the actual operating statement line-item title, and Precept will calculate the Other Fixed Expenses as the greater of (1) the fixed expenses for the prior 12-month period or (2) the three-year average for fixed expenses, if available. In the event that Other Fixed Expenses account for more than 3.0% of the Total Expenses, Precept will require explanations of such expenses and will summarize such information in either the Cash Flow Summary or Operating Statement Reconciliation section of the underwriting summary. Two of the more common Other Fixed Expense categories are Personal Property Tax and Ground Rent.

Personal Property Tax. The *Personal Property Tax* line item includes state and local taxes on vehicles and equipment. For multifamily properties, this expense is generally small. If expenses in this category exceed

3.0% of Total Expenses, Precept will check the historical expense information against the most recent tax bills if they are available.

Ground Rent (If Applicable). Precept will generally underwrite *Ground Rent* using 75% of the proposed amortization schedule of the loan amount.

Total Expenses

Standard Definition. Upon drawing conclusions for each of the Other Variable and Other Fixed Expense categories, Precept will compare the Total Expenses on a per-unit and percentage basis to market and industry averages and ranges.

The sources of market and industry data will include the appraisal report, the Institute of Real Estate Management, the National Apartment Association, the Multifamily Housing Institute, and the Urban Land Institute. In the event that the underwritten level of Total Expenses is not supported by this data, Precept will review its conclusions for each of the expense line items, paying particular attention to those that are closer to the lower end of the market and/or industry range. Precept will adjust these expenses either individually or in the aggregate so that the Total Expenses level underwritten is supported by market and industry statistics.

Capital Expenditures

Reserves for Replacement

Standard Definition. *Reserves for Replacement* costs are an estimate of the average annual expenditures required for replacement of building components that have shorter useful lives than the structure itself. Building components that require periodic replacement include roofs, parking lot asphalt, HVAC equipment, carpets, and appliances.

Method of Derivation. Reserves for Replacement will be concluded based on the greater of (1) $250 per unit per year and (2) the total ongoing physical needs annual average estimated in the Property Condition Assessment Summary section of the underwriting summary.

Additional Considerations. Precept will review the property condition assessment conclusions for reasonableness, taking into account the property's age, common-area structures, and overall improvement required to generate the underwritten Effective Gross Rental Income.

Other Capital Expense–1 and 2

Standard Definition. *Other Capital Expense—1 and 2* includes generic line items that are reserved for capital expenditures that were not represented in the property condition assessment's ongoing physical needs analysis or that Precept determines to be more meaningful as separate line items.

Other Capital Expenses, for example, could include an improvement recommended by the environmental engineer. Precept will require explanations of such expenses and will summarize such information in either the Cash Flow Summary or Operating Statement Reconciliation sections of the underwriting summary.

CHAPTER 5

Mobile Home Parks–Cash Flow Analysis

Mobile home parks (MHPs), or manufactured home communities, are very similar to apartment properties in terms of cash flow analysis. Lease negotiations between a landlord and tenant are largely limited to the rental rate and length of the lease agreement, and the expenses associated with operating MHPs are generally easy to understand and reconcile to industry averages. However, there are key differences between MHPs and apartment buildings.

First, the aboveground improvements are far less extensive due to the fact that the manufactured homes are typically owned by the individual tenants. Therefore, buildings within the MHP are usually limited to a management office and recreation and meeting facilities. Additional aboveground improvements are common-area landscaping, the pad slabs themselves, and stubbed utility connections. Therefore, repairs and maintenance costs for MHPs are usually significantly less than for apartment buildings on a per-unit/pad basis.

The rental of MHP pads is dependent on the availability of manufactured homes. Likewise, manufactured home dealerships are dependent on the availability of MHP pads. Therefore, manufactured home dealerships are sometimes operated in conjunction and on location with a MHP. Moreover, the ability of an MHP to satisfy demand from owners of varying types and sizes of manufactured homes (e.g., single-wides, double-wides, park models, etc.) is limited to the pad sizes of the MHP.

Given the cost associated with moving a manufactured home and the relative maturity of the average MHP tenant, tenants tend to remain in place longer, with rollovers occurring less frequently. Used manufactured homes are usually sold in-place, so that tenants change without any rollover consequence to the MHP itself. For the same reason, manufactured housing lenders are often guarantors of individual tenant leases by default, due to the fact that their collateral is dependent on the leasehold for the pad where the manufactured home resides. In a default scenario, the manufactured home lender often becomes the MHP tenant in order to maximize the value of its collateral.

At times the remote location of MHPs in suburban areas dictates that the MHPs operate their own on-site sewage treatment facilities. Proper underwriting of repair and maintenance costs for these facilities requires careful consideration.

As a result of the straightforward nature of apartment properties, income and expense conclusions (which are made for the purpose of establishing stabilized cash flow conclusions) can be drawn on a more systematic basis. Of course, multifamily properties with less traditional uses (single demand generators, shared living arrangements, etc.) create challenges to underwriting within very specific guidelines.

The following is Precept's systematic approach to cash flow analysis for MHP land uses. As previously stated, it is intentionally rigid. The value of the rigidity is that the ultimate user of its results will know exactly what is being provided. This does not imply that all MHP properties should be underwritten in strict accordance to the specific income and expense line-item derivations outlined herein. Rather, it provides a framework from which to evaluate MHP cash flows on a consistent basis, with clear documentation of exceptions to the systematic method of derivations for each component of operating cash flow.

Please refer to Chap. 4 for the relevant sections of the Precept Underwriting Summary pertaining to the concepts and methodologies contained in this chapter. Similar to its use for multifamily uses, the underwriting summary should be utilized for the capture, analysis, and maintenance of due diligence data for office and industrial properties. It is anticipated that the underwriter will complete the underwriting summary while conducting the underwriting analysis.

STEP 1: PROPERTY STATEMENT COLLECTION

Operating Statements

Precept will require the borrower to submit certified cash flow statements for (1) the past three full years (calendar or fiscal), (2) the current partial year (year to date), and (3) the prior partial year (for the same months relative to the current partial year). The borrower may substitute a complete trailing-12-month cash flow statement for the partial-year statements. In addition to the historical cash flow statements, Precept will require the borrower to submit a certified budget or pro forma for the current full year.

Additional Considerations. Precept will make every effort to obtain partial-year or trailing-12-month statements for periods that end within 3 months (partial months excluded) of the effective underwriting date.

Rent Rolls

Precept will require the borrower to provide a certified current list of tenants and their monthly financial rental obligations. Information on each tenant/apartment will include at a minimum the following information or other information sufficient to allow Precept to derive the following:

1. Pad number
2. Pad description (single-wide, double-wide, etc.)
3. Lease start date
4. Original and current lease term (month-to-month, one-year, etc.)
5. Security deposit and financial rental obligations (pad rent, storage rent, etc.)

In addition to the information just listed, Precept will also request a rent roll as of the end of each operating statement period.

Additional Considerations. In the event that rent rolls are not available as of the end of the operating statement periods, Precept will obtain rent rolls for historical points-in-time that are available.

Summary of Annual Occupancy

Precept will request that the borrower provide corresponding physical and/or economic occupancy figures for the operating statement periods. This is not a required item, given that economic occupancy during historical periods can at least be estimated by comparing actual rent collections from the operating statements to Gross Potential Rent for the same periods. Precept may request monthly occupancy statistics where either seasonality or severe income fluctuations exist.

Additional Considerations. Precept will compare the summary of annual occupancy numbers with point-in-time occupancy indicated by historical rent rolls (explained later).

Summary of Delinquencies (or Aging Report)

Precept will require the borrower to provide a current summary of tenants that are delinquent in their financial rental obligations, including the length of time each tenant has been delinquent and the dollar amount of the delinquency (summary of delinquencies). Precept will also request a summary of delinquencies as of the end of each operating statement period.

Additional Considerations. In the event that a summary of delinquencies is not available as of the end of each operating statement period, Precept will request that the borrower provide the summary for historical points-in-time that are available.

Summary of Historical Capital Expenditures

Precept will request that the borrower provide a brief description of capital expenditures made to the property made within the operating statement periods (past three years), including the timing and cost of such capital expenditures. In addition to providing relevant detail regarding the property's physical improvements, this summary will be utilized to make any necessary adjustments for nonrecurring expenditures in the Operating Statement Reconciliation section of the underwriting summary.

Additional Considerations. In addition to providing relevant detail regarding the property's physical improvements, this summary will be utilized to make any necessary adjustments for nonrecurring expenditures in the Operating Statement Reconciliation section of the underwriting summary.

STEP 2. OPERATING STATEMENT NORMALIZATION

Standard Cash Flow Line Items

Precept will use the Operating Statement Reconciliation section of the underwriting summary to normalize the operating statements as set forth herein. For mobile home park land uses, Precept's standard cash flow line items are indicated in bold typeface in the following table:

Revenues

Gross Potential Rent
 or Collected Rent
Vacancy
Credit Loss
Concessions

Effective Gross Rental Income

Other Income—1
Other Income—2
Other Income—3

Total Effective Gross Income

Expenses

Variable

Management Fee
Payroll and Benefits
Utilities
Repairs and Maintenance
Marketing and Advertising
Administrative
Other Variable Expense—1
Other Variable Expense—2
Other Variable Expense—3

Total Variable Expense

Fixed

Real Property Taxes
Insurance
Other Fixed Expense—1
Other Fixed Expense—2
Other Fixed Expense—3

Total Fixed Expense

Total Expenses

Net Operating Income

Capital Expenditures

Reserves for Replacement
Other Capital Expense—1
Other Capital Expense—2

Total Capital Expenditures

Net Cash Flow

The headings in the preceding table are group descriptions and the line items in bold italics are calculated fields. The generic line items (e.g., Other Income—1, Other Fixed Expense—1, etc.) are reserved for income and/or expenditures from the operating statements that either do not clearly fit within Precept's standard line items or that Precept determines to be more meaningful as separate line items (e.g., storage income, ground rent, etc.). In these cases, the generic Precept line-item title in the table will be replaced with the actual operating statement line-item title. For example, an operating statement line item entitled "Pad prep and leasing fee" would be difficult to divide between Precept's standard Repairs and Maintenance and Administrative line items. Therefore, Pad Prep and Leasing Fee would be given its own title, replacing Other Variable Expense—1.

Precept anticipates that a portion of borrower-provided historical operating statements will reflect Collected Rent in lieu of Gross Potential Rent and corresponding Vacancy. Therefore, Precept's standard cash flow line items allow for one or the other, but not both.

Compiling a Trailing-12-Month or Annualized Operating Statement

In some cases the borrower will have provided Precept with a current trailing-12-month operating statement that can be directly entered into the Operating Statement Reconciliation portion of the underwriting summary. In this event, Precept will compile a trailing-12-month statement or create an annualized statement, provided that the operating statements obtained from the borrower allow Precept to do so in a meaningful manner. For example, if the borrower is able to provide operating statements for the past full calendar year *A*, the current partial year *B* (year to date), and the prior partial year *C* (for the same months relative to the current partial year), the trailing-12-month cash flow would be compiled by subtracting *C*, the prior partial year, from *A*, the past full calendar year, and adding *B*, the current partial year, to the result. This compilation would be completed on a line-by-line basis, and results would appear in the Operating Statement Reconciliation portion of the model, with a "trailing-12" or "TTM" designation. Whenever possible this method of compiling the trailing-12-month cash flow will be used.

This calculation will not always be possible, given, for example, the absence of prior partial-year statements that correspond to the same number of months as the statements for the current partial year. In this event, the trailing-12-month cash flow may be calculated using the partial-year formula, or the trailing-12 may be replaced with annualized figures.

Partial-Year Formula

$$\text{TTM} = \text{current partial year} + \left[\frac{\text{most recent full year}}{12} \times (12 - x)\right]$$

where x = the number of months of operating statements used for the current partial year

Precept will determine whether to calculate the trailing-12-month cash flow using the partial-year formula or to simply annualize the current partial year on the following basis:

Current Partial-Year Operating Statements	Prior Full-Year Operating Statements	Action
Less than 6 months	None	Do not calculate TTM
Less than 6 months	Yes	Use the partial-year formula
6 months or greater	None	Annualize the period available
6 months or greater	Yes	Use the partial-year formula

STEP 3: DATA CONFIRMATION

In addition to the collection and normalization of the property's operating statements, Precept will conduct other various procedures confirming the property's operating history. If these procedures identify inaccuracies or misrepresentations within the normalized operating history, corresponding adjustments will be made and footnoted within the appropriate section of the underwriting summary, and/or the borrower may be asked to resubmit one or more property statements. Moreover, if individual income and expense line items presented in the property's operating statements are volatile from year to year, Precept may increase the sample size (length of the operating period) for data confirmation purposes.

Federal Income Tax Return Review

Precept will reconcile the property's operating statements to the borrower or current owner's most recent available federal income tax returns. Precept expects that total income reported in the tax return will be within 5% of Total Effective Gross Income reported in the operating statements. If this expectation is not met, Precept will require an explanation from the borrower, which will be noted within the Income Tax Reconciliation section of the underwriting summary.

While individual expense line-item titles often differ between tax returns and operating statements (making line-item comparisons difficult), overall expenses are expected to be consistent. To the greatest extent possible, Precept will group individual expense line items from the tax returns so that they are consistent with the expense line items of operating statements. For example, Precept may total all expense line items except Real Property Taxes and Insurance, and compare the result to the same from the operating statements. At a minimum, Precept will compare overall expenses from the tax returns, with obvious adjustments for interest and depreciation, to overall expenses from the corresponding operating statement. If comparable line items, line-item groupings, and/or Total Expenses differ between the two sources by more than 10%, Precept will require borrower explanations that will be noted within the Income Tax Reconciliation section of the underwriting summary.

Additional Considerations. Federal income tax returns may not always be available, given that some borrowers may be using the contemplated financing as purchase money. If this is the case, Precept will continue the data confirmation procedures outlined here in lieu of the income tax reconciliation.

Bank Statement Review

Precept will reconcile Total Effective Gross Income from the operating statements for the most recent 12-month period to actual bank statements reflecting property income. This reconciliation will not be conducted if the federal income tax return review is completed and yields no discrepancies with respect to property income.

Lease Reviews

Precept will review the property's standard lease agreement form to confirm basic rental payment terms.

Occupancy Review

Precept will compare the summary of annual occupancy numbers provided by the borrower with point-in-time occupancy indicated by historical rent rolls and estimated economic occupancy (derived by comparing actual rent collections from the operating statements to Gross Potential Rent for the same periods). If the operating statements do not provide a Gross Potential Rent figure, Precept will estimate it based on the historical rent rolls.

Management Fee Review

Precept will reconcile historical Management Fee expenses from the operating statements to the current management contract.

Payroll and Benefits Expense Review

Precept will reconcile historical Payroll and Benefits expenses to the borrower's summary of property employees and payroll.

Utilities Expense Review

Precept will reconcile Utilities expenses from the operating statements to actual utility bills for the most recent 12-month period.

Real Property Tax Expense Review

Precept will reconcile Real Property Taxes from the operating statements to actual tax bills for the most recent 12-month period.

Capital Expenditures Review

Precept will reconcile capital expenditures from the operating statements to the summary of historical capital expenditures provided by the borrower.

Other

Depending on (1) the results of the procedures outlined previously, (2) the sophistication of the borrower's accounting system, and (3) the volatility of individual operating statement figures, Precept may conduct additional procedures, including, but not limited to, a detailed income and expense ledger review for certain periods of time in order to better understand the components of the property's operations.

STEP 4: ESTIMATION OF STABILIZED PROPERTY CASH FLOW

As previously described, Precept will conclude an underwritten Net Cash Flow on a trailing-12-month (TTM) basis and on a leases-in-place (LIP) basis. While the process of deriving underwritten operating expenses is the same for each of these methodologies, the derivation of underwritten revenues is different.

Revenues

Gross Potential Rent

Standard Definition. *Gross Potential Rent* is an estimate of the annual fixed base rent that would be collected if the property were 100% occupied for one year.

Method of Derivation

LIP. Gross Potential Rent is calculated by annualizing the sum of (1) the total monthly rent in place for occupied pads (based on the most current rent roll) and (2) the monthly Market Rent for each vacant pad:

Gross Potential Rent (LIP) = (total monthly base rent for current tenants + monthly Market Rent for each vacant pad) × 12 months

TTM. Gross Potential Rent will equal the Gross Potential Rent figure provided in the trailing-12-month operating statement. Precept will not conclude Gross Potential Rent if the trailing-12-month operating statement does not provide such a figure.

MARKET RENT. *Market Rent* is derived by comparing property-level rental rate data from the rent roll with market data from the site inspection report and appraisal report. The primary source of the Market Rent conclusion will be actual leasing history provided by the most current rent roll. First, the rental rates from the most recent leases for each property's comparable pad type will be averaged. Second, the average comparable rental rate within the property will be compared to the market rent conclusions in the site inspection report and appraisal report to confirm that the three sources are supportive of each other. Last, provided that the site inspection report and appraisal report conclusions do not deviate from the property's comparable rental rate average by more than 5%, the Market Rent conclusion will be equal to the property's comparable rental rate average. In the event that either the site inspection or appraisal report monthly market rent conclusions deviate by more than 5% from the property's comparable rental rate average, the Market Rent conclusion will be between the high and low of the three indicators. The exact Market Rent conclusion will depend on the reason(s) for the deviations. In all cases, the exact source of the Market Rent conclusion will be noted in the underwriting summary.

Additional Considerations. Regardless of whether existing rent is below market or management has been successful in implementing rent increases, Precept will not give credit for future rental rate increases beyond the inclusion of Market Rent for vacant pads in the Gross Potential Rent calculation. For purposes of establishing Gross Potential Rent, Precept will include only rental income from pads. Precept will not give credit for manufactured home rental income in addition to pad rental income for manufactured homes owned by the borrower or related entities.

Collected Rent

Standard Definition—TTM Only. *Collected Rent* is an estimate of the annual fixed base rent that will be collected over the first year of the loan term net of actual Vacancy, Credit Loss, and Concessions. Collected Rent is reserved for the TTM methodology and will not be included if Gross Potential Rent is available.

Method of Derivation. Collected Rent is concluded based on actual rent received during the trailing-12-month period.

Additional Considerations. For purposes of establishing Collected Rent, Precept will include only rental income from pads. Precept will not give credit for manufactured home rental income in addition to pad rental income for manufactured homes owned by the borrower or related entities.

Vacancy

Standard Definition. *Vacancy* is an estimate of the annual economic loss that the property will experience from Gross Potential Rent due to a portion of the property being unoccupied and/or not leased.

Method of Derivation

LIP. Vacancy is calculated by taking the product of (1) Gross Potential Rent and (2) the greater of MHP Minimum Vacancy Percentage, Actual Vacancy Percentage, or Market Vacancy Percentage.

TTM. If Gross Potential Rent is concluded, Vacancy will equal the greater of (1) the corresponding vacancy figure from the normalized trailing-12-month operating statement or (2) the product of the MHP Minimum Vacancy Percentage and Gross Potential Rent. Otherwise, if Collected Rent is concluded, Vacancy will be calculated as follows:

$$\text{Vacancy} = \text{the greater of zero and } \{[(\text{the greater of MHP Minimum Vacancy Percentage, Actual Vacancy Percentage, or Market Vacancy Percentage}) - \text{Actual Vacancy Percentage}] \times [\text{Collected Rent}/(1 - \text{Actual Vacancy Percentage})]\}$$

where MHP Minimum Vacancy Percentage = 5%.

Note: In the event that Collected Rent is concluded in lieu of Gross Potential Rent, underwritten Vacancy percentage represents the difference between Actual Vacancy Percentage and the greater of Minimum Vacancy Percentage or Market Vacancy Percentage.

Actual Vacancy Percentage

LIP. *Actual Vacancy Percentage* is derived by dividing the sum of annual Market Rent for all vacant pads by Gross Potential Rent.

TTM. *Actual Vacancy Percentage* is equal to the reported vacancy figure for the trailing-12-month period. If a vacancy figure is not reported for the trailing-12-month period, Actual Vacancy Percentage will be derived as follows:

$$\text{Actual Vacancy Percentage} = 1 - \frac{\text{Collected Rent}}{\text{LIP Gross Potential Rent}}$$

Market Vacancy Percentage. *Market Vacancy Percentage* shall be determined by Precept after conducting a reconciliation analysis of the appraisal report's concluded market vacancy (or one minus the appraiser's concluded market occupancy) and the site inspection report's concluded market vacancy for the property. The Market Vacancy Percentage will be a number between the appraiser's concluded market vacancy (or one minus the appraiser's concluded market occupancy) and the site inspection report's concluded market vacancy.

Additional Considerations. When reviewing the appraisal and site inspection reports, Precept will pay particular attention to demand growth versus anticipated new supply and how these factors relate to stabilized occupancy for the property. Precept will also investigate the number of pads that are nonowner occupied and will increase vacancy in situations where nonowner occupancy is material.

Credit Loss

Standard Definition. *Credit Loss* is an estimate of the annual economic loss that the property will experience due to the inability to collect scheduled rent from various tenants.

Method of Derivation

LIP. Credit Loss is concluded based on a comparison of historical Credit Loss at the property to market data from the site inspection report and appraisal report. The primary basis for the Credit Loss conclusion will be the property's actual three-year historical Credit Loss, with emphasis placed on the most recent 12-month period and most recent tenant arrearage report. If Credit Loss over the three-year history is volatile or declining, Precept will use an average of Credit Loss for the collected three-year history. If historical Credit Loss is systematically increasing, Precept's conclusion will be consistent with the most recent 12-month period. The Credit Loss conclusion will be compared to similar data in the site inspection report and appraisal report to ensure that these sources are supportive of historical levels.

TTM. Credit Loss will be concluded on the same basis as LIP, except in cases where Collected Rent is used in lieu of Gross Potential Rent. In this case, the underwritten Credit Loss will represent the difference, if any, between the actual Credit Loss reflected in Collected Rent and the total stabilized Credit Loss concluded using the LIP methodology.

Additional Considerations. Many times operating statements do not separately identify Credit Loss. Precept will endeavor to determine

Credit Loss history in these cases through conversations with the borrower and, if necessary, by reconciling historical rent rolls to the appropriate operating statements. In many cases the Credit Loss adjustment to Gross Potential Rent will be incorporated in the Vacancy adjustment because property-level data and market-level data are not discerning enough for Precept to draw individual conclusions.

Concessions

Standard Definition. *Concessions* adjustments are an estimate of the annual cost of incentives that the property will offer in order to induce tenants to sign leases and take occupancy.

Method of Derivation

LIP. The Concessions adjustment is concluded based on a comparison of historical Concessions at the property to market data from the site inspection and appraisal reports. The primary basis for the Concessions conclusion will be the property's actual three-year historical Concessions in relation to Gross Potential Rent and Vacancy, with emphasis placed on the most recent 12-month period and current rent roll. The history-based Concessions conclusion will be compared to similar data in the site inspection report and appraisal report to ensure that these sources are supportive of historical levels.

TTM. Concessions will be concluded on the same basis as LIP, except in cases where Collected Rent is used in lieu of Gross Potential Rent. In this case, the underwritten Concessions will represent the difference, if any, between the actual Concessions reflected in Collected Rent and the total stabilized Concessions loss concluded using the LIP methodology.

Additional Considerations. Many times operating statements do not separately account for Concessions. In many cases the Concessions adjustment to Gross Potential Rent will be incorporated in the Vacancy adjustment because property-level data and market-level data are not discerning enough for Precept to draw individual conclusions.

Other Income—1, 2, and 3

Standard Definition. *Other Income* is an estimate of the annual recurring income generated from sources that are ancillary or incidental to the property's base rental revenue. Examples include parking fees, laundry, storage, cable, application fees, nonsufficient funds fees, and late fees.

Method of Derivation—LIP and TTM. Precept will include as underwritten revenue only those items individually or in aggregate having consistent history and strong expectations for future collections. If such amounts comprise more than 5.0% of Total Effective Gross Income, Precept will request documentation confirming and explaining the sources of revenue. Precept will base the underwritten amount of Other Income on the most recent 12-month collections or an average of historical collections for which Precept has operating statements. Underwritten Other Income in excess of 5.0% of Total Effective Gross Income will be noted as to source in either the Cash Flow Summary section or the Operating Statement Reconciliation page of the underwriting summary. The underwriting summary allows for Other Income to be categorized into three separate line items.

Additional Considerations. In cases where Other Income includes utility payments (where the borrower bills tenants for utilities using either fixed charges or submeters), Precept will include this income only to the extent that it is historically consistent and the amount of revenue from this source does not exceed the actual aggregate corresponding Utilities expense. Precept will exclude interest income from Other Income, provided that operating statements give sufficient detail from which to do so.

Expenses

Management Fee

Standard Definition. *Management Fee* is an estimate of the annual amount an independent management company would charge to comprehensively oversee the property's operations. The Management Fee does not include the cost of on-site management personnel or on-site administrative costs.

Method of Derivation. Precept will underwrite the Management Fees to equal the greater of the following:

- The management fees set forth in the current management contract.
- The market Management Fee Precept determines would be required to engage a competent third-party property management firm.

- 5% of Total Effective Gross Income (e.g., base rent plus other income less deductions) for lending situations involving 300 or less pads, or 4% of Total Effective Gross Income for lending situations involving more than 300 pads.

Additional Considerations. Precept will determine the market Management Fee based on its review of the site inspection and appraisal reports. In the event that the property is borrower managed, the borrower's fee or related Payroll and Benefits will be evaluated in lieu of the Management Fee for purposes of the preceding analysis.

Payroll and Benefits

Standard Definition. *Payroll and Benefits* are the total annual amount of wages paid to all personnel, including the allowable rental value of pads given to employees as part of their compensation, payroll taxes, workman's compensation insurance, health insurance, and other employee benefits that have not been allocated directly to other expense categories.

Method of Derivation. Payroll and Benefits are determined based on a comparison of historical Payroll and Benefits at the property to market and industry data. The primary basis for the Payroll and Benefits conclusion will be the property's actual three-year historical Payroll and Benefits, with emphasis placed on the most recent 12-month period for which Precept has sufficient data. If Payroll and Benefits over the three-year history are volatile or declining, Precept will use an average of Payroll and Benefits for the collected three-year history. If historical Payroll and Benefits are systematically increasing, Precept's conclusion will be consistent with the most recent 12-month period. The Payroll and Benefits conclusion will be compared to market data from one or more of the following sources: Institute of Real Estate Management (IREM), Urban Land Institute (ULI), Manufactured Housing Institute, and the appraisal report.

Additional Considerations. The first step in concluding underwritten Payroll and Benefits is to determine how the borrower has accounted for such expenses. In cases where the borrower accounts for personnel costs in functional categories (e.g., maintenance personnel under Repairs and Maintenance expenses and leasing staff under Administration) as opposed to aggregating labor costs in one line item, Precept will conduct its analysis on the functional category level. In doing so, Precept will seek assurances that the level of staffing and staff compensation levels are adequate to operate the property in a commercially reasonable and prudent manner. When comparing the property's historical figures to market data, Precept will ensure that comparisons are meaningful in terms of accounting methodology. Precept will pay particular attention to Payroll and Benefits expenses in situations involving an owner-operated property because of the increased likelihood that reported expenses are not true indications of the Payroll and Benefits expenses necessary to operate a property with third-party management.

Utilities

Standard Definition. *Utilities* are the total annual amount of water, sewer, electricity, gas, and other applicable utility expenses.

Method of Derivation. Utilities expenses are concluded based on historical utilities expenses. The primary basis for the Utilities conclusion will be the property's actual three-year historical Utilities expenses, with emphasis placed on the most recent 12-month period. If Utilities expenses over the three-year history are volatile or declining, Precept will utilize an average of Utilities expenses for the collected three-year history. If historical Utilities expenses are systematically increasing, Precept's conclusion will be consistent with the most recent 12-month period.

Additional Considerations. Utilities expenses are often seasonal in nature and are sometimes billed less frequently than on a monthly basis. Therefore, Precept will underwrite Utilities expenses based on a full year of operating history (if available) rather than annualizing a partial year's operating statements. Precept will include an inflation factor if the information on which the Utilities costs are calculated is older than one year. Precept will reconcile Utilities expenses from either the trailing-12-month or most recent year-end operating statements to actual utility bills for that same period, or portion thereof if a full 12 months is not available.

Repairs and Maintenance

Standard Definition. *Repairs and Maintenance* expenses are estimates of the total annual costs of general interior and exterior repairs and maintenance exclusive of capital expenditures. Repairs and Maintenance costs include gardening; landscaping; exterior spot painting; swimming pool service contracts; heating, ventilation, and air-conditioning (HVAC) service contracts; plumbing, electrical, and window repairs; plastering; carpentry; masonry; street sweeping; and light maintenance. Payroll and Benefits of the maintenance personnel may or may not be included in this category, depending on the accounting system of the borrower. Repairs and Maintenance expenses are limited to improvements owned by the mobile home park itself, such as the clubhouse, pads, streets, and other common area improvements exclusive of tenant-owned manufactured homes.

Method of Derivation. Repairs and Maintenance expenses are concluded based on a comparison of historical Repairs and Maintenance expenses at the property to market and industry data. The primary basis for the Repairs and Maintenance conclusion will be the property's actual three-year historical Repairs and Maintenance costs, with emphasis placed on the most recent 12-month period. If Repairs and Maintenance expenses over the three-year history are volatile or declining, Precept will use an average of Repairs and Maintenance expenses for the collected three-year history. If historical Repairs and Maintenance expenses are systematically increasing, Precept's conclusion will be consistent with the most recent 12-month period. The Repairs and Maintenance conclusion will be compared to market data from one or more of the following sources: Institute of Real Estate Management (IREM), Urban Land Institute (ULI), Manufactured Housing Institute, and the appraisal report.

Additional Considerations. Capital expenses that add significant longevity to the remaining life of the property (e.g., street or driveway resurfacing) should not be included in this line item. Repairs to such items, however, should be included in Repairs and Maintenance.

Marketing and Advertising

Standard Definition. *Marketing and Advertising* expenses are estimates of the annual costs to advertise and market the property to prospective tenants in order to maintain occupancy and rental rates at the level underwritten.

Method of Derivation. Marketing and Advertising expenses are concluded based on a comparison of historical Marketing and Advertising costs at the property to market and industry data. The primary basis for the Marketing and Advertising conclusion will be the property's actual three-year historical Marketing and Advertising costs, with emphasis placed on the most recent 12-month period. If Marketing and Advertising expenses over the three-year history are volatile or declining, Precept will use an average of Marketing and Advertising expenses for the collected three-year history. If historical Marketing and Advertising expenses are systematically increasing, Precept's conclusion will be consistent with the most recent 12-month period. The Marketing and Advertising conclusion will be compared to market data from one or more of the following sources: Institute of Real Estate Management (IREM), Urban Land Institute (ULI), Manufactured Housing Institute, and the appraisal report.

Additional Considerations. The Marketing and Advertising expense line item will include costs associated with advertising, marketing administration, and property promotions.

Administrative

Standard Definition. *Administrative* expenses are an estimate of the annual total costs of all administrative costs necessary to operate the property, exclusive of Management Fees. Administrative expenses include legal and accounting fees, dues to professional organizations, and all on-site telephone and building office expenses. Depending on the borrower's method of accounting, this category may also include Payroll and Benefits for related staff.

Method of Derivation. Administrative expenses are concluded based on a comparison of historical Administrative expenses at the property to apartment market and industry data. The primary basis for the Administrative conclusion will be the property's actual three-year historical Administrative expenses, with emphasis placed on the most recent 12-month period. If Administrative expenses over the three-year history are volatile or declining, Precept will use an average of Administrative expenses for the collected three-year history. If historical Administrative expenses are systematically increasing, Precept's conclusion will be consistent with the most recent 12-month period. The Administrative conclusion will be compared to market data from one or more of the following sources: Institute of Real Estate Management (IREM), Urban Land Institute (ULI), Manufactured Housing Institute, and the appraisal report.

Additional Considerations. Precept will separate administrative costs associated with manufactured home sales from administrative costs of operating the mobile home park in cases where the borrower conducts both businesses at the property. Administrative costs definitively attributable to manufactured home sales will be excluded from Precept's underwritten Net Cash Flow.

Other Variable Expense–1, 2, and 3

Standard Definition. *Other Variable Expense—1, 2, and 3* includes generic line items that are reserved for variable expenditures from the operating statements that either do not clearly fit within Precept's standard line items or that Precept determines to be more meaningful as separate line items.

In these cases, the generic Precept line-item title will be replaced with the actual operating statement line-item title. In the event that Other Variable Expenses account for more than 5.0% of the Total Expenses, Precept will require explanations of such expenses and will summarize such information in either the Cash Flow Summary or Operating Statement Reconciliation section of the underwriting summary.

Real Property Taxes

Standard Definition. *Real Property Taxes* are all taxes assessed against the real property of the property by a state or political subdivision of the state, such as a county or city, including assessments for public improvements.

Method of Derivation. Precept will conclude Real Property Taxes based on the greater of the following:

- The most recent tax bill adjusted for known increases in tax rates and/or impending upward reassessments, and any tax abatements that expire in less than 22.5 years.
- The *Market Real Property Tax* determined by the property's potential Real Property Tax liability assuming a current (near-term) reassessment or a periodic reassessment. For purposes of this estimation, Precept will attempt to follow the appropriate jurisdiction's reassessment methodology in conjunction with the following guidelines:

  Near-term reassessment. For jurisdictions where Real Property Taxes are recalculated upon transfer as a percentage of the transfer price or are generally not subject to systematic reassessments, Precept will estimate Market Real Property Tax by multiplying the appropriate local taxation rate by a proposed first mortgage amount. The proposed first mortgage amount will be an estimate of what Precept believes the loan amount will be based on its underwriting. If no information about the potential loan amount is available, Precept generally will use a first mortgage amount equal to 75% of the estimated current property value.

Periodic reassessment. For jurisdictions where reassessments take place on a periodic basis, Precept will estimate Market Real Property Tax, taking into account the following factors:

- Real Property Taxes at competing properties (on a per-square-foot basis, sales price basis, etc.)
- Trends in local commercial property values and taxation rates
- The assumptions made by the appraisers regarding their estimate of the Real Property Tax

Additional Considerations. Precept will not underwrite Real Property Taxes below the most recent tax bill without written correspondence from the local taxation authorities confirming the lower assessment and/or taxation rate. If Precept determines it is warranted (if unique taxation structures are identified by Precept), Precept will discuss taxation frameworks with the local tax assessor to understand and clarify these issues.

Insurance

Standard Definition. *Insurance* shall mean all policies of insurance against loss or damage by fire and against loss or damage by other risks or hazards, including, without limitation, liability, riot, civil commotion, vandalism, malicious mischief, burglary, theft, flood, or earthquake.

Method of Derivation. Precept will underwrite Insurance expense at the greater of (1) the most recent insurance bill, or (2) market insurance premiums for Precept standard coverage levels for a single-property policy.

Additional Considerations. Precept will adjust the Insurance expense item, described in point (2) of the preceding paragraph, upward in those instances where a property has inadequate coverage levels or below-market insurance rates (which could not be replicated by a new owner or are due to the fact that a property is covered by a blanket insurance policy covering a property and other properties that are not part of the collateral).

Other Fixed Expense—1, 2, and 3

Standard Definition. *Other Fixed Expense—1, 2, and 3* includes generic line items that are reserved for fixed expenditures from the operating statements that either do not clearly fit within Precept's standard line items or that Precept determines to be more meaningful as separate line items.

In these cases, the generic Precept line-item title will be replaced with the actual operating statement line-item title, and Precept will calculate the Other Fixed Expenses as the greater of (1) the fixed expenses for the prior 12-month period or (2) the three-year average for fixed expenses, if available. In the event that Other Fixed Expenses account for more than 3.0% of the Total Expenses, Precept will require explanations of such expenses and will summarize such information in either the Cash Flow Summary or Operating Statement Reconciliation sections of the underwriting summary. Two of the more common Other Fixed Expense categories are Personal Property Tax and Ground Rent.

Personal Property Tax. The *Personal Property Tax* line item includes state and local taxes on vehicles and equipment. For mobile home park properties, this expense is generally small. If expenses in this category exceed 3.0% of Total Expenses, Precept will check the historical expense information against the most recent tax bills if they are available.

Ground Rent (If Applicable). Precept will generally underwrite *Ground Rent* using 75% of the proposed amortization schedule of the loan amount.

Total Expenses

Standard Definition. Upon drawing conclusions for each of the Other Variable and Other Fixed Expense categories, Precept will compare the Total Expenses on a per-pad and percentage basis to market and industry averages and ranges.

The sources of market and industry data will include the appraisal report, Institute of Real Estate Management, the Manufactured Housing Institute, and the Urban Land Institute. In the event that the underwritten level of Total Expenses is not supported by this data, Precept will review its conclusions for each of the expense line items, paying particular attention to those that are closer to the lower end of the market and/or industry range. Precept will adjust these expenses either individually or in the aggregate so that the Total Expenses level underwritten is supported by market and industry statistics.

Capital Expenditures

Reserves for Replacement

Standard Definition. *Reserves for Replacement* costs are an estimate of the average annual expenditures required for replacement of the improvement components that have shorter useful lives than the improvements themselves. Property improvements that require periodic replacement include driveway asphalt and common area structures.

Method of Derivation. Reserves for Replacement will be concluded based on the greater of (1) $50 per pad per year and (2) the total ongoing physical needs annual average estimated in the Property Condition Assessment Summary section of the underwriting summary.

Additional Considerations. Precept will review the property condition assessment's conclusions for reasonableness, taking into account the property's age, common-area structures, and overall improvement condition required to generate the underwritten Effective Gross Rental Income.

Other Capital Expense–1 and 2

Standard Definition. *Other Capital Expense—1 and 2* includes generic line items that are reserved for capital expenditures that were not represented in the property condition assessment's ongoing physical needs analysis or that Precept determines to be more meaningful as separate line items.

Other capital expenses, for example, could include an improvement recommended by the environmental engineer. Precept will require explanations of such expenses and will summarize such information in either the Cash Flow Summary or Operating Statement Reconciliation sections of the underwriting summary.

CHAPTER 6

Office and Industrial Properties—Cash Flow Analysis

The complexity of underwriting office and industrial cash flows are largely attributed to the leased-fee nature of the estates. Cash flow from these land uses is subject to the terms provided for in tenant lease agreements. As a result, an in-depth review of tenant lease provisions is critical to accurate cash flow analysis. What makes this especially difficult is the fact that lease agreements are often customized to represent complicated negotiations between the tenant and landlord.

The custom nature of tenant lease agreements makes it difficult to compare rental rates to one another for purposes of evaluating their relationship to market levels. The length of lease terms can render current contractual rents irrelevant for purposes of establishing market rent for the subject property. Unless the property has recent leasing activity, the underwriter is required to rely on lease comparables from other properties and/or perform occupancy cost analysis in order to determine market rental rates.

Complicated reimbursement calculations make it difficult to reconcile actual reimbursement collections to actual expenses for the same period of time. The complicated nature of reimbursements can lead to errors in landlord billings to tenants, which can either understate or overstate actual collections when compared to contractual entitlements. At times, other landlords will not actively bill tenants for certain reimbursable expenses in light of market conditions or pending lease negotiations. Thus, reimbursements require careful consideration from the underwriter.

Physical characteristics of improvements can have a wide range of demand implications. Divisibility of space, floor-plate size and configuration, parking, turning radiuses, clearance heights, and docking are some of the more important considerations.

Finally, office and industrial cash flow analysis requires an evaluation of costs associated with re-leasing vacant space and renegotiating new leases for existing tenants upon expiration. The components of these costs include tenant improvement allowances, brokerage commissions, and free rent. Tenant improvements and free rent are negotiated in conjunction with numerous other lease provisions—most notably, rent and term. This requires that the underwriter evaluate these costs on an effective basis.

The following is Precept's systematic approach to cash flow analysis for office and industrial properties. Overall, it is intentionally rigid. The value of the rigidity is that the ultimate user of its results will know exactly what it is being provided. This does not imply that all office and industrial properties should be underwritten in strict accordance to the specific income and expense line-item derivations outlined herein. In fact, there are several areas of the following methodology that require subjective judgments by the user. However, Precept's approach does provide a framework from which to evaluate office and industrial cash flows on a consistent basis, with clear documentation of exceptions to the systematic method of derivations for each component of operating cash flow.

Please refer to Chap. 3 for the relevant sections of the Precept Underwriting Summary pertaining to the concepts and methodologies contained in this chapter. Similar to its use for retail land uses, the underwriting summary should be utilized for the capture, analysis, and maintenance of due diligence data for office and industrial properties. It is anticipated that the underwriter will complete the underwriting summary while conducting the underwriting analysis.

STEP 1: PROPERTY STATEMENT COLLECTION

Operating Statements

Precept will require the borrower to submit certified cash flow statements for (1) the past three full years (calendar or fiscal), (2) the current partial year (year to date) and (3) the prior partial year (for the same months relative to the current partial year). The borrower may substitute a complete trailing-12-month cash flow statement for the partial year statements. In addition to the historical cash flow statements, Precept will require the borrower to submit a certified budget or pro forma for the current full year.

Additional Considerations. Precept will make every effort to obtain partial year or trailing-12-month statements for periods that end within 3 months (partial months excluded) of the effective underwriting date.

Rent Rolls

Precept will require the borrower to provide a certified current list of tenants and their monthly financial rental obligations. Information on each tenant space will include at a minimum the following information or other information sufficient to allow Precept to derive the following:

1. Tenant name
2. Space identifier
3. Square footage
4. Lease start and end dates
5. Lease options
6. Financial rental obligations (base rent, reimbursements, etc.)

In addition to the information just listed, Precept will also request a rent roll as of the end of each operating statement period.

Additional Considerations. In the event that rent rolls are not available as of the end of the operating statement periods, Precept will obtain rent rolls for historical points-in-time that are available.

Summary of Annual Occupancy

Precept will request that the borrower provide corresponding physical and/or economic occupancy figures for the operating statement periods. Precept may request monthly occupancy statistics where severe income fluctuations exist. This is not a required item, given that economic occupancy during historical periods can be estimated by comparing actual rent collections from the operating statements to estimated

Gross Potential Rent for the same periods. Precept may request monthly occupancy statistics where severe income fluctuations exist.

Additional Considerations. Precept will compare the summary of annual occupancy numbers with point-in-time occupancy indicated by historical rent rolls (explained later).

Summary of Delinquencies (or Aging Report)

Precept will require the borrower to provide a current summary of tenants that are delinquent in their financial rental obligations, including the length of time each tenant has been delinquent and the dollar amount of the delinquency. Precept will also request a summary of delinquencies as of the end of each operating statement period.

Additional Considerations. In the event that a summary of delinquencies is not available as of the end of each operating statement period, Precept will request that the borrower provide the summary for historical points-in-time that are available.

Summary of Historical Capital Expenditures

Precept will request that the borrower provide a brief description of capital expenditures made to the property within the operating statement periods (past three years), including the timing and cost of such capital expenditures.

Additional Considerations. In addition to providing relevant detail regarding the property's physical improvements, this summary will be utilized to make any necessary adjustments for nonrecurring expenditures in the Operating Statement Reconciliation section of the underwriting summary.

STEP 2: OPERATING STATEMENT NORMALIZATION

Standard Cash Flow Line Items

Precept will use the Operating Statement Reconciliation section of the underwriting summary to normalize the operating statements as set forth herein. For office and industrial land uses, Precept's standard cash flow line items are indicated in bold typeface in the following table:

Revenues

Gross Potential Rent
or Collected Rent
Expense Reimbursements
Common Area Maintenance (CAM)
Real Estate Taxes
Insurance
Other Expense Recoveries

Total Expense Reimbursements

Other Income—1
Other Income—2

Total Gross Income

Mark-to-Market
Vacancy
Credit Loss

Total Effective Gross Income

Expenses

Variable
Management Fee
Payroll and Benefits
Utilities
Repairs and Maintenance
Common Area Maintenance (CAM)
Administrative
Other Variable Expense—1
Other Variable Expense—2
Other Variable Expense—3

Total Variable Expense

Fixed
Real Estate Taxes
Insurance
Other Fixed Expense—1
Other Fixed Expense—2
Other Fixed Expense—3

Total Fixed Expense

Total Expenses

Net Operating Income

Capital Expenditures
Reserves for Replacement
Retenanting Costs
Other Capital Expense—1
Other Capital Expense—2
Total Capital Expenditures
Net Cash Flow

The headings in the preceding table are group descriptions, and the line items in bold italics are calculated fields. The generic line items (e.g., Other Income—1, Other Fixed Expenses—1, etc.) are reserved for income and/or expenditures from the operating statements that either do not clearly fit within Precept's standard line items or that Precept determines to be more meaningful as separate line items (e.g., ground rent, etc.). In these cases, the generic Precept line-item title in the table will be replaced with the actual operating statement line-item title.

Precept anticipates that a portion of borrower-provided historical operating statements will reflect Collected Rent in lieu of Gross Potential Rent and corresponding Vacancy. Therefore, Precept's standard cash flow line items allow for one or the other, but not both.

Compiling a Trailing-12-Month or Annualized Operating Statement

In some cases the borrower will not have provided Precept with a current trailing-12-month operating statement that can be directly entered into the Operating Statement Reconciliation section of the underwriting summary. In this event, Precept will compile a trailing-12-month statement or create an annualized statement, provided that the operating statements obtained from the borrower allow Precept to do so in a meaningful manner. For example, if the borrower is able to provide operating statements for the past full calendar year *A*, the current partial year *B* (year to date), and the prior partial year *C* (for the same months relative to the current partial year), the trailing-12-month cash flow would be compiled by subtracting *C*, the prior partial year, from *A*, the past full calendar year, and adding *B*, the current partial year, to the result. This compilation would be completed on a line-by-line basis, and results would appear in the Operating Statement Reconciliation section of the model, with a "trailing-12" or "TTM" designation. Whenever possible this method of compiling the trailing-12-month cash flow will be used.

This calculation will not always be possible, given, for example, the absence of prior partial-year statements that correspond to the same number of months as the statements for the current partial year. In this event, the trailing-12-month cash flow may be calculated using the partial-year formula, or the trailing-12 may be replaced with annualized figures.

Partial-Year Formula

$$\text{TTM} = \text{current partial year} + \left[\frac{\text{most recent full year}}{12} \times (12 - x)\right]$$

where x = the number of months of operating statements used for the current partial year

Precept will determine whether to calculate the trailing-12-month cash flow using the partial-year formula or to simply annualize the current partial year on the following basis:

Current Partial-Year Operating Statements	Prior Full-Year Operating Statements	Action
Less than 6 months	None	Do not calculate TTM
Less than 6 months	Yes	Use the partial-year formula
6 months or greater	None	Annualize the period available
6 months or greater	Yes	Use the partial-year formula

Rent Roll Reconciliation

Precept anticipates that most borrower rent rolls will not (1) provide sufficient individual lease details and/or (2) be organized in a manner such that Precept can efficiently summarize and analyze individual lease terms for underwriting purposes. Therefore, Precept will reconstruct the rent roll provided by the borrower within the underwriting summary. This process begins by transposing the rent roll to Precept's standard rent roll summary within the underwriting summary. Precept will add to this information leasing details provided in documents separate from the rent roll (e.g., a summary of tenant improvement costs, lease termination provisions, etc.) and will show lease details on a varying basis (e.g., rent per square foot per year versus rent per square foot per month, etc.). Precept will also add to the rent roll summary market rental data and will conduct analysis such as occupancy cost and average rental rate calculations.

STEP 3: DATA CONFIRMATION

In addition to the collection and normalization of property operating statements, Precept will conduct other various procedures confirming the property's operating history. In the event that these procedures identify inaccuracies or misrepresentations within the normalized operating history, corresponding adjustments will be made and footnoted within the appropriate section of the underwriting summary, and/or the borrower may be asked to resubmit one or more property statements. Moreover, if individual income and expense line items presented in the property operating statements are volatile from year to year, Precept may increase the sample size (length of the operating period) for data confirmation purposes.

Federal Income Tax Return Review

Precept will reconcile the property operating statements to the borrower or current owner's most recent available federal income tax returns. Precept expects that total income reported in the tax return will be within 5% of Total Effective Gross Income reported in the operating statements. If this expectation is not met, Precept will require an explanation from the borrower, which will be noted within the Income Tax Reconciliation section of the underwriting summary.

While individual expense line-item titles often differ between tax returns and operating statements (making line-item comparisons difficult), overall expenses are expected to be consistent. To the greatest extent possible, Precept will group individual expense line items from the tax returns so that they are consistent with the expense line items of operating statements. For example, Precept may total all expense line items except Real Property Taxes and Insurance, and compare the result to the same from the operating statements. At a minimum, Precept will compare overall expenses from the tax returns, with obvious adjustments for interest and depreciation, to overall expenses from the corresponding operating statement. If comparable line items, line-item groupings, and/or Total Expenses differ between the two sources by more than 10%, Precept will require borrower explanations that will be noted within the Income Tax Reconciliation section of the underwriting summary.

Additional Considerations. Federal income tax returns may not always be available, given that some borrowers may be using the contemplated financing as purchase money. If this is the case, Precept will continue the data confirmation procedures outlined here in lieu of the income tax reconciliation.

Bank Statement Review

Precept will reconcile Total Effective Gross income from the operating statements for the most recent 12-month period to actual bank statements reflecting property income. This reconciliation will not be conducted if the federal income tax return review is completed and yields no discrepancies with respect to property income.

Lease Reviews

In order to confirm lease terms outlined within the current rent roll and identify special lease provisions that may materially impact the Property's future operations, Precept will review tenant lease agreements. This procedure begins by sorting the tenants by the amount of base rent payable by each tenant. Precept will then conduct a "flip" review of each lease to determine the various types of lease forms, followed by a full lease review for each tenant that represents at least 5% of the total base rental revenue up to a cumulative total of at least 70% of the Property's base rental revenue. Precept will continue beyond the 70% to the extent that a full lease review has not been performed on each lease form identified during the flip review. The results of the lease reviews will be documented in Precept's lease review form.

Additional Considerations. To the extent that financial lease terms within the leases differ from those presented in the rent roll, Precept will seek explanations from the borrower. Depending on the explanations, Precept may ask the borrower to adjust the rent roll or leases, or both. In addition, Precept may require a full lease review for 100% of the leases in order to eliminate further potential for discrepancies.

Estoppel Certificate Review

Precept will review all estoppel certificates provided by the borrower. Precept will reconcile the terms outlined in the estoppel certificates to the current rent roll and lease agreements. Precept will also investigate all tenant notes on the estoppel certificates that indicate potential problems with the physical improvements, disputes between the borrower and the tenant, etc. Precept will pay particular attention to estoppel certificates from tenants that have past-due balances reflected in the summary of delinquencies.

Occupancy Review

Precept will compare the summary of annual occupancy numbers with point-in-time occupancy indicated by historical rent rolls and estimated economic occupancy derived by comparing actual rent collections from the operating statements to Gross Potential Rent for the same periods. If the operating statements do not provide a Gross Potential Rent figure, Precept will estimate it based on the historical rent rolls.

Expense Reimbursements Review

Utilizing the indicative expense reimbursement formulas from the rent rolls and the lease reviews on an aggregate basis, Precept will recalculate total Expense Reimbursements for historical periods and compare these estimates to actual collections outlined within the operating statements.

Management Fee Review

Precept will reconcile historical Management Fee expenses from the operating statements to the current management contract.

Payroll and Benefits Expense Review

Precept will reconcile historical Payroll and Benefits expenses to the borrower's summary of property employees and payroll.

Utilities Expense Review

Precept will reconcile Utilities expenses from the operating statements to actual utility bills for the most recent 12-month period.

Real Property Tax Expense Review

Precept will reconcile Real Property Taxes from the operating statements to actual tax bills for the most recent 12-month period.

Capital Expenditures Review

Precept will reconcile capital expenditures from the operating statements to the summary of historical capital expenditures provided by the borrower.

Other

Depending on (1) the results of the procedures outlined previously, (2) the sophistication of the borrower's accounting system, and (3) the volatility of individual operating statement figures, Precept may conduct additional procedures, including, but not limited to, a detailed income and expense ledger review for certain periods of time in order to better understand the components of the property's operations.

STEP 4: ESTIMATION OF STABILIZED PROPERTY CASH FLOW

As previously described herein, Precept will conclude an underwritten Net Cash Flow on a trailing-12-month (TTM) basis and on a leases-in-place (LIP) basis. While the process of deriving underwritten operating expenses is the same for each of these methodologies, the derivation of underwritten revenues is different.

Revenues

Gross Potential Rent

Standard Definition. *Gross Potential Rent* is an estimate of the annual fixed base rent that would be collected if the property were 100% occupied for one year.

Method of Derivation

LIP. Gross Potential Rent is calculated by annualizing the sum of (1) the total monthly rent in place for occupied space (based on the most current rent roll) and (2) the monthly Market Rent for each vacant space:

Gross Potential Rent (LIP) = (total monthly base rent for current tenants + monthly Market Rent for each vacant space) × 12 months

To be considered in occupancy for purposes of the foregoing calculation, existing noncredit tenants must have paid full rent for at least one month and credit tenants must be in occupancy pursuant to an executed lease (collectively, a *qualifying lease*). Precept will review the most recent three months of rent collections to determine which tenants meet these criteria. Precept will request explanations of any discrepancies between the rent roll and actual collections, and will adjust underwritten current rent accordingly.

MARKET RENT. *Market Rent* is determined by comparing property-level rental rate data from the rent roll with market data from the site inspection report and appraisal report. Upon reviewing the site inspection report and appraisal report, Precept may also conduct direct interviews of leasing brokers in order to clarify market conditions. The primary source of the Market Rent conclusion will be actual leasing at the property within the past two years as determined from the most current rent roll.

First, Precept will average the rental rates from the most recent leases for each of the Property's comparable spaces (low-floor, medium-floor, high-floor, 0 to 1000 square feet, 1000 to 3000 square feet, etc.). Second, the average comparable rental rate within the property will be compared to the market rent conclusions in the site inspection report and appraisal report to confirm that the three sources are supportive of each other. Third, provided that the site inspection report and appraisal report conclusions do not deviate from the property's comparable rental rate average by more than 5%, the Market Rent conclusion will be equal to the property's comparable rental rate average. If either the site inspection or appraisal report market monthly rental rate conclusions deviate by more than 5% from the property's comparable rental rate average, the Market Rent conclusion will be between the high and low of the three indicators. The exact Market Rent conclusion will depend on the reason(s) for the deviations. The exact source of the Market Rent conclusion will be noted in the underwriting summary.

For purposes of the preceding analysis, rental rates will be compared on an effective basis to account for offsets or additions in the form of free rent, abnormal expense reimbursements, and tenant improvements costs that deviate dramatically from underwritten levels (discussed later). *Effective Rental Rates* will be calculated as follows:

Effective Rental Rate, $ per square foot = (base rent for the full term of the lease, $ – deviation from underwritten Expense Reimbursements and underwritten tenant improvement allowances, $ + total value of free rent for the lease term, $)/lease term, years

ADDITIONAL CONSIDERATIONS. Precept expects that the largest deviations from current Market Rent will be found for older leases. Precept will review the most recently executed leases and calculate Effective Rental Rates for a large enough sample (as determined by Precept) of tenants to determine the Effective Rental Rate levels the property is currently achieving. Precept will also calculate effective market rental rates for competitive space when possible. Overall, Precept will use its analysis of market leasing conditions to determine the relative attractiveness of the financial terms under which a tenant occupies its space and determine the leasing packages a property can expect to achieve for new leases.

Regardless of whether existing rent is below market or management has been successful in implementing rent increases upon tenant rollover, Precept will not give credit for future rental rate increases beyond the inclusion of Market Rent for vacant square footage in the Gross Potential Rent calculation.

TTM. Gross Potential Rent will equal the Gross Potential Rent figure provided in the trailing-12-month operating statement. Precept will not conclude Gross Potential Rent if the trailing-12-month operating statement does not provide such a figure.

Collected Rent

Standard Definition—TTM Only. *Collected Rent* is an estimate of the annual fixed base rent that will be collected over the first year of the loan term net of actual Vacancy and Credit Loss. Collected Rent is reserved for the TTM methodology and will not be included if Gross Potential Rent is concluded.

Method of Derivation. Collected Rent is concluded based on actual rent received in the trailing-12-month period.

Expense Reimbursements

Standard Definition. *Expense Reimbursements* are estimates of the annual amount of income the property will receive from tenants to offset variable and fixed operating expenses. Precept organizes reimbursements into four categories: (1) real property taxes, (2) insurance premiums, (3) common area maintenance (CAM), and (4) other.

Method of Derivation—LIP and TTM. Precept first concludes the actual expense levels for each of the four Expense Reimbursement categories (see the Expenses subsection of this chapter). Precept then calculates historical recovery percentages for each of the four Expense Reimbursement categories by analyzing the historical recovery percentages for trends and general stability. If the data randomly fluctuates between historical periods, Precept will use the average recovery percentage for the historical three-year period. If the recovery percentage is declining over time, Precept will use a figure at or below the most recent recovery percentage level, depending on the cause of the decline. Under the TTM methodology, Precept calculates underwritten Expense Reimbursements by multiplying the underwriting reimbursement percentage by the underwritten expense for each Expense Reimbursement category, subject to a cap at the lower of the following:

- Contractual expense recovery obligations of the tenants
- Underwritten expenses

Under the LIP methodology, the preceding derivation will include justifiable reimbursements associated with new qualifying leases.

Additional Considerations. Precept will verify tenant reimbursement obligations by performing lease reviews. Of particular importance will be reimbursement provisions for expense categories (e.g., Real Property Taxes) that Precept underwrites at a level materially in excess of the historical expense. In this case, Precept will verify that a commensurate increase in reimbursement based on the preceding methodology is supportable based on the tenant's lease obligations and overall Market Rent. Moreover, Precept may reconcile historical reimbursements to the borrower's billing summary (or actual bills if a summary is not available) to confirm collections. It is anticipated that other expense recoveries will most often represent Utilities expense reimbursements.

Other Income—1 and 2

Standard Definition. *Other Income* is an estimate of the annual recurring income generated from sources that are ancillary or incidental to the property's base rental revenue. Examples include parking fees, storage rentals, resale of utilities, and signage and antenna fees.

Method of Derivation—LIP and TTM. Precept will include as underwritten revenue only those items individually or in aggregate having consistent history and strong expectations for future collections. If such amounts comprise more than 5.0% of Total Effective Gross Income, Precept will request documentation confirming and explaining the sources of revenue. Precept will base the underwritten amount of Other Income on the most recent 12-month collections or an average of historical collections for which Precept has operating statements. Underwritten Other Income in excess of 5.0% of Total Effective Gross Income will be noted as to source in either the Cash Flow Summary section or the Operating Statement Reconciliation page of the underwriting summary. The underwriting summary allows for Other Income to be categorized into three separate line items.

Additional Considerations. Precept will exclude interest income from Other Income provided that operating statements give sufficient detail from which to do so.

Mark-to-Market

Standard Definition. *Mark-to-Market* is a downward adjustment made to Gross Potential Rent or Collected Rent to reflect the overall amount by which the property's current rental rates exceed market rates.

Method of Derivation. First, the current base rent for each comparable type of space within the property will be subtracted from the corresponding Market Rent conclusion (explained previously under Gross Potential Rent). The comparable type of space within the property will depend on the property's individual characteristics but may include low-floor, mid-floor, high-floor, 0 to 1000 square feet, 1000 to 3000 square feet, etc. Next, Precept will determine the Mark-to-Market adjustment by taking the lesser of zero or the sum of the following two subtotals:

- The sum of Market Rent less current base rent (on an annual basis) for each tenant space that is currently leased with a remaining term less than three years
- The sum of Market Rent less current base rent (on an annual basis) for each tenant space that is currently leased at a base rent that exceeds Market Rent by more than 10% and has a remaining lease term greater than three years

Vacancy

Standard Definition. *Vacancy* is an estimate of the annual economic loss that the property will experience from Gross Potential Rent, or the annual additional economic loss that the property will experience from

Collected Rent, due to a portion of the property being unoccupied and/or not leased.

Method of Derivation

LIP. Vacancy is calculated by taking the product of (1) Gross Potential Rent and (2) the greater of Office and Industrial Minimum Vacancy Percentage, Actual Vacancy Percentage, and Market Vacancy Percentage.

TTM. If Gross Potential Rent is concluded, Vacancy will equal the corresponding vacancy figure from the normalized trailing-12-month operating statement. Otherwise, if Collected Rent is concluded, Vacancy will be calculated as follows:

Vacancy = the greater of zero and {[(the greater of Office and Industrial Minimum Vacancy Percentage, Actual Vacancy Percentage, and Market Vacancy Percentage) – Actual Vacancy Percentage] × [the sum of Collected Rent/(1 – Actual Vacancy Percentage)]}

Office and Industrial Minimum Vacancy Percentage is the economic weighted average of concluded minimum vacancy for each type of space. Concluded minimum vacancy will be 0 to 5% for anchor office space, and 5 to 12% for nonanchor office space and industrial space.

In the event that Collected Rent is concluded in lieu of Gross Potential Rent, underwritten Vacancy represents the difference between Actual Vacancy Percentage and the greater of Office and Industrial Minimum Vacancy Percentage and Market Vacancy Percentage.

Anchor Office Space. For office buildings, an anchor tenant is one that: (1) comprises 20% or more of the revenue or square footage of a property, (2) has a remaining lease term of 12 years or greater, (3) does not have early lease cancellation options unless the lease contains a termination provision requiring the tenant to pay an amount that roughly equals the base rent payable through the end of the lease term, and (4) has strong credit quality as determined by Precept.

Nonanchor Office and Industrial Space. Certainty of cash flow from tenants varies greatly depending on the quality of a Property, tenant credit quality, location of the building, historical vacancy, and historical credit losses. Precept will determine minimum vacancy for nonanchor office space tenants and industrial properties by evaluating the following:

MODERATE TO STRONG PROPERTIES. For moderate to strong properties (e.g., properties at which greater than 50% of the rent roll, as determined by the number of tenants, is comprised of national and regional tenants with an Average Lease Term in excess of seven years), Precept will use a standard minimum vacancy of 5% for office land uses and 5% for industrial land uses.

WEAK PROPERTIES. Precept will use a standard minimum vacancy of 7.5% for weak properties. Precept considers a property weak if 75% of the tenants are local or small regional companies, or actual vacancy has exceeded 10% for three consecutive years.

PROPERTIES IN WEAK MARKETS. Precept will use a standard minimum vacancy of 7.5% for properties in weak markets. Precept considers a market weak if (1) market vacancy is in excess of 12%, (2) the market's economy is stagnant or is suffering from declining regional economic growth, or (3) the market's annual base rent is below $12 per square foot for office space and $2.50 per square foot for industrial space.

Actual Vacancy Percentage

LIP. *Actual Vacancy Percentage* is derived by dividing the sum of annual Market Rent for all unoccupied and/or unleased units by Gross Potential Rent.

TTM. *Actual Vacancy Percentage* is equal to the reported vacancy figure for the trailing-12-month period. If a vacancy figure is not reported for the trailing-12-month period, Actual Vacancy Percentage will be derived as follows:

$$\text{Actual Vacancy Percentage} = 1 - \frac{\text{collected rent}}{\text{LIP gross potential rent}}$$

Market Vacancy Percentage. *Market Vacancy Percentage* shall be determined by Precept after conducting a reconciliation analysis of the appraisal report's concluded market vacancy (or one minus the appraiser's concluded market occupancy) and the site inspection report's concluded market vacancy. When reviewing the appraisal report and site inspection report, Precept will pay particular attention to demand growth versus anticipated new supply and how these factors relate to stabilized occupancy for the property. The Market Vacancy Percentage will be a number between the appraiser's concluded market vacancy (or one minus the appraiser's concluded market occupancy) and the site inspection report's concluded market vacancy.

Credit Loss

Standard Definition. *Credit Loss* is an estimate of the annual economic loss that the property will experience due to the inability to collect scheduled rent from various tenants.

Method of Derivation

LIP. Credit Loss is concluded based on a comparison of historical Credit Loss at the property to market data from the site inspection report and appraisal report. The primary basis for the Credit Loss conclusion will be the property's actual three-year historical Credit Loss, with emphasis placed on the most recent 12-month period and most recent tenant arrearage report. If Credit Loss over the three-year history is volatile or declining, Precept will use an average of Credit Loss for the collected three-year history. If historical Credit Loss is systematically increasing, Precept's conclusion will be consistent with the most recent 12-month period. The Credit Loss conclusion will be compared to similar data in the site inspection and appraisal reports to ensure that these sources are supportive of historical levels.

TTM. Credit Loss will be concluded on the same basis as LIP, except in cases where Collected Rent is used in lieu of Gross Potential Rent. In this case, the underwritten Credit Loss will represent the difference, if any, between the actual Credit Loss reflected in Collected Rent and the total stabilized Credit Loss concluded using the LIP methodology.

Additional Considerations. Many times operating statements do not separately identify Credit Loss. Precept will endeavor to determine Credit Loss history in these cases through conversations with the borrower and, if necessary, by reconciling historical rent rolls to the appropriate operating statements. In many cases the Credit Loss adjustment to Gross Potential Rent will be incorporated in the Vacancy adjustment because property-level data and market-level data are not discerning enough for Precept to draw individual conclusions.

Expenses

Management Fee

Standard Definition. *Management Fee* is an estimate of the annual amount an independent management company would charge to comprehensively oversee the property's operations.

Method of Derivation. Precept will underwrite the Management Fees to equal the greater of the following:

- The management fees set forth in the current management contract
- The market Management Fee Precept determines would be required to engage a competent third-party property management firm
- 5% of Total Effective Gross Income (e.g., Gross Potential Rent + Percentage Rent + Expense Reimbursements + Other Income – Mark-to-Market – Vacancy and Credit Loss) except as noted here:
  - Single-tenant property: 3 to 4% of Total Effective Gross Income.
  - Greater than 350,000-square-feet Class A central business district properties: 4 to 4.5% of Total Effective Gross Income. For purposes of this analysis, Class A central business district properties are defined as office buildings that generally command the highest rental rates within the market, do not have any physical obsolescence, and have primary locations.
  - Single-tenant Class A central business district properties: 3 to 4% of Total Effective Gross Income.

Additional Considerations. Precept will determine the market Management Fee based on its review of the site inspection and appraisal reports. If the property is borrower-managed, the borrower's fee or related payroll and benefits will be evaluated in lieu of the Management Fee for purposes of the preceding analysis.

Payroll and Benefits

Standard Definition. *Payroll and Benefits* are the total annual amount of wages paid to all personnel, including payroll taxes, workman's compensation insurance, health insurance, and other employee benefits that have not been allocated directly to other expense categories.

Method of Derivation. Payroll and Benefits are concluded based on a comparison of historical Payroll and Benefits at the property to market and industry data. The primary basis for the Payroll and Benefits conclusion will be the property's actual three-year historical Payroll and Benefits, with emphasis placed on the most recent 12-month period for which Precept has sufficient data. If Payroll and Benefits over the three-year history are volatile or declining, Precept will use an average of Payroll and Benefits for the collected three-year history. If historical Payroll and Benefits are systematically increasing, Precept's conclusion will be consistent with the most recent 12-month period. The Payroll and Benefits conclusion will be compared to market data from one or more of the following sources: Institute of Real Estate Management (IREM), Urban Land Institute (ULI), Building Owners and Managers Association (BOMA), and the appraisal report.

Additional Considerations. The first step in concluding underwritten Payroll and Benefits is to determine where the borrower has accounted for such expenses. In cases where the borrower accounts for personnel costs in functional categories (e.g., maintenance personnel under Repairs and Maintenance expenses and leasing staff under administration) as opposed to aggregating labor costs in one line item, Precept will conduct its analysis on the functional category level. In doing so, Precept will seek assurances that the level of staffing and staff compensation levels are adequate to operate the property in a commercially reasonable and prudent manner. When comparing the property's historical figures to market data, Precept will ensure that comparisons are meaningful in terms of accounting methodology. Precept will pay particular attention to Payroll and Benefits expenses in situations involving an owner-operated property because of the increased likelihood that reported expenses are not true indications of the Payroll and Benefits expenses necessary to operate a property with third-party management. Precept will reconcile Payroll and Benefits expenses from either the trailing-12-month or most recent year-end operating statements to the borrower's written summary of all property-related labor expenses.

Utilities

Standard Definition. *Utilities* are the total annual amount of water, sewer, electricity, gas, and other applicable utility expenses.

Method of Derivation. Utilities expenses are concluded based on a historical utilities expense. The primary basis for the Utilities conclusion will be the property's actual three-year historical Utilities expenses, with emphasis placed on the most recent 12-month period. If Utilities expenses over the three-year history are volatile or declining, Precept will utilize an average of Utilities expenses for the collected three-year history. If historical Utilities expenses are systematically increasing, Precept's conclusion will be consistent with the most recent 12-month period.

Additional Considerations. Utilities expenses are often seasonal in nature and are sometimes billed less frequently than on a monthly basis. Therefore, Precept will underwrite Utilities expenses based on a full year of operating history (if available) rather than annualizing a partial year's operating statements. Precept will include an inflation factor if the information on which the Utilities costs are calculated is older than one year. Precept will reconcile Utilities expenses from either the trailing-12-month or most recent year-end operating statements to actual utility bills for that same period, or portion thereof if a full 12 months is not available.

Repairs and Maintenance

Standard Definition. *Repairs and Maintenance* expenses are estimates of the total annual costs of general interior and exterior repairs and maintenance exclusive of capital expenditures. Repairs and Maintenance costs include gardening; landscaping; exterior spot painting; elevator maintenance contracts; boiler inspection and repair contracts; heating, ventilating, and air-conditioning (HVAC) service contracts; plumbing, electrical, and window repairs; plastering; carpentry; masonry; street sweeping; light maintenance; and tenant turnover cleaning and painting. Payroll and Benefits of the maintenance personnel may or may not be included in this category, depending on the accounting system of a borrower. *Note:* All or a portion of Repairs and Maintenance expenses may be classified as CAM for underwriting purposes (see Common Area Maintenance expense category).

Method of Derivation. Repairs and Maintenance expenses are concluded based on a comparison of historical Repairs and Maintenance expenses at the property to market and industry data. The primary basis for the Repairs and Maintenance conclusion will be the property's actual three-year historical Repairs and Maintenance costs, with emphasis placed on the most recent 12-month period. If Repairs and Maintenance expenses over the three-year history are volatile or declining, Precept will use an average of Repairs and Maintenance expenses for the collected three-year history. If historical Repairs and Maintenance expenses are systematically increasing, Precept's conclusion will be consistent with the most recent 12-month period. The Repairs and Maintenance conclusion will be compared to market data from one or more of the following sources: Institute of Real Estate Management (IREM), Urban Land Institute (ULI), Building Owners and Managers Association (BOMA), and the appraisal report.

Additional Considerations. Capital expenses that add significant longevity to the remaining life of the property (e.g., new roof, new boiler, or parking lot resurfacing) should not be included in this line item. Repairs to such items, however, should be included in Repairs and Maintenance.

Common Area Maintenance

Standard Definition. *Common Area Maintenance* (CAM) is an estimate of Repairs and Maintenance expenses that are necessary to maintain property components common to all tenants. For underwriting purposes, this category is reserved for expenses that are contractually reimbursed by tenants in whole or in part. The CAM line item will be underwritten only if the property's operating statements provide sufficient detail to differentiate CAM expenses from overall Repairs and Maintenance. Absent this detail, all CAM expenses will be grouped with overall Repairs and Maintenance expenses under the heading Repairs and Maintenance as previously noted, and the CAM line item will be left blank.

Method of Derivation. CAM is concluded based on a comparison of historical CAM at the property to market and industry data. The primary basis for the CAM conclusion will be the property's actual three-year historical CAM, with emphasis placed on the most recent 12-month period. If CAM over the three-year history is volatile or declining, Precept will use an average of CAM for the collected three-year history. If historical CAM is systematically increasing, Precept's conclusion will be consistent with the most recent 12-month period. The sum of the CAM and Repairs and Maintenance conclusions will be compared to overall Repairs and Maintenance market data from one or more of the following sources: Institute of Real Estate Management (IREM), Urban Land Institute (ULI), Building Owners and Managers Association (BOMA), and the appraisal report.

Administrative

Standard Definition. *Administrative* expenses are an estimate of the annual total of all administrative costs necessary to operate the property, exclusive of Management Fees. Administrative expenses include legal and accounting fees, marketing and advertising, dues to professional organizations, and all on-site telephone and building office expenses. Depending on the borrower's method of accounting, this category may also include Payroll and Benefits for related staff.

Method of Derivation. Administrative expenses are concluded based on a comparison of historical Administrative expenses at the property to market and industry data. The primary basis for the Administrative expense conclusion will be the property's actual three-year historical Administrative expenses, with emphasis placed on the most recent 12-month period. If Administrative expenses over the three-year history are volatile or declining, Precept will use an average of Administrative expenses for the collected three-year history. If historical Administrative expenses are systematically increasing, Precept's conclusion will be consistent with the most recent 12-month period. The Administrative expense conclusion will be compared to market data from one or more of the following sources: Institute of Real Estate Management (IREM), Urban Land Institute (ULI), Building Owners and Managers Association (BOMA), and the appraisal report.

Additional Considerations. Administrative expenses include the annual cost to advertise and market the property to prospective tenants in order to maintain occupancy and rental rates at the level underwritten. To the extent that marketing and advertising expenses represent more than 25% of total Administrative costs, Precept will separate marketing and advertising from Administrative expenses by utilizing one of the Other Variable Expense line items noted in the next subsection. The marketing and advertising expense line item may include, among other things, costs associated with advertising, marketing administration, property promotions, and merchant association contributions. To the extent that the property's space is not leased using third-party broker representation, Precept will attempt to recategorize in-house and on-site leasing expenses from Administration to Retenanting Costs (described later).

Other Variable Expense–1, 2, and 3

Standard Definition. *Other Variable Expense—1, 2, and 3* includes generic line items that are reserved for variable expenditures from the operating statements that either do not clearly fit within Precept's standard line items or that Precept determines to be more meaningful as separate line items.

In these cases, the generic Precept line-item title will be replaced with the actual operating statement line-item title. In the event that Other Variable Expenses account for more than 5.0% of the Total Expenses, Precept will require explanations of such expenses and will summarize such information in either the Cash Flow Summary or Operating Statement Reconciliation section of the underwriting summary.

Real Property Taxes

Standard Definition. *Real Property Taxes* are all taxes assessed against the real property of the property by a state or political subdivision of the state, such as a county or city, including assessments for public improvements.

Method of Derivation. Precept will conclude Real Property Taxes based on the greater of the following:

- The most recent tax bill adjusted for known increases in tax rates and/or impending upward reassessments, and any tax abatements that expire in less than 22.5 years.
- The *Market Real Property Tax* determined by the property's potential Real Property Tax liability assuming a current (near-term) reassessment or a periodic reassessment. For purposes of this estimation, Precept will attempt to follow the appropriate jurisdiction's reassessment methodology in conjunction with the following guidelines:

  Near-term reassessment. For jurisdictions where Real Property Taxes are recalculated upon transfer as a percentage of the transfer price or are generally not subject to systematic reassessments, Precept will estimate Market Real Property Tax by multiplying the appropriate local taxation rate by a proposed first mortgage amount. The proposed first mortgage amount will be an estimate of what Precept believes the loan amount will be based on its underwriting. If no information about the potential loan amount is available, Precept generally will use a first mortgage amount equal to 75% of the estimated current property value.

  Periodic reassessment. For jurisdictions where reassessments take place on a periodic basis, Precept will estimate Market Real Property Tax, taking into account the following factors:

  - Real property taxes at competing properties (on a per-square-foot basis, sales price basis, etc.)
  - Trends in local commercial property values and taxation rates
  - The assumptions made by the appraisers regarding their estimate of the Real Property Tax

Additional Considerations. Precept will not underwrite Real Property Taxes below the most recent tax bill without written correspondence from the local taxation authorities confirming the lower assessment and/or taxation rate. If Precept determines it is warranted (if unique taxation structures are identified by Precept), Precept will discuss taxation frameworks with the local tax assessor to understand and clarify these issues.

Insurance

Standard Definition. *Insurance* shall mean all policies of insurance against loss or damage by fire and against loss or damage by other risks or hazards, including, without limitation, liability, riot, civil commotion, vandalism, malicious mischief, burglary, theft, flood, or earthquake.

Method of Derivation. Precept will underwrite Insurance expense at the greater of (1) the most recent insurance bill, or (2) market insurance premiums for Precept standard coverage for a single property policy.

Precept will adjust the Insurance expense item, described in point (2) of the preceding paragraph, upward in those instances where a property has inadequate coverage levels or below-market insurance rates (which could not be replicated by a new owner or are due to the fact that a property is covered by a blanket insurance policy covering a property and other properties that are not part of the collateral).

Other Fixed Expense–1, 2, and 3

Standard Definition. *Other Fixed Expense—1, 2, and 3* includes generic line items that are reserved for fixed expenditures from the operating statements that either do not clearly fit within Precept's standard line items or that Precept determines to be more meaningful as separate line items.

In these cases, the generic Precept line-item title will be replaced with the actual operating statement line-item title, and Precept will calculate the Other Fixed Expenses as the greater of (1) the fixed expenses for the prior 12-month period and (2) the three-year average for fixed expenses, if available. In the event that Other Fixed Expenses account for more than 3.0% of the Total Expenses, Precept will require explanations of such expenses and will summarize such information in either the Cash Flow Summary or Operating Statement Reconciliation section of the underwriting summary. One of the more common Other Fixed Expense categories is Ground Rent.

Ground Rent (If Applicable). Precept will generally underwrite *Ground Rent* using 75% of the proposed amortization schedule of the loan amount.

Total Expenses

Standard Definition. Upon drawing conclusions for each of the Other Variable and Other Fixed Expense categories, Precept will compare the Total Expenses on a per-unit and percentage basis to market and industry averages and ranges.

The sources of market and industry data will include the appraisal report, the Institute of Real Estate Management, and the Urban Land Institute. In the event that the underwritten level of Total Expenses is not supported by this data, Precept will review its conclusions for each of the expense line items, paying particular attention to those that are closer to the lower end of the market and/or industry range. Precept will adjust these expenses either individually or in the aggregate so that the Total Expenses level underwritten is supported by market and industry statistics.

Capital Expenditures

Reserves for Replacement

Standard Definition. *Reserves for Replacement* costs are an estimate of the average annual expenditures required for replacement of building components that have shorter useful lives than the structure itself. Building components that require periodic replacement include roofs, parking lot asphalt, elevators, HVAC equipment, windows, etc.

Method of Derivation. Reserves for Replacement will be concluded based on the greater of (1) $0.20 per square foot of total leasable area per year for office properties or $0.10 per square foot of total leasable area per year for industrial properties and (2) the total ongoing physical needs annual average estimated in the Property Condition Assessment summary section of the underwriting summary.

Additional Considerations. Precept will review the property condition assessment's conclusions for reasonableness, taking into account the property's age, common-area structures, and overall improvement condition required to generate the underwritten Effective Gross Rental Income.

Retenanting Costs

Standard Definition. *Retenanting Costs* are broken into two categories: (1) tenant improvements (TIs) and (2) leasing commissions (LCs). TIs include the costs associated with improving space in order to induce tenants to execute leases and take occupancy. LCs are fees paid to brokers involved in bringing the property and tenant together.

Method of Derivation. Precept will first group each tenant into logical categories similar to the comparable space groupings made during the Market Rent analysis (low-floor, mid-floor, high-floor, 0 to 1000 square feet, 1000 to 3000 square feet etc.). For each space grouping, Precept will then make assumptions for renewal probability, average lease term, average lease rental rate, tenant improvement allowances, and leasing commissions. Using the following formula, below, Precept will calculate the estimated *Average Annual Tenant Improvement Amount* and *Leasing Commission Amount* for each space grouping, the aggregate sum of which will be used by Precept as the underwritten Retenanting Costs:

Average Annual Tenant Improvement Amount, \$ = (Retenanting Square Footage per Annum × Renewal Probability, % × renewal tenant improvement per square foot, \$) + [Retenanting Square Footage per Annum × (1 – Renewal Probability, %) × new tenant improvement per square foot, \$]

Leasing Commission Amount, \$ = (Retenanting Square Footage per Annum × average rental rate per square foot per year, \$ × Renewal Probability, % × renewal leasing commission, %) + [Retenanting Square Footage per Annum × average rental rate per square foot per year, \$ × (1 – Renewal Probability, %) × new leasing commission, %]

Note: for purposes of the preceding calculation, the *Retenanting Square Footage per Annum* = total square footage of space for which rental revenue was underwritten/Average Lease Term, years.

Renewal Probability. *The Renewal Probability* value is the estimated probability that a tenant will renew its lease upon expiration. Precept will assume that 60% of the tenants (measured by square footage) will renew their leases upon expiration. Notwithstanding this rule, Precept may assign renewal probabilities of greater than 60% (but in no event higher than 70%) if Precept is provided with evidence proving historical tenant retention in excess of 60% for leases which have expired over the previous five years. This evidence is not required as part of the loan submission package and will need to be obtained specifically for buildings with high retention rates. Furthermore, Precept may assign renewal probabilities of less than 60% when Precept believes that more than 60% of the tenants (by square footage) will vacate upon lease expiration (e.g., tenant base does not appear stable, a property has significantly higher vacancy than its competitors, or tenant sales are rapidly declining).

Average Lease Term. An *Average Lease Term* assumption is necessary for each space grouping when calculating Retenanting Costs. To estimate the stabilized annual square footage rollover, Precept will divide the total square footage for each tenant space grouping by an assumed Average Lease Term for each space grouping. In making lease term assumptions, Precept will review the following: (1) leases executed within the last two years at the property, (2) the remaining average lease terms for the tenants at the property, and (3) the average lease term for comparable leases in the market, to establish supportable assumptions. Precept will use an Average Lease Term that is consistent with leases being signed in the market unless property leasing activity supports a deviation from the market term. Nonmarket leases may also have nonmarket TIs, as TIs are correlated with lease terms (e.g., longer lease terms receive higher tenant improvement amounts). Lease terms longer than those being signed at a property should be used in rollover calculations only when tenant improvement amounts are being underwritten at amounts higher than those being given at the property.

Lease Rental Rate. Precept will use the lower of the average rental rate in place at a property or the Market Rent for each space grouping. Precept does not use a higher rental rate in situations where the lease rates for the current tenants are below market because the increased cost for leasing commissions associated with new leases will be offset by the increase in rental revenue from these same leases. Precept's underwritten rental revenue does not include the potentially higher rental revenue associated with retenanting, and, therefore, does not include the associated higher leasing commissions.

Tenant Improvements. For purposes of this analysis, TIs include free rent given by the owner in lieu of or in addition to a tenant improvement allowance. Precept evaluates these two components of Retenanting Costs together, given the dependency that improvement allowances and free rent often have on each other during lease negotiations (e.g., free rent during the build-out of space, free rent in lieu of tenant improvements, etc.). The amount of TI required to sign new tenants customarily is two to three times the amount of concessions required to sign renewal tenants. Precept will determine underwritten TI and free rent on a per-square-foot basis for each space grouping. Precept will make two calculations, one for new leases and the other for renewal leases using market data and the Average Lease Term for each space grouping. Precept's assumptions regarding TI and free rent will be similar to those found in comparable leases with the same average lease term. Better than average credit quality tenants, larger tenants, and longer lease terms will generally receive a higher level of concessions.

Leasing Commissions. LCs are fees paid to brokers that represent the owner of a property (*listing broker*) or that represent a tenant (*procuring broker*). Precept will review the LC schedule for the market in which a property is located and identify the party responsible for paying the LCs. In some instances, space can be leased directly from an owner to a tenant without a broker. In most instances, however, the owner and the tenant each have a broker. A property owner almost always pays the listing broker and usually pays the procuring broker. Depending on the market, the brokers will each get paid separate commissions or split a total commission (calculated as a percentage of the total base rent payable over the term of the lease) ranging from 2.5% to 4.0% for renewal leases and 4.0 to 6.0% for new leases. In some markets and more typically for large spaces, LCs are calculated on a square-foot basis rather than as a percentage of total base rent due. Commissions taking this form generally range from $2 to $5 per square foot. Precept will make two calculations for LCs, one for new leases and one for renewal leases. For underwriting purposes, Precept will determine the LC rate for each space grouping and the total commissions paid in the market by landlords assuming all leases are signed using third-party leasing brokers. Precept will not underwrite LCs at less than 4% of total lease term rental revenue for new leases and 2% for renewals (without adequate support).

Unlike other expense categories, underwriting Retenanting Costs is largely independent of the historical cost. Retenanting Costs fluctuate significantly from year to year, depending on the quantity and type of space being leased and whether the leases involve new or renewal tenants. The cost of both TIs and LCs tend to be higher (historically at least double) for new leases than for renewal leases. Precept will underwrite Retenanting Costs on a lease-specific basis by grouping the existing tenants into logical groups and estimating future Retenanting Costs for each group.

Additional Considerations. Precept may look to the following sources of information to determine current market conditions for TIs and LCs, free rent, and lease terms:

- All leases executed over the last three years at a property
- The current leasing package offered at a property for each space grouping, using information from discussions with the borrower and the borrower's leasing representative
- The appraiser's rollover cost assumptions using the appraisal report
- Leasing packages for comparable space currently available and comparable signed leases in the market during the last two years

Other Capital Expense–1 and 2

Standard Definition. *Other Capital Expense—1 and 2* includes generic line items that are reserved for capital expenditures that were not represented in the property condition assessment's ongoing physical needs analysis or that Precept determines to be more meaningful as separate line items.

Other Capital Expenses, for example, could include an improvement recommended by the property condition assessment report. Precept will require explanations of such expenses and will summarize such information in either the Cash Flow Summary or Operating Statement Reconciliation section of the underwriting summary.

CHAPTER 7

Hospitality Properties—Cash Flow Analysis

Hospitality properties can also be very complex assets to underwrite, for three basic reasons. First, hospitality properties operate under what may be considered a daily lease structure, where, based on a variety of external factors, rental rates can change instantly. It is for this reason that underwriters must be extremely careful about additions to room supply in the subject market. Second, this asset class generally has the highest operating leverage, which means that a relatively minor change in revenues can have a major proportional impact on net cash flows. Third, regardless of the limited- or full-service nature of a given property, in all instances the underwriter is analyzing an operating business where a good portion of the customer experience and subsequent retention remains management driven.

The following is Precept's systematic approach to cash flow analysis for hotels. Overall, it is intentionally rigid. The value of the rigidity is that the ultimate user of its results will know exactly what is being provided. This does not imply that all hotel properties should be underwritten in strict accordance to the specific income and expense line-item derivations outlined herein. In fact, there are several areas of the following methodology that require subjective judgments by the user. However, Precept's approach does provide a framework from which to evaluate retail cash flows on a consistent basis, with clear documentation of exceptions to the systematic method of derivations for each component of operating cash flow.

For your reference, following are the relevant sections of the Precept

Underwriting Summary pertaining to the concepts and methodologies contained in this chapter and specific to hotels. This underwriting summary should be utilized for the capture, analysis, and maintenance of underwriting-related due diligence data. It is anticipated that the underwriter will complete the underwriting summary while conducting the underwriting analysis.

PRECEPT™

CASH FLOW SUMMARY

Property Name

Type of Financials: | | Income | |

Property Number: 0000

Deal Number: 0000

Rooms: 0

	RevPAR: 1998		RevPAR: 1999		RevPAR: TTM		RevPAR: Precept TTM		Comments
	# of Days in Year	365	# of Days in Year	365	# of Days in Year	365	# of Days in Year	365	
	# of Rooms	0	# of Rooms	0	# of Rooms	0	# of Rooms	0	
N	Occupancy %	0.00%	Occupancy %	0.00%	Occupancy %	0.00%	Occupancy %	0.00%	
O	ADR	$0.00	ADR	$0.00	ADR	$0.00	ADR	$0.00	
T	Total Occ. Rooms	0	Total Occ. Rooms	0	Total Occ. Rooms	0	Total Occ. Rooms	0	
E	Total Rooms Avail.	0	Total Rooms Avail.	0	Total Rooms Avail.	0	Total Rooms Avail.	0	
S									

	1998 $PAR	1998 $POR	1998 % REV	1998	1999 $PAR	1999 $POR	1999 % REV	1999	TTM $PAR	TTM $POR	TTM % REV	TTM	Precept TTM $PAR	Precept TTM $POR	Precept TTM % REV	Precept TTM
	Through: 12/31/1998				Through: 12/31/1999											
REVENUES																
Room Revenue	-	-	-	-	-	-	-	-	-	-	-	-	-	-	-	-
Food & Beverage	-	-	-	-	-	-	-	-	-	-	-	-	-	-	-	-
Telecommunications	-	-	-	-	-	-	-	-	-	-	-	-	-	-	-	-
Other Operated Departments	-	-	-	-	-	-	-	-	-	-	-	-	-	-	-	-
Other Departmental Revenue	-	-	-	-	-	-	-	-	-	-	-	-	-	-	-	-
Total Revenue	-	-	-	-	-	-	-	-	-	-	-	-	-	-	-	-
EXPENSES																
Departmental																
Room Expense	-	-	-	-	-	-	-	-	-	-	-	-	-	-	-	-
Food & Beverage	-	-	-	-	-	-	-	-	-	-	-	-	-	-	-	-
Telecommunications	-	-	-	-	-	-	-	-	-	-	-	-	-	-	-	-
Other Operated Departments	-	-	-	-	-	-	-	-	-	-	-	-	-	-	-	-
Other Departmental Expense	-	-	-	-	-	-	-	-	-	-	-	-	-	-	-	-
Total Departmental Expense	-	-	-	-	-	-	-	-	-	-	-	-	-	-	-	-
GROSS OPERATING INCOME	-	-	-	-	-	-	-	-	-	-	-	-	-	-	-	-
Undistributed																
Management	-	-	-	-	-	-	-	-	-	-	-	-	-	-	-	-
Franchise Fees	-	-	-	-	-	-	-	-	-	-	-	-	-	-	-	-
Marketing	-	-	-	-	-	-	-	-	-	-	-	-	-	-	-	-
Administrative	-	-	-	-	-	-	-	-	-	-	-	-	-	-	-	-
Operation and Maintenance	-	-	-	-	-	-	-	-	-	-	-	-	-	-	-	-
Utilities	-	-	-	-	-	-	-	-	-	-	-	-	-	-	-	-
Other Undistributed Expense	-	-	-	-	-	-	-	-	-	-	-	-	-	-	-	-
Total Undistributed Expense	-	-	-	-	-	-	-	-	-	-	-	-	-	-	-	-
GROSS OPERATING PROFIT	-	-	-	-	-	-	-	-	-	-	-	-	-	-	-	-
Fixed													-	-		
Real Estate Taxes	-	-	-	-	-	-	-	-	-	-	-	-	-	-	-	-
Insurance	-	-	-	-	-	-	-	-	-	-	-	-	-	-	-	-
Other Fixed Expense - 1	-	-	-	-	-	-	-	-	-	-	-	-	-	-	-	-
Other Fixed Expense - 2	-	-	-	-	-	-	-	-	-	-	-	-	-	-	-	-
Other Fixed Expense - 3	-	-	-	-	-	-	-	-	-	-	-	-	-	-	-	-
Total Fixed Expense	-	-	-	-	-	-	-	-	-	-	-	-	-	-	-	-
Capital Expenditures																
FF&E (Reserve)	-	-	-	-	-	-	-	-	-	-	-	-	-	-	-	-
Other Capital Expense - 1	-	-	-	-	-	-	-	-	-	-	-	-	-	-	-	-
Other Capital Expense - 2	-	-	-	-	-	-	-	-	-	-	-	-	-	-	-	-
Total Capital Expenditures	-	-	-	-	-	-	-	-	-	-	-	-	-	-	-	-
NET CASH FLOW	-	-	-	-	-	-	-	-	-	-	-	-	-	-	-	-

Notes:

PRECEPT™

Property Number: 0000
Deal Number: 0000

CASH FLOW SUMMARY (Continued)
Property Name

Property Number: 0000
Deal Number: 0000
Rooms: 0

RevPAR: Precept TTM		RevPAR: Rating Agency		RevPAR: Bidder	
# of Days in Year	365	# of Days in Year	365	# of Days in Year	365
# of Rooms	0	# of Rooms	0	# of Rooms	0
Occupancy %	0.00%	Occupancy %		Occupancy %	
ADR	$0.00	ADR		ADR	
Total Occ. Rooms	0	Total Occ. Rooms	0	Total Occ. Rooms	
Total Rooms Avail.	0	Total Rooms Avail.	0	Total Rooms Avail.	0

	Precept TTM $PAR	$POR	% REV		NOTES	Rating Agency $PAR	$POR	% REV		NOTES	Comments	Bidder $PAR	$POR	% REV		NOTES	Comments
REVENUES																	
Room Revenue	-	-	-	-		-	-	-	-			-	-	-	-		
Food & Beverage	-	-	-	-		-	-	-	-			-	-	-	-		
Telecommunications	-	-	-	-		-	-	-	-			-	-	-	-		
Other Operated Departments	-	-	-	-		-	-	-	-			-	-	-	-		
Other Departmental Revenue	-	-	-	-		-	-	-	-			-	-	-	-		
Total Revenue	-	-	-	-		-	-	-	-			-	-	-	-		
EXPENSES																	
Departmental																	
Room Expense	-	-	-	-		-	-	-	-			-	-	-	-		
Food & Beverage	-	-	-	-		-	-	-	-			-	-	-	-		
Telecommunications	-	-	-	-		-	-	-	-			-	-	-	-		
Other Operated Departments	-	-	-	-		-	-	-	-			-	-	-	-		
Other Departmental Expense	-	-	-	-		-	-	-	-			-	-	-	-		
Total Departmental Expense	-	-	-	-		-	-	-	-			-	-	-	-		
GROSS OPERATING INCOME	-	-	-	-		-	-	-	-			-	-	-	-		
Undistributed																	
Management	-	-	-	-		-	-	-	-			-	-	-	-		
Franchise Fees	-	-	-	-		-	-	-	-			-	-	-	-		
Marketing	-	-	-	-		-	-	-	-			-	-	-	-		
Administrative	-	-	-	-		-	-	-	-			-	-	-	-		
Operation and Maintenance	-	-	-	-		-	-	-	-			-	-	-	-		
Utilities	-	-	-	-		-	-	-	-			-	-	-	-		
Other Undistributed Expense	-	-	-	-		-	-	-	-			-	-	-	-		
Total Undistributed Expense	-	-	-	-		-	-	-	-			-	-	-	-		
GROSS OPERATING PROFIT	-	-	-	-		-	-	-	-			-	-	-	-		
Fixed	-	-										-	-				
Real Estate Taxes	-	-	-	-		-	-	-	-			-	-	-	-		
Insurance	-	-	-	-		-	-	-	-			-	-	-	-		
Other Fixed Expense - 1	-	-	-	-		-	-	-	-			-	-	-	-		
Other Fixed Expense - 2	-	-	-	-		-	-	-	-			-	-	-	-		
Other Fixed Expense - 3	-	-	-	-		-	-	-	-			-	-	-	-		
Total Fixed Expense	-	-	-	-		-	-	-	-			-	-	-	-		
Capital Expenditures																	
FF&E (Reserve)	-	-	-	-		-	-	-	-			-	-	-	-		
Other Capital Expense - 1	-	-	-	-		-	-	-	-			-	-	-	-		
Other Capital Expense - 2	-	-	-	-		-	-	-	-			-	-	-	-		
Total Capital Expenditures	-	-	-	-		-	-	-	-			-	-	-	-		
NET CASH FLOW	-	-	-	-		-	-	-	-			-	-	-	-		

Notes:

PRECEPT™

Property Number: 0000
Deal Number: 0000

CASH FLOW SUMMARY (Continued)

Property Name

Type of Financials:

Property Number: 0000
Deal Number: 0000
Rooms: 0

RevPAR:	
# of Days in Year	
# of Rooms	
Occupancy %	0.00%
ADR	$0.00
Total Occ. Rooms	
Total Rooms Avail.	
$PAR $POR % REV	

RevPAR:	
# of Days in Year	
# of Rooms	
Occupancy %	0.00%
ADR	$0.00
Total Occ. Rooms	
Total Rooms Avail.	
$PAR $POR % REV	

Comments

RevPAR: Appraiser	
# of Days in Year	365
# of Rooms	0
Occupancy %	0.00%
ADR	$0.00
Total Occ. Rooms	0
Total Rooms Avail.	0
$PAR $POR % REV	

RevPAR: Budget	
# of Days in Year	365
# of Rooms	0
Occupancy %	0.00%
ADR	$0.00
Total Occ. Rooms	0
Total Rooms Avail.	0
$PAR $POR % REV	

Comments

Comments

	Appraiser	$PAR	$POR	% REV	Budget	$PAR	$POR	% REV
REVENUES								
Room Revenue	-	-	-	-	-	-	-	-
Food & Beverage	-	-	-	-	-	-	-	-
Telecommunications	-	-	-	-	-	-	-	-
Other Departmental Revenue	-	-	-	-	-	-	-	-
Total Revenue	-	-	-	-	-	-	-	-
EXPENSES								
Departmental								
Room Expense	-	-		-	-	-		-
Food & Beverage	-	-		-	-	-		-
Telecommunications	-	-		-	-	-		-
Other Departmental Expense	-	-		-	-	-		-
Total Departmental Expense	-	-	-	-	-	-	-	-
GROSS OPERATING INCOME	-	-	-	-	-	-	-	-
Undistributed								
Management	-	-	-	-	-	-	-	-
Franchise Fees	-	-	-	-	-	-	-	-
Marketing	-	-	-	-	-	-	-	-
Administrative	-	-	-	-	-	-	-	-
Operation and Maintenance	-	-	-	-	-	-	-	-
Utilities	-	-	-	-	-	-	-	-
Other Undistributed Expense	-	-	-	-	-	-	-	-
Total Undistributed Expense	-	-	-	-	-	-	-	-
GROSS OPERATING PROFIT	-	-	-	-	-	-	-	-
Fixed								
Real Estate Taxes	-	-	-	-	-	-	-	-
Insurance	-	-	-	-	-	-	-	-
Other Fixed Expense - 1	-	-	-	-	-	-	-	-
Other Fixed Expense - 2	-	-	-	-	-	-	-	-
Other Fixed Expense - 3	-	-	-	-	-	-	-	-
Total Fixed Expense	-	-	-	-	-	-	-	-
Capital Expenditures								
FF&E (Reserve)	-	-	-	-	-	-	-	-
Other Capital Expense - 1	-	-	-	-	-	-	-	-
Other Capital Expense - 2	-	-	-	-	-	-	-	-
Total Capital Expenditures	-	-	-	-	-	-	-	-
NET CASH FLOW	-	-	-	-	-	-	-	-

PRECEPT™

OP STMT RECONCILIATION

Property Name

Property Number: 0000
Deal Number: 0000
Rooms: 0

	1	2	3	4
	1997	**1998**	**1999**	**TTM**
# of Days in Year	365	365	365	365
# of Rooms	0	0	0	0
Occupancy %	0.00%	0.00%	0.00%	0.00%
ADR	$0.00	$0.00	$0.00	$0.00
Occ. Rooms during Year	0	0	0	0
Avail. Rooms during Year	0	0	0	0
Through:	12/31/1997	12/31/1998	12/31/1999	
Stmt. Type:			Income	

NOTES

REVENUES

	1997 Statement	1997 Adjustment	1997 Operating	1998 Statement	1998 Adjustment	1998 Operating	1999 Statement	1999 Adjustment	1999 Operating	TTM Statement	TTM Adjustment	TTM Operating
Room Revenue												
-	-	-	-	-	-	-	-	-	-	-	-	-
-	-	-	-	-	-	-	-	-	-	-	-	-
-	-	-	-	-	-	-	-	-	-	-	-	-
Room Revenue	-	-	-	-	-	-	-	-	-	-	-	-
Food & Beverage												
-	-	-	-	-	-	-	-	-	-	-	-	-
-	-	-	-	-	-	-	-	-	-	-	-	-
-	-	-	-	-	-	-	-	-	-	-	-	-
Food & Beverage	-	-	-	-	-	-	-	-	-	-	-	-
Telecommunications												
-	-	-	-	-	-	-	-	-	-	-	-	-
-	-	-	-	-	-	-	-	-	-	-	-	-
-	-	-	-	-	-	-	-	-	-	-	-	-
Telecommunications	-	-	-	-	-	-	-	-	-	-	-	-
Other Operated Departments												
-	-	-	-	-	-	-	-	-	-	-	-	-
-	-	-	-	-	-	-	-	-	-	-	-	-
-	-	-	-	-	-	-	-	-	-	-	-	-
-	-	-	-	-	-	-	-	-	-	-	-	-
Other Operated Departments	-	-	-	-	-	-	-	-	-	-	-	-
Other Departmental Revenue												
-	-	-	-	-	-	-	-	-	-	-	-	-
-	-	-	-	-	-	-	-	-	-	-	-	-
-	-	-	-	-	-	-	-	-	-	-	-	-
Other Departmental Revenue	-	-	-	-	-	-	-	-	-	-	-	-
Total Revenue	-	-	-	-	-	-	-	-	-	-	-	-

PRECEPT™

OP STMT RECONCILIATION

Property Name

Property Number: 0000
Deal Number: 0000
Rooms: 0

	1		2		3		4	
	1997		1998		1999		TTM	
# of Days in Year	365		365		365		365	
# of Rooms	0	N	0	N	0	N	0	N
Occupancy %	0.00%	O	0.00%	O	0.00%	O	0.00%	O
ADR	$0.00	T	$0.00	T	$0.00	T	$0.00	T
Occ. Rooms during Year	0	E	0	E	0	E	0	E
Avail. Rooms during Year	0	S	0	S	0	S	0	S
Through:	12/31/1997		12/31/1998		12/31/1999			
Stmt. Type:					Income			

EXPENSES (Departmental)

	1997 Statement	1997 Adjustment	1997 Operating	1998 Statement	1998 Adjustment	1998 Operating	1999 Statement	1999 Adjustment	1999 Operating	TTM Statement	TTM Adjustment	TTM Operating
Room Expense												
-	-	-	-	-	-	-	-	-	-	-	-	-
-	-	-	-	-	-	-	-	-	-	-	-	-
-	-	-	-	-	-	-	-	-	-	-	-	-
Room Expense	-	-	-	-	-	-	-	-	-	-	-	-
Food & Beverage												
-	-	-	-	-	-	-	-	-	-	-	-	-
-	-	-	-	-	-	-	-	-	-	-	-	-
-	-	-	-	-	-	-	-	-	-	-	-	-
Food & Beverage	-	-	-	-	-	-	-	-	-	-	-	-
Telecommunications												
-	-	-	-	-	-	-	-	-	-	-	-	-
-	-	-	-	-	-	-	-	-	-	-	-	-
-	-	-	-	-	-	-	-	-	-	-	-	-
Telecommunications	-	-	-	-	-	-	-	-	-	-	-	-
Other Operated Departments												
-	-	-	-	-	-	-	-	-	-	-	-	-
-	-	-	-	-	-	-	-	-	-	-	-	-
-	-	-	-	-	-	-	-	-	-	-	-	-
-	-	-	-	-	-	-	-	-	-	-	-	-
-	-	-	-	-	-	-	-	-	-	-	-	-
Other Operated Departments	-	-	-	-	-	-	-	-	-	-	-	-
Other Departmental Expense												
-	-	-	-	-	-	-	-	-	-	-	-	-
-	-	-	-	-	-	-	-	-	-	-	-	-
-	-	-	-	-	-	-	-	-	-	-	-	-
-	-	-	-	-	-	-	-	-	-	-	-	-
-	-	-	-	-	-	-	-	-	-	-	-	-
Other Departmental Expense	-	-	-	-	-	-	-	-	-	-	-	-
Total Departmental Expenses	-	-	-	-	-	-	-	-	-	-	-	-
Gross Operating Income	-	-	-	-	-	-	-	-	-	-	-	-

PRECEPT™

OP STMT RECONCILIATION

Property Name

Property Number: 0000
Deal Number: 0000
Rooms: 0

	1		2		3		4	
	1997		1998		1999		TTM	
# of Days in Year	365		365		365		365	
# of Rooms	0	N	0	N	0	N	0	N
Occupancy %	0.00%	O	0.00%	O	0.00%	O	0.00%	O
ADR	$0.00	T	$0.00	T	$0.00	T	$0.00	T
Occ. Rooms during Year	0	E	0	E	0	E	0	E
Avail. Rooms during Year	0	S	0	S	0	S	0	S
Through:	12/31/1997		12/31/1998		12/31/1999			
Stmt. Type:					Income			

EXPENSES (Undistributed)

	1997 Statement	1997 Adjustment	1997 Operating	1998 Statement	1998 Adjustment	1998 Operating	1999 Statement	1999 Adjustment	1999 Operating	TTM Statement	TTM Adjustment	TTM Operating
Management												
-	-	-	-	-	-	-	-	-	-	-	-	-
-	-	-	-	-	-	-	-	-	-	-	-	-
Management	-	-	-	-	-	-	-	-	-	-	-	-
Franchise Fees												
-	-	-	-	-	-	-	-	-	-	-	-	-
-	-	-	-	-	-	-	-	-	-	-	-	-
Franchise Fees	-	-	-	-	-	-	-	-	-	-	-	-
Marketing												
-	-	-	-	-	-	-	-	-	-	-	-	-
-	-	-	-	-	-	-	-	-	-	-	-	-
Marketing	-	-	-	-	-	-	-	-	-	-	-	-
Administrative												
-	-	-	-	-	-	-	-	-	-	-	-	-
-	-	-	-	-	-	-	-	-	-	-	-	-
-	-	-	-	-	-	-	-	-	-	-	-	-
-	-	-	-	-	-	-	-	-	-	-	-	-
-	-	-	-	-	-	-	-	-	-	-	-	-
-	-	-	-	-	-	-	-	-	-	-	-	-
-	-	-	-	-	-	-	-	-	-	-	-	-
Administrative	-	-	-	-	-	-	-	-	-	-	-	-
Operation and Maintenance												
-	-	-	-	-	-	-	-	-	-	-	-	-
-	-	-	-	-	-	-	-	-	-	-	-	-
-	-	-	-	-	-	-	-	-	-	-	-	-
-	-	-	-	-	-	-	-	-	-	-	-	-
-	-	-	-	-	-	-	-	-	-	-	-	-
-	-	-	-	-	-	-	-	-	-	-	-	-
-	-	-	-	-	-	-	-	-	-	-	-	-
-	-	-	-	-	-	-	-	-	-	-	-	-
-	-	-	-	-	-	-	-	-	-	-	-	-
-	-	-	-	-	-	-	-	-	-	-	-	-
-	-	-	-	-	-	-	-	-	-	-	-	-
Operation and Maintenance	-	-	-	-	-	-	-	-	-	-	-	-
Utilities												
-	-	-	-	-	-	-	-	-	-	-	-	-
-	-	-	-	-	-	-	-	-	-	-	-	-
-	-	-	-	-	-	-	-	-	-	-	-	-
-	-	-	-	-	-	-	-	-	-	-	-	-
-	-	-	-	-	-	-	-	-	-	-	-	-
Utilities	-	-	-	-	-	-	-	-	-	-	-	-

PRECEPT™

OP STMT RECONCILIATION

Property Name

Property Number: 0000
Deal Number: 0000
Rooms: 0

	1 (1997)	2 (1998)	3 (1999)	4 (TTM)
# of Days in Year	365	365	365	365
# of Rooms	0	0	0	0
Occupancy %	0.00%	0.00%	0.00%	0.00%
ADR	$0.00	$0.00	$0.00	$0.00
Occ. Rooms during Year	0	0	0	0
Avail. Rooms during Year	0	0	0	0
Through:	12/31/1997	12/31/1998	12/31/1999	
Stmt. Type:			Income	

NOTES

	1997 Statement	1997 Adjustment	1997 Operating	1998 Statement	1998 Adjustment	1998 Operating	1999 Statement	1999 Adjustment	1999 Operating	TTM Statement	TTM Adjustment	TTM Operating
Other Undistributed Expense												
-	-	-	-	-	-	-	-	-	-	-	-	-
-	-	-	-	-	-	-	-	-	-	-	-	-
-	-	-	-	-	-	-	-	-	-	-	-	-
Other Undistributed Expense	-	-	-	-	-	-	-	-	-	-	-	-
Total Undistributed Expenses	-	-	-	-	-	-	-	-	-	-	-	-
Gross Operating Profit	-	-	-	-	-	-	-	-	-	-	-	-
Fixed Expenses												
Real Estate Taxes												
-	-	-	-	-	-	-	-	-	-	-	-	-
-	-	-	-	-	-	-	-	-	-	-	-	-
-	-	-	-	-	-	-	-	-	-	-	-	-
Real Estate Taxes	-	-	-	-	-	-	-	-	-	-	-	-
Insurance												
-	-	-	-	-	-	-	-	-	-	-	-	-
-	-	-	-	-	-	-	-	-	-	-	-	-
-	-	-	-	-	-	-	-	-	-	-	-	-
Insurance	-	-	-	-	-	-	-	-	-	-	-	-
Other Fixed Expense - 1												
-	-	-	-	-	-	-	-	-	-	-	-	-
-	-	-	-	-	-	-	-	-	-	-	-	-
-	-	-	-	-	-	-	-	-	-	-	-	-
Other Fixed Expense - 1	-	-	-	-	-	-	-	-	-	-	-	-
Other Fixed Expense - 2												
-	-	-	-	-	-	-	-	-	-	-	-	-
-	-	-	-	-	-	-	-	-	-	-	-	-
-	-	-	-	-	-	-	-	-	-	-	-	-
Other Fixed Expense - 2	-	-	-	-	-	-	-	-	-	-	-	-
Other Fixed Expense - 3												
-	-	-	-	-	-	-	-	-	-	-	-	-
-	-	-	-	-	-	-	-	-	-	-	-	-
-	-	-	-	-	-	-	-	-	-	-	-	-
Other Fixed Expense - 3	-	-	-	-	-	-	-	-	-	-	-	-
Total Fixed Expenses	-	-	-	-	-	-	-	-	-	-	-	-

PRECEPT

OP STMT RECONCILIATION

Property Name

Property Number: 0000
Deal Number: 0000
Rooms: 0

	1		2		3		4	
	1997		1998		1999		TTM	
# of Days in Year	365	N	365	N	365	N	365	N
# of Rooms	0	O	0	O	0	O	0	O
Occupancy %	0.00%	T	0.00%	T	0.00%	T	0.00%	T
ADR	$0.00	E	$0.00	E	$0.00	E	$0.00	E
Occ. Rooms during Year	0	S	0	S	0	S	0	S
Avail. Rooms during Year	0		0		0		0	
Through:	12/31/1997		12/31/1998		12/31/1999			
Stmt. Type:					Income			

Capital Expenditures

	1 Statement	1 Adjustment	1 Operating	2 Statement	2 Adjustment	2 Operating	3 Statement	3 Adjustment	3 Operating	4 Statement	4 Adjustment	4 Operating
FF&E (Reserve)												
-	-	-	-	-	-	-	-	-	-	-	-	-
-	-	-	-	-	-	-	-	-	-	-	-	-
-	-	-	-	-	-	-	-	-	-	-	-	-
FF&E (Reserve)	-	-	-	-	-	-	-	-	-	-	-	-
Other Capital Expense - 1												
-	-	-	-	-	-	-	-	-	-	-	-	-
-	-	-	-	-	-	-	-	-	-	-	-	-
-	-	-	-	-	-	-	-	-	-	-	-	-
Other Capital Expense - 1	-	-	-	-	-	-	-	-	-	-	-	-
Other Capital Expense - 2												
-	-	-	-	-	-	-	-	-	-	-	-	-
-	-	-	-	-	-	-	-	-	-	-	-	-
-	-	-	-	-	-	-	-	-	-	-	-	-
Other Capital Expense - 2	-	-	-	-	-	-	-	-	-	-	-	-
Total Capital Expenditures	-	-	-	-	-	-	-	-	-	-	-	-

Net Cash Flow	-	-	-	-	-	-	-	-	-	-	-	-

OCCUPANCY	1 ADR	1 Occupancy	2 ADR	2 Occupancy	3 ADR	3 Occupancy	4 ADR	4 Occupancy
31 January								
28 February								
31 March								
30 April								
31 May								
30 June								
31 July								
31 August								
30 September								
31 October								
30 November								
31 December								
Weighted Avg ADR and Avg Occ								
Conc ADR & Room Rev Occ Calc		0.00%		0.00%		0.00%		0.00%

PRECEPT™

OP STMT RECONCILIATION

Property Name

Property Number: 0000
Deal Number: 0000
Rooms: 0

	5		6		7		8	
	YTD	NOTES	YTD Prior	NOTES	Appraiser	NOTES	Budget	NOTES
# of Days in Year	365		365		365		365	
# of Rooms	0		0		0		0	
Occupancy %	0.00%		0.00%		0.00%		0.00%	
ADR	$0.00		$0.00		$0.00		$0.00	
Occ. Rooms during Year	0		0		0		0	
Avail. Rooms during Year	0		0		0		0	
Through:								
Stmt. Type:								

REVENUES

	YTD Statement	YTD Adjustment	YTD Operating	YTD Prior Statement	YTD Prior Adjustment	YTD Prior Operating	Appraiser Statement	Appraiser Adjustment	Appraiser Operating	Budget Statement	Budget Adjustment	Budget Operating
Room Revenue												
-	-	-	-	-	-	-	-	-	-	-	-	-
-	-	-	-	-	-	-	-	-	-	-	-	-
-	-	-	-	-	-	-	-	-	-	-	-	-
Room Revenue	-	-	-	-	-	-	-	-	-	-	-	-
Food & Beverage												
-	-	-	-	-	-	-	-	-	-	-	-	-
-	-	-	-	-	-	-	-	-	-	-	-	-
-	-	-	-	-	-	-	-	-	-	-	-	-
Food & Beverage	-	-	-	-	-	-	-	-	-	-	-	-
Telecommunications												
-	-	-	-	-	-	-	-	-	-	-	-	-
-	-	-	-	-	-	-	-	-	-	-	-	-
-	-	-	-	-	-	-	-	-	-	-	-	-
Telecommunications	-	-	-	-	-	-	-	-	-	-	-	-
Other Operated Departments												
-	-	-	-	-	-	-	-	-	-	-	-	-
-	-	-	-	-	-	-	-	-	-	-	-	-
-	-	-	-	-	-	-	-	-	-	-	-	-
-	-	-	-	-	-	-	-	-	-	-	-	-
Other Operated Departments	-	-	-	-	-	-	-	-	-	-	-	-
Other Departmental Revenue												
-	-	-	-	-	-	-	-	-	-	-	-	-
-	-	-	-	-	-	-	-	-	-	-	-	-
-	-	-	-	-	-	-	-	-	-	-	-	-
Other Departmental Revenue	-	-	-	-	-	-	-	-	-	-	-	-
Total Revenue	-	-	-	-	-	-	-	-	-	-	-	-

PRECEPT™

OP STMT RECONCILIATION
Property Name

Property Number: 0000	5 YTD			6 YTD Prior			7 Appraiser			8 Budget		
Deal Number: 0000	# of Days in Year		365	# of Days in Year		365	# of Days in Year		365	# of Days in Year		365
Rooms: 0	# of Rooms		0	# of Rooms		0	# of Rooms		0	# of Rooms		0
	Occupancy %		0.00%	Occupancy %		0.00%	Occupancy %		0.00%	Occupancy %		0.00%
	ADR		$0.00	ADR		$0.00	ADR		$0.00	ADR		$0.00
	Occ. Rooms during Year		0	Occ. Rooms during Year		0	Occ. Rooms during Year		0	Occ. Rooms during Year		0
	Avail. Rooms during Year		0	Avail. Rooms during Year		0	Avail. Rooms during Year		0	Avail. Rooms during Year		0
	Statement	**Adjustment**	**Operating**	**Statement**	**Adjustment**	**Operating**	**Statement**	**Adjustment**	**Operating**	**Statement**	**Adjustment**	**Operating**
	Through:			**Through:**			**Through:**			**Through:**		
	Stmt. Type:			**Stmt. Type:**			**Stmt. Type:**			t		

NOTES

EXPENSES (Departmental)

	YTD Statement	YTD Adjustment	YTD Operating	YTD Prior Statement	YTD Prior Adjustment	YTD Prior Operating	Appraiser Statement	Appraiser Adjustment	Appraiser Operating	Budget Statement	Budget Adjustment	Budget Operating
Room Expense												
-	-	-	-	-	-	-	-	-	-	-	-	-
-	-	-	-	-	-	-	-	-	-	-	-	-
-	-	-	-	-	-	-	-	-	-	-	-	-
Room Expense	-	-	-	-	-	-	-	-	-	-	-	-
Food & Beverage												
-	-	-	-	-	-	-	-	-	-	-	-	-
-	-	-	-	-	-	-	-	-	-	-	-	-
-	-	-	-	-	-	-	-	-	-	-	-	-
Food & Beverage	-	-	-	-	-	-	-	-	-	-	-	-
Telecommunications												
-	-	-	-	-	-	-	-	-	-	-	-	-
-	-	-	-	-	-	-	-	-	-	-	-	-
-	-	-	-	-	-	-	-	-	-	-	-	-
Telecommunications	-	-	-	-	-	-	-	-	-	-	-	-
Other Operated Departments												
-	-	-	-	-	-	-	-	-	-	-	-	-
-	-	-	-	-	-	-	-	-	-	-	-	-
-	-	-	-	-	-	-	-	-	-	-	-	-
-	-	-	-	-	-	-	-	-	-	-	-	-
-	-	-	-	-	-	-	-	-	-	-	-	-
Other Operated Departments	-	-	-	-	-	-	-	-	-	-	-	-
Other Departmental Expense												
-	-	-	-	-	-	-	-	-	-	-	-	-
-	-	-	-	-	-	-	-	-	-	-	-	-
-	-	-	-	-	-	-	-	-	-	-	-	-
-	-	-	-	-	-	-	-	-	-	-	-	-
-	-	-	-	-	-	-	-	-	-	-	-	-
Other Departmental Expense	-	-	-	-	-	-	-	-	-	-	-	-
Total Departmental Expenses	-	-	-	-	-	-	-	-	-	-	-	-
Gross Operating Income	-	-	-	-	-	-	-	-	-	-	-	-

PRECEPT™

OP STMT RECONCILIATION

Property Name

Property Number: 0000
Deal Number: 0000
Rooms: 0

	5 YTD		6 YTD Prior		7 Appraiser		8 Budget	
# of Days in Year	365		365		365		365	
# of Rooms	0	N	0	N	0	N	0	N
Occupancy %	0.00%	O	0.00%	O	0.00%	O	0.00%	O
ADR	$0.00	T	$0.00	T	$0.00	T	$0.00	T
Occ. Rooms during Year	0	E	0	E	0	E	0	E
Avail. Rooms during Year	0	S	0	S	0	S	0	S

	Statement	Adjustment	Operating	Statement	Adjustment	Operating	Statement	Adjustment	Operating	Statement	Adjustment	Operating
Through:												
Stmt. Type:												

EXPENSES (Undistributed)

	5 Statement	5 Adjustment	5 Operating	6 Statement	6 Adjustment	6 Operating	7 Statement	7 Adjustment	7 Operating	8 Statement	8 Adjustment	8 Operating
Management												
-	-	-	-	-	-	-	-	-	-	-	-	-
-	-	-	-	-	-	-	-	-	-	-	-	-
Management	-	-	-	-	-	-	-	-	-	-	-	-
Franchise Fees												
-	-	-	-	-	-	-	-	-	-	-	-	-
-	-	-	-	-	-	-	-	-	-	-	-	-
Franchise Fees	-	-	-	-	-	-	-	-	-	-	-	-
Marketing												
-	-	-	-	-	-	-	-	-	-	-	-	-
-	-	-	-	-	-	-	-	-	-	-	-	-
Marketing	-	-	-	-	-	-	-	-	-	-	-	-
Administrative												
-	-	-	-	-	-	-	-	-	-	-	-	-
-	-	-	-	-	-	-	-	-	-	-	-	-
-	-	-	-	-	-	-	-	-	-	-	-	-
-	-	-	-	-	-	-	-	-	-	-	-	-
-	-	-	-	-	-	-	-	-	-	-	-	-
-	-	-	-	-	-	-	-	-	-	-	-	-
-	-	-	-	-	-	-	-	-	-	-	-	-
Administrative	-	-	-	-	-	-	-	-	-	-	-	-
Operation and Maintenance												
-	-	-	-	-	-	-	-	-	-	-	-	-
-	-	-	-	-	-	-	-	-	-	-	-	-
-	-	-	-	-	-	-	-	-	-	-	-	-
-	-	-	-	-	-	-	-	-	-	-	-	-
-	-	-	-	-	-	-	-	-	-	-	-	-
-	-	-	-	-	-	-	-	-	-	-	-	-
-	-	-	-	-	-	-	-	-	-	-	-	-
-	-	-	-	-	-	-	-	-	-	-	-	-
-	-	-	-	-	-	-	-	-	-	-	-	-
-	-	-	-	-	-	-	-	-	-	-	-	-
-	-	-	-	-	-	-	-	-	-	-	-	-
Operation and Maintenance	-	-	-	-	-	-	-	-	-	-	-	-
Utilities												
-	-	-	-	-	-	-	-	-	-	-	-	-
-	-	-	-	-	-	-	-	-	-	-	-	-
-	-	-	-	-	-	-	-	-	-	-	-	-
-	-	-	-	-	-	-	-	-	-	-	-	-
-	-	-	-	-	-	-	-	-	-	-	-	-
Utilities	-	-	-	-	-	-	-	-	-	-	-	-

PRECEPT™

OP STMT RECONCILIATION

Property Name

	5		6		7		8	
	YTD		YTD Prior		Appraiser		Budget	
Property Number: 0000	# of Days in Year	365	# of Days in Year	365	# of Days in Year	365	# of Days in Year	365
Deal Number: 0000	# of Rooms	0	# of Rooms	0	# of Rooms	0	# of Rooms	0
Rooms: 0	Occupancy %	0.00%	Occupancy %	0.00%	Occupancy %	0.00%	Occupancy %	0.00%
	ADR	$0.00	ADR	$0.00	ADR	$0.00	ADR	$0.00
	Occ. Rooms during Year	0	Occ. Rooms during Year	0	Occ. Rooms during Year	0	Occ. Rooms during Year	0
	Avail. Rooms during Year	0	Avail. Rooms during Year	0	Avail. Rooms during Year	0	Avail. Rooms during Year	0

NOTES

	Statement	Adjustment	Operating	Statement	Adjustment	Operating	Statement	Adjustment	Operating	Statement	Adjustment	Operating
	Through:			**Through:**			**Through:**			**Through:**		
	Stmt. Type:			**Stmt. Type:**			**Stmt. Type:**			**Stmt. Type:**		
Other Undistributed Expense												
-	-	-	-	-	-	-	-	-	-	-	-	-
-	-	-	-	-	-	-	-	-	-	-	-	-
-	-	-	-	-	-	-	-	-	-	-	-	-
Other Undistributed Expense	-	-	-	-	-	-	-	-	-	-	-	-
Total Undistributed Expenses	-	-	-	-	-	-	-	-	-	-	-	-
Gross Operating Profit	-	-	-	-	-	-	-	-	-	-	-	t -
Fixed Expenses												
Real Estate Taxes												
-	-	-	-	-	-	-	-	-	-	-	-	-
-	-	-	-	-	-	-	-	-	-	-	-	-
-	-	-	-	-	-	-	-	-	-	-	-	-
Real Estate Taxes	-	-	-	-	-	-	-	-	-	-	-	-
Insurance												
-	-	-	-	-	-	-	-	-	-	-	-	-
-	-	-	-	-	-	-	-	-	-	-	-	-
-	-	-	-	-	-	-	-	-	-	-	-	-
Insurance	-	-	-	-	-	-	-	-	-	-	-	-
Other Fixed Expense - 1												
-	-	-	-	-	-	-	-	-	-	-	-	-
-	-	-	-	-	-	-	-	-	-	-	-	-
-	-	-	-	-	-	-	-	-	-	-	-	-
Other Fixed Expense - 1	-	-	-	-	-	-	-	-	-	-	-	-
Other Fixed Expense - 2												
-	-	-	-	-	-	-	-	-	-	-	-	-
-	-	-	-	-	-	-	-	-	-	-	-	-
-	-	-	-	-	-	-	-	-	-	-	-	-
Other Fixed Expense - 2	-	-	-	-	-	-	-	-	-	-	-	-
Other Fixed Expense - 3												
-	-	-	-	-	-	-	-	-	-	-	-	-
-	-	-	-	-	-	-	-	-	-	-	-	-
-	-	-	-	-	-	-	-	-	-	-	-	-
Other Fixed Expense - 3	-	-	-	-	-	-	-	-	-	-	-	-
Total Fixed Expenses	-	-	-	-	-	-	-	-	-	-	-	-

PRECEPT™

OP STMT RECONCILIATION

Property Name

Property Number: 0000
Deal Number: 0000
Rooms: 0

	5	6	7	8
	YTD	YTD Prior	Appraiser	Budget
# of Days in Year	365	365	365	365
# of Rooms	0	0	0	0
Occupancy %	0.00%	0.00%	0.00%	0.00%
ADR	$0.00	$0.00	$0.00	$0.00
Occ. Rooms during Year	0	0	0	0
Avail. Rooms during Year	0	0	0	0

NOTES

	YTD Statement	YTD Adjustment	YTD Operating	YTD Prior Statement	YTD Prior Adjustment	YTD Prior Operating	Appraiser Statement	Appraiser Adjustment	Appraiser Operating	Budget Statement	Budget Adjustment	Budget Operating
Through:												
Stmt. Type:												
Capital Expenditures												
FF&E (Reserve)												
-	-	-	-	-	-	-	-	-	-	-	-	-
-	-	-	-	-	-	-	-	-	-	-	-	-
-	-	-	-	-	-	-	-	-	-	-	-	-
FF&E (Reserve)	-	-	-	-	-	-	-	-	-	-	-	-
Other Capital Expense - 1												
-	-	-	-	-	-	-	-	-	-	-	-	-
-	-	-	-	-	-	-	-	-	-	-	-	-
-	-	-	-	-	-	-	-	-	-	-	-	-
Other Capital Expense - 1	-	-	-	-	-	-	-	-	-	-	-	-
Other Capital Expense - 2												
-	-	-	-	-	-	-	-	-	-	-	-	-
-	-	-	-	-	-	-	-	-	-	-	-	-
-	-	-	-	-	-	-	-	-	-	-	-	-
Other Capital Expense - 2	-	-	-	-	-	-	-	-	-	-	-	-
Total Capital Expenditures	-	-	-	-	-	-	-	-	-	-	-	-
Net Cash Flow	-	-	-	-	-	-	-	-	-	-	-	-

OCCUPANCY	ADR	Occupancy	ADR	Occupancy	ADR	Occupancy	ADR	Occupancy
31 January								
28 February								
31 March								
30 April								
31 May								
30 June								
31 July								
31 August								
30 September								
31 October								
30 November								
31 December								
Weighted Avg ADR and Avg Occ								
Conc ADR & Room Rev Occ Calc		0.00%		0.00%		0.00%		0.00%

PRECEPT™

OP STMT RECONCILIATION
Property Name

MONTHLY SCHEDULE IF NEEDED - need to reference back to columns on right in order to flow through

	0	0	0	0	0	0	0	0	0	0	0	0
Property Number: 0000	**January**	**February**	**March**	**April**	**May**	**June**	**July**	**August**	**September**	**October**	**November**	**December**
Deal Number: 0000	31	28	31	30	31	30	31	31	30	31	30	31
Rooms: 0	0	0	0	0	0	0	0	0	0	0	0	0
	0	0	0	0	0	0	0	0	0	0	0	0
	0	0	0	0	0	0	0	0	0	0	0	0

0	0 Months		
# of Days in Year		365	N
# of Rooms		0	O
Occupancy %		0.00%	T
ADR		$0.00	E
Occ. Rooms during Year		0	S
Avail. Rooms during Year		0	
Statement	**Adjustment**	**Operating**	
Through:			
Financials:			

REVENUES

	January	February	March	April	May	June	July	August	September	October	November	December	Statement	Adjustment	Operating
Room Revenue															
-	-	-	-	-	-	-	-	-	-	-	-	-	-	-	-
-	-	-	-	-	-	-	-	-	-	-	-	-	-	-	-
-	-	-	-	-	-	-	-	-	-	-	-	-	-	-	-
Room Revenue	-	-	-	-	-	-	-	-	-	-	-	-	-	-	-
Food & Beverage															
-	-	-	-	-	-	-	-	-	-	-	-	-	-	-	-
-	-	-	-	-	-	-	-	-	-	-	-	-	-	-	-
-	-	-	-	-	-	-	-	-	-	-	-	-	-	-	-
Food & Beverage	-	-	-	-	-	-	-	-	-	-	-	-	-	-	-
Telecommunications															
-	-	-	-	-	-	-	-	-	-	-	-	-	-	-	-
-	-	-	-	-	-	-	-	-	-	-	-	-	-	-	-
-	-	-	-	-	-	-	-	-	-	-	-	-	-	-	-
Telecommunications	-	-	-	-	-	-	-	-	-	-	-	-	-	-	-
Other Operated Departments															
-	-	-	-	-	-	-	-	-	-	-	-	-	-	-	-
-	-	-	-	-	-	-	-	-	-	-	-	-	-	-	-
-	-	-	-	-	-	-	-	-	-	-	-	-	-	-	-
-	-	-	-	-	-	-	-	-	-	-	-	-	-	-	-
Other Operated Departments	-	-	-	-	-	-	-	-	-	-	-	-	-	-	-
Other Departmental Revenue															
-	-	-	-	-	-	-	-	-	-	-	-	-	-	-	-
-	-	-	-	-	-	-	-	-	-	-	-	-	-	-	-
-	-	-	-	-	-	-	-	-	-	-	-	-	-	-	-
Other Departmental Revenue	-	-	-	-	-	-	-	-	-	-	-	-	-	-	-
Total Revenue	-	-	-	-	-	-	-	-	-	-	-	-	-	-	-

PRECEPT™

OP STMT RECONCILIATION

Property Name

MONTHLY SCHEDULE IF NEEDED - need to reference back to columns on right in order to flow through

	January	February	March	April	May	June	July	August	September	October	November	December
	0	0	0	0	0	0	0	0	0	0	0	0
Property Number: 0000												
Deal Number: 0000	31	28	31	30	31	30	31	31	30	31	30	31
Rooms: 0	0	0	0	0	0	0	0	0	0	0	0	0
	0	0	0	0	0	0	0	0	0	0	0	0
	0	0	0	0	0	0	0	0	0	0	0	0

0	**0 Months**
# of Days in Year	365
# of Rooms	0
Occupancy %	0.00%
ADR	$0.00
Occ. Rooms during Year	0
Avail. Rooms during Year	0

Statement	**Adjustment**	**Operating**
Through:		
Financials:		

NOTES

EXPENSES (Departmental)

	January	February	March	April	May	June	July	August	September	October	November	December	Statement	Adjustment	Operating
Room Expense															
-	-	-	-	-	-	-	-	-	-	-	-	-	-	-	-
-	-	-	-	-	-	-	-	-	-	-	-	-	-	-	-
-	-	-	-	-	-	-	-	-	-	-	-	-	-	-	-
Room Expense	-	-	-	-	-	-	-	-	-	-	-	-	-	-	-
Food & Beverage															
-	-	-	-	-	-	-	-	-	-	-	-	-	-	-	-
-	-	-	-	-	-	-	-	-	-	-	-	-	-	-	-
-	-	-	-	-	-	-	-	-	-	-	-	-	-	-	-
Food & Beverage	-	-	-	-	-	-	-	-	-	-	-	-	-	-	-
Telecommunications															
-	-	-	-	-	-	-	-	-	-	-	-	-	-	-	-
-	-	-	-	-	-	-	-	-	-	-	-	-	-	-	-
-	-	-	-	-	-	-	-	-	-	-	-	-	-	-	-
Telecommunications	-	-	-	-	-	-	-	-	-	-	-	-	-	-	-
Other Operated Departments															
-	-	-	-	-	-	-	-	-	-	-	-	-	-	-	-
-	-	-	-	-	-	-	-	-	-	-	-	-	-	-	-
-	-	-	-	-	-	-	-	-	-	-	-	-	-	-	-
-	-	-	-	-	-	-	-	-	-	-	-	-	-	-	-
-	-	-	-	-	-	-	-	-	-	-	-	-	-	-	-
Other Operated Departments	-	-	-	-	-	-	-	-	-	-	-	-	-	-	-
Other Departmental Expense															
-	-	-	-	-	-	-	-	-	-	-	-	-	-	-	-
-	-	-	-	-	-	-	-	-	-	-	-	-	-	-	-
-	-	-	-	-	-	-	-	-	-	-	-	-	-	-	-
-	-	-	-	-	-	-	-	-	-	-	-	-	-	-	-
-	-	-	-	-	-	-	-	-	-	-	-	-	-	-	-
Other Departmental Expense	-	-	-	-	-	-	-	-	-	-	-	-	-	-	-
Total Departmental Expenses	-	-	-	-	-	-	-	-	-	-	-	-	-	-	-
Gross Operating Income	-	-	-	-	-	-	-	-	-	-	-	-	-	-	-

PRECEPT™

OP STMT RECONCILIATION

Property Name

	0	0	0	0	0	0	0	0	0	0	0	0
Property Number: 0000	**January**	**February**	**March**	**April**	**May**	**June**	**July**	**August**	**September**	**October**	**November**	**December**
Deal Number: 0000	31	28	31	30	31	30	31	31	30	31	30	31
Rooms: 0	0	0	0	0	0	0	0	0	0	0	0	0
	0	0	0	0	0	0	0	0	0	0	0	0
	0	0	0	0	0	0	0	0	0	0	0	0

0			
0 Months			
# of Days in Year		365	N
# of Rooms		0	O
Occupancy %		0.00%	T
ADR		$0.00	E
Occ. Rooms during Year		0	S
Avail. Rooms during Year		0	
Statement	**Adjustment**	**Operating**	
Through:			
Financials:			

EXPENSES (Undistributed)

	January	February	March	April	May	June	July	August	September	October	November	December	Statement	Adjustment	Operating
Management															
-	-	-	-	-	-	-	-	-	-	-	-	-	-	-	-
-	-	-	-	-	-	-	-	-	-	-	-	-	-	-	-
Management	-	-	-	-	-	-	-	-	-	-	-	-	-	-	-
Franchise Fees															
-	-	-	-	-	-	-	-	-	-	-	-	-	-	-	-
-	-	-	-	-	-	-	-	-	-	-	-	-	-	-	-
Franchise Fees	-	-	-	-	-	-	-	-	-	-	-	-	-	-	-
Marketing															
-	-	-	-	-	-	-	-	-	-	-	-	-	-	-	-
-	-	-	-	-	-	-	-	-	-	-	-	-	-	-	-
Marketing	-	-	-	-	-	-	-	-	-	-	-	-	-	-	-
Administrative															
-	-	-	-	-	-	-	-	-	-	-	-	-	-	-	-
-	-	-	-	-	-	-	-	-	-	-	-	-	-	-	-
-	-	-	-	-	-	-	-	-	-	-	-	-	-	-	-
-	-	-	-	-	-	-	-	-	-	-	-	-	-	-	-
-	-	-	-	-	-	-	-	-	-	-	-	-	-	-	-
-	-	-	-	-	-	-	-	-	-	-	-	-	-	-	-
-	-	-	-	-	-	-	-	-	-	-	-	-	-	-	-
Administrative	-	-	-	-	-	-	-	-	-	-	-	-	-	-	-
Operation and Maintenance															
-	-	-	-	-	-	-	-	-	-	-	-	-	-	-	-
-	-	-	-	-	-	-	-	-	-	-	-	-	-	-	-
-	-	-	-	-	-	-	-	-	-	-	-	-	-	-	-
-	-	-	-	-	-	-	-	-	-	-	-	-	-	-	-
-	-	-	-	-	-	-	-	-	-	-	-	-	-	-	-
-	-	-	-	-	-	-	-	-	-	-	-	-	-	-	-
-	-	-	-	-	-	-	-	-	-	-	-	-	-	-	-
-	-	-	-	-	-	-	-	-	-	-	-	-	-	-	-
-	-	-	-	-	-	-	-	-	-	-	-	-	-	-	-
-	-	-	-	-	-	-	-	-	-	-	-	-	-	-	-
-	-	-	-	-	-	-	-	-	-	-	-	-	-	-	-
Operation and Maintenance	-	-	-	-	-	-	-	-	-	-	-	-	-	-	-
Utilities															
-	-	-	-	-	-	-	-	-	-	-	-	-	-	-	-
-	-	-	-	-	-	-	-	-	-	-	-	-	-	-	-
-	-	-	-	-	-	-	-	-	-	-	-	-	-	-	-
-	-	-	-	-	-	-	-	-	-	-	-	-	-	-	-
-	-	-	-	-	-	-	-	-	-	-	-	-	-	-	-
Utilities	-	-	-	-	-	-	-	-	-	-	-	-	-	-	-

PRECEPT™

OP STMT RECONCILIATION

Property Name

MONTHLY SCHEDULE IF NEEDED - need to reference back to columns on right in order to flow through

	0	0	0	0	0	0	0	0	0	0	0	0
Property Number: 0000	**January**	**February**	**March**	**April**	**May**	**June**	**July**	**August**	**September**	**October**	**November**	**December**
Deal Number: 0000	31	28	31	30	31	30	31	31	30	31	30	31
Rooms: 0	0	0	0	0	0	0	0	0	0	0	0	0
	0	0	0	0	0	0	0	0	0	0	0	0
	0	0	0	0	0	0	0	0	0	0	0	0

0			
0 Months			**N O T E S**
# of Days in Year	365		
# of Rooms	0		
Occupancy %	0.00%		
ADR	$0.00		
Occ. Rooms during Year	0		
Avail. Rooms during Year	0		
Statement	**Adjustment**	**Operating**	
Through:			
Financials:			

	January	February	March	April	May	June	July	August	September	October	November	December	Statement	Adjustment	Operating
Other Undistributed Expense															
-	-	-	-	-	-	-	-	-	-	-	-	-	-	-	-
-	-	-	-	-	-	-	-	-	-	-	-	-	-	-	-
-	-	-	-	-	-	-	-	-	-	-	-	-	-	-	-
Other Undistributed Expense	-	-	-	-	-	-	-	-	-	-	-	-	-	-	-
Total Undistributed Expenses	-	-	-	-	-	-	-	-	-	-	-	-	-	-	-
Gross Operating Profit	-	-	-	-	-	-	-	-	-	-	-	-	-	-	-
Fixed Expenses															
Real Estate Taxes															
-	-	-	-	-	-	-	-	-	-	-	-	-	-	-	-
-	-	-	-	-	-	-	-	-	-	-	-	-	-	-	-
-	-	-	-	-	-	-	-	-	-	-	-	-	-	-	-
Real Estate Taxes	-	-	-	-	-	-	-	-	-	-	-	-	-	-	-
Insurance															
-	-	-	-	-	-	-	-	-	-	-	-	-	-	-	-
-	-	-	-	-	-	-	-	-	-	-	-	-	-	-	-
-	-	-	-	-	-	-	-	-	-	-	-	-	-	-	-
Insurance	-	-	-	-	-	-	-	-	-	-	-	-	-	-	-
Other Fixed Expense - 1															
-	-	-	-	-	-	-	-	-	-	-	-	-	-	-	-
-	-	-	-	-	-	-	-	-	-	-	-	-	-	-	-
-	-	-	-	-	-	-	-	-	-	-	-	-	-	-	-
Other Fixed Expense - 1	-	-	-	-	-	-	-	-	-	-	-	-	-	-	-
Other Fixed Expense - 2															
-	-	-	-	-	-	-	-	-	-	-	-	-	-	-	-
-	-	-	-	-	-	-	-	-	-	-	-	-	-	-	-
-	-	-	-	-	-	-	-	-	-	-	-	-	-	-	-
Other Fixed Expense - 2	-	-	-	-	-	-	-	-	-	-	-	-	-	-	-
Other Fixed Expense - 3															
-	-	-	-	-	-	-	-	-	-	-	-	-	-	-	-
-	-	-	-	-	-	-	-	-	-	-	-	-	-	-	-
-	-	-	-	-	-	-	-	-	-	-	-	-	-	-	-
Other Fixed Expense - 3	-	-	-	-	-	-	-	-	-	-	-	-	-	-	-
Total Fixed Expenses	-	-	-	-	-	-	-	-	-	-	-	-	-	-	-

PRECEPT™

OP STMT RECONCILIATION
Property Name

MONTHLY SCHEDULE IF NEEDED - need to reference back to columns on right in order to flow through

	0	0	0	0	0	0	0	0	0	0	0	0
Property Number: 0000	**January**	**February**	**March**	**April**	**May**	**June**	**July**	**August**	**September**	**October**	**November**	**December**
Deal Number: 0000	31	28	31	30	31	30	31	31	30	31	30	31
Rooms: 0	0	0	0	0	0	0	0	0	0	0	0	0
	0	0	0	0	0	0	0	0	0	0	0	0
	0	0	0	0	0	0	0	0	0	0	0	0

0			
0 Months			
# of Days in Year		365	**N**
# of Rooms		0	**O**
Occupancy %		0.00%	**T**
ADR		$0.00	**E**
Occ. Rooms during Year		0	**S**
Avail. Rooms during Year		0	
Statement	**Adjustment**	**Operating**	
Through:			
Financials:			

Capital Expenditures

	January	February	March	April	May	June	July	August	September	October	November	December	Statement	Adjustment	Operating
FF&E (Reserve)															
-	-	-	-	-	-	-	-	-	-	-	-	-	-	-	-
-	-	-	-	-	-	-	-	-	-	-	-	-	-	-	-
-	-	-	-	-	-	-	-	-	-	-	-	-	-	-	-
FF&E (Reserve)	-	-	-	-	-	-	-	-	-	-	-	-	-	-	-
Other Capital Expense - 1															
-	-	-	-	-	-	-	-	-	-	-	-	-	-	-	-
-	-	-	-	-	-	-	-	-	-	-	-	-	-	-	-
-	-	-	-	-	-	-	-	-	-	-	-	-	-	-	-
Other Capital Expense - 1	-	-	-	-	-	-	-	-	-	-	-	-	-	-	-
Other Capital Expense - 2															
-	-	-	-	-	-	-	-	-	-	-	-	-	-	-	-
-	-	-	-	-	-	-	-	-	-	-	-	-	-	-	-
-	-	-	-	-	-	-	-	-	-	-	-	-	-	-	-
Other Capital Expense - 2	-	-	-	-	-	-	-	-	-	-	-	-	-	-	-
Total Capital Expenditures	-	-	-	-	-	-	-	-	-	-	-	-	-	-	-
Net Cash Flow	-	-	-	-	-	-	-	-	-	-	-	-	-	-	-

OCCUPANCY

31 January
28 February
31 March
30 April
31 May
30 June
31 July
31 August
30 September
31 October
30 November
31 December
Weighted Avg ADR and Avg Occ
Conc ADR & Room Rev Occ Calc

Notes and Comments:

PRECEPT™

Property Name
SEASONALITY ANALYSIS

Property Number: 0000
Deal Number: 0000

	Days	Occ	ADR	Basis For Seasonality: Calculated Room Rev	Basis For Seasonality: Calculated NCF A	Basis For Seasonality: Actual NCF\Other B	Concluded NCF("A"/"B")	% Of Concluded NCF	Allocated U/W NCF	Calculated DSCR	Overage/ (Shortfall) @ DSCR of	Required (Reserve)/ Distribution	Final Structured DSCR
JAN	31												
FEB	28												
MAR	31												
APR	30												
MAY	31												
JUN	30												
JUL	31												
AUG	31												
SEP	30												
OCT	31												
NOV	30												
DEC	31												
Average		0.00%	$0.00	$0	$0	$0	$0	0.00%	$0	0.00	$0	$0	0.00

Comments (explain source of "Actual NCF/Other" if applicable)

Calculated Room Rev. Comparable Years		
JAN		
FEB		
MAR		
APR		
MAY		
JUN		
JUL		
AUG		
SEP		
OCT		
NOV		
DEC		

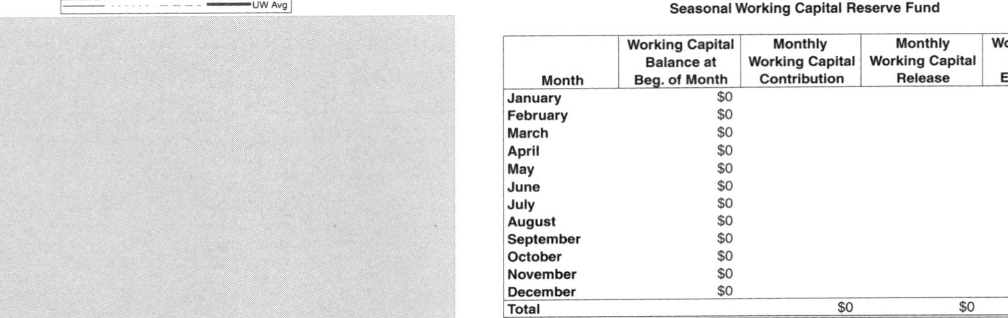
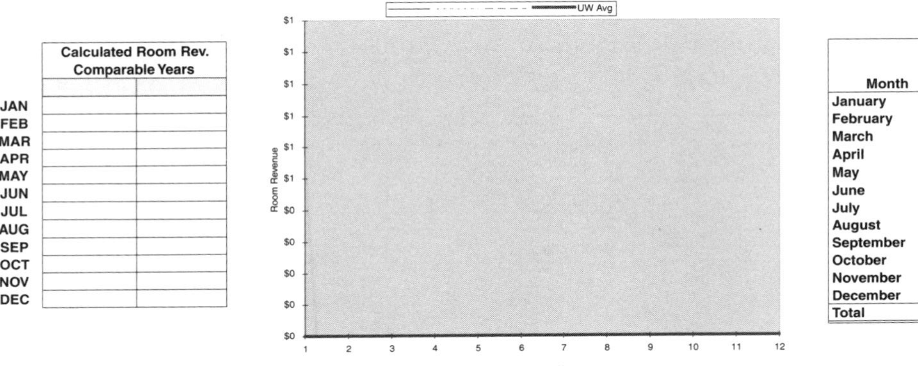

Seasonal Working Capital Reserve Fund

Month	Working Capital Balance at Beg. of Month	Monthly Working Capital Contribution	Monthly Working Capital Release	Working Capital Balance at End of Month
January	$0			$0
February	$0			$0
March	$0			$0
April	$0			$0
May	$0			$0
June	$0			$0
July	$0			$0
August	$0			$0
September	$0			$0
October	$0			$0
November	$0			$0
December	$0			$0
Total		$0	$0	

PRECEPT™

Property Name
OCCUPANCY, RENTAL RATES AND SALES DATA

Property Number: 0000
Deal Number: 0000

Is property stabilized?	
If "No," est. stabilization date:	

Current Occupancy:

		Occupancy	ADR	As of Date	Source	Comments
Market					Appraisal	
Sub-market					Appraisal	
TTM	(Property)					
1999	(Property)					
1998	(Property)					
1997	(Property)					

Tenant Concentration	Subject (%)	Market (%)
Commercial		
Group		
Transient/Leisure		
Discount		
	0%	0%

Comments on Occupancy:

Competitive Property Summary:

#	Property Name/Location	Distance from Subject	Rooms	Physical Occupancy	ADR	Year Built	Compare to subject (+, -, =) Location	Compare to subject (+, -, =) Condition	Source	Comments
S	**Property Name, City**		0			0				
1										
2										
3										
4										
5										

Comments on Comparable Property:

Sales Comparable Summary:

#	Property Name/Location	Rooms	Year Built	Date Sold	Sale Price	Value Per Room	Seller	Buyer	Estimated Cap Rate	Estimated NOI/Room
1										
2										
3										
4										
5										

Comments on Sales Comparable (i.e. source of information and general comments on each property, etc,):

PRECEPT™

Property Name
PROPERTY DESCRIPTION

Property Number: 0000
Deal Number: 0000

General Property Characteristics:

Property Type / Style	Hotel				
Property Class (A, B, C)		Largest meeting space SF		Type of parking	
Number of rooms		Total land area (acres)		Total parking spaces	
Gross SF		Excess land area (acres)		Exterior façade	
Year built		Number of floors		Roof type	
Year last renovated		Number of buildings		Sprinklered (yes / no)	

Property Description Comments (e.g., space, usage, etc.):

Exterior Condition ("Ex/Good/Avg/Poor/NA"):

Overall quality of the exterior	
Landscaping	
Adequacy of roads / parking	
Paving	
Adequacy of lighting	
Pool(s) / Spa(s)	
Paint	
Windows	
Roof	
Façade	

Interior Condition ("Ex/Good/Avg/Poor/NA"):

Lobby / Common Areas	
Overall quality of the interior	
Carpet	
Furniture	
Convention / meeting space	
Elevators	
Lighting	
Restaurant / Lounge / Bar	
Rooms	
Bathrooms	
Kitchen	
Walls	
Carpet	
Lighting	
Heating / Cooling units	
Furniture	

Amenities (yes / no):

Security service	
Valet parking	
Laundry service	
Indoor pool(s)	
Outdoor pool(s)	
Health club	
Vending machines	
Meeting space	
Restaurant / Lounge / Bar	
Concierge	
Room service	

Room

Cable TV	
Kitchen in room	
Jacuzzi tubs	
Patio / Balcony	
Bar	

Neighborhood Description:

PRECEPT™

Property Name
PROPERTY DESCRIPTION

Property Number: 0000
Deal Number: 0000

Product Mix

Type of Room	# of Rooms	% of Total
2 Doubles		
Queens		
Kings		
1BD Suite		
2BD Suite		
Other		
Other		
Other		
Total	-	**0%**

Commercial Space

Type of space	Income
Total	$ -
% of Total	

Location Characteristics:

Corner (yes / no)	
Traffic volume (low, medium, high)	
Access to major arteries	
Access to local amenities	
Street appeal	
Ingress / Egress	
Ease of left hand turn into property	
Visibility	
Signage	
Overall quality of the location	

Major off-site demand generators:

Occupancy Mix

Business	
Leisure	
Other	

Location comments:

Franchisor and Management Information:

Franchisor	
Franchise fee	
Contract expiration date	
Manager / Operator	
Management fee	
Contract expiration date	
Years Mgmt Co. has been associated with Property	
Manages properties for other owner	

Property Management Firm's History/Experience:

REAL ESTATE TAX SUMMARY

General Tax Information:

Tax identification	
Assessor's phone number	
Tax abatements? (yes / no)	
Tax abatement expiration date(s)	

Last re-assessment Date (month/year)	
Assessment currently under appeal?	
Next assessment date (month/year)	

Real Estate Tax Assessment History:

Fiscal Year Ending	Market Value	Conversion Factor	Assessed Value	Millage Rate	Total Property Tax	Other Assessments	Total Tax Liability	Comments
1996							$0	
1997							$0	
1998							$0	
1999							$0	

Comments On Real Estate Taxes (Status of tax appeals and description of other assessments):

STEP 1: PROPERTY STATEMENT COLLECTION

Operating Statements

Precept will require the borrower to submit certified cash flow statements for (1) the past three full years (calendar or fiscal), (2) the current partial year (year to date) and (3) the prior partial year (for the same months relative to the current partial year). The borrower may substitute a complete trailing-12-month cash flow statement for the partial-year statements. In addition to the historical cash flow statements, Precept will require the borrower to submit a certified budget or pro forma for the current full year.

Precept will request that the borrower provide statements that have been generally prepared in accordance with the Ninth Revised Edition of the *Uniform System of Accounts for the Lodging Industry*, published by the Hotel Association of New York City and the American Hotel and Motel Association. If the borrower-provided operating statements do not substantially comply with this accounting methodology and/or do not include sufficient detail from which Precept can adequately reconstruct the operating figures for analytical purposes, Precept may require the borrower to engage a Certified Public Accountant to reprepare the operating statements for Precept's review.

Additional Considerations. Precept will make every effort to obtain partial-year or trailing-12-month statements for periods that end within 3 months (partial months excluded) of the effective date.

Summary of Annual and Monthly ADR

Precept will require the borrower to provide either a certified summary of average daily rates (ADRs) for each month and year corresponding to operating statements provided, or provide certified information sufficient in order for Precept to calculate the same. If ADR (as defined later) statistics are included in the operating statements, a separate summary will not be required.

Additional Considerations. In the absence of ADR statistics provided by the borrower, Precept will calculate ADRs from room revenue (as defined later), occupancy, and room-count figures.

Summary of Annual and Monthly Occupancy

Precept will require the borrower to either provide a summary of occupancy figures for each month and year corresponding to operating statements provided, or provide information sufficient in order for Precept to calculate the same. If occupancy statistics are included in the operating statements, a separate summary will not be required.

Additional Considerations. In the absence of occupancy statistics provided by the borrower, Precept will calculate occupancy from Room Revenue, ADR, and room-count figures.

Summary of Historical Capital Expenditures

Precept will require that the borrower provide a brief description of capital expenditures made to the property within the operating statement periods (prior three years), including the timing and cost of such capital expenditures. In addition to providing relevant detail regarding the property's physical improvements, this summary will be utilized to make any necessary adjustments for nonrecurring expenditures in the Operating Statement Reconciliation section of the underwriting summary.

STEP 2. OPERATING STATEMENT NORMALIZATION

Standard Cash Flow Line Items

Precept will use the Operating Statement Reconciliation section of the underwriting summary to normalize the operating statements as set forth herein. For hotel land uses, Precept's standard cash flow line items are indicated in bold typeface in the following table:

Revenues
Rooms
Food and Beverage
Telecommunications
Other Operated Departments
Other Departmental Revenue
Total Revenue

Expenses
Departmental
Rooms
Food and Beverage
Telecommunications
Other Operated Departments
Other Departmental Expense
Total Departmental Expenses
Gross Operating Income
Undistributed
Management Fee
Franchise Fees
Marketing
Administrative
Operation and Maintenance
Utilities
Other Undistributed Expense
Total Undistributed Expenses
Gross Operating Profit
Fixed
Real Property Taxes
Insurance
Other Fixed Expense—1
Other Fixed Expense—2
Other Fixed Expense—3
Total Fixed Expenses

Capital Expenditures
Reserves for FF&E
Other Capital Expense—1
Other Capital Expense—2
Total Capital Expenditures
Net Cash Flow

The headings in the preceding table are group descriptions and the line items in bold italics are calculated fields. The line item entitled "Other Operated Departments" is reserved for all other sources of income derived from departments operated by the hotel (e.g., parking, golf, etc.). The line item entitled "Other Departmental Revenue" is reserved for all other sources of income derived from departments that are not operated by the hotel (e.g., space rentals, commissions, etc.). Each revenue line item has a corresponding expense line item, given its departmental nature.

Precept's standard cash flow line items were developed in general conformance to the departmental statements/accounts methodology from the Ninth Revised Edition of the *Uniform System of Accounts for the Lodging Industry,* published by the Hotel Association of New York City and the American Hotel and Motel Association. However, Precept's standard cash flow line items are not intended to be in complete conformance with that particular standard.

With respect to Franchise Fees (hereinafter defined), Precept will aggregate all fees paid to a franchisor (including those fees associated with royalties, marketing, and reservations) provided that the operating statements contain sufficient detail from which to do so. Nonfranchise or marketing expenses (local advertising and marketing expenses) will be included in the line item entitled "Marketing."

Comparative Statistics for Standard Cash Flow Items

Within the Cash Flow section of the underwriting summary, Precept will present each of the standard cash flow items in separate columns as dictated by the corresponding operating periods. Adjacent to each of these columns, Precept will calculate and present each standard cash flow item per occupied room (POR) and per available room (PAR). Precept will use these figures for comparative analytical purposes during its estimation of stabilized cash flow.

Compiling a Trailing-12-Month Operating Statement

In some cases the borrower will have provided Precept with a current trailing-12-month operating statement that can be entered directly into the Operating Statement Reconciliation portion of the underwriting summary. In this event, Precept will compile a trailing-12-month statement, provided that the operating statements obtained from the borrower allow Precept to do so in a meaningful manner. For example, if the borrower is able to provide operating statements for the past full calendar year *A*, the current partial year *B* (year to date), and the prior partial year *C* (for the same months relative to the current partial year), the trailing-12-month cash flow would be compiled by subtracting *C*, the prior partial year, from *A*, the past full calendar year, and adding *B*, the current partial year, to the result. This compilation would be completed on a line-by-line basis, and results would appear in the Operating Statement Reconciliation portion of the model, with a "trailing-12" or "TTM" designation. Under no circumstances will Precept accept annualized partial-year operating figures in lieu of a borrower-provided TTM statement or TTM compilation.

STEP 3. DATA CONFIRMATION

In addition to the collection and normalization of property operating statements, Precept will conduct other various procedures confirming the property's operating history. If these procedures identify inaccuracies or misrepresentations within the normalized operating history, corresponding adjustments will be made and footnoted within the appropriate section of the underwriting summary, and/or the borrower may be asked to resubmit one or more property statements. Moreover, if individual income and expense line items presented in the property operating statements are volatile from year to year, Precept may increase the sample size (length of the operating period) for data confirmation purposes.

Federal Income Tax Return Review

Precept will reconcile the property operating statements to the borrower or current owner's most recent available federal income tax returns. Precept expects that total income reported in the tax return will be within 5% of Total Effective Gross Income reported in the operating statements. If this expectation is not met, Precept will require an explanation from the borrower, which will be noted within the Income Tax Reconciliation section of the underwriting summary.

While individual expense line-item titles often differ between tax returns and operating statements (making line-item comparisons difficult), overall expenses are expected to be consistent. To the greatest extent possible, Precept will group individual expense line items from the tax returns so that they are consistent with the expense line items of operating statements. For example, Precept may total all expense line items except Real Property Taxes and Insurance, and compare the result to the same from the operating statements. At a minimum, Precept will compare overall expenses from the tax returns, with obvious adjustments for interest and depreciation, to overall expenses from the corresponding operating statement. If comparable line items, line-item groupings, and/or Total Expenses differ between the two sources by more than 10%, Precept will require borrower explanations that will be noted within the Income Tax Reconciliation section of the underwriting summary.

Additional Considerations. Federal income tax returns may not always be available, given that some borrowers may be using the contemplated financing as purchase money. If this is the case, Precept will continue the data confirmation procedures outlined here in lieu of the income tax reconciliation.

Bank Statement Review

Precept will reconcile Total Revenue from the operating statements for the most recent 12-month period to actual bank statements reflecting property income. This reconciliation will not be conducted if the federal income tax return review is completed and yields no discrepancies with respect to property income.

Franchise Agreement Review

For franchised hotels, Precept will review the property's current franchise agreement in order to confirm basic financial terms (e.g., Franchise Fees). Precept will recalculate franchise-related fees for historical periods based on the terms of the franchise agreement and historical revenue and reservation figures from the operating statements. Precept will reconcile the recalculated franchise related fees to actual expenditures from the operating statements. For purposes of this analysis, franchise-related fees include those associated with royalties, reservations, and marketing.

Occupancy and ADR Review

Precept will use borrower-provided occupancy and ADR figures (along with room count) to recalculate Room Revenue for purposes of reconciliation to Room Revenue reported in the operating statements. To the extent that there is a material discrepancy, Precept will attempt to determine whether the discrepancy is in occupancy, ADR, or both, and will make adjustments accordingly.

Additional Considerations. The product of reported ADR and occupancy (along with room count) may not always yield a Room Revenue figure that exactly matches the operating statement. Such discrepancies may be due to rounding of ADR and occupancy figures, or inconsistencies in accounting methodology over a given period of time. For minor discrepancies, Precept will not attempt to determine the exact cause; rather, Precept will maintain the borrower's reported ADR figure and Room Revenue figure and recalculate the corresponding occupancy percentage for the underwriting summary. Precept will provide the reported occupancy figures for comparison to calculated occupancy within the Operating Statement Reconciliation section of the underwriting summary.

Management Fee Review

Precept will reconcile historical Management Fee expenses from the operating statements to the current management contract.

Payroll and Benefits Expense Review

Precept will reconcile historical Payroll and Benefits expenses to the borrower's summary of property employees and payroll. Precept will pay particular attention to the actual level of staffing in relation to industry standards for similar hotels. Precept will also evaluate whether the borrower (including the borrower's family) performs necessary operating functions without reflecting corresponding Payroll and Benefits expenses within the operating statements.

Utilities Expense Review

Precept will reconcile Utilities expenses from the operating statements to actual utility bills for the most recent 12-month period. Precept will not perform this reconciliation if the Precept's review of the borrower's federal income tax return yields no discrepancies with respect to Utilities expenses.

Real Property Tax Expense Review

Precept will reconcile Real Property Taxes from the operating statements to actual tax bills for the most recent 12-month period.

Capital Expenditures Review

Precept will reconcile capital improvement expenses from the operating statements to the summary of historical capital expenditures provided by the borrower. Precept will pay particular attention to the last soft- and case-good renovations completed at the property.

Other

Depending on (1) the results of the procedures outlined previously, (2) the sophistication of the borrower's accounting system, and (3) the volatility of individual operating statement figures, Precept may conduct additional procedures, including, but not limited to, a detailed income and expense ledger review for certain periods of time in order to better understand the components of the property's operations.

STEP 4. ESTIMATION OF STABILIZED PROPERTY CASH FLOW

Precept will conclude an underwritten Net Cash Flow on a trailing-12-month (TTM) basis.

Revenues

Room Revenue

Standard Definition. *Room Revenue* is an estimate of the stabilized annual revenue the property will generate from renting rooms and suites for part of a day, a week, a month, or longer period of time.

Method of Derivation. Room Revenue is derived by drawing conclusions for ADR (as defined later) and Occupancy (as defined later) and incorporating these conclusions into the following calculation:

Room Revenue = Occupancy × ADR × hotel room count × days in the year

ADR. Average daily rate (ADR) will equal the actual ADR from the trailing-12-month operating statement.

Additional Considerations. Rather than attempt to adjust both ADR and Occupancy from historical levels to achieve estimated stabilized Room Revenue, Precept will concentrate on adjusting Occupancy alone, given the property's actual ADR. However, Precept may conclude ADR based on an adjustment to the actual trailing 12 months (with or without an Occupancy conclusion that represents an adjustment from the actual trailing 12 months) if making such an adjustment more clearly supports Precept's Room Revenue conclusion. This may be the case, for example, if (1) a property's ADR is consistently declining, (2) the general manager indicates his or her intention to lower ADR in light of new competition, and/or (3) the appraiser draws an ADR conclusion that is well supported and deviates from the actual trailing 12 months. In no case, however, will Precept's ADR conclusion be greater than the actual trailing 12 months.

Occupancy. *Occupancy* is concluded as either *maximum hotel occupancy* or *adjusted TTM occupancy,* as follows.

MAXIMUM HOTEL OCCUPANCY. *Maximum Hotel Occupancy* shall be defined as follows:

- 70% for limited-service hotels
- 75% for full-service hotels (including convention facilities) with less than five years of stabilized occupancy history above 80%
- 80% for extended-stay hotels and full-service hotels (including convention facilities) with five years of history above 80% occupancy and strong barriers to entry

ADJUSTED TTM OCCUPANCY. Trailing-12-months Occupancy will be adjusted downward in order to reflect the anticipated negative impact of recent and future market events (as defined later). For example, recent and future market events might include the relocation of a large corporate employer (a change in demand) or the opening of a new hotel (a change in supply).

Additional Considerations. The most important distinction between Recent Market Events (defined later) and Future Market Events is that Recent Market Events will likely provide at least some actual history from which to base adjustments. In addition, the identification of Future Market Events is more geared toward supply than demand, given the simplicity and at least short-term predictability of real estate development versus the unpredictability and complexity of demand characteristics. Recent Market Events are therefore more likely to involve a demand component because they have already surfaced and been identified (for example, it is much easier to identify that a major employer has left a market than to predict that a major employer plans to leave in the future). On the other hand, given the fairly standardized and accessible channels of investigation for potential real estate development (local building and planning departments, etc.), short-term prediction of future supply is more easily made.

Recent Market Events that have occurred within two months of Precept's underwriting will be treated as Future Market Events if actual operating history since the Recent Market Event is not available at the time of underwriting.

Recent Market Events. Precept will identify *Recent Market Events* through the site inspection report, appraisal report, and direct interviews of (1) local planning/building department personnel, (2) the property's general manager, (3) management of competing hotels, and (4) the local Chamber of Commerce. Precept will pay particular attention to declines in room revenue from the 12-month period immediately preceding the trailing-12-month (TTM) period.

Precept will begin by evaluating the exact timing of the Recent Market Event(s) in relation to changes in the property's monthly Room Revenue. Next, Precept will compare each month of operation after the Recent Market Event to the corresponding months from the previous calendar year, noting the percentage decline in Room Revenue. Precept will then evaluate whether the Property's operations have stabilized by comparing the percentage declines for the three most recent months of the TTM (after the Recent Market Event). Provided that the percentage decline from the prior year is consistent (or improving) during the TTM's most recent three months, Precept will adjust the Room Revenue for the TTM prior to the Recent Market Event by an average of the actual percentage decline indicated by post–Recent Market Event operations:

Adjusted TTM = actual room revenue for portion of TTM post–market event
+ [actual room revenue for portion of TTM pre–market event
× (actual room revenue for portion of TTM following market event
/ actual room revenue from prior year for same number of months
as the portion of TTM following market event)]

If the percentage decline from the prior calendar year is continuing to increase for the most recent three months of the TTM, Precept will consider the magnitude of the Recent Market Event to be unpredictable. In this case, Precept will postpone the cash flow underwriting process for the property until the borrower can provide an updated TTM (by one to three months, depending on the severity of the operating decline) that demonstrates that the property's operations have stabilized since the occurrence of the Recent Market Event, at which point Precept will repeat the Recent Market Event analysis.

Additional Considerations. When evaluating the impact that a Recent Market Event has had on the TTM, Precept will pay particular attention to whether the post–Recent Market Event portion of the TTM represents the strongest or weakest months within the market's demand cycle. If this is the case, Precept may increase or decrease the severity of the TTM adjustment previously described for specific months in order to reflect typical seasonal fluctuations that will likely diminish or exacerbate the Recent Market Event's impact on the property's operations. For example, assume the property is located in a desert location, where the winter months (November through March) represent the peak season, and a new hotel that would appear to be directly competitive opened in November 2000. Further assume that Precept will conduct the underwriting in April 2001 with a TTM through March 2001. TTM Room Revenue for the property is almost equal to the TTM one year, earlier and each of the most recent three months of the TTM are consistent with the same months from the prior year. Based on this operating history, it would appear that no adjustment is necessary. However, because the new hotel opened in the middle of the peak season, when the market is typically undersupplied, the new hotel would have little effect from November to March, but would be likely to impact the property during the slower months, when the market would be oversupplied. In such a case, Precept would adjust the TTM to reflect the likely impact the new hotel will have on the property from April through October only.

Depending on the complexity of the market and the Recent Market Event, including whether the Recent Market Event is primarily a change in supply or a change in demand, Precept will adjust the TTM in any number of ways. The basis for Precept's adjustment might include, for example, a detailed fair-share analysis with changes in supply and demand and individual hotel market penetration rates from pre– to post–market event. It may also include a more simplified demand-fixed fair-share analysis, such as the one explained later under Future Market Events. In all cases, Precept will attempt to use the property's actual operating history (before and after the Recent Market Event) as an indicator of how the TTM should be adjusted to more accurately reflect future stabilized cash flow. Ultimately, Precept will clearly outline within the underwriting summary how and to what extent the TTM was adjusted for the Recent Market Event(s).

Future Market Events. Precept will identify anticipated *Future Market Events* through the site inspection report, appraisal report, and direct interviews of (1) local planning/building department personnel, (2) the property's general manager, (3) management of competing hotels, and (4) the local Chamber of Commerce. Given the difficulty of identifying Future Market Events which may affect demand, Precept will pay particular attention to the potential for additional hotels that will compete directly or indirectly with the property.

Adjusting TTM Occupancy for anticipated new hotel room supply involves a downward adjustment of a property's market share of total occupied hotel room nights in proportion to the future growth in room supply, assuming no change in total occupied room nights for the market. Precept will adjust new room supply in a manner that attempts to measure the degree to which the impending new hotel room supply directly competes with the property. For example, new supply located a significant distance from the property will not affect Occupancy at the property nearly as much as new supply directly across the street. Similarly, Occupancy will be affected more from a new hotel in a market with 500 rooms than if the hotel is added to a market with 5000 rooms. Therefore, in analyzing the impact of the distant hotel, Precept may adjust down by 75% the number of rooms at the new hotel to reach an *effective* new room supply of 25% of the actual new room count. Precept will analyze each new hotel project and determine the appropriate adjustment factor. The following list provides examples of adjustment factors and accompanying situations:

- 25% of actual room count for a *noncompetitive hotel*—e.g., a new limited-service hotel one mile from the property, which is a full-service hotel.
- 50% of actual room count for a *semicompetitive hotel*—e.g., a new limited-service hotel across the street from the property, which is a full-service hotel.
- 75% of actual room count for a *competitive hotel*—e.g., a new full-service hotel within the market of the property, which is a full-service hotel.

- 100% of the actual room count for a *highly competitive hotel*—e.g., a new full-service hotel within the market that will fully cannibalize on a share basis the property, which is a full-service hotel. This situation occurs only when Precept determines that the new supply is directly competitive with a property being underwritten.
- 125% of the actual room count for a *superior hotel*—e.g., a new limited-service hotel within the market that has the potential to reduce the property's market penetration (where the property is a limited-service hotel).

After choosing an adjustment factor for each new hotel in the market, Precept will adjust the TTM Occupancy for the property to determine *Adjusted TTM Occupancy* using the following equation:

Adjusted TTM Occupancy = TTM Occupancy × {total number of rooms in the market / [total number of rooms in the market + sum of: (new rooms in each hotel × adjustment factor for each new hotel)]}

The following table shows an example of adjusting historical occupancy for new room supply:

Description	Room Count	Adjustment Factor	Effective Room Count
Property's TTM Occupancy	80.0%		
Property room count	100		
TTM market room count	1000		1000
New supply summary:			
New hotel 1	100	0.25	25
New hotel 2	150	0.75	112.5
Total Effective Market Room Count			**1137.5**
Adjusted TTM Occupancy = 80% occupancy × 1000/1137.5 = 70.33%			

Additional Considerations. While evaluating the potential impact of a Future Market Event, Precept will consider the property's recent historical reaction to similar events, if any, in terms of operating performance.

Food and Beverage Revenue

Standard Definition. *Food and Beverage Revenue* is an estimate of the stabilized annual revenue the property will generate from the sale of food and beverages, including alcoholic and soft drinks, coffee, tea, juice, and milk from outlets such as restaurants, lounges, room service, banquets, and minibars.

Method of Derivation. Food and Beverage Revenue is determined by drawing a conclusion for stabilized food and Beverage Revenue per occupied room and incorporating the result into the following calculation:

Food and Beverage Revenue = concluded Food and Beverage Revenue per occupied room × underwritten TTM Occupancy × number of hotel rooms × number of days in the year

Precept will conclude Food and Beverage Revenue per occupied room using the property's actual three-year historical operations, with emphasis placed on the most recent 12-month period. If Food and Beverage Revenue per occupied room over the three-year history is volatile or increasing, Precept will use an average of Food and Beverage Revenue per occupied room for the three-year period. If, however, Food and Beverage Revenue per occupied room is declining, Precept will use a figure at or below the most recent 12-month period, depending on the cause of the decline.

Precept will then evaluate whether the amount of Food and Beverage Revenue is consistent with the type of hotel (budget, limited-service, full-service, etc.) and industry standards. Precept will pay particular attention to levels of Food and Beverage Revenue that are at the high end of industry norms, in which case Precept will evaluate whether the hotel derives a material amount of profit from sources outside the hotel (e.g., off-site catering) and/or from non-hotel-room guests (e.g., night club or restaurant guests), and will make adjustments accordingly. For purposes of this analysis, Precept will use industry statistics from the appraisal report and publications by Smith Travel Research and PKF Consulting.

Additional Considerations. If the property has not been in operation for three years, Precept will use the average Food and Beverage Revenue per occupied room over the life of the property. Precept recognizes that while Food and Beverage Revenue may fluctuate dramatically from year to year, food and beverage profit (revenue less expenses) may be consistent, in which case Precept will adjust Food and Beverage Revenue as previously noted, but will also make a corresponding adjustment to Food and Beverage Expense (as defined later) to reflect the historical profit level.

Telecommunications Revenue

Standard Definition. *Telecommunications Revenue* is an estimate of the stabilized annual revenue the property will receive from telecommunication facilities used by guests, including, but not limited to, revenue from local and long-distance in-room calls, facsimile services, modem services, commissions received from nonowned pay stations, revenue from owned pay stations, and service charges.

Method of Derivation. Telecommunications Revenue is determined by drawing a conclusion for stabilized Telecommunications Revenue per occupied room and incorporating the result into the following calculation:

Telecommunications Revenue = concluded Telecommunications Revenue per occupied room × underwritten TTM Occupancy × number of hotel rooms × number of days in the year

Precept will conclude Telecommunications Revenue per occupied room using the property's actual three-year historical operations, with emphasis placed on the most recent 12-month period. If Telecommunications Revenue per occupied room over the three-year history is volatile or increasing, Precept will use an average of Telecommunications Revenue per occupied room for the three-year period. If, however, Telecommunications Revenue per occupied room is declining, Precept will use a figure at or below the most recent 12-month period, depending on the cause of the decline.

Precept will then evaluate whether the amount of Telecommunications Revenue is consistent with the type of hotel (budget, limited-service, full-service, etc.) and industry standards, paying particular attention to levels of Telecommunications Revenue that are at the high end of industry norms. For purposes of this analysis, Precept will use industry statistics from the appraisal report and publications by Smith Travel Research and PKF Consulting.

Additional Considerations. If the property has not been in operation for three years, Precept will use the average Telecommunications Revenue per occupied room over the life of the property. Precept recognizes that while Telecommunications Revenue may fluctuate dramatically from year to year, telecommunications profit (revenue less expenses) may be consistent, in which case Precept will adjust Telecommunications Revenue as previously noted, but will also make a corresponding adjustment to Telecommunications Expense (as defined later) to reflect the historical profit level.

Other Operated Departments Revenue

Standard Definition. *Other Operated Departments Revenue* is an estimate of the stabilized annual revenue the property will receive from other guest services and/or merchandise sales that are operated as departments within the property and not contracted through rental or concession agreements. Other operated departments may include garage/parking, golf course, golf pro shop, guest laundry, health center, swimming pool, tennis, tennis pro shop, barber/beauty shop, and gift shop.

Method of Derivation. Other Operated Departments Revenue is determined by drawing a conclusion for stabilized Other Operated Departments revenue per occupied room and incorporating the result into the following calculation:

Other Operated Departments Revenue = concluded Other Operated Departments Revenue per occupied room × underwritten TTM Occupancy × number of hotel rooms × number of days in the year

Precept will conclude Other Operated Departments Revenue per occupied room using the property's actual three-year historical operations, with emphasis placed on the most recent 12-month period. If Other Operated Departments Revenue per occupied room over the three-year history is volatile or increasing, Precept will use an average of Other Operated Departments Revenue per occupied room for the three-year period. If, however, Other Operated Departments Revenue per occupied room is declining, Precept will use a figure at or below the most recent 12-month period, depending on the cause of the decline.

Precept will then evaluate whether the amount of Other Operated Departments Revenue is consistent with the type of hotel (budget, limited-service, full-service, etc.) and industry standards, paying particular attention to levels of Other Operated Departments Revenue that are at the high end of industry norms. For purposes of this analysis, Precept will use industry statistics from the appraisal report and publications by Smith Travel Research and PKF Consulting.

Additional Considerations. If the property has not been in operation for three years, Precept will use the average Other Operated Departments Revenue per occupied room over the life of the property. Precept recognizes that while Other Operated Departments Revenue may fluctuate dramatically from year to year, Other Operated Departments profit (revenue less expenses) may be consistent, in which case Precept will still adjust Other Operated Departments Revenue as previously noted, but will also make a corresponding adjustment to Other Operated Departments Expense (as defined later) to reflect the historical profit level.

Other Departmental Revenue

Standard Definition. *Other Departmental Revenue* is an estimate of the stabilized annual revenue the property will receive from other guest services and/or merchandise sales that are not operated as departments within the property and/or are provided by others through rental and concession agreements.

Method of Derivation. Precept will include as Other Departmental Revenue only those items individually or in aggregate having consistent history and strong expectations for future collections. If such amounts comprise more than 5.0% of Total Revenue, Precept will request documentation confirming and explaining such sources of revenue. Otherwise, Precept will base the underwritten amount on the most recent 12-month collections or an average of historical collections, depending on the source and historical fluctuations. If Precept determines the sources of Other Departmental Revenue to be sensitive to Occupancy fluctuations, Precept may adjust historical revenues for underwritten Occupancy in accordance with the derivation of Other Departmental Revenues. The Operating Statement Reconciliation section of the underwriting summary will identify the specific source of income.

Expenses

Room Expense

Standard Definition. *Room Expense* is an estimate of the stabilized annual expenses the property will incur in order to operate the rooms department at the level of revenue underwritten. Room Expense includes Payroll and Benefits for room personnel (front office manager, concierge, guest service agents, house attendants, housekeepers, linen control staff, reservations staff, service staff, etc.), cable television, travel agency commissions, complimentary guest services, guest relocation, guest transportation, soft-good maintenance, and employee uniforms.

Method of Derivation. Room Expense is determined by drawing a conclusion for the ratio of Room Expense to Room Revenue and multiplying the result by underwritten Room Revenue. First, Precept will calculate the ratio of Room Expense to Room Revenue for each of the prior three years. The underwritten ratio of Room Expense to Room Revenue will then be concluded based on the greater of (1) the TTM expense ratio or (2) the average of the expense ratios for the prior three years. The concluded ratio is then multiplied by underwritten Room Revenue.

As a final step, the Room Expense conclusion will be compared to market data from one or more of the following sources: Smith Travel Research, PKF Consulting, and the appraisal report. Precept will evaluate whether the ratio of Room Expense to Room Revenue is consistent with the type of hotel (limited-service, full-service, etc.) and industry averages. Provided that the underwritten expense ratio is within the range of national statistics for similar hotel types, Precept will make no adjustment to the underwritten expense outlined previously. If the expense ratio is beneath the low end of the range of national statistics for similar hotel types, Precept will explore the reason for the property's superior operating efficiency. In this case, Precept will conclude an expense ratio that is between the low end of the range of national statistics and the actual (either TTM or average of historical periods), depending on the borrower's explanation regarding the property's actual expense ratios, and will recalculate Room Expense as previously outlined.

Additional Considerations. A portion of typical Room Expense may be fixed, and therefore Room Expense is not directly variable with Room Revenue. Similarly, various undistributed expenses (such as energy) are not entirely fixed. Rather than attempt to establish the exact variability of both departmental and undistributed expenses, Precept assumes that departmental expenses are completely variable and that undistributed expenses are completely fixed.

Food and Beverage Expense

Standard Definition. *Food and Beverage Expense* is an estimate of the stabilized annual expenses the property will incur in order to operate the combined food and beverage departments at the revenue level underwritten, including, but not limited to, Payroll and Benefits of food and beverage personnel (departmental management, food preparation staff, food and beverage service staff, room service staff, minibar staff, etc.), glassware, eating utensils, gratis food, licenses, miscellaneous banquet expenses, music and entertainment, and employee uniforms.

Method of Derivation. Food and Beverage Expense is determined by drawing a conclusion for the ratio of Food and Beverage Expense to Food and Beverage Revenue and multiplying the result by underwritten Food and Beverage Revenue. First, Precept will calculate the ratio of Food and Beverage Expense to Food and Beverage Revenue for each of the prior three years. The underwritten ratio of Food and Beverage Expense to Food and Beverage Revenue will then be concluded based on the greater of (1) the TTM expense ratio or (2) the average of the expense ratios for the prior three years. The concluded ratio is then multiplied by underwritten Food and Beverage Revenue.

As a final step, the food and beverage conclusion will be compared to market data from one or more of the following sources: Smith Travel Research, PKF Consulting, and the appraisal report. Precept will evaluate whether the ratio of Food and Beverage Expense to Food and Beverage Revenue is consistent with the type of hotel (limited-service, full-service, etc.) and industry averages. Provided that the underwritten expense ratio is within the range of national statistics for similar hotel types, Precept will make no adjustment to the underwritten expense outlined previously. If the expense ratio is beneath the low end of the range of national statistics for similar hotel types, Precept will explore the reason for the property's superior operating efficiency. In this case, Precept will conclude an expense ratio that is between the low end of the range of national statistics and the actual (either TTM or average of historical periods), depending on the borrower's explanation regarding the property's actual expense ratio, and will recalculate Food and Beverage Expense as previously outlined.

Additional Considerations. A portion of typical Food and Beverage Expense is fixed, and therefore Food and Beverage Expense is not directly variable with Food and Beverage Revenue. Similarly, various undistributed expenses (such as energy) are not entirely fixed. Rather than attempt to establish the exact variability of both departmental and undistributed expenses, Precept assumes that departmental expenses are completely variable and that undistributed expenses are completely fixed.

Telecommunications Expense

Standard Definition. *Telecommunications Expense* is an estimate of the stabilized annual expenses the property will incur in order to operate the telecommunications department at the revenue level underwritten, including, but not limited to, Payroll and Benefits of telecommunications personnel (departmental management, supervisors, telephone operators, technicians, etc.).

Method of Derivation. Telecommunications Expense is determined by drawing a conclusion for the ratio of Telecommunications Expense to Telecommunications Revenue and multiplying the result by underwritten Telecommunications Revenue. First, Precept will calculate the ratio of Telecommunications Expense to Telecommunications Revenue for each of the prior three years. The underwritten ratio of Telecommunications Expense to Telecommunications Revenue will then be concluded based on the greater of (1) the TTM expense ratio or (2) the average of the expense ratios for the prior three years. The concluded ratio is then multiplied by underwritten Telecommunications Revenue.

As a final step, the telecommunications conclusion will be compared to market data from one or more of the following sources: Smith Travel Research, PKF Consulting, and the appraisal report. Precept will evaluate whether the ratio of Telecommunications Expense to Telecommunications Revenue is consistent with the type of hotel (limited-service, full-service, etc.) and industry averages. Provided that the underwritten expense ratio is within the range of national statistics for similar hotel types, Precept will make no adjustment to the underwritten expense outlined previously. If the expense ratio is beneath the low end of the range of national statistics for similar hotel types, Precept will explore the reason for the property's superior operating efficiency. In this case, Precept will conclude an expense ratio that is between the low end of the range of national statistics and the actual (either TTM or average of historical periods), depending on the borrower's explanation regarding the property's actual expense ratio, and will recalculate Telecommunications Expense as previously outlined.

Additional Considerations. A portion of typical Telecommunications Expense is fixed, and therefore Telecommunications Expense is not directly variable with Telecommunications Revenue. Similarly, various undistributed expenses (such as energy) are not entirely fixed. Rather than attempt to establish the exact variability of both departmental and undistributed expenses, Precept assumes that other department expenses are completely variable and that undistributed expenses are completely fixed.

Other Operated Departments Expense

Standard Definition. *Other Operated Departments Expense* is an estimate of the stabilized annual expenses the property will incur in order to operate other departments.

Method of Derivation. Other Operated Departments Expense is determined by drawing a conclusion for the ratio of Other Operated Departments Expense to Other Operated Departments Revenue and multiplying the result by underwritten Other Operated Departments Revenue. First, Precept will calculate the ratio of Other Operated Departments Expense to Other Operated Departments Revenue for each of the prior three years. The underwritten ratio of Other Operated Departments Expense to Other Operated Departments Revenue will then be concluded based on the greater of (1) the TTM expense ratio or (2) the average of the expense ratios for all historical periods available. The concluded ratio is then multiplied by underwritten Other Operated Departments Revenue.

Other Departmental Expense

Standard Definition. *Other Departmental Expense* is an estimate of the stabilized annual expenses the property will incur to maintain other guest services and/or merchandise sales that are not operated as departments within the property.

Method of Derivation. Other Departmental Expense is determined by drawing a conclusion for the ratio of Other Departmental Expense to Other Departmental Revenue and multiplying the result by underwritten Other Departmental Revenue. First, Precept will calculate the ratio of Other Departmental Expense to Other Departmental Revenue for each of the prior three years. The underwritten ratio of Other Departmental Expense to Other Departmental Revenue will then be concluded based on the greater of (1) the trailing-12-month expense ratio or (2) the average of the expense ratios for all historical periods available. The concluded ratio is then multiplied by the underwritten Other Departmental Revenue.

Management Fee

Standard Definition. *Management Fee* is an estimate of the annual amount an independent management company would charge to comprehensively oversee the property's operations.

Method of Derivation. Precept will underwrite the Management Fees to equal the greater of the following:

- The management fees set forth in the current management contract
- The market Management Fee that Precept determines would be required to engage a competent third-party property management firm

In concluding the Management Fees, Precept shall use the following Management Fee minimums:

- Limited-service hotel, full-service hotel, and extended-stay hotel with ADR less than or equal to $100—4.5% of underwritten Total Revenue
- Limited-service hotel, full-service hotel, and extended-stay hotel with ADR greater than $100—3.5% of underwritten Total Revenue
- Convention hotels (with major management contracts and no franchise)—5.5% of underwritten Total Revenue

Additional Considerations. Precept will determine the market Management Fee based on its review of the site inspection and appraisal reports. In the event that the property is borrower managed, the borrower's fee or related Payroll and Benefits will be evaluated in lieu of the Management Fee for purposes of the preceding analysis.

Franchise Fees

Standard Definition. *Franchise Fees* are estimates of the annual amount the property will pay to a "branded" hotel company (the *franchisor*) in exchange for the right to use the franchise name, benefit from national marketing, access a centralized reservation system managed by the hotel company, and generally receive operating support from the franchisor.

Method of Derivation. Franchise Fees are derived by multiplying underwritten Room Revenue by the greater of (1) Precept's minimum Franchise Fees percentage, (2) the contractual Franchise Fees percentage (concession periods ignored), (3) the TTM ratio of actual Franchise Fees to Room Revenue, or (4) the average ratio of Franchise Fees to Room Revenue for the prior three years. Precept's minimum Franchise Fees percentage of underwritten Room Revenue by hotel type is outlined in the following table:

Hotel Type	Franchise Fee, %
Limited service	6.0
Full service	5.0
Extended stay	5.0
Convention (full service)	0.0

Precept shall apply these minimums to nonfranchised hotels for underwriting purposes. However, Precept will offset the Franchise Fees resulting from the preceding derivation by the amount that Marketing expenses exceed 3% of Total Revenue for independent (nonfranchised) hotels.

Additional Considerations. In some cases, not all components of the Franchise Fees will be based on a percentage of Room Revenue. For example, reservation fees may be charged on a flat rate per reservation. In such cases, Precept will place emphasis on the actual fees paid during historical periods as a percentage of historical Room Revenue for purposes of establishing which Franchise Fee percentage to use for underwriting.

When reviewing the franchise agreement, Precept will pay particular attention to whether the formula for calculating Franchise Fees varies from year to year and/or the Franchise Fees are stepped for an initial term in order to provide the franchisee a short-term concession. In such cases, Precept will use the fee calculation yielding the greatest Franchise Fee over the remaining term of the franchise agreement.

Marketing

Standard Definition. *Marketing* expense is an estimate of the annual nonfranchise costs the property will incur in order to create and maintain the property's image and develop, promote, and further new business.

Method of Derivation. Marketing expense is concluded based on a comparison of historical Marketing expense at the property to hotel industry data. The primary basis for the Marketing conclusion will be the property's actual three-year historical Marketing expense, with emphasis placed on the most recent 12-month period. If the Marketing expense over the three-year history is volatile or declining, Precept will use an average of the Marketing expense for the collected three-year history. If historical Marketing expense is systematically increasing, Precept's conclusion will be consistent with the most recent 12-month period. The Marketing conclusion will be compared to industry data from one or more of the following sources: Smith Travel Research, PKF Consulting, and the appraisal report. Provided that the ratio of underwritten Marketing expense to Total Revenue is within the range of national statistics for similar hotel types, Precept will make no adjustment to the underwritten expense outlined previously. If the expense ratio is beneath the low end of the range of national statistics for similar hotel types, Precept will explore the reason. In this case, Precept will conclude an expense ratio that is between the low end of the range of national statistics and the actual, depending on the results of Precept's investigation, and will recalculate Marketing expense as previously outlined.

Additional Considerations. The cost of marketing a property will vary depending on the location and condition of the property as well as the strength and services provided by the franchisor (if any). Hotels without a franchise affiliation (unflagged) are expected to have Marketing expenses that exceed those of similar franchised (flagged) hotels. For nonfranchised hotels, Precept will offset Franchise Fees by the amount that Marketing expenses exceed 3% of Total Revenue. For franchised hotels, Precept will attempt to isolate hotel-specific local marketing expenses from Marketing Fees paid as part of a franchise agreement when reconciling the historical operating statements.

Administrative

Standard Definition. *Administrative* expenses are an estimate of the stabilized annual expenses that are applicable to the entire property and are not easily allocated to operated departments. The type of expenses allocated to this category will vary depending on the needs and requirements of the property. Administrative expenses include, but are not limited to, bank charges, communication systems, credit and collection, credit card commissions, donations, dues and subscriptions, head-office expense allocations, information systems, internal audits, operating supplies, postage, professional fees, security, training, travel, and Payroll and Benefits for administrative staff.

Method of Derivation. Administrative expenses are concluded based on a comparison of historical Administrative expenses at the property to hotel industry data. The primary basis for the Administrative expense conclusion will be the property's actual three-year historical Administrative expenses, with emphasis placed on the most recent 12-month period. If Administrative expenses over the three-year history are volatile or declining, Precept will use an average of Administrative expenses for the collected three-year history. If historical Administrative expenses are systematically increasing, Precept's conclusion will be consistent with the most recent 12-month period. The Administrative expense conclusion will be compared to industry data from one or more of the following sources: Smith Travel Research, PKF Consulting, and the appraisal report. Provided that the ratio of underwritten Administrative expense to total revenue is within the range of national statistics for similar hotel types, Precept will make no adjustment to the underwritten expense outlined previously. If the expense ratio is beneath the low end of the range of national statistics for similar hotel types, Precept will explore the reason for the property's superior operating efficiency. In this case, Precept will conclude an expense ratio that is between the low end of the range of national statistics and the actual, depending on the results of Precept's investigation, and will recalculate administrative expenses as previously outlined.

Additional Considerations. The amount of historical Administrative expense will vary, depending on, among other things, the sophistication of the property's accounting systems and proper departmentalization of expenses. If it is unclear why the property's historical Administrative expenses are below industry averages, Precept will compare the property's overall expenses and Gross Operating Profit (as defined later) to industry statistics. If Gross Operating Profit as a percentage of Total Revenue is consistent with or less than industry norms, Precept will not underwrite Administrative expenses in excess of actual expenditures (either TTM or an average of prior periods). If Gross Operating Profit is greater than industry norms, Precept will underwrite Administrative expenses at a level that is consistent with the range of industry statistics.

Operations and Maintenance

Standard Definition. *Operations and Maintenance* expenses are estimates of the stabilized annual expenses to repair and maintain the property's physical improvements, including furniture fixtures and improvements. The type of expenses allocated to this category will vary depending on the needs and requirements of the property. Operations and Maintenance expenses include, but are not limited to, building supplies, locks and keys, lightbulbs, trash removal, uniforms for departmental personnel, internal telecommunications, and payroll and benefits for administrative staff, as well as repairs and maintenance of curtains and draperies, electrical systems, plumbing, elevators, floor coverings, grounds and landscaping, kitchen equipment, laundry equipment, and hotel vehicles.

Method of Derivation. Operations and Maintenance expenses are concluded based on a comparison of historical operations and Maintenance expenses at the property to hotel industry data. The primary basis for the Operations and Maintenance conclusion will be the property's actual three-year historical Operations and Maintenance expenses, with emphasis placed on the most recent 12-month period. If Operations and Maintenance expenses over the three-year history are volatile or declining, Precept will use an average of Operations and Maintenance expenses for the collected three-year history. If historical Operations and Maintenance expenses are systematically increasing, Precept's conclusion will be consistent with the most recent 12-month period. The Operations and Maintenance conclusion will be compared to industry data from one or more of the following sources: Smith Travel Research, PKF Consulting, and the appraisal report. The property's actual operating history will be compared to industry statistics on a per-room basis and on a ratio basis (Operations and Maintenance expense to Total Revenue). If the property's actual performance is within the range of national statistics for similar hotel types, Precept will make no adjustment to the underwritten expense outlined previously. If the property's expenses are beneath the low end of the range of national statistics, Precept will explore the reason for the property's superior operating efficiency. In this case, Precept will conclude an expense ratio that is between the low end of the range of national statistics and the actual, depending on the results of Precept's investigation, and will recalculate Operations and Maintenance expenses as previously outlined.

Additional Considerations. If it is unclear why a property's historical Operations and Maintenance expenses are below industry averages, Precept will compare the property's overall expenses and Gross Operating Profit to industry statistics. If Gross Operating Profit as a percentage of Total Revenue is consistent with or less than industry norms, Precept will not underwrite Operations and Maintenance expenses in excess of actual expenditures (either TTM or an average of prior periods). If Gross Operating Profit is greater than industry norms, Precept will underwrite Operations and Maintenance expenses at a level that is consistent with the range of industry statistics.

Utilities

Standard Definition. *Utilities* are the total annual amount of water, sewer, electricity, gas, and other applicable utility expenses.

Method of Derivation. Utilities expenses are concluded based on a historical Utilities expense. The primary basis for the Utilities conclusion will be the property's actual three-year historical Utilities expenses, with emphasis placed on the most recent 12-month period. If Utilities expenses over the three-year history are volatile or declining, Precept will use an average of Utilities expenses for the collected three-year history. If historical Utilities expenses are systematically increasing, Precept's conclusion will be consistent with the most recent 12-month period.

Additional Considerations. Utilities expenses are often seasonal in nature and are sometimes billed less frequently than on a monthly basis. As with all other hotel cash flow line items, Precept will underwrite Utilities expenses based on a full year of operating history. Precept will reconcile Utilities expenses from either the trailing-12-month or most recent year-end operating statements to actual utility bills for that same period, or portion thereof if a full 12 months is not available.

Other Undistributed Expense

Standard Definition. *Other Undistributed Expense* is a generic line item that is reserved for a single grouping of nonfixed expenditures from the operating statements that Precept determines would be more meaningfully presented as a separate line item.

In these cases, the generic Precept's line-item title will be replaced with the actual operating statement line-item title. In the event that

Other Undistributed Expenses account for more than 5.0% of the Total Expenses, Precept will require explanations of such expenses and will summarize such information in either the Cash Flow Summary or Operating Statement Reconciliation section of the underwriting summary.

Gross Operating Profit

Standard Definition. Upon drawing conclusions for each of the departmental and undistributed expense categories, Precept will compare the Gross Operating Profit as a percentage of Total Revenue to industry averages and ranges.

This comparison will account for hotel type as well as geographic location to the extent allowed by industry statistics. The sources of industry data will include Smith Travel Research, PKF Consulting, and the appraisal report. In the event that the underwritten level of Total Expenses is not supported by this data, Precept will review its conclusions for each of the expense line items, paying particular attention to those that are closer to the lower end of the industry range. Precept will adjust these expenses either individually or in the aggregate so that underwritten Gross Operating Profit is supported by market and industry statistics.

Real Property Taxes

Standard Definition. *Real Property Taxes* are all taxes assessed against the real property of the property by a state or political subdivision of the state, such as a county or city, including assessments for public improvements.

Method of Derivation. Precept will conclude Real Property Taxes based on the greater of the following:

- The most recent tax bill adjusted for known increases in tax rates and/or impending upward reassessments, and any tax abatements that expire in less than 22.5 years.
- The *Market Real Property Tax* determined by the property's potential Real Property Tax liability assuming a current (near-term) reassessment or a periodic reassessment. For purposes of this estimation, Precept will attempt to follow the appropriate jurisdiction's reassessment methodology in conjunction with the following guidelines:

Near-term reassessment. For jurisdictions where Real Property Taxes are recalculated upon transfer as a percentage of the transfer price or are generally not subject to systematic reassessments, Precept will estimate Market Real Property Tax by multiplying the appropriate local taxation rate by a proposed first mortgage amount. The proposed first mortgage amount will be an estimate of what Precept believes the loan amount will be, based on its underwriting. If no information about the potential loan amount is available, Precept generally will use a first mortgage amount equal to 75% of the estimated current property value.

Periodic reassessment. For jurisdictions where reassessments take place on a periodic basis, Precept will estimate Market Real Property Tax, taking into account the following factors:

- Real property taxes at competing properties (on a per-square-foot basis, sales price basis, etc.)
- Trends in local commercial property values and taxation rates
- The assumptions made by the appraisers regarding their estimate of the Real Property Tax

Additional Considerations. Precept will not underwrite Real Property Taxes below the most recent tax bill without written correspondence from the local taxation authorities confirming the lower assessment and/or taxation rate. If Precept determines it is warranted (if unique taxation structures are identified by Precept), Precept will discuss taxation frameworks with the local tax assessor to understand and clarify these issues.

Insurance

Standard Definition. *Insurance* shall mean all policies of insurance against loss or damage by fire and against loss or damage by other risks or hazards, including, without limitation, liability, riot, civil commotion, vandalism, malicious mischief, burglary, theft, flood, or earthquake.

Method of Derivation. Precept will underwrite Insurance expense at the greater of (1) the most recent insurance bill, or (2) market insurance premiums for Precept standard coverage for a single property policy.

Additional Considerations. Precept will adjust the Insurance expense item, described in point (2) of the preceding paragraph, upward in those instances where a property has inadequate coverage levels or below-market insurance rates (which could not be replicated by a new owner or are due to the fact that a property is covered by a blanket insurance policy covering a property and other properties that are not part of the collateral).

Other Fixed Expense–1, 2, and 3

Standard Definition. *Other Fixed Expense—1, 2, and 3* are generic line items that are reserved for fixed expenditures from the operating statements that either do not clearly fit within Precept's standard line items or that Precept determines to be more meaningful as separate line items.

In these cases, the generic Precept line-item title will be replaced with the actual operating statement line-item title, and Precept will calculate the Other Fixed Expenses as the greater of (1) the fixed expenses for the prior 12-month period or (2) the three-year average for fixed expenses, if available. In the event that Other Fixed Expenses account for more than 3.0% of the Total Expenses, Precept will require explanations of such expenses and will summarize such information in either the Cash Flow Summary or Operating Statement Reconciliation sections of the underwriting summary. One of the more common Other Fixed Expense categories is Ground Rent.

Ground Rent (If Applicable). Precept will generally underwrite *Ground Rent* using 75% of the proposed amortization schedule of the loan amount.

Capital Expenditures

Reserves for FF&E

Standard Definition. *Reserves for FF&E* (furniture, fixtures, and equipment) are estimates of the average annual expenditures needed in order to replace improvement components that have shorter useful lives than the structure itself. Improvement components that require periodic replacement include roofs, parking lot asphalt, elevators, HVAC equipment, windows, guest room and lobby furniture, linens, and tableware.

Method of Derivation. Reserves for FF&E will be concluded based on the greater of 4.5% of underwritten Total Revenue for hotel properties and the property condition assessment's ongoing physical needs annual average estimate.

Additional Considerations. Precept will review the property condition assessment's conclusions for reasonableness, taking into account the property's age, common-area structures, and overall improvement condition required to generate the underwritten level of Total Revenue. The engineer preparing the property condition assessment will review the property's furniture, fixtures, and equipment only from a function/useful-life standpoint, and not from a market/guest-appeal perspective. Therefore, Precept will pay particular attention to the site inspection report's comments regarding the condition of FF&E and their guest appeal. For franchised hotels, Precept will also review the property's last three franchisor inspection reports for improvement condition comments, suggestions, and upgrade requirements. Based on a review of these items, Precept may increase the underwritten Reserves for FF&E to be in excess of 4.5% of Total Revenue.

Other Capital Expense–1 and 2

Standard Definition. *Other Capital Expense—1 and 2* includes generic line items that are reserved for capital expenditures that were not represented in the property condition assessment's ongoing physical needs analysis or that Precept determines to be more meaningful as separate line items.

Other Capital Expenses, for example, could include an improvement recommended by the environmental engineer. Precept will require explanations of such expenses and will summarize such information in either the Cash Flow Summary or Operating Statement Reconciliation sections of the underwriting summary.

CHAPTER 8

Borrower Credit Analysis

The decision-making process involved in underwriting a commercial mortgage is not limited to just an investigation of the property's qualities. It also includes a credit review of the property's owner(s), which can be a single person, partnership, corporation, or other business entity involving a number of different investors. The ownership structure of a property can be simple or complicated; but in either case, lenders have long found it prudent to investigate the creditworthiness of the borrower in as much depth as is reasonably possible.

In the event that the contemplated loan will be fully recourse to the borrower, clearly the creditworthiness of the borrower and its principals is relevant since the lender is looking to other assets of the borrower (in addition to the property) for repayment of the loan. Therefore, with a recourse loan, a credit investigation of the borrower is extremely important.

However, even when a contemplated loan will be nonrecourse to the borrower, it has become common practice for lenders to investigate the credit history of the borrower because there may be instances in the borrower's past that would cause the lender some concern. Issues such as fraud lawsuits filed against the borrower, a fraud conviction, or a bankruptcy would certainly necessitate further investigation. There could be a number of different events in the borrower's credit history which would lead a lender, in the worst-case scenario, to elect not to make the loan, or at least to restructure the loan or to increase pricing in order to compensate the lender for its higher perceived risk of default.

In order to standardize and therefore expedite the process of collecting information, Precept has created simple, easy-to-use data collection forms. These forms address the borrower's credit history and, in some cases, also request information regarding any contingent liabilities of the borrower—information which can be relevant to both credit analysis and financial analysis.

The first eight questions on the primary form address credit history. Precept will review the borrower's responses to these questions and then perform due diligence in order to verify, as much as is possible, the accuracy of the borrower's answers. At times, answers will appear in the negative, but information may be discovered through the underwriter's due diligence regarding the borrower's credit history that contradicts the answer. This does not necessarily mean the borrower has been deceitful; it may just be that it happened long enough ago that specifics had been forgotten, or the borrower may have assumed such information was not material. Under these circumstances, Precept will request a written explanation of the discrepancy.

The forms are designed not to overburden the borrower with unnecessarily detailed questions, which might have the effect of alienating or angering the borrower. Therefore, they are designed to ask only those questions which are deemed to be reasonably necessary in order to enable Precept to accurately assess any risks presented by the credit history. Precept's goal with the information requested in the data collection forms is to find a happy medium, using a minimum of questions to obtain the most relevant information.

The credit information gathered from the data collection forms, as well as independently from these forms, can then be easily summarized on the Borrower Credit Summary portion of the underwriting summary (shown following), providing as much detailed information about credit-related risk factors as possible. Lenders can then easily review all the information and assess the risks disclosed by such information.

GENERAL

This chapter describes the process by which Precept will review the credit history of the borrower. It includes an outline of Precept's standard credit history documentation and an explanation of how the borrower's credit history will be summarized within the underwriting summary (referred to herein as the *Precept Credit Analysis*). The goal of the Precept Credit Analysis is to identify and underwrite the occurrence of events, if any, within the past several years which indicate that the borrower might be unable, or might not act in good faith, to satisfy its obligations under the loan.

For purposes of the Precept Credit Analysis, the *borrower* shall include the borrowing entity and any of its principals. The *principals* of the borrowing entity are considered to be (1) any general partner, managing member, or controlling shareholder, as applicable, of the borrowing entity; (2) persons or entities which individually own or control, directly or indirectly, 20% or more of the equity interests of the borrowing entity; and/or (3) persons or entities which individually own or control, directly or indirectly, 20% or more of the equity interests of any general partner, managing member, or controlling shareholder of the borrowing entity.

The Precept Credit Analysis is organized into three steps: (1) borrower credit disclosures, (2) credit database record searches, and (3) physical public record searches. Steps 2 and 3 are conducted primarily to confirm the accuracy of information provided by the borrower in Step 1.

STEP 1: BORROWER CREDIT DISCLOSURES

Precept will require the borrower to make various written disclosures. Each of these required disclosures has a corresponding standard form that Precept will deliver to the borrower for execution (collectively, the *credit disclosure forms*). An explanation of each credit disclosure form and its intended use follows.

Borrower Structure and Credit Investigation Authorization

Borrower Structure. Precept will require the borrower to execute and deliver to Precept a Borrower Structure and Credit Investigation Authorization form (shown later in this section). The purpose of the "borrower structure" portion of the Borrower Structure and Credit Investigation Authorization form is to disclose the borrower's legal and organizational structure and to identify the ownership percentages of the borrower's principals. This document will also provide Precept with information regarding the management of the borrowing entity. Precept will also use this information to determine which persons and entities should be further investigated by identifying the borrower's principals.

BORROWER CREDIT SUMMARY

Village Square Shopping Center

#	Legal Name Entities & Individual(s)	Clean Credit History (Y/N)	Bankruptcy within last 10 years (Y/N)

BORROWER

#	Legal Name Entities & Individual(s)	Clean Credit History (Y/N)	Bankruptcy within last 10 years (Y/N)
1	Real Estate Investment Partners	No	No

CONSUMER/COMMERCIAL CREDIT REPORT:
PHYSICAL RECORDS SEARCH:
A) Judgments: One (1) outstanding judgment
tenant over its underrefunded security deposit.
lien is not yet reflected in the county records.
B) Litigation: One (1) lawsuit currently pending
damages. Borrower has provided coverage letters
other seeking unspecified damages) were filed
settlements.
C) Tax Liens: Clear.
D) Criminal Records: N/A
E) UCC Filings: One (1) UCC filing in the county
Delaware UCC filing; all 3 of these UCC filings
terminated at closing.

BORROWER'S PRINCIPALS

A "Principal" is (a) any general partner,
entities which individually own or control,
persons or entities which individually own or
managing member or controlling shareholder,

#	Legal Name Entities & Individual(s)	Clean Credit History (Y/N)	Bankruptcy within last 10 years (Y/N)
2	John Doe Holdings, Inc.	No	No

CONSUMER/COMMERCIAL CREDIT REPORT:
PHYSICAL RECORDS SEARCH:
A) Judgments: Clear.
B) Litigation: Three (3) lawsuits are currently
above); the other two (2) lawsuits relate to
partnerships involving John Doe Holdings, Inc.
seeking more than $7500 in damages) were filed
C) Tax Liens: Clear.
D) Criminal Records: N/A
E) UCC Filings: Clear.

Property Number: 0000
Financing Number: 0000

Consumer/ Commercial Credit Report		Physical Record Search	
Date(s)	**Clear (Y/N/NA)**	**Date(s)**	**Clear (Y/N/NA)**
07/12/2001	Yes	7/25/01	No

Clear (other than public records filings described below).

lien (in the amount of $2000) has been filed against the Borrower relating to a dispute with a former
Documentation provided by the Borrower indicates that it has paid off such judgment, but release of

in CA state court; arising from "slip and fall" personal injuries; plaintiff is seeking $15,000 in
from its liability insurance carrier. Two (2) similar lawsuits (one seeking $5000 in damages, the
within the last two (2) years; both were dismissed with prejudice, as a result of insurance company

where the Property is located; one (1) State of California UCC filing and one (1) State of
relate to the same, existing financing (from ABC Bank) currently encumbering the Property; to be

managing member or controlling shareholder, as applicable, of the borrowing entity, (b) persons or directly or indirectly, 20% or more of the equity interests of the borrowing entity, and/or (c) control, directly or indirectly, 20% or more of the equity interests of any general partner, as applicable, of the borrowing entity.

N/A	N/A	7/25/01	No

No business credit report was available for John Doe Holdings, Inc.

pending in CA state court; one (1) arising from "slip and fall" personal injuries at the Property (see
contractual disputes with contractors performing work at other properties owned by affiliated
Five (5) other past lawsuits (alleging breaches of contracts or personal injuries, with no single lawsuit
within the last five (5) years; all were dismissed with prejudice.

BORROWER CREDIT SUMMARY

Village Square Shopping Center

#	Legal Name Entities & Individual(s)	Credit and Banking References	
		Lenders (Form 4) Clear? (Y/N/NA)	Depositories (Form 4) Clear? (Y/N/NA)

BORROWER

1	Real Estate Investment Partners	Yes	Yes

CREDIT AND BANKING REFERENCES: ABC
for the Property, indicated that the Borrower's
loan. The Banking & Credit Reference was
CREDIT HISTORY AND CONTINGENT LIABILITY:
Liability Certification, the Borrower disclosed each
Borrower Credit Summary. In answering Question
Borrower disclosed the outstanding judgment lien
answering Question #5 of the Contingent Liability
assets of the Borrower are currently pledged as
VOM/VOD: See above; otherwise, clear.

BORROWER'S PRINCIPALS

**A "Principal" is (a) any general partner, managing
entities which individually own or control, directly
persons or entities which individually own or
managing member or controlling shareholder,**

2	John Doe Holdings, Inc.	Yes	Yes

CREDIT AND BANKING REFERENCES: ABC
CREDIT HISTORY AND CONTINGENT LIABILITY:
Liability Certification, John Doe Holdings, Inc.,
section of this Borrower Credit Summary. In
Certification, John Doe Holdings, Inc., disclosed
analysis section of the Borrower Summary. These
partnerships which are owned in part by John Doe
VOM/VOD: N/A

Property Number: 0000
Financing Number: 0000

Credit History Certification (Form 5 Sec. A) Clear? (Y/N/NA)	Contingent Liability Certification (Form 5 Sec. B) Clear? (Y/N/NA)	Verification of Mortgage (Form 7) (Y/N/NA)	Verification of Deposit (Form 8) (Y/N/NA)
Yes	Yes	Yes	N/A

Bank is the only Banking & Credit Reference for the Borrower. ABC Bank, which is the current lender mortgage payment has been late (by less than ten (10) days) on two (2) occasions during the life of the otherwise clear.

In answering Question #9 of the Credit History section of the Credit History and Contingent of the items of past and present litigation described in the Physical Records Search section of this #1 of the Contingent Liability section of the Credit History and Contingent Liability Certification, the against it described in the Physical Records Search section of this Borrower Credit Summary. In section of the Credit History and Contingent Liability Certification, the Borrower disclosed that all security for repayment of the existing mortgage currently encumbering the Property.

member or controlling shareholder, as applicable, of the borrowing entity, (b) persons or or indirectly, 20% or more of the equity interests of the borrowing entity, and/or (c) control, directly or indirectly, 20% or more of the equity interests of any general partner, as applicable, of the borrowing entity.

Yes	Yes	N/A	N/A

Bank and XYZ Bank are the Banking & Credit References. Both references were clear.

In answering Question #9 of the Credit History section of the Credit History and Contingent disclosed each of the items of past and present litigation described in the Physical Records Search answering Question #3 of the Contingent Liability section of the Credit History and Contingent Liability the terms of the payment and performance guaranties issued by it which are described in the financial guaranties relate to mortgages on other commercial real estate assets owned by affiliated Holdings, Inc.

BORROWER CREDIT SUMMARY

Village Square Shopping Center

#	Legal Name Entities & Individual(s)	Clean Credit History (Y/N)	Bankruptcy within last 10 years (Y/N)
3	James Doe Holdings, Inc.	No	No

CONSUMER/COMMERCIAL CREDIT REPORT:
PHYSICAL RECORDS SEARCH:

A) Judgments: Clear.

B) Litigation: Four (4) lawsuits are currently above); the other three (3) lawsuits relate to partnerships involving James Doe Holdings, Inc.; (alleging breaches of contracts or personal injuries, years; all were dismissed with prejudice.

C) Tax Liens: Clear.

D) Criminal Records: N/A

E) UCC Filings: Clear.

Property Number: 0000
Financing Number: 0000

Consumer/ Commercial Credit Report		Physical Record Search	
Date(s)	Clear (Y/N/NA)	Date(s)	Clear (Y/N/NA)
N/A	N/A	7/25/01	No

No business credit report was available for James Doe Holdings, Inc.

pending in CA state court; one (1) arising from "slip and fall" personal injuries at the Property (see contractual disputes with contractors performing work at other properties owned by affiliated no single pending lawsuit is seeking more than $15,000 in damages. Five (5) other past lawsuits with no single lawsuit seeking more than $10,000 in damages) were filed within the last five (5)

BORROWER CREDIT SUMMARY

Village Square Shopping Center

#	Legal Name Entities & Individual(s)	Credit and Banking References	
		Lenders (Form 4) Clear? (Y/N/NA)	Depositories (Form 4) Clear? (Y/N/NA)
3	James Doe Holdings, Inc.	Yes	Yes

CREDIT AND BANKING REFERENCES: ABC
CREDIT HISTORY AND CONTINGENT LIABILITY:
Liability Certification, James Doe Holdings, Inc.,
section of this Borrower Credit Summary. In
Certification, James Doe Holdings, Inc., disclosed
financial analysis section of the Borrower Summary.
partnerships which are owned in part by James
VOM/VOD: N/A

Property Number: 0000
Financing Number: 0000

Credit History Certification (Form 5 Sec. A) Clear? (Y/N/NA)	Contingent Liability Certification (Form 5 Sec. B) Clear? (Y/N/NA)	Verification of Mortgage (Form 7) (Y/N/NA)	Verification of Deposit (Form 8) (Y/N/NA)
Yes	Yes	N/A	N/A

Bank and XYZ Bank are the Banking & Credit References. Both references were clear.
In answering Question #9 of the Credit History section of the Credit History and Contingent
disclosed each of the items of past and present litigation described in the Physical Records Search
answering Question #3 of the Contingent Liability section of the Credit History and Contingent Liability
the terms of the payment and performance guaranties issued by it which are described in the
These guaranties relate to mortgages on other commercial real estate assets owned by affiliated
Doe Holdings, Inc.

BORROWER CREDIT SUMMARY

Village Square Shopping Center

#	Legal Name Entities & Individual(s)	Clean Credit History (Y/N)	Bankruptcy within last 10 years (Y/N)

PRINCIPALS (cont'd)

#	Legal Name Entities & Individual(s)	Clean Credit History (Y/N)	Bankruptcy within last 10 years (Y/N)
4	John Doe	No	No

CONSUMER/COMMERCIAL CREDIT REPORT:
PHYSICAL RECORDS SEARCH:
A) Judgments: Clear.
B) Litigation: One (1) lawsuit currently pending damages. Borrower has provided coverage letters other seeking unspecified damages) were filed settlements.
C) Tax Liens: Clear.
D) Criminal Records: John Doe was convicted
E) UCC Filings: Clear.

#	Legal Name Entities & Individual(s)	Clean Credit History (Y/N)	Bankruptcy within last 10 years (Y/N)
5	James Doe	No	No

CONSUMER/COMMERCIAL CREDIT REPORT: payments by 30 days or more on three (3) occasions James Doe's personal credit history contains no
PHYSICAL RECORDS SEARCH:
A) Judgments: Clear.
B) Litigation: One (1) lawsuit currently pending damages. Borrower has provided coverage letters other seeking unspecified damages) were filed company settlements.
C) Tax Liens: A federal tax lien in the amount of 1995. Mr. Doe explained that the tax lien related Mr. Doe's 1993 personal tax return. Copies of released the lien thereafter.
D) Criminal Records: Clear.
E) UCC Filings: Clear.

Property Number: 0000
Financing Number: 0000

Consumer/ Commercial Credit Report		Physical Record Search	
Date(s)	Clear (Y/N/NA)	Date(s)	Clear (Y/N/NA)
07/15/2001	Yes	7/25/01	No

Clear.

in CA state court; arising from "slip and fall" personal injuries; plaintiff is seeking $15,000 in
from its liability insurance carrier. Two (2) similar lawsuits (one seeking $5000 in damages, the
within the last two (2) years; both were dismissed with prejudice, as a result of insurance company

of first-offense, misdemeanor DUI in March 1998. No other criminal record disclosed.

Date(s)	Clear (Y/N/NA)	Date(s)	Clear (Y/N/NA)
07/15/2001	No	7/25/01	No

James Doe's consumer credit report indicates that he has been late on certain credit card
in the last two (2) years, and by 60 days or more on one (1) occasion in the last two (2) years.
other material adverse information.

in CA state court; arising from "slip and fall" personal injuries; plaintiff is seeking $15,000 in
from its liability insurance carrier. Two (2) similar lawsuits (one seeking $5000 in damages, the
within the last two (2) years; both were dismissed with prejudice, as a result of insurance

$23,000 was filed against James Doe in July 1995 and subsequently released in September
to a dispute with the IRS over certain alleged income which the IRS believed went unreported on
correspondence to and from the IRS clearly indicates that the IRS reversed its position and

BORROWER CREDIT SUMMARY

Village Square Shopping Center

#	Legal Name Entities & Individual(s)	Credit and Banking References	
		Lenders (Form 4) Clear? (Y/N/NA)	Depositories (Form 4) Clear? (Y/N/NA)

PRINCIPALS (cont'd)

#	Legal Name	Lenders	Depositories
4	John Doe	Yes	Yes

CREDIT AND BANKING REFERENCES: ABC
CREDIT HISTORY AND CONTINGENT LIABILITY:
Liability Certification, John Doe disclosed that estate planning vehicles for the benefit of his 2 Liability Certification, John Doe disclosed his March History and Contingent Liability Certification, John Search section of this Borrower Credit Summary. In Liability Certification, John Doe disclosed the terms analysis section of the Borrower Summary. These are indirectly owned in part by John Doe. In Certification, John Doe disclosed that his home of their respective acquisition financing.
VOM/VOD: N/A

#	Legal Name	Lenders	Depositories
5	James Doe	Yes	Yes

CREDIT AND BANKING REFERENCES: ABC
CREDIT HISTORY AND CONTINGENT LIABILITY:
Liability Certification, James Doe disclosed that as estate planning vehicles for the benefit of his and Contingent Liability Certification, James Doe section of this Borrower Credit Summary. In Certification, James Doe disclosed the terms of the section of the Borrower Summary. These guaranties which are indirectly owned in part by James Doe. In Liability Certification, James Doe disclosed that his repayment of their respective acquisition financing.
VOM/VOD: N/A

Property Number: 0000
Financing Number: 0000

Credit History Certification (Form 5 Sec. A) Clear? (Y/N/NA)	Contingent Liability Certification (Form 5 Sec. B) Clear? (Y/N/NA)	Verification of Mortgage (Form 7) (Y/N/NA)	Verification of Deposit (Form 8) (Y/N/NA)
Yes	Yes	N/A	N/A

Bank and XYZ Bank are the Banking & Credit References. Both references were clear.
In answering Question #6 of the Credit History section of the Credit History and Contingent
approximately $5,000,000 of his assets are currently held in two (2) living trusts, established by him as
children. In answering Question #7 of the Credit History section of the Credit History and Contingent
1998 conviction for DUI. In answering Question #9 of the Credit History section of the Credit
Doe disclosed each of the items of past and present litigation described in the Physical Records
answering Question #3 of the Contingent Liability section of the Credit History and Contingent
of the payment and performance guaranties issued by him which are described in the financial
guaranties relate to mortgages on other commercial real estate assets owned by partnerships which
answering Question #5 of the Contingent Liability section of the Credit History and Contingent Liability
(worth approximately $1,500,000) and each of his cars are currently pledged as security for repayment

Yes	Yes	N/A	N/A

Bank and XYZ Bank are the Banking & Credit References. Both references were clear.
In answering Question #6 of the Credit History section of the Credit History and Contingent
approximately $15,000,000 of his assets are currently held in three (3) living trusts, established by him
wife and his 3 children. In answering Question #9 of the Credit History section of the Credit History
disclosed each of the items of past and present litigation described in the Physical Records Search
answering Question #3 of the Contingent Liability section of the Credit History and Contingent Liability
payment and performance guaranties issued by him which are described in the financial analysis
relate to mortgages on other commercial real estate assets owned by affiliated partnerships
answering Question #5 of the Contingent Liability section of the Credit History and Contingent
home (worth approximately $5,000,000) and each of his cars are currently pledged as security for

BORROWER OWNERSHIP & CONTROL

Village Square Shopping Center

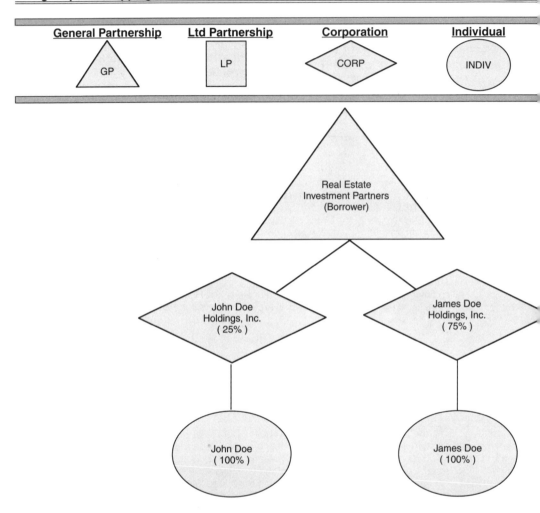

Comments:

Real Estate Investment Partners, a Delaware general partnership, was organized in December 1999, for the sole purpose of acq general partners in the Borrower are (1) John Doe Holdings, Inc., a Delaware corporation, which owns a 25% interest in the Borr corporation, which owns a 75% interest in the Borrower. John Doe Holdings, Inc., is owned 100% by John Doe, an individual. Ja an individual.

A "Principal" is (a) any general partner, managing member or controlling shareholder, as applicable, of the borrowing e control, directly or indirectly, 20% or more of the equity interests of the borrowing entity, and/or (c) persons or entities w 20% or more of the equity interests of any general partner, managing member or controlling shareholder, as applicable,

Property Number: 0000
Financing Number: 0000

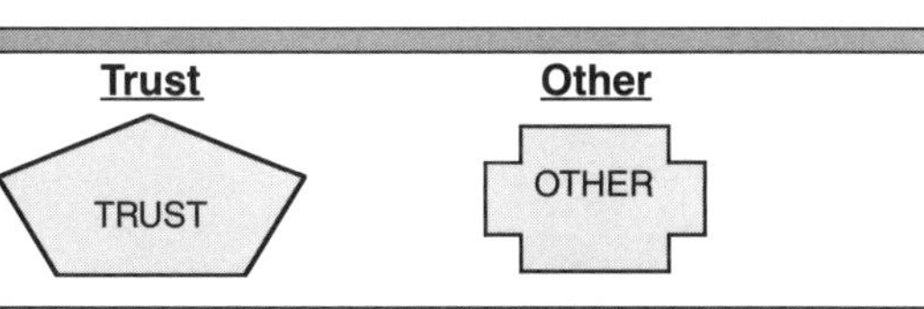

and operating Village Square Shopping Center. The
and (2) James Doe Holdings, Inc., a Delaware
Doe Holdings, Inc., is owned 100% by James Doe,

(b) persons or entities which individually own or
individually own or control, directly or indirectly,
the borrowing entity.

FORM 3	BORROWER STRUCTURE AND CREDIT INVESTIGATION AUTHORIZATION (IF BORROWER IS A GENERAL PARTNERSHIP)

Instructions: Applicant must complete this Borrower Structure and Credit Investigation Authorization based upon the anticipated Borrower structure, and obtain authorization signatures from the following parties: (A) Applicant, (B) Borrower (if Borrower is different from Applicant), (C) an Affiliated Management Company, and (D) all Principals of Borrower. For purposes of this form "Principal" shall include (a) any general partner, managing member or controlling shareholder, as applicable, of the Borrower, (b) persons or entities which individually own or control, directly or indirectly, 20% or more of the equity interests of the Borrower, and (c) persons or entities which individually own or control, directly or indirectly, 20% or more of the equity interests of any general partner, managing member or controlling shareholder of the Borrower. Please see your Pre-Auction Checklist Completion Instructions for more detailed instructions.

PART I	CREDIT INVESTIGATION AUTHORIZATION

Each of the persons and entities listed as "Authorized Representatives" in Part II below, by executing this instrument, hereby authorizes Precept Corporation ("Precept") (a) to order credit, litigation and other related reports and records searches on the entities and individuals identified above, (b) to contact credit, banking and other references provided by the entities and individuals, and (c) to utilize, summarize and/or disclose any or all of such information, as well as any or all other information compiled by or delivered to Precept by or concerning such entities and individuals, on the Precept internet website, or otherwise, for the sole purpose of facilitating Borrower's participation in the Precept system of underwriting and auctioning the proposed Financing.

The Authorized Representatives, on behalf of themselves and the entities and individuals listed above, hereby forever release Precept and its members, officers, employees, agents, affiliates, successors and assigns, as well as all prospective lenders registered with Precept, and their members, officers, employees, agents, affiliates, successors and assigns (collectively, the "Released Parties"), from any and all liability in connection with any credit investigation performed by, and any information obtained by, the Released Parties, or the use, summarization or disclosure by the Released Parties of any confidential information concerning such entities and individuals. The Authorized Representatives, on behalf of themselves and the entities and individuals listed above, also hereby forever release any and all third parties from any liability pertaining to their use of any information provided to the Released Parties in connection with any credit investigation activities conducted by the Released Parties or such third parties.

The Authorized Representatives hereby certify that, to the best of their knowledge, all the information set forth above is true, accurate and complete, and that each of them is duly authorized (i) to make the certifications contained herein, and to (ii) agree to the release of the Released Parties on behalf of each entity or individual identified above.

PART II	GENERAL INFORMATION
TO: Precept Corporation **5375 Mira Sorrento Place, Suite 540** **San Diego, CA 92121**	Legal Name of Borrower: Real Estate Investment Partners
State or Jurisdiction in which Borrower is organized: Delaware	Federal Tax Identification Number (TIN): 12-3456789
Will the Property be the only asset owned by the Borrower? ☒ yes ☐ no If "no," please describe the other assets that Borrower will own: N/A	
Are any Principals of Borrower or any of its shareholders a foreign individual or entity? ☐ yes ☒ no If "yes", please indicate country of citizenship or formation:	

Please list the Borrower and each of its general partners and their respective percentage interests in Borrower (attach additional sheets as needed). PLEASE NOTE: If any general partner(s) is not an individual, please identify all constituents of such general partner(s) on a separate sheet of paper.

Borrower	***Authorized Representative***
Name, Address & TIN	***(see "Part I" above)***
Name: Real Estate Investment Partners Address: 123 Elm Street San Diego, CA 92121 TIN: 12-3456789	X ________________ (Sign) X John Doe ________ (Print)

General Partner(s)		***Authorized Representative***
Name, Address & TIN	*Percentage Interest*	***(see "Part I" above)***
Name: John Doe Holdings, Inc. Address: 123 Elm Street San Diego, CA 92121 TIN: 13-2456789	25 %	X ________________ (Sign) X John Doe ________ (Print)
Name: James Doe Holdings, Inc. Address: 345 Elm Street San Diego, CA 92121 TIN: 15-2346789	75 %	X ________________ (Sign) X James Doe ________ (Print)
Name: Address: TIN:	____%	X ________________ (Sign) X ________________ (Print)
Name: Address: TIN:	____%	X ________________ (Sign) X ________________ (Print)
TOTAL	***100%***	

Comments:

____

____

____

If Borrower has any General Partner(s) which is not an individual, please complete the following:

(a) Legal Form of General Partner: ☒ Corporation ☐ Limited Liability Company ☐ Other: ______

(b) CORPORATE GENERAL PARTNER OF BORROWER:

If the General Partner is a corporation, please list its shareholders and their respective percentage interests (attach additional sheets as needed):

Shareholder	***Percentage Interest***	***Authorized Representative (see "Part I" above)***
Name: John Doe Address: 123 Elm Street San Diego, CA 92121 TIN: 123-45-6789	100 % of John Doe Holdings, Inc.	X ____________ (Sign) X John Doe (Print)
Name: James Doe Address: 123 Elm Street San Diego, CA 92121 TIN: 124-35-6789	100 % of John Doe Holdings, Inc.	X ____________ (Sign) X James Doe (Print)
Name: Address: TIN:	____%	X ____________ (Sign) X ____________ (Print)
Name: Address: TIN:	____%	X ____________ (Sign) X ____________ (Print)
TOTAL	***100%***	

(c) LIMITED LIABILITY COMPANY AS GENERAL PARTNER OF BORROWER:

If any General Partner(s) is a limited liability company, please list its members and their respective percentage interests (attach additional sheets as needed):

Managing Member(s)		***Authorized Representative***
Name, Address & TIN	*Percentage Interest*	*(see "Part I" above)*
Name: Address: TIN:	____%	X ____________ (Sign) X ____________ (Print)
Name: Address: TIN:	____%	X ____________ (Sign) X ____________ (Print)
TOTAL		

Non-Managing Members		Authorized Representative
Name, Address & TIN	*Percentage Interest*	*(see "Part I" above)*
Name: Address: TIN:	____%	X ____________________ (Sign) X ____________________ (Print)
Name: Address: TIN:	____%	X ____________________ (Sign) X ____________________ (Print)
Name: Address: TIN:	____%	X ____________________ (Sign) X ____________________ (Print)
Name: Address: TIN:	____%	X ____________________ (Sign) X ____________________ (Print)
Name: Address: TIN:	____%	X ____________________ (Sign X ____________________ (Print)
TOTAL	***100%***	

(d) If any General Partner(s) of the Borrower is a form of entity other than a corporation or limited liability company, please detail the ownership structure of such General Partner: N/A ____________________

(e) If an Affiliated Management Company manages the Property, please complete the following:

Affiliated Management Company	Authorized Representative
Name, Address & TIN	*(see "Part I" above)*
Name: Doe Management, Inc. Address: 123 Elm Street San Diego, CA 92121 TIN: 16-2345789	X ____________________ (Sign) X John Doe ____________ (Print)

PART III BORROWER/PROPERTY INDIVIDUAL DECISION-MAKER

Please provide the name of the individual responsible for the daily decision-making with respect to the Borrower and the Property: John Doe

Address: 123 Elm Street

City: San Diego CA Zip Code: 92121

Phone: 858-555-1234 Facsimile: 858-555-4321

E-mail Address: john.doe@doemanagement.com

TIN/SS#: 123-45-6789

Additional Considerations. Precept anticipates that a particular borrower's organizational structure may change during the underwriting process before the loan is closed. Therefore, Precept and outside counsel to the lender will compare the borrower structure disclosed in the Borrower Structure and Credit Investigation Authorization form to the organizational documents for the actual borrowing entity prior to closing. If the ownership structure of the actual borrowing entity appears to differ from that disclosed in the Borrower Structure and Credit Investigation Authorization form, Precept will modify and/or expand accordingly the scope of the Precept Credit Analysis performed.

Credit Investigation. The purpose of the Credit Investigation Authorization portion of the Borrower Structure and Credit Investigation Authorization form is to obtain the written consent of the borrower to conduct a credit investigation and to obtain necessary information regarding the borrower to enable the completion of the Precept Credit Analysis (e.g., addresses of principal places of business, tax identification numbers, Social Security numbers, etc.).

Credit History and Contingent Liability Certification

Precept will require the borrower to execute and deliver to Precept a Credit History and Contingent Liability Certification form (shown later in this section). The purpose of the "credit history certification" portion thereof is to obtain a written statement from the borrower indicating whether the Borrower (1) has filed, or has had filed against it, a petition for bankruptcy protection within the last 10 years; (2) holds title to any assets in trust, in an estate, or in any other name or capacity; (3) has ever defaulted in the repayment of any indebtedness or been involved in any loan forbearance or modification agreements; (4) has been a party to any lawsuits within the past 10 years; (5) has ever lost a property to foreclosure or deed in lieu; (6) has ever been notified of any existing violations of law with respect to the property; (7) has any knowledge of any past litigation (not involving the borrower) concerning the property; and (8) has ever been convicted of, or pleaded guilty to, a criminal offense other than a minor traffic violation. If the borrower answers affirmatively to any of the questions on the credit history certification, Precept will require the borrower to provide a detailed written explanation of such

FORM 5 CREDIT HISTORY AND CONTINGENT LIABILITY CERTIFICATION

Instructions: Each of the following parties must complete, duly execute and return this form to Precept: (A) Applicant, (B) Borrower (if Borrower is different from Applicant), (C) an Affiliated Management Company, and (D) all Principals of Borrower. For purposes of this form "Principal" shall include (a) any general partner, managing member or controlling shareholder, as applicable, of the Borrower, (b) persons or entities which individually own or control, directly or indirectly, 20% or more of the equity interests of the Borrower, and (c) persons or entities which individually own or control, directly or indirectly, 20% or more of the equity interests of any general partner, managing member or controlling shareholder of the Borrower. **Applicant/Borrower must duplicate this form as necessary and provide to Precept one completed form for each of the persons and entities described above.**

TO: **Precept Corporation**
5375 Mira Sorrento Place, Suite 540
San Diego, CA 92121

RE: Credit History and Contingent Liability Certification of:
John Doe
(Name of person or entity)

In Connection With The Requested Financing To Be Secured By:
Village Square Shopping Center, (the "Property")

PART I SUMMARY OF CREDIT HISTORY

1. Has the undersigned, or any entity in which the undersigned was or is a Principal, filed or had filed against it a petition for bankruptcy protection within the last ten years? ☒ No ☐ Yes

2. Has the undersigned ever transferred title to a property in whole or partial satisfaction of a debt or obligation? ☒ No ☐ Yes

3. Has the undersigned been involved in any forbearance / modification agreements? ☒ No ☐ Yes

4. Has the undersigned been, or is the undersigned currently, in default on any obligations to pay principal or interest to any creditor? ☒ No ☐ Yes

5. Is the undersigned aware of any existing, cited or likely to be cited upon inspection by any governmental official or authority, violations with respect to any current property holdings? ☒ No ☐ Yes

6. Are any of the undersigned's assets held in trust, in an estate or in any other name or capacity? ☐ No ☒ Yes
Amount:
Two living trusts as estate planning vehicles for my two children. $ 5,000,000

7. Has the undersigned ever been convicted of, or pleaded guilty to, a criminal offense, other than a minor traffic violation? ☐ No ☒ Yes
One misdemeanor conviction for first-time DUI in March 1998.

8. Has the undersigned any knowledge of any past litigation (not involving the undersigned) concerning the Property? ☒ No ☐ Yes

9. Has the undersigned been a party to any litigation within the last 10 years? ☐ No ☒ Yes
See attached description of litigation.

PART II	SUMMARY OF CONTINGENT LIABILITY

1. Is the undersigned currently a party to any suit/legal action or are there any unsatisfied judgments against the undersigned? ☐ No ☒ Yes Amount $ 15,000

   See Below

2. Are any of the undersigned's tax returns currently being audited or contested? If so, what tax year(s)? ☒ No ☐ Yes

3. Is the undersigned a guarantor, co-maker or endorser of any debt of an individual, corporation or partnership? ☐ No ☒ Yes Amount $ 4,000,000

   Two Payment and Performance Guarantees executed by me in connection with financing for two other real estate investments.

4. Is the undersigned contingently liable on any lease or contract? ☒ No ☐ Yes Amount $______

5. Are any of the undersigned's assets pledged or debts secured? ☐ No ☒ Yes Amount $ 1,600,000

   Personal residence is mortgaged (~ $1,500,000)
   Two car loans (~ $50,000 each)

6. Were any of the undersigned's assets (i) owned or claimed by the undersigned's spouse before marriage; or (ii) acquired by the undersigned's spouse during marriage by gift or inheritances; or (iii) recovered for personal injuries sustained by the undersigned's spouse during marriage; or (iv) acquired from the proceeds of liquidation of any of the preceding? (NOTE: Applicable if residing in community property states only.) ☒ No ☐ Yes Amount $______

PART III	EXPLANATIONS

If any of the questions in Parts I or II above have been answered in the affirmative, please provide a detailed explanation indicating the circumstances (including relevant dates, places and names), and where applicable, the amount of the contingent liability outstanding and the amount that has been paid. Also, indicate whether or not the undersigned is likely to be called upon to honor this liability (add additional sheets if necessary):

Litigation:

1) One "slip and fall" lawsuit pending in California state court where the plaintiff is seeking $15,000 in damages. My insurance company is defending me in this lawsuit.

2) Two similar lawsuits, also in California state court, related to other properties I own, were filed against me in June 1999 and December 1999. Both were settled by my insurance company.

The undersigned hereby certifies to Precept and each of its respective successors, assigns and affiliates (collectively, the "Parties") that all of the information contained in the foregoing Questionnaire is true, correct and complete as of the date hereof, and is a fair presentation of all the contingent liabilities affecting, or which might reasonably be expected to affect, the financial condition of the undersigned. The undersigned agrees to provide prompt written notice to the Parties of any material change in the facts that would render the foregoing statements untrue or misleading, after the date hereof until immediately prior to the closing of the loan.

The undersigned further certifies to the Parties that each of the certifications contained in this Questionnaire have been duly authorized, and that the undersigned has been duly authorized to execute and deliver this Questionnaire to the Parties.

The undersigned acknowledges that (i) Precept will rely on the information contained in this Questionnaire in conducting its underwriting activities and determining the creditworthiness of Borrower and Applicant, and (ii) any lender will rely on the information contained in this Questionnaire in evaluating a requested financing and in determining whether to extend credit to Borrower.

Sincerely,

Dated: July 3, 2001

By: ______________________

Name: John Doe

responses. Depending on the circumstances, Precept may require the borrower to provide additional information or documentation (e.g., copies of lawsuit complaints, contact information for related creditors) for Precept's review.

The "contingent liability certification" portion of the Credit History and Contingent Liability Certification form is discussed in the next chapter.

Additional Considerations. The credit history certification will include within its scope the spouses of relevant individuals in an effort to identify individuals with poor credit histories who may have covertly transferred assets to their spouses in order to hide their poor credit histories.

Credit and Banking References

The purpose of the Credit and Banking References form (shown later in this section) is to provide Precept with contact information for banks and lending institutions of which the borrower is a client, and to obtain the borrower's permission to contact such lending institutions regarding the borrower's credit history. Precept will use this information to conduct telephone interviews and/or mail written requests for information regarding the borrower's past performance under other credit relationships. If possible, Precept will obtain at least three references for each borrower, with an emphasis placed on individuals exercising managerial responsibility over the borrowing entity. Precept will require additional references in the event that Precept determines that the borrower's credit history is inconsistent. Moreover, the credit references discussed in this section will be in addition to lender interviews, if any, conducted by Precept in order to confirm or clarify circumstances surrounding specific borrower credit problems disclosed by the borrower or discovered by Precept. Precept's inability to reach and/or hold discussions with at least three such credit references will be noted in the underwriting summary.

Request for Mortgage Information

Precept will require the borrower to execute and deliver to Precept a Request for Mortgage Information form. The purpose of the Request for Mortgage Information form is to provide Precept with contact

FORM 4	CREDIT AND BANKING REFERENCES

Instructions: Each of the following parties must complete and return this form to Precept: (A) Applicant, (B) Borrower (if Borrower is different from Applicant), (C) a property manager for the Property which is affiliated with Borrower and/or Applicant, and (D) all Principals of Borrower. For purposes of this form "Principal" shall include (a) any general partner, managing member or controlling shareholder, as applicable, of the Borrower, (b) persons or entities which individually own or control, directly or indirectly, 20% or more of the equity interests of the Borrower, and (c) persons or entities which individually own or control, directly or indirectly, 20% or more of the equity interests of any general partner, managing member or controlling shareholder of the Borrower. **Applicant/Borrower must duplicate this form as necessary and provide to Precept one completed form for each of the persons and entities described above.**

TO: **Precept Corporation**
5375 Mira Sorrento Place, Suite 540
San Diego, CA 92121

RE: Credit and Banking References For:

Real Estate Investment Partners
(Name of person or entity)

PART I LENDER INFORMATION

Please provide the following information for at least two lenders with whom the entity or above-referenced person has entered into a loan:

Lender 1	Lender 2
Name & Address of Lender: ABC Bank	Name & Address of Lender: XYZ Bank
Account #: 123-456789-0	Account #: 12345-67890
Contact Person: Mark Thompson	Contact Person: Brian Phelps
Telephone #: 858-555-5555	Telephone #: 858-555-1111
Facsimile #: 858-555-5678	Facsimile #: 858-555-2222

PART II CURRENT DEPOSITORY INSTITUTION INFORMATION

Please provide the following information for at least two depository institutions with which the entity or above-referenced person has a banking relationship:

Depository Institution 1	Depository Institution 2
Name & Address of Depository: ABC Bank	Name & Address of Depository: XYZ Bank
Account #: 098-765432-1	Account #: 09876-54321
Contact Person: Mark Thompson	Contact Person: Brian Phelps
Telephone #: 858-555-5555	Telephone #: 858-555-1111
Facsimile #: 858-555-5678	Facsimile #: 858-555-2222

FORM 6 AUTHORIZATION TO RELEASE INFORMATION

Instructions: Applicant, Borrower and all Principals of Borrower must complete the following form for each of Borrower's current mortgage lender(s), and for all Credit and Banking References provided on Form 4. Precept will submit this form, under its own signature, to such mortgage lenders and Credit and Banking References. **Applicant/Borrower must duplicate this form as necessary and provide to Precept one completed form for each of the persons and entities described above.**

To Whom It May Concern:

1. I/We have applied to Precept Corporation ("Precept") for the underwriting of a mortgage loan. As part of the underwriting process, Precept may, at any time, verify information provided to Precept in various documents required by Precept in connection with their underwriting of the proposed loan.

2. I/We authorize you to provide to Precept, and to any financial or lending institution considering making a loan to me/us, any and all information and documentation that Precept or any such lender may request. Such information may include, without limitation, employment history and income information; bank, money market and similar account balances; credit history; loan payment history; and copies of income tax returns.

3. You may accept a photocopy of this Authorization to Release Information form as an original.

4. I/We will appreciate a prompt response to any inquiry as specified above.

5. Your response is solely a matter of courtesy for which no responsibility is attached to your institution or any of your officers.

Sincerely,

REAL ESTATE INVESTMENT PARTNERS

Dated: July 3, 2001

By: ____________________________
Name: John Doe
Title: President of John Doe Holdings, Inc.,
its general partner

information for the property's current mortgagee and to obtain written consent of the borrower for the mortgagee to release information regarding the mortgage and the borrower's past performance under the mortgage.

Verification of Deposit

Typically used in the case of an acquisition, Precept will require the borrower to execute and deliver to Precept a Request for Verification of Deposit form. The purpose of the Request for Verification of Deposit form is to provide Precept with contact information for a depository with which the borrower has an account and to obtain written consent of the borrower for the depository to verify the account and/or loan balances. This information is typically used to verify, in the case of an acquisition, that the borrower has sufficient funds to purchase the property.

STEP 2: CREDIT DATABASE RECORD SEARCHES

Upon receipt of the borrower's credit investigation authorization, Precept will conduct consumer and commercial credit database searches on the borrower in order to obtain a summary of the borrower's history as a debtor with creditors that report to credit bureaus, and to identify, as early in the process as possible, bankruptcies, outstanding legal judgments, and other derogatory credit information concerning the borrower.

Consumer Credit Reports (for Individuals)

Consumer credit reports provide a summary of information contained within a credit bureau's database (or a combination of databases) regarding an individual. A credit bureau's database for an individual generally consists of information (a) provided to the credit bureau by companies that provide credit, and (b) from selected public records.

Precept will obtain copies of consumer credit reports for the borrower (or order summary reports thereof prepared by an independent search firm). These reports will give Precept access to the credit bureau databases and result in the preparation of a summary report. Precept will review the summary report and note the following within the Borrower Credit section of the underwriting summary:

FORM 7	REQUEST FOR MORTGAGE INFORMATION

INSTRUCTIONS: Applicant – Complete Parts I & II
Lender – Complete Part III and return DIRECTLY to Precept

PART I NAME AND ADDDRESS OF CURRENT LENDER

TO: (FILL IN NAME & ADDRESS OF CURRENT LENDER):	MORTGAGE NUMBER:
ABC Bank 12345 Oak Street San Diego, CA 92121	123-456789-0
ATTN: VERIFICATION OF MORTGAGE:	PROPERTY ADDRESS: 1330 Pacific Street Bellingham, WA 38225

PART II APPLICANT(S) INFORMATION & AUTHORIZATION

BORROWER'S NAME:	SOCIAL SECURITY NO or TAX ID NO:
Real Estate Investment Partners	12-3456789
ADDRESS: 123 Elm Street, San Diego, CA 92121	

I/WE THE UNDERSIGNED AUTHORIZE THE RELEASE OF INFORMATION REQUESTED BY PRECEPT CORPORATION.

[ ] *SEE ATTACHED FOR AUTHORIZATION*

X ______ 7/10/01 X ______ 7/10/01
APPLICANT SIGNATURE DATE APPLICANT SIGNATURE DATE

PART III TO BE COMPLETED BY CURRENT LENDER

To Whom It May Concern:

The borrower(s) named above authorized the release of the below information in conjunction with an application for a loan. Your response is solely a matter of courtesy for which no responsibility is attached to your institution or any of your officers. Please furnish us with this information. Thank you.

MORTGAGE INFORMATION: *(TO BE COMPLETED BY LENDER)*

LOAN TYPE /RATE		MONTHLY PAYMENT P & I:	ESCROW ACCOUNTS:
FIXED: 8.25 %	ADJUSTABLE:______%	$64,608.93	TAXES $: 0 INSURANCE $: 0 OTHER $: 0
DATE MADE: April 11, 1998	ORIGINAL AMOUNT: $8,600,000	PRESENT BALANCE: $8,427,293	NEXT PAYMENT DUE DATE: August 1, 2001
TERMS: 30/10	MATURITY DATE: March 31, 2000	INTEREST RATE: 8.25%	SECOND MORTGAGE ALLOWED? No

PRESENT STATUS OF LOAN: CURRENT [X] IN ARREARS [ ] AMOUNT ______

NUMBER OF TIMES LATE IN THE PAST 24 MONTHS: 0

PAYMENT RECORD: GOOD [X] SLOW [ ] POOR [ ]

HAS BORROWER SOUGHT OR OBTAINED FORBEARANCE OF FORECLOSURE DURING THE TERM OF THIS LOAN?

YES [ ] NO [X] IF YES, PLEASE EXPLAIN: ______

SIGNATURE OF LENDING OFFICIAL: ______ DATE: 7/20/01

FORM 8	REQUEST FOR VERIFICATION OF DEPOSIT

INSTRUCTIONS: APPLICANT - Complete Items 1, 7, 8 and 9
DEPOSITORY - Please complete Items 10 through 15 and return DIRECTLY to Precept

PART I REQUEST

1. TO: *(Name and Address of Depository)* ATTN: VERIFICATION OF DEPOSIT	2. FROM: *(Name and Address of Lender)* **Precept Corporation** **5375 Mira Sorrento Place, Suite 540** **San Diego, CA 92121**

I certify that this verification has been sent directly to the bank or depository and has not been passed through the hands of the applicant or any other party.

3. SIGNATURE OF PRECEPT OFFICIAL Signature	4. TITLE	
	5. DATE	6. Precept No.

7. INFORMATION TO BE VERIFIED

Type of Account and/or Loan	Account and/or Loan Name of	Account and/or Loan Number	Balance
			$
			$
			$
			$
			$
			$

TO DEPOSITORY: I have applied for a loan and state that the balances on deposit with you are as shown above. You are authorized to verify this information and to supply Precept with the information requested in items 10 through 12. Your response solely a matter of courtesy for which no responsibility is attached to your institution or any of your officers.

8. NAME AND ADDRESS OF APPLICANT(S)	9. SIGNATURE OF APPLICANT(S) X X

PART II VERIFICATION OF PRESENT DEPOSITORY TO BE COMPLETED BY DEPOSITORY

10. DEPOSIT ACCOUNTS OF APPLICANT(S)

Type of Account	Account Number	Current Balance	Average balance for Previous Two Months	Date Opened
		$	$	
		$	$	
		$	$	
		$	$	

11. LOANS OUTSTANDING TO APPLICANT(S)

Loan Number	Date of Loan	Original Amount	Current Balance	Installments Monthly/Quarterly	Secured By	No. of Late Payments
		$	$	$ per		
		$	$	$ per		
		$	$	$ per		

12. ADDITIONAL INFORMATION WHICH MAY BE OF ASSISTANCE IN DETERMINATION OF CREDITWORTHINESS: Please include information on loans paid-in-full as in Item 11 above.

13. SIGNATURE OF DEPOSITORY OFFICIAL	14. TITLE	15. DATE

The confidentiality of the information you have furnished will be preserved except where disclosure of this information is required by applicable law. The completed form is to be transmitted directly to Precept and is not to be transmitted through the applicant or any other party.

- Number of loans or credit lines (including aggregate dollar amount) currently in default and the nature of the default (past due, collection, etc.)
- Number of loans or credit lines (including aggregate dollar amount) previously in default and the nature of the default (past due, collection, etc.)
- Description of any bankruptcies, outstanding legal judgments, and other derogatory credit information customarily contained in credit bureau databases.

Precept will also review the consumer credit reports (and commercial credit reports, as discussed later) for recent changes in a borrower's place(s) of business, or material credit facilities originated in jurisdictions other than (1) where the property is located, and (2) where the borrower conducts a significant portion of its business. The results of this review will be utilized when selecting the appropriate jurisdictions for which to conduct the physical public record searches (as discussed later).

Commercial Credit Reports (for Businesses)

Commercial credit reports provide a summary of information contained within a credit bureau database (or a combination of databases) for a business. A credit bureau's database for a business generally consists of information (1) provided to the credit bureau by companies that provide trade credit, and (2) from selected public records. Commercial credit reports are available for legal entities, such as corporations, limited partnerships, and limited liability companies, as well as individuals and sole proprietorships that conduct business under fictitious business names.

Precept will obtain copies of commercial credit reports for the borrower (or order summary reports thereof prepared by an independent search firm). Precept will review and analyze the summary reports in the same manner in which consumer credit reports are analyzed (see preceding subsection), and Precept will note within the Borrower Credit section of the underwriting summary the same types of information as are discussed in the preceding subsection regarding individuals.

STEP 3: PHYSICAL PUBLIC RECORD SEARCHES

Precept will engage an independent public records search firm to perform physical searches of certain types of public records concerning the borrower and generate a summary report for Precept's review. This service involves a search firm representative visiting selected county, state, and federal courthouses and real estate recorder's offices to search available public records for recent filings concerning the searched individual or entity. For legal entities (corporations, limited partnerships, and limited liability companies), physical record searches will be conducted in order to locate any bankruptcies, outstanding legal judgments, federal and state pending civil litigation, tax liens, and Uniform Commercial Code (UCC) filings. For individuals, the search will also be expanded to include any public records concerning criminal prosecutions and convictions (local, state, and federal). In addition to the summary report, if requested by Precept, the search firm will provide copies of certain requested documents, and unlike the consumer credit reports and the commercial credit reports, the physical public records search report will specify whether identified lawsuits were dismissed "with prejudice" or "without prejudice."

Physical public record searches for the borrower will ordinarily be ordered only concerning the county, state, and federal records located in the following jurisdictions: (1) the location of the property, (2) the location of the borrower's place(s) of business (as identified by the borrower), (3) the address of the residence of the borrower's principals (as identified by the borrower), and (4) if applicable, the filing location of any previously discovered derogatory credit information. In determining whether to search any other jurisdictions, Precept will pay particular attention to the results of the credit database record searches. If a consumer credit report or commercial credit report indicates that the borrower has engaged in extensive business activity in a particular location, has recently moved, or has operated under a different name in the past 10 years, additional physical public records searches in the corresponding counties, states, and federal districts will be ordered.

If the management company for the property is an affiliate of the borrower, physical public record searches will also be conducted for the management company in the county, state, and federal district in which the property is located, as well as the county, state, and federal district in which the management company maintains its principal place of business (as identified by the borrower).

Precept will review the summary report, analyze the disclosed information, and present a written summary in the Borrower Credit section of the underwriting summary, which summary will typically include the total number of disclosed items for each type of derogatory information listed here, the number of disclosed items requiring an explanation from the borrower (if less than the total), and an analysis of the disclosed items as described here:

- *Criminal records (for individuals only).* If the summary report discloses any state or federal criminal records concerning the borrower within the last seven years, Precept will examine selected court records concerning all such criminal charges, and require the borrower to provide a detailed, written explanation of the circumstances surrounding all such criminal charges. Precept's summary of this information in the Borrower Credit section of the underwriting summary will include (1) the crime(s) charged; (2) the status and/or disposition of the case (pending, dismissal, acquittal, or conviction); (3) if convicted, the sentence imposed; and (4) the result of Precept's reconciliation of the borrower's written explanation with Precept's analysis of any actual court records reviewed.
- *Bankruptcies.* If the summary report discloses the occurrence of any bankruptcies or other insolvency proceedings involving the borrower within the last 10 years, Precept will examine selected court records concerning all such proceedings, and require the borrower to provide a detailed, written explanation of the circumstances surrounding all such proceedings. Precept's summary of this information in the Borrower Credit section of the underwriting summary shall include (1) the nature of the insolvency proceeding (e.g., federal bankruptcy or state law proceeding, liquidation or reorganization, voluntary or involuntary), (2) the status and/or disposition of the case (e.g., pending, dismissal, plan confirmation), and (3) the result of Precept's reconciliation of the borrower's written explanation with Precept's analysis of any actual court records reviewed.
- *Outstanding legal judgments.* If the summary report discloses the existence of any outstanding civil judgments against the borrower, Precept will examine selected court records concerning such judgments, and require the borrower to provide a detailed, written explanation of the circumstances surrounding all such outstanding judgments. Precept's summary of this information in the Borrower Credit section of the underwriting summary shall include (1) the nature of the lawsuit producing such judgment (e.g., breach of contract, fraud), (2) the nature of the judgment

(e.g., amount of damages, injunction), and (3) the result of Precept's reconciliation of the borrower's written explanation with Precept's analysis of the actual court records reviewed. In addition, all outstanding legal judgments will be reconciled with Precept's analysis of borrower's financial statements and/or disclosed contingent liabilities (see Chap. 9). In the event of any discrepancies, Precept will require the borrower to provide a detailed written explanation thereof.

- *Pending and dismissed civil litigation.* If the summary report discloses the existence of any state court civil litigation involving the borrower (as plaintiff or a defendant) within the last 7 years (or any federal court civil litigation within the last 10 years), whether currently pending or dismissed, Precept will analyze such litigation as follows:

  Borrower as plaintiff. Precept will require the borrower to provide a detailed, written explanation of the circumstances surrounding any litigation involving the borrower as plaintiff, including, without limitation, an explanation of the borrower's relationship with the defendant(s) in such litigation. Precept's summary of this information in the Borrower Credit section of the underwriting summary shall include (1) the nature of the lawsuit (e.g., breach of contract, fraud) and (2) a summary of the borrower's written explanation.

  Pending. Precept will examine selected court documents concerning all pending litigation against the borrower, and will require the borrower to provide a detailed, written explanation of the circumstances surrounding such proceedings. Precept's summary of this information in the Borrower Credit section of the underwriting summary shall include (1) the nature of the lawsuit (e.g., breach of contract, fraud), (2) the remedy sought (e.g., damages, injunction), and (3) the result of Precept's reconciliation of the borrower's written explanation with Precept's analysis of the actual court records reviewed. In addition, all pending litigation against the borrower will be reconciled with Precept's analysis of the borrower's financial statements and/or disclosed contingent liabilities. In the event of any discrepancies, Precept will require the borrower to provide a detailed written explanation thereof.

  Dismissed with prejudice. Precept will examine selected court documents concerning any litigation against the borrower dismissed with prejudice within the last three years, and will require the borrower to provide a detailed, written explanation of the circumstances surrounding such proceedings (and the terms of settlement, if applicable). Precept's summary of this information in the Borrower Credit section of the underwriting summary shall include (1) the nature of the lawsuit against the borrower (e.g., breach of contract, fraud), (2) the remedy sought against the borrower (e.g., damages, injunction), and (3) the result of Precept's reconciliation of the borrower's written explanation with Precept's analysis of the actual court records reviewed.

Dismissed without prejudice. Precept will examine selected court documents concerning any litigation against the borrower dismissed without prejudice within the last five years, and will require the borrower to provide a detailed, written explanation of the circumstances surrounding such proceedings. Precept's summary of this information in the Borrower Credit section of the underwriting summary shall include (1) the nature of the lawsuit against the borrower (e.g., breach of contract, fraud), (2) the remedy sought against the borrower (e.g., damages, injunction), and (3) the result of Precept's reconciliation of the borrower's written explanation with Precept's analysis of the actual court records reviewed.

- *Tax liens.* If the summary report discloses the existence of any tax liens filed within the last seven years against any assets of the borrower (whether pending or released), Precept will examine selected documentation concerning such liens, and will require the borrower to provide a detailed, written explanation of the circumstances surrounding the imposition of such liens. Precept's summary of this information in the Borrower Credit section of the underwriting summary shall include (1) the nature of the tax lien against the borrower (e.g., local, state, or federal; income tax or property tax), (2) the amount of the lien, and (3) the result of Precept's reconciliation of the borrower's written explanation with Precept's analysis of the actual lien records reviewed. In addition, any disclosed tax liens will be reconciled with Precept's analysis of the borrower's financial statements and/or disclosed contingent liabilities. In the event of any discrepancies, Precept will require the borrower to provide a detailed written explanation thereof.

- *UCC filings (hotel loans only).* If the summary report discloses the existence of UCC filings within the last 5 years (or 12 years in the state of Maryland) indicating the borrowing entity as the debtor, Precept will examine copies of such UCC filings in an attempt to verify that none of such filings relate to existing debt secured by the property (other than existing mortgage debt to be repaid at or before closing of the loan). If Precept cannot verify with reasonable certainty that no such existing UCC filings relate to other debt secured by a lien on the property, then Precept will require a written explanation from the borrower (or will require such UCC filings to be terminated at or before closing of the loan).

CHAPTER 9

Borrower Financial Analysis

While borrower credit analysis is principally aimed at identifying risks in the borrower's past (e.g., litigation, bankruptcy, delinquent bill paying, etc.), borrower financial analysis is an examination of the borrower's current financial status as of a recent point in time.

The relevance of this information may differ according to the contemplated loan structure. On one hand, if the contemplated loan is a recourse loan (i.e., in the event of default, the lender will have recourse to the personal assets of the borrower in addition to the real property security), then the borrower's financial condition will be relevant to the lender in determining the borrower's ability to pay off the loan in full. On the other hand, if the contemplated loan is a nonrecourse loan (i.e., if the borrower defaults, the lender's recourse is limited to foreclosing on the real property security), then the lender has already made the business decision to look solely to the underwritten asset (the real property) in satisfaction of the debt, and not to any other personal assets of the borrower. Nevertheless, an examination of the borrower's financial position may yield some insight into the borrower's ability to invest further equity in the property in the event of hard times.

Since borrowers often tend to be secretive about their financial information, borrower financial analysis can often be very difficult—especially where there are a number of investors involved. To avoid getting overwhelmed in instances of complicated ownership structures (for example, where many individual investors own small percentages of the real estate being financed), Precept limits its due diligence to individuals who have a controlling interest in the property, or have a material economic interest in the property.

Precept requests a detailed financial statement from the borrower and each of its material principals. In the event the borrower objects to providing a financial statement, Precept may use a net worth certification instead of a financial statement, whereby the borrower certifies in writing that it possesses a specific minimum net worth and liquid net worth.

GENERAL

This chapter describes the process by which Precept will review the basic financial condition of the borrower. It includes an outline of the documentation that Precept will require from the borrower and an explanation of how the borrower's financial information will be analyzed and presented within the underwriting summary, an example of which is displayed in this chapter (collectively referred to herein as the *Precept Borrower Financial Analysis*). The goal of the Precept Borrower Financial Analysis is to summarize for all Precept lenders the current basic financial condition of the borrower.

For purposes of the Precept Borrower Financial Analysis, the *borrower* includes the borrowing entity and any of its principals. The *principals* of the borrowing entity are considered to be (1) any general partner, managing member, or controlling shareholder (as applicable) of the borrowing entity; (2) persons or entities which individually own or control, directly or indirectly, 20% or more of the equity interests of the borrowing entity; and/or (3) persons or entities which individually own or control, directly or indirectly, 20% or more of the equity interests of any general partner, managing member, or controlling shareholder of the borrowing entity.

BORROWER FINANCIAL DISCLOSURES

Precept will require the borrower to provide certified financial statements for the borrowing entity and each of its principals. The information contained in the requested financial statements will enable Precept to conduct the Precept Borrower Financial Analysis.

Additional Considerations. Precept anticipates that obtaining financial statements from certain principals of the borrowing entity may be difficult or impractical, especially with regard to those principals who exercise no management responsibility for, and are otherwise unaffiliated with, the borrowing entity, and instead simply own an equity interest therein. Under those circumstances, financial statements for such persons or entities may not be collected by Precept. In such cases, Precept will instead request a *net worth certification* from the person or entity who is unwilling or unable to deliver the requested financial statements.

PRECEPT BORROWER FINANCIAL ANALYSIS

Precept will use the borrower's financial statements to calculate and include within the Borrower Summary section of the underwriting summary the following certified financial information regarding the borrowing entity and each of its principals: (1) total assets, (2) liquid assets, (3) assets invested in real estate, (4) net worth, and (5) liquid net worth. In addition, Precept will reconcile the borrower's contingent liability certification (discussed in the following section) to the borrower's financial statements, summarize all contingent liabilities disclosed by the borrower, and indicate whether (and to what extent) any such contingent liabilities are reflected in the borrower's financial statements.

Additional Considerations.

In the event that Precept utilizes a net worth certification instead of financial statements for a particular entity or person, the underwriting summary will contain only the following certified financial information regarding such person or entity: (1) minimum net worth, and (2) minimum liquid net worth.

CONTINGENT LIABILITY CERTIFICATION

As discussed and shown in the previous chapter, Precept will require the borrower to execute and deliver to Precept a Credit History and Contingent Liability Certification form which, among other things, requires the borrower to certify that it is not subject to any contingent liabilities (or, if so, to provide a detailed written explanation of the circumstances thereof, including relevant dates, places, and names, and the amount outstanding [and, if applicable, paid] of such contingent liabilities). The borrower's responses provided in the contingent liability certification will be reconciled against Precept's review of its financial statements and credit reports, as well as the results of public records searches, and Precept will require the borrower to provide a detailed written explanation of any discrepancies. The results of Precept's analysis of the borrower's contingent liability certification, as well as any discrepancies in the information provided by the borrower, will be summarized within the Borrower Credit section of the underwriting summary.

BORROWER SUMMARY

Village Square Shopping Center

#	Legal Name Entities & Individual(s)	Total Ownership % in Borrower
BORROWER		
1	Real Estate Investment Partners	100.0%
		Resume: Real Estate December 1999, for general partners in the in the Borrower, and in the Borrower. The held by the Borrower.
BORROWER'S PRINCIPALS		**A "Principal" is (a) any entity, (b) persons or interests of the indirectly, 20% or more as applicable, of the**
2	John Doe Holdings, Inc.	25.0%
		Resume: John Doe holding company for including office, retail, no business other
3	James Doe Holdings, Inc.	75.0%
		Resume: James Doe holding company for cluding several office ployees and conducts

Property Number: 0000
Financing Number: 0000

Ownership Role	Entity Type (Indiv., Corp., GP, LP, LLC or Trust)	State of Domicile	Yrs. of RE Experience
Owner	GP	DE	2

Investment Partners, a Delaware special-purpose general partnership, was organized in the sole purpose of acquiring and operating Village Square Shopping Center. The Borrower are (1) John Doe Holdings, Inc., a Delaware corporation, which owns a 25% interest (2) James Doe Holdings, Inc., a Delaware corporation, which owns a 75% interest Borrower acquired the Property in December 1999, and the Property is the only asset

general partner, managing member or controlling shareholder, as applicable, of the borrowing entities which individually own or control, directly or indirectly, 20% or more of the equity borrowing entity, and/or (c) persons or entities which individually own or control, directly or of the equity interests of any general partner, managing member or controlling shareholder, borrowing entity.

Ownership Role	Entity Type	State of Domicile	Yrs. of RE Experience
GP of Borrower	Corporation	DE	12

Holdings, Inc., a Delaware corporation, has served as John Doe's real estate portfolio the past 12 years. It currently holds John Doe's interest in 11 real estate projects, and multifamily properties. John Doe Holdings, Inc., has no employees and conducts than as a holding company.

Ownership Role	Entity Type	State of Domicile	Yrs. of RE Experience
GP of Borrower	Corporation	DE	17

Holdings, Inc., a Delaware corporation, has served as James Doe's real estate portfolio the past 17 years. It currently holds James Doe's interest in 16 real estate projects, in- buildings, retail centers, and multifamily properties. James Doe Holdings, Inc., has no em- no business other than as a holding company.

BORROWER SUMMARY

Village Square Shopping Center

#	Legal Name Entities & Individual(s)	Financial Statements	
		Date(s)	Type

BORROWER

#	Legal Name	Date(s)	Type
1	Real Estate Investment Partners	06/30/2001	Balance Sheet and Income Stmt.

Comments: Balance Sheet and Income dated as of December 31, 2000, which have

BORROWER'S PRINCIPALS

A "Principal" is (a) any general partner, managing individually own or control, directly or indirectly, own or control, directly or indirectly, 20% or more the borrowing entity.

#	Legal Name	Date(s)	Type
2	John Doe Holdings, Inc.	06/30/2001	Balance Sheet

Comments: Balance Sheet is unaudited. and performance guaranties executed by it of $5,895,000.

#	Legal Name	Date(s)	Type
3	James Doe Holdings, Inc.	06/30/2001	Balance Sheet

Comments: Balance Sheet is unaudited. and performance guaranties executed by it of $5,895,000.

Total Assets	Liquid Assets	Assets in RE (%)	Stated Net Worth	Current Assets/ Current Liabilities
$10,610,562	$410,562	97%	$3,682,914	5.43

Statement are unaudited. Precept also reviewed a balance and an income statement, both of which are been audited by Borrower's CPA in accordance with GAAP.

member or controlling shareholder, as applicable, of the borrowing entity, (b) persons or entities which 20% or more of the equity interests of the borrowing entity, and/or (c) persons or entities which individually of the equity interests of any general partner, managing member or controlling shareholder, as applicable, of

Total Assets	Liquid Assets	Assets in RE (%)	Stated Net Worth	Current Assets/ Current Liabilities
$22,354,654	$424,200	98%	$6,331,279	2.12

John Doe Holdings, Inc., discloses contingent liabilities on its balance sheet, which are related to payment in connection with 3 other real estate investments. These contingent liabilities are in the aggregate amount

Total Assets	Liquid Assets	Assets in RE (%)	Stated Net Worth	Current Assets/ Current Liabilities
$37,829,323	$712,870	98%	$8,915,670	1.91

James Doe Holdings, Inc., discloses contingent liabilities on its balance sheet, which are related to payment in connection with 3 other real estate investments. These contingent liabilities are in the aggregate amount

BORROWER SUMMARY

Village Square Shopping Center

#	Legal Name Entities & Individual(s)	Total Ownership % in Borrower
4	John Doe	100.0%
		Resume: John Doe finance from the Doe, he is a coowner San Diego, California.
5	James Doe	100.0%
		Resume: James Doe computer science, as coowner of Doe Realty California.

Property Number: 0000
Financing Number: 0000

Ownership Role	Entity Type (Indiv., Corp., GP, LP, LLC or Trust)	State of Domicile	Yrs. of RE Experience
Shareholder of GP	Individual	CA	12

is a professional real estate investor and property manager. John Doe holds a BA in University of California, Berkeley, and an MBA from UCLA. With his older brother, James of Doe Realty Services, the third-largest real estate advisory and management company in

Ownership Role	Entity Type (Indiv., Corp., GP, LP, LLC or Trust)	State of Domicile	Yrs. of RE Experience
Shareholder of GP	Individual	CA	20

is a professional real estate investor and property manager. James Doe holds a BS in well as a JD and an MBA, from UCLA. With his younger brother, John Doe, he is a Services, the third-largest real estate advisory and management company in San Diego,

BORROWER SUMMARY

Village Square Shopping Center

#	Legal Name Entities & Individual(s)	Financial Statements	
		Date(s)	Type
4	John Doe	06/30/2001	Balance Sheet
		Comments: Balance Sheet is unaudited. performance guaranties executed by him in $4,000,000.	
5	James Doe	06/30/2001	Balance Sheet
		Comments: Balance Sheet is unaudited. performance guaranties executed by him in $4,000,000.	

Property Number: 0000
Financing Number: 0000

Total Assets	Liquid Assets	Assets in RE (%)	Stated Net Worth	Current Assets/ Current Liabilities
$29,808,912	$1,129,300	72%	$9,658,000	22.17

John Doe discloses contingent liabilities on his balance sheet, which are related to payment and connection with 2 other real estate investments. These contingent liabilities are in the aggregate amount of

Total Assets	Liquid Assets	Assets in RE (%)	Stated Net Worth	Current Assets/ Current Liabilities
$48,127,462	$962,800	83%	$16,898,000	17.81

James Doe discloses contingent liabilities on his balance sheet, which are related to payment and connection with 2 other real estate investments. These contingent liabilities are in the aggregate amount of

PART II	SUMMARY OF CONTINGENT LIABILITY		
1. Is the undersigned currently a party to any suit/legal action or are there any unsatisfied judgments against the undersigned? (See Below)	☐ No	☐ Yes Amount $_________
2. Are any of the undersigned's tax returns currently being audited or contested? If so, what tax year(s)?	☐ No	☐ Yes
3. Is the undersigned a guarantor, co-maker or endorser of any debt of an individual, corporation or partnership? Two Payment and Performance Guaranties executed by me in connection with financing for two other real estate investments.	☐ No	☐ Yes Amount $_________
4. Is the undersigned contingently liable on any lease or contract?	☐ No	☐ Yes Amount $_________
5. Are any of the undersigned's assets pledged or debts secured?	☐ No	☐ Yes Amount $_________
6. Were any of the undersigned's assets (i) owned or claimed by the undersigned's spouse before marriage; or (ii) acquired by the undersigned's spouse during marriage by gift or inheritances; or (iii) recovered for personal injuries sustained by the undersigned's spouse during marriage; or (iv) acquired from the proceeds of liquidation of any of the preceding? (NOTE: Applicable if residing in community property states only.)	☐ No	☐ Yes Amount $_________

PART III — EXPLANATIONS

If any of the questions in Parts I or II above have been answered in the affirmative, please provide a detailed explanation indicating the circumstances (including relevant dates, places and names), and where applicable, the amount of the contingent liability outstanding and the amount that has been paid. Also, indicate whether or not the undersigned is likely to be called upon to honor this liability (add additional sheets if necessary):

____
____
____
____
____
____
____
____
____
____
____
____
____
____

FORM 5 CREDIT HISTORY AND CONTINGENT LIABILITY CERTIFICATION

Instructions: Each of the following parties must complete, duly execute and return this form to Precept: (A) Applicant, (B) Borrower (if Borrower is different from Applicant), (C) an Affiliated Management Company, and (D) all Principals of Borrower. For purposes of this form "Principal" shall include (a) any general partner, managing member or controlling shareholder, as applicable, of the Borrower, (b) persons or entities which individually own or control, directly or indirectly, 20% or more of the equity interests of the Borrower, and (c) persons or entities which individually own or control, directly or indirectly, 20% or more of the equity interests of any general partner, managing member or controlling shareholder of the Borrower. **Applicant/Borrower must duplicate this form as necessary and provide to Precept one completed form for each of the persons and entities described above.**

TO: Precept Corporation
5375 Mira Sorrento Place, Suite 540
San Diego, CA 92121

RE: Credit History and Contingent Liability Certification of:
John Doe
(Name of person or entity)

In Connection With The Requested Financing To Be Secured By:
Village Square Shopping Center, (the "Property")

PART I SUMMARY OF CREDIT HISTORY

1. Has the undersigned, or any entity in which the undersigned was or is a Principal, filed or had filed against it a petition for bankruptcy protection within the last ten years? ☒ No ☐ Yes

2. Has the undersigned ever transferred title to a property in whole or partial satisfaction of a debt or obligation? ☒ No ☐ Yes

3. Has the undersigned been involved in any forbearance / modification agreements? ☒ No ☐ Yes

4. Has the undersigned been, or is the undersigned currently, in default on any obligations to pay principal or interest to any creditor? ☒ No ☐ Yes

5. Is the undersigned aware of any existing, cited or likely to be cited upon inspection by any governmental official or authority, violations with respect to any current property holdings? ☐ No ☐ Yes

6. Are any of the undersigned's assets held in trust, in an estate or in any other name or capacity? ☐ No ☒ Yes
Amount:
Two living trusts as estate planning vehicles for my two children. $ 5,000,000

7. Has the undersigned ever been convicted of, or pleaded guilty to, a criminal offense, other than a minor traffic violation? ☐ No ☒ Yes
One misdemeanor conviction for first-time DUI, in March 1998.

8. Has the undersigned any knowledge of any past litigation (not involving the undersigned) concerning the Property? ☒ No ☐ Yes

9. Has the undersigned been a party to any litigation within the last 10 years? ☐ No ☒ Yes
See attached description of litigation.

PART II	SUMMARY OF CONTINGENT LIABILITY		
1. Is the undersigned currently a party to any suit/legal action or are there any unsatisfied judgments against the undersigned? (See Below)	☐ No	☒ Yes Amount $ 15,000	
2. Are any of the undersigned's tax returns currently being audited or contested? If so, what tax year(s)?	☒ No	☐ Yes	
3. Is the undersigned a guarantor, co-maker or endorser of any debt of an individual, corporation or partnership? Two Payment and Performance Guaranties executed by me in connection with financing for two other real estate investments.	☐ No	☒ Yes Amount $ 4,000,000	
4. Is the undersigned contingently liable on any lease or contract?	☒ No	☐ Yes Amount $	
5. Are any of the undersigned's assets pledged or debts secured?	☐ No	☒ Yes Amount $ 1,600,000	
6. Were any of the undersigned's assets (i) owned or claimed by the undersigned's spouse before marriage; or (ii) acquired by the undersigned's spouse during marriage by gift or inheritances; or (iii) recovered for personal injuries sustained by the undersigned's spouse during marriage; or (iv) acquired from the proceeds of liquidation of any of the preceding? (NOTE: Applicable if residing in community property states only.)	☒ No	☐ Yes Amount $	

PART III — EXPLANATIONS

If any of the questions in Parts I or II above have been answered in the affirmative, please provide a detailed explanation indicating the circumstances (including relevant dates, places and names), and where applicable, the amount of the contingent liability outstanding and the amount that has been paid. Also, indicate whether or not the undersigned is likely to be called upon to honor this liability (add additional sheets if necessary):

Litigation:

1) One "slip and fall" lawsuit pending in California state court where the plaintiff is seeking $15,000 in damages. My insurance company is defending me in this lawsuit.

2) Two similar lawsuits, also in California state court, related to other properties I own, were filed against me in June 1999 and December 1999. Both were settled by my insurance company.

The undersigned hereby certifies to Precept and each of its respective successors, assigns and affiliates (collectively, the "Parties") that all of the information contained in the foregoing Questionnaire is true, correct and complete as of the date hereof, and is a fair presentation of all the contingent liabilities affecting, or which might reasonably be expected to affect, the financial condition of the undersigned. The undersigned agrees to provide prompt written notice to the Parties of any material change in the facts that would render the foregoing statements untrue or misleading, after the date hereof until immediately prior to the closing of the loan.

The undersigned further certifies to the Parties that each of the certifications contained in this Questionnaire have been duly authorized, and that the undersigned has been duly authorized to execute and deliver this Questionnaire to the Parties.

The undersigned acknowledges that (i) Precept will rely on the information contained in this Questionnaire in conducting its underwriting activities and determining the creditworthiness of Borrower and Applicant, and (ii) any lender will rely on the information contained in this Questionnaire in evaluating a requested financing and in determining whether to extend credit to Borrower.

Sincerely,

Dated: July 3, 2001

By: ____________________

Name: John Doe

Its: ____________________

CHAPTER 10

Third-Party Scopes of Work

Fortunately for the commercial real estate industry, there exist various standardized scopes of work for the third-party reports: the *appraisal,* the *environmental report,* and the *engineering report.* Standard & Poor's published third-party report scopes, along with those developed by various vendor associations such as the Appraisal Institute and the American Society of Testing and Materials, have fairly widespread adoption among industry participants. This is important because it enables a more consistent delivery of such reports from any given third-party report provider. Accordingly, variances in reports generally result from individual lenders' preferences to include or exclude certain elements of the analysis, and in some instances relate to the quality of the provider. For example, in an environmental analysis, a lender may or may not require testing for radon. Radon is an environmental hazard that, while potentially dangerous, is of concern only under very specific circumstances, and even a positive test for radon would cause the lender to require remedy only if such circumstances existed. Thus, inclusion of this component in the analysis may be considered irrelevant.

It is important to understand that the producer and the end user of the third-party reports (the third-party report provider and the lender, respectively) have different perspectives on the actual reports. The report providers are attempting to provide a certain basis for understanding the condition of the property, while the lender is trying to relate such condition to the challenge of making a credit decision. For example, while the appraiser will take several standardized approaches to concluding a reconciled valuation for a particular property with an emphasis on what a "market" buyer would pay for the property, the lender will use certain components of the appraiser's value analysis to support conclusions on appropriate debt levels for that same property. The perspectives are different in this example because the appraiser and the lender have different analysis objectives.

As a result of these different analysis objectives and perspectives, it is critical that the details supporting report conclusions be properly documented. In addition, the lender must be able to reconcile isolated components of the analysis to the underwriting analysis. For example, the lender must be able to extract market rents from the appraisal report and effectively compare them to the rental rate structure at the subject property. This requires that rents be discussed in a consistent manner, specifically with regard to the inclusion or exclusion of passed-through expenses and leasing concessions.

Consistent with other aspects of the Precept underwriting methodology, Precept requires third-party reports that have been consistently produced. Precept was able to assemble its own scopes of work from existing scopes that were already applied in practice. Each of the three scopes of work is written in such a way that all of the required deliverables should be self-evident without additional interaction between the underwriter and the third-party report provider. Scopes of work are provided for appraisal, environmental, and engineering reports and require specific deliverables intended for integration into the applicable sections of the Precept Underwriting Summary, which are also provided in this chapter.

APPRAISAL

The primary objective of scope of work for the appraisal report is the delivery of an independent assessment (the appraiser's view) of market rents, occupancy rates, competition to the subject property, and expected future supply of competitive properties and to test the reasonableness of expense ratios and the resulting operating margins. In addition, the report should serve as a supplemental overview of the physical characteristics of the property, its improvements, and its site layout.

ENVIRONMENTAL

There are two objectives of scope of work for the environmental report: first, to surmise environmental impact of surrounding environmental conditions on the subject property, and second, to surmise existing environmental conditions on the subject property that may either: (1) affect the borrower's ability to operate the property and satisfy debt service, or (2) negatively impact surrounding properties, thus creating liability for the borrower. As important as *which* contaminants are tested for is *how* such contaminants are tested for. Recommended tests, as well as testing methods, are outlined in the environmental analysis scope of work.

ENGINEERING

The primary objective of scope of work for the engineering report is to estimate the remaining economic useful life of the property. In making this determination, the engineer must assess the current physical condition of the property, identify items that require immediate repair, and estimate the cost associated with such repairs. In addition, the engineer must outline a schedule of ongoing maintenance, calculated in some usable measure (e.g., square feet, units, or rooms). Finally, the engineer must conclude that adherence to the ongoing maintenance schedule as specifically outlined in combination with the initial upfront improvements will allow the property to be operated over the anticipated remaining economically useful life of the property.

Appraisal Information:

Firm	Hawk Consulting Group
Name and Accreditation	John Venstra
Type (Narrative or Other)	Narrative
Effective Date	01/05/2001

Appraised Value:	Total Value	Per SF			DCF Assumptions
Discounted Cash Flow	$11,531,000	$	89.77	Terminal Cap Rate	10.00%
Income Approach	$11,500,000	$	89.53	Going-In Cap Rate	9.72%
Sales Comparison Approach	$11,605,000	$	90.35	Discount Rate	10.75%
Cost Approach	$11,260,000	$	87.66	Rent Growth Rate	3.00%
Reconciled Value	$11,500,000	$	89.53	Hold Period (Yrs.)	7

Market Analysis Summary (Supply and Demand Trends):

Bellingham is the largest metropolitan area within Whatcom County, comprising 39% of the total population.
with Canada had a strong impact on the County, enhancing cross-border investment and employment. Due
agreement has encouraged investment by larger companies, the trend of Canadians doing all of their retail
this affects overall retail sales, it will not impact a neighborhood retail center to the extent it would a regional

Discussion of Market Rent, Occupancy, and Subject's Competitive Position:

The subject is well located next to Western Washington University, a residential growth area, and other supporting
grocery and drug store anchor tenants make the subject very competitive. The location next to the University is

Competitive Supply (Minimum of Three Properties):

Item #	Property Name	Address	Distance From Subject
1	Barkley Village	5412 Bellingham Blvd., Bellingham	10 miles
2			
3			
4			

New Supply - Historical/Current/Future Construction:

There are no new retail developments planned in the area per the Bellingham Planning Department. The only

Area and Neighborhood Analysis Summary (Economic and Demographic Factors):

The subject is the dominant retail development in the immediate neighborhood. The surrounding neighborhood
west. Notable neighborhood landmarks include Interstate 5, which is adjacent to the subject, and Western

Market/Sub-Market Demographics & Statistics:

Source: Research

Market Name	Whatcom County		
Employment	71,400	As of Date:	1999
Employment Growth	28.0%	As of Date:	1997-1999
Population	148,300	As of Date:	1999
Population Growth	39.0%	As of Date:	1980-1999
Unemployment Rate	7.3%	As of Date:	11/1999
Median Household Income	$37,082	As of Date:	06/1999
Med. Household Inc. Growth	N/A	As of Date:	N/A

Source: Research

Sub-Market Name	Bellingham		
Population	57,830	As of Date:	1999
Population Density	10.83%	As of Date:	1995-1999
Median Household Income	$24,714	As of Date:	1999
Per Capita Income	3.50%	As of Date:	1995-1999

Village Square Center
APPRAISAL REPORT SUMMARY

Property Number: 0238
Financing Number: 0128

Property Information:	
Class (A,B,C)	B
Overall Condition	Good
Highest & Best Use? (Y/N)	Yes
Ownership Rights Appraised	Fee Simple
Est. Marketing Period (Mos.)	6 months
Zoning Classification	Commercial
Compliance with Zoning? (Y/N)	Yes

Market/Sub-Market Rent and Occupancy:	Projected	Current	Year End 1999	Year End 1998
Mkt Occupancy	90.0%	92.0%	90.0%	91.0%
Sub-Mkt Occupancy	91.5%	90.0%	90.0%	90.0%
Subject Occupancy	92.5%	91.0%	91.0%	93.0%
Prop Penetration Rate				
Mkt Rent/SF Range				
Sub-Mkt Rent/SF Range				
Mkt Absorption Rate				

Source: Appraisal

The economy has shifted from one based on logging and fishing to a more service and retail oriented base. The signing of a 1989 Free Trade Agreement to a lower labor cost and relatively inexpensive land, there has been a considerable amount of Canadian investment in the County. While the trade shopping in the area has been greatly diminished since the early 1990s due to a closer parity on the exchange rate and incentives in Canadian retailers. While mall.

Source: Appraiser

commercial uses. The property was totally renovated and expanded within the past five years, the tenant mix is well suited for the area, and the strong considered superior by other shopping center owners in the market.

Source: Property Manager

Estimated Compl. Date	Square Footage	Estimated Rents	Developer	Development Status	Comparative Ranking	Comments
2001	150,000	$18-$19	Ligent Development	Near Completion	+	Not competitive b/c of distance

Source: Appraiser

new project, which is not considered competitive, is Barkley Village, mentioned above.

Source:

consists of commercial development to the north (retail, office, hotel, etc.), and multifamily and single-family residential development to the east, south, and Washington University and its on-campus housing, within 1/4 mile.

Top 5 Market Industries/Employers: Source: Appraisal

#	Industry	%	#	Employer
1	Wholesale Trade	28%	1	Bellis Faire Mall
2	Services	25%	2	Western Washington
3	Government	17%	3	University
4	Manufacturing	15%	4	Intalco
5	Mining & Constr.	7%	5	St. Josephs Hospital

Real Estate Tax Data:	
Est. 1st Year Tax Expense	$70,524
Tax Assessing Property Value	$5,930,000
Est.Tax Growth Rate	3.0%
Delinquent Tax Amount	$0

Real Estate Tax and Assessment Issues: Source: County Tax Recorder

Millage can only go up 6% per year by law. When millage goes up assessments usually decrease to avoid unreasonable increases. Tax Acct No's. 370306-390535-0002 & 370306-4

	Date of Report:	Date of Site Observation:	
Phase I Report Prepared:	01/06/2001	12/22/2000	Name
Phase II Report Prepared:	N/A	N/A	Name
Desktop Review Report:	N/A	N/A	Name of Firm

Environmental Engineer's Recommendations:

Item #	Investigation Type	Addressed In Report (Yes/No)	Testing Performed (Yes/No)	Code Level	O & M Plans Recommended
1	ACM (asbestos)	Yes		2	No
2	Lead Paint	No		1	
3	UST & LUST Searches	Yes		1	
4	PCBs (transformers)	Yes		1	
5	Radon	Yes		1	
6	Water Potability	Yes		1	
7	Hazardous Waste Mgmt	Yes		1	
8	Solid Waste Mgmt	Yes		1	
9	Chemical Storage	Yes		1	
10	Prior Use History	Yes		2	Yes
11	Environmental Database Review	Yes		1	
12	Other				

Comments Related to Additional Investigation and Other Issues:

1. Locate prior studies, circa 1989, relating to the presence of asbestos-containing building materials at contaminated an area behind the property. Quarterly testing of monitoring wells began in March of 1996. as of 11/8/96. The letter, however, does not relieve them of any long-term monitoring or maintenance at the filed restrictive covenants.

Results of Phase II Environmental Report, if performed:

N/A

Comment:

Misc.: Monitor dumping of trash on adjacent upgradient site.
Seismic review - A Level 1 seismic review prepared by Project Resources, Inc., dated February 20, 1997, only and 11%, including the low liquefaction potential.

Code Level:

Level 1 = Very Low Risk. No issues requiring action identified.
Level 2 = Low Risk. Acceptable but requires routine solutions (i.e., implementation of O&M plan or addition of secondary
Level 3 = Moderate Risk. Not acceptable but may be cured by corrective action. A Phase II may be required for items in this
Level 4 = Potential High Risk. Unable to conclude based on available data. A Phase II may be required for items in this
Level 5 = High Risk. Not acceptable and cannot be cured by any corrective action.

Village Square Center
ENVIRONMENTAL ASSESSMENT SUMMARY

Property Number: 0238
Financing Number: 0128

of Firm that Provided the Phase I Report:	Galloway Environmental, Inc.
of Firm that Provided the Phase II Report:	N/A
that Provided the Desktop Review Report:	N/A

Additional Investigation Recommended	Recommended Amount of Reserve	Engineer's Recommendation Regarding Additional Investigation:
Yes	$0	Locate prior ACBM studies
Yes	$0	Ongoing testing of monitoring wells
RESERVE TOTAL	**$0**	

the time of renovation to confirm that all ACBMs have been removed. 10. In the mid-1980s, dry-cleaning fluid
The Washington Department of the Environment (WDOE) issued a "NFA" letter indicating no further action is necessary
site and requires that semiannual testing of the wells be performed. It additionally requires them to abide by previously

indicates that for a 100-yr. average recurrence interval, the estimated probable maximum loss (PML) is 10% for shaking

containment around aboveground tank). No environmental problems exist that require additional investigation.
category to identify cost of corrective action.
category to identify extent of and cost to cure potential concerns.

Name of Firm: Project Resources

Up-front Holdbacks:

Item #	Capital Expenditure or Deferred Maintenance Item
1	Driveway/Parking
2	Truck Well Repair
3	Concrete Paving, Curb, and Gutter Repair
4	Trash Dumpster Enclosure Repair
5	Building Exterior
6	Roofing and Parapet
7	Preventive Maintenance
8	Drywall Soffit
9	Ceiling Tiles
10	

Ongoing Physical Needs Assessment:

Item #	Building Components	Avg Life	Remaining Life	Action
1	Parking Lot	N/A	N/A	Slurry Seal
2	Parking Lot	N/A	N/A	Striping
3	Exterior Walls	N/A	N/A	Paint/Finish
4	Roof	N/A	N/A	Repairs
5	Water Heaters	N/A	N/A	Replace
6	HVAC	N/A	N/A	Refurbish
7				
8				
9				
10				
11				
12				

Percentage of Total Physical Needs Occurring During the First Three (3) Years: 24.00%

Seismic Assessment

Seismic Zone: None performed

PML Results (if applicable): N/A

Explanation of Seismic Issues (if any):

N/A

Termite Analysis:

N/A

ADA Analysis:

While the scope of the Engineering Report did not specifically address ADA compliance, it was noted that a sufficient number of handicapped

Comments:

The sump pump for the truck well at space 400 should be surveyed to ensure proper working order. Costs not included in the above schedules.

Village Square Center

PROPERTY CONDITION ASSESSMENT SUMMARY

Property Number: 0238

Financing Number: 0128

Date of Report: 01/08/2001

Observation Date: 12/22/2000

Total SF: 128,451

Required Actions	Recommended Total Capital Expenditure
Repair, Slurry Seal, Restripe	$20,460
Replace damaged concrete (space 400)	$4,300
Replace where needed	$3,300
Repair	$200
Repair T-111 siding, caulk and paint	$2,500
Repair roof drains and waterproof parapet	$2,500
Seal cap sheet metals at roof	$5,000
Repair from roof leak (space 226)	$100
Replace water-damaged tiles	$150
Total Up-front Holdbacks	$38,510

Qty.	Unit Cost	Unit	Year 1	Total Physical Needs Years 2 through 12	Annual Average	Cost per Unit per Year
162,000	$ 0.06	SF	See Upfront Holdbacks	$9,720	$810	$0.01
400	$ 3.00	Stalls		1,200	$100	$0.00
2	$ 11,000.00	Bldg		22,000	$1,833	$0.01
2	$ 5,000.00	EA		10,000	$833	$0.01
5	$ 160.00	Units		800	$67	$0.00
5	$ 2,500.00	EA		12,500	$1,042	$0.01
	Total Ongoing Physical Needs			$56.220	$4,685	$0.04

parking spaces (13), ramps, and door sizes sufficient for access to all tenant spaces is provided.

This is the tenant's responsibility, and the tenant has been notified.

APPRAISAL REPORT

Scope of Work

PURPOSE

1. Inspect the subject property and objectively assess the subject's ability to compete within its market and submarket. The appraiser should provide a complete and accurate description of the property, market, and an estimate of the market value of the property. All conclusions reached should be supported by market data, logical analysis, and professional judgment.
2. Prepare an appraisal report in accordance with the terms of this scope of work (each an "appraisal report"). Each appraisal report should be in a complete, self-contained format describing the results of the procedures performed and be consistent with the criteria set forth in this scope of work.

SCOPE OF WORK

This appraisal report and scope of work (the "scope of work") for Precept Corporation ("Precept") should be reviewed and approved by an MAI (Member of Appraisal Institute) appraiser specializing in appraisals of the type and quality of the properties identified by Precept (collectively the "property") owned by a borrower or any other party (collectively the "borrower").

All appraisal reports should be prepared as complete, self-contained appraisal reports, in accordance with (1) the requirements of the Code of Professional Ethics and Standards of Professional Conduct of the Appraisal Institute, (2) the *Uniform Standards of Professional Appraisal Practice* (USPAP) *Guidelines,* 2000 edition, and (3) the Federal Financial Institutions Reform, Recovery, and Enforcement Act of 1989 (FIRREA). If for any reason the appraiser is unable to prepare a complete appraisal report, Precept should be notified immediately. Furthermore, if it is not possible to prepare a complete appraisal report (as defined by USPAP), the appraisal process should be stopped until the appraiser receives further notice from Precept.

The executive summary of the appraisal report (discussed later) should be completed and e-mailed to Precept and located in the front of the final appraisal report.

REPORT

Prepare an Appraisal Report document (the "report") that follows the following outline:

1. Letter of Transmittal
2. Standard Disclosures
3. Executive Summary
4. Introduction
5. Area and Neighborhood Analysis
   a. Area
   b. Neighborhood
6. Site Analysis and Property Description
   a. Site Analysis
   b. Property Description
7. Real Estate Tax and Assessment Data
8. Zoning
9. Market Analysis
   a. Supply Analysis
   b. Demand Analysis
10. Highest and Best Use
11. Valuation Analysis
    a. Cost Approach
    b. Sales Comparison Approach
    c. Income Approach
12. Reconciliation and Conclusion of Value
13. Exhibits

Letter of Transmittal

The letter of transmittal should contain the property name, address, and size, and the purpose of appraisal, date of appraisal, inspection date, and final appraised value, as well as any specific assumptions or limiting conditions. In addition, in compliance with USPAP, all appraisals performed on properties with personal property must separate total value into realty and personalty components. The personalty value should be expressed in dollar terms and as a percentage of the overall value of the property.

Standard Disclosures

All appraisal reports should contain the appraiser's signed certification as well as a statement of assumptions and limiting conditions.

Executive Summary

All appraisal reports should contain an executive summary. This summary should include a general property description; property location, land area, site, improvement, and valuation descriptions; highest and best use description; key assumptions; and a summary of the various value estimates allocated to land and improvements. In addition, the value indications via the utilized approaches to value should be included.

Introduction

The introduction to the appraisal report should include the following: purpose and function of the appraisal report, property identification (including the estimated remaining useful life), ownership rights appraised, definition of market value, date of report, date of value, date of inspection, property rights appraised, definition of fee simple or leasehold estate (whichever is applicable), scope of the report, exposure time, marketing period, history and current ownership (to include a disclosure of prior financing and sales of the property that occurred within three years of the valuation date), scope of the appraisal, and estimated marketing period. Please note that the estimated marketing period must be based on and supported by market data.

Area and Neighborhood Analysis

The Area and Neighborhood section of the appraisal report should include an overview of the economic and demographic factors impacting both the area and the neighborhood.

Area. The area overview should include a discussion of the following factors: climate, major boundaries, roadways and transportation, historical and projected population, household formation, major employers, employment and income trend, major and potential demand generators, business and commercial activity, general class (Class A, B, or C) and overall appearance of commercial properties and tourist and recreational attractions. For hotel appraisals, also include a discussion of convention center and airport activities and trends. In addition, the area's major demand generators should be identified, as well as their respective proximity to the property.

The local political climate and governmental actions, such as zoning restrictions and moratoriums on new development, as well as landlord/tenant rights and remedies under local law, should be discussed.

The conclusion of this section should summarize the appraiser's overall impression of the area. Exhibits should highlight population, household formation, and income and employment trends as provided by local census and labor departments. In the case of hotel appraisals, the conclusion should also explain how the area's characteristics might impact the area's hotel demand.

Neighborhood. The neighborhood analysis should include a discussion of the following factors: an overview of the subject's neighborhood, starting specifically with adjacent sites surrounding the property and expanding outward; neighborhood boundaries; land use and development patterns; public transportation; proximity to schools (e.g., local elementary schools, middle schools, and high schools); proximity to general retail services, including grocery, drugstore, and community shopping; proximity to health care facilities; railroad trackage, industrial properties, and basic neighborhood characteristics; and local access and visibility. Neighborhood analysis should also include a discussion of the social, economic, governmental, and environmental forces on property values. In addition, the analysis should provide an overall conclusion about the neighborhood.

Site Analysis and Property Description

Site Analysis. This section should describe the following:

- Street address
- Dimensions and area
- Shape
- Identification of nearby major routes
- Accessibility to/from major routes
- Visibility from major routes
- Easements
- Topography and drainage

- Soil and subsoil conditions
- Availability and description of utilities, especially water and sewer
- Street improvements
- Street frontage and location in block (corner or inside, etc.)
- Functional adequacy of the subject site
- Number of open and covered parking spaces and adequacy thereof
- Relationship of the subject site to its surroundings
- Nuisances and hazards, including floodplain and hazardous waste
- Railroad trackage, if available
- Any land and building lease agreements, if applicable
- Ground lease analysis, if applicable
- Site analysis conclusion, summarizing the functional adequacy of the subject site

A plat or sketch should be included in this section or referred to and included as an exhibit.

Property Description. A thorough description of the improvements should be included in the report. Whenever items of deferred maintenance exist, there should be a discussion, which provides a foundation for accrued depreciation in the development of the cost approach (discussed later). An outline form of the description of improvements is generally desirable. The improvement description should include the following:

- Current use or uses.
- Age and condition of the improvements.
- Dimensions and area, including an overview of square footage of the property as well as an appropriate unit breakdown (such as the size per unit, per hotel room, etc.).
- Design and layout, including description of facility amenities (e.g., tennis court, swimming pool, parking, etc.) and any other site improvements.
- Details of interior and exterior construction and finish, including quality, condition and workmanship, and identification of major components of construction (i.e., foundation, walls, etc.).
- Details of mechanical systems and other equipment.

- Condition of improvements (interior, common areas and amenities, exterior structure, landscaping), including any deferred maintenance noted or needed repairs. Instances of graffiti or any other vandalism should also be noted.
- Description of recent/proposed rehabilitation or renovation, if any.
- Discussion of functional utility of the improvements.
- Conclusion of effective age, remaining economic life, and remaining physical life. This data should support and provide the foundation for conclusions as to the highest and best use of the property, as improved.

Photographs of the subject's exterior, common areas and amenities, and the interior of the property should be included in this section. A plot plan and floor plan (or typical floor plan) should be included here or among the exhibits with a reference thereto at this point.

Real Estate Tax and Assessment Data

This section should set forth the identity of the responsible taxing authority, the local tax policy, the existing assessment, real property tax comparables, and the estimated assessment. It should conclude with an estimate of the property's Year 1 tax expense and real estate tax expense growth throughout the estimate period. Any ongoing appeals and pending or proposed special tax assessments or rebates affecting the property should be thoroughly discussed, with the probable economic effects to the property clearly stated. Furthermore, any delinquent taxes for the subject should be stated. A tax map should be included in this section or referred to and included as an exhibit.

Zoning

This section should identify the property's zoning district, list the permitted uses within the zoning district, summarize the applicable zoning laws or ordinances, and discuss any and all zoning issues, concluding with the subject's conformance (or nonconformance) with all applicable zoning ordinances and building codes. In addition, any deed restrictions or other restrictions to the property should be discussed. A zoning map should be included in this section or referred to and included as an exhibit.

Market Analysis

This section should address the various supply and demand factors affecting the property's defined market. It should begin with an overview of the property's general market condition, including a historical supply-and-demand trend analysis, which spans a minimum and a target of five years. This analysis should note any special annual or one-time events that may have had a significant impact on the market's performance. The historical analysis should be followed by a discussion of upcoming events or issues which may impact the market's performance in the future. All historical, present, and future new construction should be summarized and analyzed in relation to the property.

Supply Analysis. This section should include a discussion of the following factors:

- Existing supply for the entire market (e.g., total number of hotel rooms, total gross leasable retail space, etc.)
- The property's competitive supply (including discussion of at a minimum three competitive properties, and preferably six)
- The historical absorption/occupancy trends (whichever is applicable) for a minimum of three years for each competitive property
- Each comparable property's competitive advantages and disadvantages (noting the occupancy and rate leaders of the market and why the author believes these properties hold the positions) and comments on any important issues regarding the property (e.g., upcoming expansion plans, change in management, etc.)
- Properties under construction, and proposed construction

The appraiser should review and discuss the status of building permits for properties of similar type in the submarket.

Exhibits. Generally, exhibits should summarize the comparative attributes of the competitive properties relative to the property on the basis of unit mix, rental rate, opening and renovation dates, concessions, and amenities.

- Photographs of the competitive properties as well as a map detailing the locations of the competitive properties in relation to the property should be included in this section or referred to and included as exhibits.

- Multifamily comparables exhibits (as demonstrated in Exhibit A-1) should summarize the comparative attributes of the competitive properties relative to the property on the basis of unit mix, rental rate, concessions, current occupancy, and amenities; and relative ranking on the basis of condition, location, and overall factors. Photographs of the competitive properties should also be enclosed as exhibits.
- Hotel property comparables exhibits (as demonstrated in Exhibit A-2) should summarize the comparative attributes of the competitive properties relative to the property on the basis of number of rooms, published room rates, opening and most recent renovation dates, available meeting space (where applicable), and any other important amenities (e.g., pool, concierge, business center, exercise room, etc.). This analysis should also include historical occupancy and average daily rate for a minimum of three years, and the most recent year's market segmentation, as well as the demand penetration and room revenue yields for each property. If statistics for individual properties are not available, industry trends (e.g., Smith Travel Research) should be utilized. Photographs of the competitive properties should also be enclosed as exhibits.
- Commercial property comparables exhibits (as demonstrated in Exhibit A-3) should summarize the comparative attributes of the competitive properties relative to the property on the basis of square footage, rental rate, concessions, current occupancy, and amenities; and relative ranking on the basis of condition, location, and overall factors. Photographs of the competitive properties should also be enclosed as exhibits.

Demand Analysis. This section should include a discussion of the following factors affecting the property: current demand in the market, segmentation of the demand, future growth in demand (by segment), future market occupancy levels, and projected occupancy levels for the subject. Historical occupancy levels and market segmentation for the property should also be discussed in this section.

Estimated Stabilized Occupancy and Rental Rate of Property. This section should present the following:

- The property's historical occupancy.
- The property's historical penetration rate by market segment (if applicable).

- Projected penetration rates for the subject by market segment, and discussion justifying the projections.
- Present estimated occupancy and rental rates for the property for the analysis period. Discussion should include any necessary reconciliation to the historical figures presented previously.
- Tenant base, including the following factors:
  Multifamily properties. Percentage of students, military, or corporate leases, as well as any subsidies. Any significant tenant concentration should be described.
  Commercial properties. Percentage of any anchor tenants; credit tenants should be described.
  Hotel properties. The historical average daily room rate for the subject and competitive properties, along with a discussion detailing the property's historical position within the market (i.e., traditionally leads or lags market), if applicable; discussion of any specific issues or events (e.g., renovations, repositioning, new supply, etc.) that may affect the property's historical market position, if applicable. Based on this historical data, the projected average room rate for the property should be discussed and shown. The appraiser should provide conclusive support for future increases in the average room rate. Applying the overall inflation rate for the property without a discussion of how the projected increases relate to historical increases is not sufficient.
- Reconciliation to competitive properties.
- Growth-rate estimates.

Highest and Best Use

This section should set forth the appraiser's conclusions as to the highest and best use for the property. These conclusions should be supported by a discussion of the area, neighborhood, site, and other analysis of the property, as well as the property history. This section of the report should include the following:

- A proper definition of the term "highest and best use" (and the source of the definition).
- The highest and best use of the raw land consisting of part of the property as legally permitted ("as if vacant") should be demonstrated and should include the kind of use as well as the size and

quality of the buildings, leading to a convincing conclusion on highest and best use.

- The highest and best use of the property ("as improved") should be analyzed, along with any reasonably probable alternate uses.
- For highest and best use of both land as if vacant and property as improved, the use should meet four criteria. The criteria are that the highest and best use must be (1) physically possible, (2) legally permissible, (3) financially feasible, and (4) maximally productive.
- The variances of the existing improvements from the ideal should be pointed out, and a conclusion should be reached as to whether such improvements add to or detract from the value of the land as if vacant.
- If the subject improvements are nonconforming or do not represent the highest and best use of the property as if vacant, further explanation is required.

Valuation Analysis

The Valuation Analysis section of the appraisal report should include a detailed description of each of the valuation approaches, as well as a discussion of each approach's applicability to the property. This section should conclude with a discussion of how the three valuation approaches will be reconciled later in the report. This section should also contain the full disclosure of any current prepurchase agreement concerning the property. The sale/purchase pricing and terms should be discussed regarding its relevance as a market sale.

Cost Approach. The following elements should be considered:

- Land value estimated from sufficient, factual market data. At least three recent sales (within the past five years when possible) should be analyzed in this section of the report. Sales and/or offerings should be adjusted for dissimilarities in size, location, zoning, date of sale, and condition of sale, and each adjustment should be shown in the report. Adjustments should be market supported if possible. Analysis of land sales should primarily be established by the appropriate unit of comparison used in the market (i.e., per square foot or acre of site area, price per unit, price per building square foot, etc.). Sales data sheets should be

included in the report, summarizing those sales used to estimate land value. The summaries should include the comparable's address, date of sale, purchase price, zoning district, condition of sale, current improvements, accessibility to major routes in the area, and any additional comments regarding the site or sale.
- All cost factors considered and justified from market data or other reliable sources. If a cost service is used, the unit price should be adequately supported and adjusted to the property. In the case of hotels, cost factors are to include the contributory value of furniture, fixtures, and equipment, as these items are normally included in the valuation of a hotel.
- Either reproduction or replacement cost new may be used. The cost estimate should be well supported and analyzed with information from local developers, cost service, or both. In addition to coverage of direct costs, the report should include indirect costs for lease-up expense, interest carry, sales commissions or permanent financing, and miscellaneous items.
- An estimate of the amount of depreciation (identified as physical, functional, or external), using an appropriate method. The analysis should describe the depreciation and explain how it affects the value of the improvements.

Sales Comparison Approach. The following elements should be considered:

- A minimum of four recent sales (within the past two years when possible) should be used. Comparables should be based on location, income characteristics, type of structure, physical condition, size, etc. The sales should be arm's-length transactions and should be adequately described and analyzed to justify all adjustment factors. A comparable sheet with a photograph should be prepared for each sale used in the analysis.
- Selection of appropriate units of comparison and justification from market data analysis. The price per square foot or price per unit should be used as a common denominator for comparative purposes. A gross income multiplier or net operating income (NOI)-per-square-foot or NOI-per-unit analysis may be used; however, it should not replace the price-per-square-foot or price-per-unit analysis. For hotel properties, a room revenue multiplier analysis may be used, but again, it should not replace the price-per-square-foot or price-per-unit analysis.

- Adjustments for differences in similarity between the comparable sales and the property. In the case of hotel properties, these adjustments should encompass any differences in condition of sale, time of sale, location, physical condition, services and amenities, and income characteristics. The adjustment should be shown in the report with supporting documentation. An adjustment grid is preferred to illustrate any adjustments.
- Specific items of depreciation, if applicable, and their effect on the market value of the property.
- Existing leases and a reasoned analysis with conclusions as to their effect, if applicable, on market value.
- Adequate reasoning and analysis leading to the conclusion of the estimate of market value.

The comparable sales should bracket the concluded value of the property above and below, on an unadjusted basis. The comparable sheets utilized in this section should include, but are not limited to, photographs; location; names of buyers, brokers, management companies, and sellers; verification of sales and date verified; date of transaction; legal description; recording data; sales price; terms of transaction; cash equivalency adjustments; age; size of structure (gross and net); type of construction and construction details; occupancy rate at sale; finished area, land area; parking area and spaces; analysis of net operating income; overall capitalization rate analysis; sales price per unit of comparison; and any additional comments or data considered appropriate. Hotel properties should also include number of units, current franchise name, amount of meeting space, amenities and services provided, main demand generators, average daily rate and net operating income at time of sale, and average daily rate and room and total revenue multipliers.

Income Approach. The appraiser should develop a reconstructed operating statement and process the net operating income into a value estimate.

Methodology. This section should describe the methodology used by the appraiser to calculate a value under the income approach.

The direct capitalization method should be employed, utilizing a stabilized net operating income and an appropriate overall capitalization rate. In addition, a discounted cash flow (DCF) analysis should be prepared. All assumptions should be market-derived and clearly explained within the text of the report. In addition, this section should contain sound conclusions as to future rental rates and occupancies. A 10-year projection period with an extra year for the reversionary value should be used.

For commercial properties with long-term leases (longer than one year), a lease-by-lease analysis software package, such as Argus, must be used to prepare the cash flow statement. For single-tenant properties and multifamily properties, a DCF analysis is not required.

Historical and Budgeted Property Operating Data. This section should describe the historical and budgeted operating and expense data gathered for the property. This information should be presented as an exhibit to the appraisal report.

The section should include an actual rent roll and appropriate comments and consideration of the effect of existing leases, if any, on the value of the property.

The actual itemized statements of expenses for recent years should be shown. These should be restated to reflect the classifications used in the stabilized operating statement.

Major Assumptions. This section should describe the following:

- Number of years for which the DCF analysis has been prepared
- Basis of the DCF analysis and discussion of comparable properties used in the analysis
- Methodology used to calculate rental occupancy and average rental rate per unit

Inflation. This section should present the estimated basis for revenue and expense assumptions for the property and include the inflation rates used for revenues and expenses.

Effective Gross Income. This section should include the following:

- *Multifamily properties.*
  Gross Potential Rent. This section should include a breakdown of the rent by apartment type (studio, one-bedroom, etc.) and by view or building, if applicable. It should also include an estimation of economic rent from recent market rental data,

with adequate data on comparable properties. These should be presented in the format shown in Exhibit A-5. The comparable rentals should be actual leases rather than rental listings. Each of the comparable rentals should be analyzed for the same characteristics as noted previously under Sales Comparison Approach. A comparable sheet with a photograph should be filled out for each rental used in the report. The analysis should present an in-depth study so that differences in rents between the property and comparable properties are readily explainable and supportable by adjustments that are representative of factual data. The explanation and justification of any adjustments should be based on careful market analysis, including, but not limited to, time, conditions of sale, location, and physical characteristics. The conclusion of market rent must be bracketed by the rental comparable on an unadjusted basis. Any subject leases that are above the estimated market rent must be analyzed to determine if they are at a market level.

Gross Potential Rent should be consistent with historical trends and include:

- Occupied units at the actual rental rate
- Vacant units at the market rental rate
- Employee units at the market rental rate
- Model units at the market rental rate

The offset to employee and model units should be included in the appropriate expense line items. Gross Potential Rent should be reduced from historical or current levels in cases where actual rents exceed market rents. Gross Potential Rent should also be reduced for any premiums derived from corporate units, furnished units, short-term leases, or government subsidies, unless such premiums are supported by the market (e.g., subsidized properties should be underwritten to the lower of market or subsidized rent levels). Gross Potential Rent should also be adjusted for any hidden concessions or reductions in service noted during the site inspection which are not reflected in the vacancy allowance and concessions line items.

Vacancy Allowance, Concessions, and Credit Loss Factor. The appraiser's conclusion of the combined Vacancy, Concessions, and Credit Loss should include the following:

- Analysis of the property's historical occupancy level for the past three years, based on available data. If the property has historically exhibited a higher vacancy level than the current rent roll indicates, the appraiser should consider applying the historical level to the Gross Potential Rent unless market data supports a higher occupancy level.
- Review of occupancy levels and concessions at comparable properties. The property's projected occupancy should not be greater than market unless supported by strong market comparable data or several years of proven historical operating performance.
- Consideration of the physical vacancy level in the market and any trends in the market which indicate increasing or decreasing occupancy levels. The property's occupancy must not be greater than the market occupancy rate unless clearly supported by historical operations or other market data.
- Consideration of whether recently completed projects or projects under construction are likely to impact occupancy of the property.
- Consideration of whether recent or planned rent increases are likely to impact occupancy of the property.
- Consideration of whether concessions or reduced tenant credit qualifications have been used to maintain current occupancy, or whether concessions in the market indicate a potential weakening in the property's occupancy.
- Consideration of the ongoing reduction in collected rents from tenant concessions. In addition, analysis of the significance of concessions in all cases where concessions have or are being granted to tenants in the market in the past year.
- Analysis of historical credit losses as indicated in historical and/or year-to-date operating statements, delinquency/accounts receivable reports, the tenant profile at the property, or other such data to identify any trends in the collection losses.
- Selections of a vacancy allowance, concession amount, and credit loss factor based on the analysis previously performed. The source for these conclusions must be well documented.

- A thorough analysis of any difference between the average vacancy rate of the submarket as indicated by a published survey, the average of the rental comparables, the subject's historical vacancy, and the conclusion of the stabilized vacancy rate chosen.

Other Income. The following sources of income should be used when calculating the Other Income amount:

- Parking income
- Laundry and vending income
- Nonreimbursable application fees
- Utility reimbursements
- Other recurring income (e.g., commercial income and pet fees)

Income from the following sources should not be used in the calculation of effective gross income:

- Interest income
- Reimbursable application fees
- Returned check fees (nonsufficient funds [NSF] fees)
- Cleaning fees
- Forfeited security deposits, unless they directly offset repair and maintenance or turnover costs that are included in the expense line items
- Furniture rental
- Late fees

The appraiser should perform a trend analysis of allowable Other Income categories to establish an appropriate Other Income amount. Other Income must be recurring to be included in the appraiser's NOI calculation.

Based on the preceding analysis, the appraiser should select the appropriate level of Other Income. As outlined, an economic vacancy factor of 5% should be applied against all other income (10% against commercial income).

- *Commercial properties.*

Gross Potential Rent. This section should include income from existing leases as well as market rent for current vacant space. It should also include an estimation of economic rent from recent market rental data, with adequate data on comparable properties. The comparable rentals should be actual leases rather than rental listings or quoted rental rates. Each of the comparable rentals should be analyzed for the same characteristics as noted previously under Sales Comparison Approach. A comparable sheet with a photograph should be filled out for each rental used in the report. The analysis should present an in-depth study so that differences in rents between the subject and comparable properties are readily explainable and supportable by adjustments that are representative of factual data. The explanation and justification of any adjustments should be based on careful market analysis, including, but not limited to, time, conditions of sale, location, and physical characteristics. In addition, recent leases signed at the property must also be considered.

Expense Reimbursements. Expense reimbursements for existing tenant leases and future leases should be included as a separate line item. Reimbursements for existing leases should be based on the terms of the lease, and future reimbursements should be supported by market conditions. Furthermore, a discussion of the individual expenses that are being reimbursed must be included. Any variance between the property's historical reimbursement income and the appraiser's estimate must be thoroughly analyzed.

Vacancy Allowance, Concessions, and Credit Loss Factor. The combined Vacancy Allowance, Concessions, and Credit Loss line items should be based on current market conditions. The appraiser's conclusion should include the following:

- Analysis of the property's historical occupancy level for the past three years, based on available data. If the property has historically exhibited a higher vacancy level than the current rent roll indicates, the appraiser should consider applying the historical level to the Gross Potential Rent unless market data supports a higher occupancy level.
- Review of occupancy levels and concessions at comparable properties. The property's projected occupancy should not be greater than market unless supported by strong market comparable data or several years of proven historical operating performance.
- Consideration of the physical vacancy level in the market and any trends in the market which indicate increasing or decreasing occupancy levels. The property's occupancy must be clearly supported by historical operations or other market data.

- Consideration of whether recently completed projects or projects under construction are likely to impact occupancy of the property.
- Consideration of whether concessions or reduced tenant credit qualifications have been used to maintain current occupancy, or whether concessions in the market indicate a potential weakening in the property's occupancy;
- Consideration of the ongoing reduction in collected rents from tenant concessions. In addition, analysis of the significance of concessions in all cases where concessions have or are being granted to tenants in the market in the past year.
- Analysis of historical credit losses as indicated in historical and/or year-to-date operating statements, delinquency/ accounts receivable reports, or other such data to identify any trends in the collection losses.
- Selections of a vacancy allowance, concessions amount, and credit loss factor based on the analysis previously performed. The source for these conclusions must be well documented.

Other Income. Other income derived at the property should be accounted for and estimated based on the historical and projected experience of the subject.

- *Hotel properties.* Hotel financial pro forma statements must follow a format consistent with the Uniform System of Accounts for Hotels (most recent edition). A comparison of the author's projections for a stabilized operating year should be to the latest edition of Smith Travel Research's HOST report or PKF's *Trends in the Hotel Industry,* using appropriate comparisons for each of the following revenue/expense categories.

Room Revenue. Room revenue should be based upon the projected occupancy and average daily rate estimates presented in the Market Analysis section of the report.

Food Revenue. Food revenue is derived from food and nonalcoholic beverage sales at all of the property's food and beverage outlets, including banquet and minibar sales, when applicable, net any allowances, rebates, overcharges, and adjustments. Public room rentals, covers, banquet sundries, and minimum charges are to be included in this department.

Beverage Revenue. Beverage revenue is derived from sales of alcoholic beverages at all of the property's food and beverage outlets, including banquet and minibar sales, when applicable, net any allowances, rebates, overcharges, and adjustments.

Telephone Revenue. Telephone revenues should include all income derived from local and long-distance calls made by the guests, as well as any commissions and service charges, net any allowances, rebates, overcharges, and adjustments. Income derived from fax and modem line use should be included in this department.

Minor Operating Departments. Income in this department is derived from sources including, but not limited to, the following, but only if the hotel operates these departments. If a third-party concessionaire provides these services, revenue derived from these sources should be included in the rental and other income. The sources are as follows:

- Parking garages
- Health club
- Hair salon
- Golf pro shop
- Tennis pro shop
- Spa services
- Gift shop
- Apparel shops
- Checkrooms and washrooms
- Cigar and newsstands
- Liquor stores
- Valet

Rental and Other Income. Income for this department is derived from sources including, but not limited to, the following:

- Rentals of hotel space for business purposes
- Concessions received from third-party businesses operating departments that would normally be operated by the hotel
- Commissions received (e.g., taxicabs, auto rentals, photographs, etc.)
- Interest income
- Vending machines
- Cash discounts earned by paying vendors within the discount period

- Salvage revenue derived from the sale of waste products, incidental articles, or obsolete equipment
- Any revenue sources not distributable under any of the previous departments

This department is always stated net of any departmental expenses.

Expenses. In narrative fashion, the individual expense items should be analyzed before developing a stabilized operating statement. Care should be taken to exclude those items that may rightfully belong in the owner's statement but not in the appraiser's stabilized statement.

In addition to a review of the past expense experience of the property, the report should include a comparison on an item-by-item basis with the expenses incurred by similar buildings in the immediate area (either through direct knowledge of the appraiser or by utilizing composite data such as is available from the National Apartment Association [NAA] or similar industry organizations); allowances may be made for anticipated increases in taxes or other items. The total expenses should be tested or supported by showing total expenses in a ratio to gross income and similar to that of other comparable properties. Adjustments upward should be made for any economies of scale achieved by the borrower or management company as an owner/manager of multiple properties. Clear justification of the appraiser's expense assumptions should be provided.

The appraiser should categorize expenses on commonly accepted categories in the marketplace for similar property types, as follows:

Management Fees
Salaries/Employee Units (multifamily)
Utilities
Water and Sewer
Repairs and Maintenance/Supplies
Grounds Maintenance and Pest Control
Snow and Trash Removal
Marketing and Model Units (multifamily)
Administrative, Legal, and Telephone
Operations and Maintenance (O&M) Program
Miscellaneous Expenses, if any
Real Estate Taxes
Insurance

Personal Property Taxes
Replacement Reserves
Other Fixed Expenses, if any

- *Guidelines for specific line items.* The appraiser should follow the following guidelines for the foregoing specific line items:
  - *Management Fee.* The management fee should be computed based on the market-derived management fees.
  - *Salaries/Employee Units (for multifamily only).* The appraiser should determine that the salary expense figure is consistent with the number of employees needed to effectively manage the property. Included in this line item should be any non-revenue-producing units provided to employees as a form of compensation (exclusive of model units, which are included in Marketing). The number of employees used in this analysis should be appropriate for the property. If current staffing levels are deemed insufficient, an appropriate upward adjustment should be made to this expense line item.
  - *Utilities.* The appraiser should analyze utility expenses (including fuel, gas, and electricity) based on a review of historical operating data as well as discussions with officials of the appropriate utility companies regarding any rate changes which have recently occurred or are contemplated. If gas and electricity are not separately metered and conversion to separate meters is anticipated, this factor should be taken into account in the expense amount calculation.
  - *Water and Sewer.* The appraiser should analyze water and sewer expense based on a review of historical operating data, as well as discussions with officials of the appropriate utility companies regarding any rate changes which have recently occurred or are contemplated.
  - *Repairs and Maintenance/Supplies.* The appraiser should determine that salaries are not included in the Repairs and Maintenance line in the historical operating statements. If the property shows signs of deferred maintenance, this expense line item should be increased to provide for adequate maintenance of the property over time. As part of the analysis of this line item, the appraiser should read the relevant service contracts. The appraiser should eliminate any capital expenditure included in this line item in the historical operating statements.

Grounds Maintenance and Pest Control and Snow and Trash Removal. The appraiser should analyze relevant service contracts to determine whether any increases are contemplated by the vendor(s). If service contracts are not available, potential increases should be discussed directly with major vendors.

Marketing/Model Units (for multifamily only). The appraiser should ensure that marketing expenses relate to the Property only and not to other properties managed by the same management entity. In addition, the appraiser should include the appropriate deduction for model units to the extent that such revenue was included in Gross Potential Rent.

Administrative, Legal, and Telephone. The appraiser should determine that these line items do not include any partnership expenses (e.g., partnership audit fees or legal fees). Administrative expenses should be for the property only and not for other properties managed by the same management entity.

Operations and Maintenance (O&M) Program. Any expenses related to the O&M program should be included in this line item.

Real Estate Taxes. The appraiser should base the real estate tax expense on the current real estate tax level as reflected on the most recent tax invoice(s) and on historical operating data, as well as the appraiser's knowledge of any increases in the millage rate or assessed value.

The potential impact of real estate tax appeals and any resulting reassessments in the property's assessed value should be reflected in the Real Estate Taxes line item only if overwhelming evidence exists to support the lower expense level. Such evidence should *not* include a letter from an attorney or tax appraiser handling the appeal, which indicates that an appeal is likely. An exception may be made if such a letter provides clear evidence that the appeal is likely based on successful appeals of similar properties in the submarket. If a successful real estate tax appeal is assumed, this assumption should be clearly indicated in the appraisal.

The appraiser should also consider the impact of the expiration of any tax abatements when developing an estimate for real estate tax expense.

The appraiser should contact the local taxing authority to confirm the current assessed value, millage rates, and assessment frequency; inquire about the targeted assessed value and status of ongoing appeals or potential changes in the millage rates; and discuss any potential delinquencies for past-due real estate taxes.

Insurance. The appraiser should calculate the cost of the required insurance, as specified in Chap. 2 of this manual, based on historical levels of insurance as well as premiums from recent quotes. Below-market-rate blanket insurance policies should be underwritten at market rate.

Personal Property Taxes and Other Taxes and Assessments. The appraiser should determine if there are any other taxes or assessments that could become liens against the real estate, excluding assessments for capital improvements or personal property taxes or special assessments. Such amounts should be included in the appraiser's analysis.

Replacement Reserves. The appraiser should use a market-derived estimate of reserves based on a review of the engineer's estimate, the physical inspection of the property, or other factors noted by the appraiser.

Total Expenses. The appraiser should correlate the total underwritten expense level on the underwriting summary to historical and year-to-date operating statements and make any necessary adjustments to the calculations.

- *Expense line items for hotel properties only.* The appraiser should observe the following guidelines for the specific line items listed here:

  Departmental Expenses. These expenses are normally stated as percentages of the respective departmental revenues. The appraiser should analyze these expenses based on a review of historical performance (if applicable) as well as on a comparison of operating statistics with properties comparable to the subject.

  - *Rooms.* Expenses for this department include, but are not limited to, salaries and wages for the front desk and housekeeping staffs, employee benefits, china and glassware, linen, contract cleaning, laundry and dry cleaning, licenses, operating supplies, cleaning supplies, guest supplies, paper supplies, printing and stationery, reservation expenses, and uniforms.

- *Food and Beverages.* Expenses for this department include, but are not limited to, salaries and wages for all food and beverage staff members, employee benefits, china and glassware, silver, linen, kitchen fuel, contract cleaning, laundry and dry cleaning, licenses, music and entertainment, operating supplies, cleaning supplies, guest supplies, paper supplies, printing and stationery, and uniforms.
- *Telephone.* Expenses for this department include, but are not limited to, cost of calls, depreciation of telephone equipment, salaries and wages for all operators, employee benefits, equipment changes, other operating expenses, printing and stationery, and uniforms.
- *Minor Operating Departments.* Expenses for this department include, but are not limited to, cost of merchandise sold by the individual departments, salaries and wages for departmental employees, employee benefits, other operating expenses, and uniforms.

Undistributed Operating Expenses. These expenses are normally stated either in dollars per available room or as a percentage of gross revenues, except where noted. The appraiser should analyze these expenses based on a review of historical performance (if applicable) as well as on a comparison of operating statistics with properties comparable to the subject.

- *Administrative and General.* Administrative expenses should be for the property only and not for other properties managed by the same management entity. General liability insurance should be included in this department.
- *Management Fees.* Traditionally stated as a percentage of gross revenue. Management fees should be calculated based on market-derived fees, or based on the existing management contract if it is assumed that the current management company will remain with the property throughout the projection period.
- *Franchise Fees.* Traditionally stated as a percentage of rooms revenue. Franchise fees should be calculated based on market-derived fees, or based on the existing franchise

agreement if it is assumed that the current franchise company will remain with the property throughout the projection period. Only the royalty portion of the franchise fee should be included in this department. Reservation expenses and advertising and marketing expenses should be included in rooms and marketing and advertising departments, respectively.

- *Marketing and Advertising.* The appraiser should ensure that marketing expenses relate to the property only and not to other properties managed by the same management entity. Any marketing component of a franchise fee should be included within this department.
- *Maintenance.* If the property shows signs of deferred maintenance, this expense line item should be increased to provide for adequate maintenance of the property over time. As part of the analysis of this line item, the appraiser should read the relevant service contracts. The appraiser should eliminate any capital expenditure included in this line item in the historical operating statements.
- *Energy.* The appraiser should analyze utility expenses (including fuel, gas, electricity, water, and sewer) based on a review of historical operating data as well as discussions with officials of the appropriate utility companies regarding any rate changes which have recently occurred or are contemplated.

Fixed Charges. These expenses are normally stated as percentages of the respective departmental revenues. The appraiser should analyze these expenses based on a review of historical performance (if applicable) as well as on a comparison of operating statistics with properties comparable to the subject.

- *Real Estate and Personal Property Taxes.* This expense should be calculated based on the analysis detailed in the Real Estate Tax and Assessment Data section of the report.
- *Property Insurance.* This expense should include only the cost of insuring the hotel building and contents against damage or destruction. General liability insurance should be included in the Administrative and General department. Worker's compensation insurance should be allocated to the various departmental expense departments based on the percentage of staff each department has, compared to the entire hotel.

- *Equipment Rentals and Other Fixed Expenses.* This includes all the costs associated with leasing capital equipment.
- *Reserve for Replacement.* This expense is normally stated as a percentage of total gross revenues. The reserve is designed to provide future funding for capital improvement projects. The expense should be calculated based on market averages or per a management or franchise agreement if it is assumed that the contract will remain in force throughout the projection period.

Net Operating Income. This should equal Effective Gross Income minus Total Expenses.

Capital Expenditures/Reserves. Clear justification for any capital expenditure should be presented. This should include an estimate of reserves for replacement of short-lived items.

Net Cash Flow. Net Cash Flow should equal Net Operating Income minus capital expenditures or reserves for replacement and capital expenditures as well as leasing commissions.

Discount Rate. The discount rate used in the valuation analysis should represent a rate which appropriately reflects the risk associated with the reliability of the estimated income stream.

Published survey information on overall investor yield expectations for multifamily properties should be analyzed in order to develop a general range. This should be defined by considering the type of facility under study.

The appraiser should consider all the economic factors affecting the subject project, such as its quality, age, location, size, historic performance levels, competitive position, estimated stabilization period, estimated holding period, and the market yield expectations for properties of this type.

Capitalization Rate. The overall or "going-in" capitalization rate should be developed based on the following considerations:

- All rates should be developed from an analysis of sales comparison data and published investor survey data for multifamily properties, commercial properties, or hotel properties where applicable. Each rate should be explained and analyzed.

- The Band of Investment technique may also be developed but not substituted for market-derived capitalization rates from the comparable sales. This method should also be supported from market data.

The concluded capitalization rate should be bracketed by the improved sales utilized in the report.

The terminal capitalization rate should be developed based on a comparison between the level of risk associated with the property now and 10 years in the future.

Direct Capitalization Value Estimate. The direct capitalization value estimate should take the estimated cash flow from operations after replacement reserves, but before debt service and income taxes, for the first fiscal year and apply a "going-in" capitalization rate to derive a value estimate.

The resulting value should be further deducted for estimated capital expenditures.

Present Value Analysis Value Estimates. This section should take the estimated cash flows from operations after replacement reserves, but before debt service and income taxes, over a 10-year period and discount them back to present value at the chosen discount rate.

Estimated Property Reversionary Proceeds. This section should specify the assumptions made concerning the sale of the property, including date of sale and the terminal capitalization rate used.

Income Approach Value Conclusion. The appraiser should discuss the reasoning behind the choice of a valuation method and conclude the market value of the property as a going concern. A copy of the Argus file must be submitted to Precept. This section should set forth the assumed marketing period.

Reconciliation and Conclusion of Value

The appraiser should consider the quantity and quality of the material available for examination under each approach. This section should discuss the inherent strengths and weaknesses of each approach to the estimate of value for the property. This should be consistent with the stated objective of the appraisal. The appraiser should point out and explain any wide discrepancies between the approaches, although agreement is not required, and demonstrate by sound reasoning the facts and basic analysis which led to the final conclusion.

Exhibits

Exhibits that contribute to a clear understanding of the written report should be part of the appraisal. These exhibits should include, but are not limited to, the following:

- Photographs which portray the property, street views, and comparable sale and rental properties. The photos should be dated and identified.
- Neighborhood maps (including strip occupancy maps for commercial properties).
- Tabulations of critical data such as sales and rentals data and competitive and market historical occupancy and rate statistics. For hotel properties, a Smith Travel Research 5 Year Trends report for the property and its defined competitors or comparable statistics should also be provided.
- Subject plot plan, drawn to scale, showing site dimensions and improvement location(s).
- Subject floor plans or typical floor plan as appropriate.
- Tax map.
- Zoning map.
- Floodplain map.
- Comparable sales sheets for the land and improvement sales utilized in the cost and sales approach, respectively.
- Support in the form of articles or surveys that support the estimated discount and capitalization rates selected in the report.
- Legal description of the property.
- Copies of the appraiser's professional qualifications.
- Site inspection form.
- Competitive lease summary form.
- Occupancy and rental rates form.
- Appraisal Report Summary form.

The report should conclude with the just listed necessary supplementary exhibits and any additional material necessary to assist the reader to visualize the property and to understand the appraisal report.

EXHIBIT A-1 Multifamily Comparables Outline

The appraiser to compare the subject and comparable properties should use the following format.

Subject	**Comp 1**	**Comp 2**	**Comp 3**
Property name			
Address			
Year built			
Square footage			
Number of units			
Vacancy, %			
Distance from subject			
Condition relative to subject			
Location relative to subject			
Monthly rent			
Studio			
One bedroom/one bath			
Two bedroom/one bath			
Two bedroom/two bath			
Three bedrooms			
Other __			
Size, SF			
Studio			
One bedroom/one bath			
Two bedroom/one bath			
Two bedroom/two bath			
Three bedrooms			
Other __			
Typical concessions			
Free rent			
Senior citizen discount			
Reduced security deposit			
Move-in allowance			
Other			
Lease length, months			
Amenities			
Subsidies			

EXHIBIT A-2 Hotel Comparables Outline

The appraiser to compare the subject and comparable properties should use the following format.

Subject	**Comp 1**	**Comp 2**	**Comp 3**
Property name			
Address			
Number of units			
Year built			
Last renovation			
Published rate			
Meeting space (where applicable)			
Square footage			
Maximum capacity			
Food and beverage outlets (where applicable)			
Upscale restaurant			
Full-day restaurant			
Lounge			
Continental breakfast			
Room service			
Other guest amenities (where applicable)			
Indoor/outdoor pool			
Exercise room			
Concierge			
Business center			
Historical occupancy			
Year 1			
Year 2			
Year 3			
Historical average daily rate			
Year 1			
Year 2			
Year 3			

(*continued*)

EXHIBIT A-2 Hotel Comparables Outline (continued)

Subject	Comp 1	Comp 2	Comp 3
Year 1 demand penetration			
Occupied rooms			
Room revenue yield			
Year 1 market segmentation			
Corporate			
Group/meeting			
Leisure			
Extended stay (where applicable)			
Government (where applicable)			
Other (where applicable)			

EXHIBIT A-3 Commercial Comparables Outline

The following format should be used by the appraiser to compare the subject and comparable properties.

Subject	**Comp 1**	**Comp 2**	**Comp 3**
Property name			
Address			
Year built			
Square footage			
Vacancy, %			
Distance from subject			
Condition relative to subject			
Location relative to subject			
Asking monthly rent			
Anchor/large spaces			
Small spaces			
Actual monthly rent			
Anchor/large spaces			
Small spaces			
Expanse structure			
Landlord-paid expenses			
Size, SF			
Tenant finish			
Leasing commissions			
Typical concessions			
Other			
Lease length, months			
Amenities			

ENVIRONMENTAL SITE ASSESSMENTS

Scope of Work

PURPOSE

1. Identify known or potential environmental concerns based on a visual survey, review of readily available documents, and the research and interrogatories as described intentionally herein.
2. Make recommendations and provide cost estimates for addressing the identified or potential environmental concerns and/or conditions.
3. Prepare a written report (the "report") that opines on the subject's environmental condition, including photographs of representative systems and identified or potential concerns.

SCOPE OF WORK

General

The consultant shall review information provided by Precept, make inquiries of the owner, review readily available regulatory databases, and make observations sufficient to identify the presence of recognized environmental concerns.

Consultant should assume that timely and complete access to the property, staff, and documents will be provided by the owner. The owner is to provide sufficient, safe, and readily available access to all areas of the building(s), including roof(s) and mechanical area(s), so as not to impede the consultant's survey procedures.

Should any document, information, or access to portions of the building(s) be requested by the consultant but knowingly withheld by the owner from the consultant, the consultant shall contact Precept. If this information is not provided before the preparation of the consultant's draft report, the consultant shall identify within the report, in the appropriate sections, any information or access requested but denied or not made readily available at the time of the consultant's site visit or the report's writing.

The level and extent of the research and report shall meet the guidelines provided in American Society of Testing and Materials (ASTM) *Standard Practice for Environmental Assessments: Phase I Environmental Site*

Assessment Process, E1527-97, and Standard & Poor's *Structured Finance Ratings: Real Estate Finance Environmental Criteria.*

Survey

Property Survey. Observe property components, systems, and elements that are easily visible and readily accessible for the purpose of identifying environmental concerns. The consultant is not required to remove materials, operate equipment not typically operated by tenants, or conduct any exploratory probing or testing. This is a nonintrusive visual survey. However, the consultant is to make a reasonable attempt at discovery. The law of reason shall prevail.

Survey procedures will consist of the following:

- Walk-around visual survey.
- Note the usage of hazardous or regulated materials and indications of improper storage, usage, or disposal of such materials.
- Identify the presence or potential presence of asbestos-containing materials (ACMs), equipment containing polychlorinated biphenyls (PCBs), aboveground storage tanks (ASTs), underground storage tanks (USTs), materials coated with lead-based paint (LBP), radon, and drinking water supplies not in compliance with applicable federal and state drinking water regulations.
- Take sufficient measurements and counts to adequately justify estimated costs to address identified concerns or to conduct the additional investigation necessary to further define and/or cost out a solution to said concern.

Research. Consultant is to provide the owner with a Presurvey Questionnaire and Disclosure Statement (the "questionnaire") which is to be completed by the owner or its representative and forwarded to the consultant. The questionnaire shall be included as an exhibit within the report, whether or not it is completed by the owner and provided to the consultant.

Research shall be conducted using tenants; service providers; local, state, and federal regulatory agencies; and other readily available resources likely to provide useful information. The following research should be conducted at a minimum. Telephone interviews may be sufficient for most inquiries.

- Interview building management, ownership, and/or tenants.
- Determine the prior use history of the subject and adjacent properties using as many of the following that are both readily available and deemed likely to provide useful information:
  Historical maps
  Aerial photographs
  Local building and zoning information
  City directories
  Ownership records

Review of Documents and Databases. Review pertinent property record and studies, as furnished by Precept and the owner; federal, state and local agency records; and regulatory databases per ASTM guidelines. In general, the documents and databases will address the past and current storage, usage, and disposal of hazardous materials at the subject and neighboring properties.

Representative Sampling. Not every tenant space must be surveyed. However, the envelope of each building, along with base building areas and systems, shall be surveyed should more than one building exist. For multifamily buildings, approximately 10% of the units should be surveyed. Should less than 10% of the units be surveyed, such a percentage shall be sufficient for the consultant to opine with confidence as to the environmental condition of all units.

Photographs. At a minimum, the consultant will take 35-mm photographs of the following:

- View of subject property from curb
- All four sides of single-building properties
- Representative mechanical systems
- Significant or commonly encountered environmental concerns (i.e., evidence of USTs or typical condition of spray-applied, asbestos-containing ceiling texture)

For most assignments, the number of photographs will range from 8 to 12. Each photograph should be captioned.

REPORT

Prepare an Environmental Site Assessment Report document (the "report") that follows the following outline:

1. Cover Page
2. Table of Contents
3. Executive Summary
   a. General Description
   b. Environmental Condition
   c. Recommendations
4. Limiting Conditions and Certifications
5. Purpose and Scope
6. Property Setting
7. Prior Use History
8. Environmental Transaction Screen
9. Regulatory Database Review
10. Exhibits
    a. Annotated Photographs
    b. Questionnaire
    c. Site Plan
    d. Regulatory Database
    e. Consultant's Qualifications

The required documentation of each environmental site assessment report is more fully described as follows. The format follows the table of contents provided.

Executive Summary

General Description. This should be no more than a short paragraph that describes the subject. It should provide salient information such as location, size, age, construction type, apparent occupancy status, etc. Sufficient information should be provided so that the reader can visualize the subject.

Environmental Condition. Each major environmental issue should be rated as (1) acceptable, (2) requires operations and maintenance (O&M), (3) standard solution, (4) concern, or (5) additional study required.

Recommendations. Should any concerns be noted or additional investigation be recommended, the consultant should provide cost estimates for addressing the concern or conducting the additional investigation. For example, conduct a limited subsurface investigation around former dry cleaning operation.

Limiting Conditions and Certifications

This includes limiting conditions, consultant's certifications, etc.

Purpose and Scope

Purpose. Consultant is to provide a short paragraph specifically stating the purpose of the engagement and identifying the subject.

Scope. Consultant is to outline the scope and the methods used to conduct the survey (as outlined herein and in accordance with the consultant's Environmental Site Assessment Agreement), and is to identify the individuals, firms, and/or government agencies interviewed for research purposes.

Property Setting

This section should provide sufficient information regarding the environmental setting of the subject property to determine the likely magnitude of on-site concerns and the likelihood of impact from neighboring properties. Specific areas to cover include topography, hydrology, and geology. The topography discussion shall include a review of a U.S. Geologic Survey (USGS) 7.5-minute series topographic map. Hydrology should include a discussion of surface water bodies on, adjacent to, or near the subject. The likely presence of wetlands should be discussed. If wetlands are suspected and construction contemplated, the consultant should determine whether a formal wetlands delineation is necessary or appropriate, given the proposed plans for construction. Geology should include the types of soil and/or bedrock underlying the subject property. Of particular interest are issues that affect the migration of contamination (i.e., the permeability of soils, depth to groundwater, and anticipated direction of groundwater flow).

Prior Use History

Consultant shall identify all obvious uses of the subject property from the present back to the subject's first developed use, or 1940, whichever is earlier. The consultant should rely on only as many sources as are necessary and both reasonably ascertainable and likely to be useful. Standard historical sources include the following:

- Aerial photographs
- Historical maps
- Property tax files and ownership records
- Local street directories
- Building and zoning department records
- Prior reports
- Interviews

When reviewing sources such as aerial photographs and local street directories that may be available for every year, reviewing these sources over five-year intervals is sufficient (i.e., 1965, 1970, 1975, etc.). If after reviewing all of the standard sources a history dating back to the earlier of the first developed use or 1940 cannot be obtained (i.e., data failure), the consultant should opine as to the level of concern (e.g., low—the property appears to have always been undeveloped or residential, or high—there has been a long history of industrial usage).

Environmental Transaction Screen

The transaction screen should cover the issues outlined in ASTM as well as the additional requirements outlined by Standard & Poor's. Specifically, the following issues should be covered:

- *Asbestos-containing materials (ACMs).* Using dates of construction and/or renovations, and the list of suspect ACMs as listed in Appendix G of *Managing Asbestos in Place—A Building Owner's Guide to Operations and Maintenance Programs for Asbestos-Containing Material* (USEPA, July 1990), determine if it is likely that ACMs are present. Based on the condition of the ACM, recommend either (1) no further action, (2) implement an O&M program, (3) remove damaged ACMs, or (4) conduct additional investigations. If removal is recommended, the presence of asbestos should be confirmed with samples analyzed by polarized light microscopy (PLM); otherwise, no sampling is to be conducted.
- *Polychlorinated biphenyl (PCB)-containing equipment.* An effort should be made to identify any transformers, capacitors, hydraulic lifts, or other equipment suspected of containing PCBs. If suspect equipment is identified, the ownership of the equipment should be identified, evidence of leakage discussed, and recommendation regarding further actions made.

- *Underground storage tanks (USTs).* The current or past presence of USTs should be determined. If USTs are or were present, an effort should be made to identify their location, size, content, and status. For USTs that are and will remain in use, the consultant shall determine if the USTs are in compliance with the technical requirements in effect as of December 1998.
- *Aboveground storage tanks (ASTs).* The condition of any above-ground storage tanks located on the subject property should be described, as should the area surrounding the tanks or any former tanks.
- *Lead-based paint (LBP).* The potential for the presence of LBP should be discussed in light of the age of the buildings, dates of renovation, and the current and proposed uses of the building. The condition of suspected LBP should be described. Based on the condition of the LBP, recommend either (1) no further action, (2) implement an O&M program, (3) remove damaged LBP, or (4) conduct additional investigations. If removal is recommended, the presence of LBP should be confirmed with paint chip samples. If miniblinds are suspected of containing lead, random blinds should be tested using chemical reaction swabs.
- *Radon.* The potential for radon to exist within any facility on the property at levels in excess of 4 picocuries per liter should be discussed, given the construction and use of the facility. For residential properties in areas with a high propensity for elevated levels of radon (Zone 1) or undetermined potential, two short-term radon samples should be collected.
- *Lead in drinking water.* The potential for elevated lead levels in drinking water should be discussed in light of the age of the building and associated piping and dates of any renovations.

It is important that a conclusion be made for each of the topics covered. The conclusions generally will consist of either (1) acceptable, (2) requires O&M, (3) standard remedy, or (4) additional investigation is warranted.

The report shall document each source that was used, even if a source revealed no findings. Sources shall be sufficiently documented, including name, date of request, date request for information was filled, and date information was last updated by the source, so as to facilitate reconstruction of the research at a later date.

Regulatory Database Review

Readily available regulatory databases shall be reviewed to identify whether the subject or neighboring properties are likely to have used, stored, generated, or released hazardous or regulated materials in a manner likely to have impacted the subject property. The following databases and radii should be reviewed:

Database	Radius
Federal National Priorities List (NPL) [Superfund] site list	1.0 mile
Federal Comprehensive Environmental Response, Compensation, and Liability Information System (CERCLIS) list	0.5 mile
Federal Resource Conservation and Recovery Act (RCRA) Corrective Action Sites Treatment, Storage, and Disposal (CORRACTS TSD) facilities list	1.0 mile
Federal RCRA non-CORRACTS TSD facilities list	0.5 mile
Federal RCRA Generators list	Property and adjoining properties
Federal Emergency Response Notification System (ERNS) list	Property only
State equivalent of NPL	1.0 mile
State equivalent of CERCLIS	0.5 mile
State landfill and/or solid waste disposal site lists	0.5 mile
State leaking UST list	0.5 mile
State registered UST list	Property and adjoining properties

Each identified site should be discussed and a conclusion made as to whether the site is likely or unlikely to have impacted the subject. The sites can be grouped for discussion purposes (e.g., 10 of the 12 identified leaking underground storage tank [LUST] sites are located downgradient of the subject and, therefore, are unlikely to impact the subject). Distance alone is not sufficient to write off a site, unless backed by studies, low permeability of intervening soils, or other information.

PROPERTY CONDITION ASSESSMENTS

Scope of Work

PURPOSE

1. Identify significant defects, deficiencies, items of deferred maintenance, and material building code violations (individually and collectively, *physical deficiencies*) as a result of a visual survey, review of documents, and the research and interrogatories as described intentionally herein.
2. Prepare estimated costs to remedy the physical deficiencies.
3. Prepare an ongoing physical needs schedule for a 12-year period. For single-tenant properties with a remaining lease term in excess of 12 years, the consultant must include an additional ongoing physical needs estimate for the remaining lease term.
4. Prepare a written report (the "report") that opines on the subject's overall physical condition, including photos of representative systems and major physical deficiencies, and provides estimated costs both to remedy physical deficiencies and for annual replacement reserves expenditures.

SCOPE OF WORK

General

The consultant shall review available information to be provided by Precept, make inquiries of the owner, make observations sufficient to establish the type and approximate extent of physical deficiencies, and take representative measurements and quantity counts to estimate the cost to remedy physical deficiencies and to prepare the replacement reserve schedule.

Consultant should assume timely and complete access to the property, staff, and vendors, and that the owner will provide documents. The owner is to provide sufficient, safe, and readily available access to all areas of the building(s), including roofs, so as not to impede the consultant's survey procedures.

Should any document, vendor access, or information be requested by the consultant but knowingly withheld by the owner from the consultant, the consultant shall contact Precept. If this information is not provided before the preparation of the consultant's draft report, the consultant shall identify within the report, in the appropriate sections, any information or access requested but denied or not made readily available at the time of the consultant's site visit or the report's writing.

Survey

Property Survey. Observe property components, systems, and elements that are easily visible and readily accessible for the purposes of identifying significant physical deficiencies. The consultant is not required to prepare detailed calculations, remove materials, operate equipment not typically operated by tenants, or conduct any exploratory probing or testing. This is a nonintrusive visual survey. However, the consultant is to make a reasonable attempt at discovery. The law of reason shall prevail.

Survey procedures will consist of the following:

- Walk-around visual survey.
- Randomly operating equipment, fixtures, and systems which are normally operated by tenants, on a sampling basis to determine system operability or operating characteristics.
- Noting material building code violations of times, systems, or design that are readily apparent as a result of the walk-through survey.
- Taking measurements and system counts to adequately justify estimated costs to remedy physical deficiencies and to estimate replacement reserve expenditures. The basis for these estimated costs (unit of measure, quantity, and unit cost) must be substantiated within the report.

Research. Consultant is to provide the owner with a Presurvey Questionnaire and Disclosure Schedule (the "questionnaire") and a Property Condition Assessment Document and Information Checklist (the "checklist"), which are to be completed by the owner or its representative and forwarded to the consultant (examples follow). The questionnaire and checklist shall be included as exhibits within the consultant's report, whether or not the owner completes and provides them to the consultant.

Research shall be conducted using tenants, service providers, and those knowledgeable about the subject as sources. The following research should be conducted at a minimum. Telephone interviews may be sufficient for most inquiries.

- Interviews of building management and ownership and tenant(s)
- Review of historical repair and improvement costs incurred by tenants and ownership, along with the following documents:
  - Certificates of occupancy
  - Maintenance reports and logs
  - Passenger and freight elevator safety
  - Inspection reports
  - Warranty information

Review of Documents. Review pertinent property records and studies as furnished by Precept and/or the owner. In general, document information will consist primarily of owner-supplied leasing literature, historical receipts for repairs and/or improvements, schedules of component replacements or improvements complete with the costs incurred for same, pending proposals, schedule of landlord responsible operating expenses, etc. There may also be previously prepared property condition survey reports, appraisals, an Americans with Disabilities Act (ADA) survey (if applicable), etc. that should be provided to the consultant as well.

Representative Sampling. Not every tenant space must be surveyed. However, the envelope of each building along with base building areas and systems shall be surveyed should more than one building exist. For multifamily buildings, as a guide, approximately 10% of the units should be surveyed. Should less than 10% of the units be surveyed, such percentage shall be sufficient for the consultant to opine with confidence as to the typical general condition of all units.

Photographs. At a minimum, the Consultant will take 35-mm photographs of the following:

- View of subject property from curb
- Representative elevations
- Typical mechanical, electrical, and plumbing systems
- Landscape photos of roof areas
- Landscape photos of parking and truck loading areas taken from roof vantage points
- Significant or commonly encountered physical deficiencies

For most assignments, the number of photographs will range from 20 to 40. Each photograph should be described.

REPORT

Prepare a Property Condition Assessment Report document (the "report") that follows this outline:

1. Cover Page
2. Table of Contents
3. Executive Summary
   a. General Description
   b. General Condition
   c. Estimated Required Expenditures
      (1) Deferred Maintenance and Physical Deficiencies
      (2) Ongoing Physical Needs
   d. Recommendations
4. Limiting Conditions and Certification
5. Purpose and Scope
6. Description and Condition
7. Cost Estimates to Remedy Deficiencies
8. Ongoing Physical Needs Analysis
9. Exhibits
   a. Annotated Photographs
   b. Presurvey Questionnaire and Disclosure Schedule
   c. Property Condition Assessment Document and Information Checklists
   d. Reduced Plot or Site Plans, etc.
   e. Consultant's Qualifications

The required content of each property condition survey report (short-form format) is more fully described as follows. The format follows the report's table of contents provided.

EXECUTIVE SUMMARY

General Description. This should be no more than a short paragraph that describes the subject. It should provide salient information such as location, size, age, construction type, apparent occupancy status, etc. Sufficient information should be provided so that the reader can visualize the subject.

General Condition. The opening paragraph should opine on the subject's general condition and the apparent level of preventive maintenance exercised, significant deferred maintenance, and material physical deficiencies. If any significant improvements were recently implemented, this information should be provided as well. Should any of the consultant's research result in either significantly positive or negative responses, provide this information. Do not dwell on minor deficiencies.

The consultant is then to provide a numbered schedule of the major physical deficiencies observed, complete with a concise description and proposed remedy.

Estimated Required Expenditures
Deferred Maintenance and Physical Deficiencies. Summarize the total of the derived cost estimates to cure physical deficiencies requiring remedy within one year of the report date.

Ongoing Physical Needs. Summarize the derived cost estimates to cure anticipated ongoing physical needs beginning 1 year after the report date and ending 11 years later (for a total evaluation period of 12 years, unless otherwise specified by Precept). For single-tenant properties with a remaining lease term in excess of 12 years, the consultant shall include an additional ongoing physical needs schedule for a period equal to the remaining lease term.

Recommendations. Should any condition be suspect and warrant further research, testing, removal of material, etc., this recommendation should be placed in this section. Examples would be recommendations for eddy current testing of chillers, roof infrared surveys, scaffold inspections, etc.

Limiting Conditions and Certification

This includes limiting conditions, consultant's certifications, etc.

Purpose and Scope

Purpose. Consultant is to provide a short paragraph specifically stating the purpose of this engagement and identifying the subject.

Scope. Consultant is to outline the scope and the methods used to conduct the survey (as outlined herein and in accordance with the consultant's Property Condition Assessment Agreement), and is to identify the individuals, firms, and/or governmental agencies interviewed for research purposes.

Description and Condition

The succeeding sections should be presented in a narrative form and may need to consist of only a few sentences and, in some cases, simply phrases. This information can be presented in either tabular or outline form. Excessively detailed descriptions, such as providing model or serial numbers of mechanical equipment, are unwarranted. If access or visual observation was impaired, denied, or limited, or if pertinent information was denied or realized as a result of the consultant's research or interviews, provide the results of same in the appropriate sections.

This section should include the following: item description; size, condition, observations, and comments; expected useful life (EUL); age; and remaining useful life (RUL). It should be presented as in the example that follows. Please provide sufficient descriptive information to support an opinion. Simply stating that the "roof is poor" is insufficient. The opinion should be adequately supported, and a recommended remedy should accompany it.

Item/ Description	Size/Condition and Comments	EUL	Age	RUL
Roofing Flat BUR ☐ Pitched shingle ☑ Clay tile ☐ Metal seam ☐ Other_____ ☐	Pitched hip roofs with asphalt composition shingles. Roofs replaced in 1991. Some leakage noted around the flashing. Repair as a physical deficiency.	20–25	7	13–18

As an exhibit, the consultant is to provide representative color photographs showing typical elevations, site improvements, common or base building areas, and commonly encountered and/or major physical deficiencies.

Text, in caption format adjacent to each photo, should identify the location, describe the system or component shown, and direct the reader to any certain condition or physical deficiencies depicted.

Seismic Requirements. For buildings located in California and Hawaii, and in all other Zone 1 and Zone 2 areas of the United States, as outlined in the earthquake seismic zone outline that follows, the following requirements shall apply:

- Review and report on available geotechnical information (geotechnical reports, soil borings, foundation system studies, etc.). Comment on the soil type and geotechnical features, and assess the potential for the following collateral hazards: liquefaction, landslide, and surface fault rupture.
- Identify and report on any catalogued active faults within a 50-mile radius (at the closest point) of the subject site. Report their expected maximum credible magnitudes and their approximate distance from the subject site.
- Review and report on available drawings as they pertain to the designed gravity (dead and live) and lateral (earthquake or wind, whichever is greater) loads and on the existing gravity- and lateral-force-resisting systems of the structures.
- Conduct a site visit to visually review as-built conditions as they comply with the drawings submitted, if any, and to identify structural deficiencies as they pertain to inadequate gravity and horizontal loading under current code requirements.

Estimate the probable maximum loss (PML) as a percentage of the current building replacement cost based on a 450-year average recurrence interval. The 450-year PML is to be based on a 10% probability of being exceeded in a 50-year period.

Cost Estimates to Remedy Deficiencies

Prepare a general scope based on (1) the consultant's observations during its site visit, and (2) information received from interviews with building management, tenants, and service personnel, which for purposes of the report will be deemed to be reliable, and include preliminary cost estimates complete with an appropriate recommended remedy for each significant physical deficiency. This remedy must be commensurate with the subject and considered a prudent expenditure. Simply stating "poor roof" and providing a lump-sum cost to cure is insufficient. Physical deficiencies shall include the following:

- Physical deficiencies that require immediate action as a result of (1) existing or potentially unsafe conditions, (2) significant negative conditions impacting tenancy or marketability, (3) material building code violations, (4) poor or deteriorated condition of critical element or system, or (5) a condition that if left as is, with an extensive delay in addressing same, would result in or contribute to critical element or system failure within one year of the report date.

- Physical deficiencies that are inclusive of deferred maintenance and that may not warrant immediate attention, but which require repairs or replacements that should be undertaken on a priority basis, taking precedence over routine preventive maintenance work within a zero- to one-year time frame. Included are such physical deficiencies resulting from improper design, faulty installation, and/or substandard quality of original system or materials. Components or systems that have realized or exceeded their expected useful life (EUL) and may require replacement within a zero- to one-year time frame are also included.

The consultant's estimated costs are deemed to be preliminary. These costs are to be net of general conditions, construction management fees, and design fees. The consultant is to use market costs or historical costs incurred by the owner that are documented and/or have been substantiated to the consultant's satisfaction. However, these costs must be reasonable market costs. The owner should document these costs by submitting paid invoices, executed or pending bona fide proposals, etc.

The basis of the derivation of these costs must be provided with respect to nominal quantities and the unit costs used; a rational approach to the derivation of the cost estimate must be provided. All cost information must be submitted in a format similar to the schedule titled "Cost Estimate to Remedy Deficiencies" that follows this guideline, complete with quantities, unit costs, and totals.

Ongoing Physical Needs Analysis

The consultant shall identify all capital components or systems typically requiring replacement or repair from 1 year after the date of the report and continuing through Year 12 of the ongoing physical needs schedule. For single-tenant properties with a remaining lease term in excess of 12 years, the consultant shall include an additional Ongoing Physical Needs Schedule document for a period equal to the remaining lease term. The consultant should include in the schedule any item or system that has a predictable expected useful life and/or is not subject to routine preventive maintenance.

The Ongoing Physical Needs Schedule form should encompass short-lived, mid-lived and long-lived recurring systems and components. Short-term recurring systems and components are typically such items as exterior caulking, pavement sealing and striping, etc. Mid-lived recurring systems are typically cooling towers, paving, roofing, domestic hot water heaters, etc. Long-lived items are typically boilers, chillers, electrical systems, infrastructure components, supply and drainage piping, etc.

The following methodology should be employed when completing the Ongoing Physical Needs Schedule form. Submit these schedules in a spreadsheet format. An example of a typical schedule follows.

Do Not Double-Dip. In other words, if the consultant identifies that the roof requires replacement as a short-term item under Cost Estimates to Remedy Deficiencies, do not require its replacement under Year 1 in the ongoing physical needs schedule. Treat the roof as if it were new, with a remaining useful life (RUL) equal to its commonly anticipated expected useful life (EUL).

Opine on EUL and EFF AGE. The consultant is allowed to use its professional judgment in determining when a system or component will require replacement. Inclement weather, exposure to the elements, initial quality and installation, extent of use, and the degree of preventive maintenance exercised are all factors that could impact the RUL of a system or component. As a result of the aforementioned items, a system or component may have an *effective age* (EFF AGE) greater or less than its *actual age* (ACT AGE). For instance, a parking lot with an EUL of 18 years that has been religiously sealed with a squeegee-applied asphaltic emulsion slurry coat may have an EFF AGE equal to 8 years although its ACT AGE is 12 years. Therefore, its RUL will be 10 years (18 – 8) instead of 6 years (18 – 12). When there is a significant deviation from common EULs, the text in the Description and Condition section must complement same. Should the owner differ from the consultant as to a component or system's EUL, the owner must substantiate this opinion with schedules, invoices, etc. The consultant is not to accept unsubstantiated EULs.

Phase Replacements. Consultant may exercise professional judgment as to the rate or phasing of replacements. For instance, suppose that an office complex has an extensive quantity of paving that will realize its EUL in Year 8. Instead of requiring the replacement of all paving in Year 8, which would be a significant cost to be incurred in any single year, the consultant may phase the work over three years; i.e., the consultant may replace 40% in Year 8, 40% in Year 9, and 20% in Year 10. However, make sure that the other replacements recommended that complement same are also completed in this phase. For instance, if the paving overlay is to be completed in phases, so must the striping. However, do not phase work that is of only limited scope, such as surfacing a 2000-square-yard parking lot, since prudent management would not phase such a small quantity of pavement resurfacing.

Phase replacement scheduling is also appropriate for allocating asbestos removal and abatement costs, inasmuch as such work commonly coincides with lease termination.

Component Replacements. Certain mechanical equipment can be broken down into commonly replaced individual major components so that funding to replace the entire piece of equipment at one time is not necessary. For example, the overall cost of a boiler may include pumps, a burner, etc., which may require replacement on a schedule different from that of the entire boiler.

Replacements Made Thus Far. Take into consideration if management has already begun a program of replacing multiple or single components that have realized their EUL. If, as a result of research, the consultant learns the extent of such replacements made to date, the consultant shall take this into consideration. In some instances, the consultant may use weighted average EULs and EFF AGEs. The onus is on management to substantiate the replacements made and the reported costs incurred by submitting documentation to the consultant. Such documents should be included as an exhibit to the report.

Term. Complete an Ongoing Physical Needs Schedule form for a term of 12 years (or as otherwise instructed by Precept).

Replacement. Replacement costs used shall be market or owner's historical incurred costs, or substantiated third-party costs. Should the owner differ from the consultant as to a component's or system's replacement cost, the owner must substantiate this opinion by submitting paid invoices, executed proposals, receipts, bona fide pending proposals, etc. The consultant is not to accept unsubstantiated replacement costs offered by the owner.

Exhibits

The consultant should append any exhibits that illustrate or clarify information presented in the body of the report. Pertinent documents such as annotated photographs, site plans, consultant's qualifications, and other relevant information should be provided where available and useful.

The Presurvey Questionnaire and Disclosure Schedule and the Property Condition Assessment Document and Information Checklist should be appended whether or not the Owner or its representative has completed them.

Text, in caption format adjacent to each photo, is to identify the location, describe the system or component shown, and direct the reader to any certain condition or physical deficiencies depicted.

Photos are to be sequentially organized into the following categories:

- Site work
- Building envelope
- Interior
- Plumbing
- HVAC
- Electrical
- Elevators

PRESURVEY QUESTIONNAIRE AND DISCLOSURE SCHEDULE

Borrower: Complete this questionnaire before the consultant's site visit. For those questions that are not applicable to the subject, please respond with "N/A." This document must be signed on the last page of this questionnaire by the borrower or its representative. If you have any questions about how to answer any of the questions, please call the consultant. If additional pages for response are necessary, please attach them to this form. Clearly mark all references to the appropriate question number(s). This document, and your written response to same, will be an exhibit in the consultant's report.

Project name: ______________________________

Property no.: ______________________________

Date: ______________________________

Address: ______________________________

Property owner: ______________________________

Fax: ______________________________

Telephone: ______________________________

Building manager: ______________________________

Fax: ______________________________

Telephone: ______________________________

1. What is the current occupancy of the building(s), expressed as a percentage?
2. If the subject is a multifamily building, what is the approximate lease turnover rate?
3. To the best of your knowledge, does the building have any of the following problems and, if so, where are they located?
   a. Roof or sidewalk leakage? Yes No
   b. Structural problems? Yes No
   c. Cellar/basement water/moisture infiltration? Yes No
   d. Heating capacity or distribution deficiencies? Yes No
   e. Air-conditioning capacity or distribution deficiencies? Yes No

f. Inadequate domestic water pressure or drainage problems? Yes No
g. Elevator service problems? Yes No
h. Inadequate electrical capacity or distribution? Yes No
i. Presence of any friable asbestos? Yes No

4. Are maintenance and/or complaint logs kept for any of the following systems? Yes No
a. Plumbing Yes No
b. Heating Yes No
c. Air conditioning Yes No
d. Elevators Yes No

5. Is the boiler water treated? If so, by whom? Yes No

6. Is the cooling-tower water treated? If so, by whom? Yes No

7. When were the chillers' last eddy-current tested? Who performed the test?

8. When was the fire alarm system last tested?

9. Has any exterior restoration or repair work been performed during the last five years? If so, what was the scope of this work and who performed the work? Yes No

10. Does the building have any structural, mechanical or electrical deficiencies or problems that you are aware of that would be of interest or concern to a possible purchaser or mortgagee? Yes No

11. Are you in receipt of or have you solicited any proposals to perform any repairs or replacement work to the building(s) or any of its components that will exceed an aggregate cost of $2000? Yes No

12. To the best of your knowledge, has the building, or any portion thereof, been surveyed during the last three years to opine on its physical condition? If so, who conducted this survey and when was it performed? Yes No

13. During the last five years, have any major capital improvements been made to the site or building? If so, please provide a schedule of same along with the approximate cost incurred. Yes No

14. Please complete the following schedule as to the status of replacement of any recurring components, items, or systems:

Item or System	Quantity Replaced Thus Far	Date Replaced	Average Cost for Replacement	
Asphalt pavement sealant			$ /SY	
Asphalt paving			$ /SY	
Roofing			$ /SY or	/bldg.
Carpeting			$ /SY or	/unit
Vinyl flooring			$ /SY or	/unit
Ceramic tiling			$ /SY or	/unit
Refrigerators			$ /each	
Rangers/stoves			$ /each	
Dishwashers			$ /each	
Garbage disposal units			$ /each	
A/C condenser units			$ /each	
Air-handling units			$ /each	
Central boiler			$ /each	
Oil/gas burner			$ /each	
Individual unit furnaces			$ /unit	
Individual domestic hot water heaters			$ /each	
Kitchen cabinets			$ /each	
Kitchen countertops			$ /each	
Heat-pump units			$ /each	
Vanities			$ /each	
Swimming pool resurfacing			$ /pool	
Swimming pool pump and filter			$ /each	
Tennis court resurfacing			$ /court	

Signature ____________________ Date ____________________

Name ____________________ ____________________

Title ____________________

Property Condition Assessment Document and Information Checklist

Please provide the consultant with the following documents and information so that the consultant may proceed with the physical evaluation of the building(s). This document, complete with consultant's comments and date of receipt of documentation and information requested, will become an exhibit in the consultant's report.

Document	Date Received	Comments
A. As-built plans and specifications		
1. Survey		
2. Site plans		
3. Structural		
4. Architectural		
5. Mechanical		
6. Electrical		
B. Municipal department documents		
1. Certificate of occupancy or temporary certificate of occupancy		
2. Building permit		
3. Schedule of building code violations		
4. Zoning variances or restrictions		
C. Promotional/leasing information		
1. Copy of the most recent appraisal		
2. Promotional leasing/sales literature		
3. Tenant SFR schedule		
4. Location map		
D. Building maintenance history		
1. Age of the building		
2. Owner's name and telephone number		
3. Building manager's name and telephone and fax numbers		
4. Building superintendent's name and telephone number		
5. Names and telephone numbers of services firms		
a. Facade repairs/restoration		
b. Roofing		
c. Plumbing		

Document	Date Received	Comments
d. Water tower		
e. Heating		
f. Boiler water treatment		
g. Air conditioning		
h. Cooling tower		
i. Electrical		
j. Elevators		
k. Sprinkler/standpipe system		
l. Swimming pool		
m. Life/safety alarm system		
E. **Miscellaneous certification/studies**		
1. Appraisal		
2. Roof condition survey		
3. Elevator inspection certificate		
4. Boiler inspection certificate		
5. Certificate of electrical compliance		
6. Asbestos survey		
7. Asbestos abatement approvals and sign-offs		
8. Phase I environmental assessment report		
9. Previously prepared due diligence condition survey reports		
10. Sprinkler system/standpipe survey prepared by insurance company		
11. Tenant complaint log		
12. Schedule of floor area measurements: gross, usable, and rentable SF		
13. Schedule of deficiencies or statement of violations—issued by a state agency		
14. Schedule of operating expenses		
15. Schedule of CAM expenses		
16. Previously prepared replacement reserve studies		
17. Fire alarm inspection report as per NFPA 72		

N/A—Not applicable or not available.

EARTHQUAKE SEISMIC ZONES

State	Zone 1 Counties	Zone 2 Counties
Alaska	All but North Slope Borough	North Slope Borough
Arkansas	None	Clay, Craighead, Crittenden, Cross, Greene, Jackson, Mississippi, Pointsett
Idaho	None	Bannock, Bear Lake, Caribou, Clark, Franklin, Freemont, and Oneida
Illinois	None	Alexander, Massac, Pulaski, and Union
Kentucky	None	Ballard, Carlisle, Fulton, Graves, Hickman, and McCracken
Mississippi	None	De Soto
Missouri	None	Bollinger, Butler, Cape Girardeau, Dunklin, Mississippi, New Madrid, Pemiscot, Scott, and Stoddard
Montana	None	Beaverhead, Broadwater, Flathead, Gallatin, Jefferson, Lewis and Clark, Park, Powell, and Yellowstone National Park
Nevada	All but Clark, Elko, Eureka, and White Pine	Lincoln
Puerto Rico	Entire commonwealth	
Tennessee	None	Crockett, Dyer, Haywood, Lake, Lauderdale, Obion, Shelby, and Tipton
Utah	None	All but Daggett, Grand, San Juan, Uintah, Beaver, Carbon, Duchesne, Emery, Garfield, Iron, Kane, Piute, Washington, and Wayne
Washington	None	Clallam Island, Jefferson, King, Kitsap, Mason, Pierce, San Juan, Skagit, Snohomish, Thurston, and Whatcom
Wyoming	None	Teton and Yellowstone National Park

COST ESTIMATE TO REMEDY DEFICIENCIES

Necessary Repairs Within One Year

Item	Quantity & Unit	Unit Cost	Repair Estimate
SITE			
Asphaltic-concrete pavement—There are several areas of pavement that need to be repaired, as cracking was observed (see photo no. 14). The stress cracks need to be filled with sealant.	2000 s.f.	$2.00	$4000
Asphalt sealing—Pavement is bleached and oil stained at parking spots. Prolong longevity and improve the complex's general aesthetics by applying an emulsion asphalt sealant. Prepare surfaces by sealing all cracks, patching deficiencies, and removing oil staining. Apply 2 coats of emulsion-based asphalt sealant, containing 4 lb of sand per gal plus 4% latex additive, to entire asphalt paved area in that location.			
Asphalt striping—Striping is faded throughout the paved parking areas (see photo no. 15). Lay out and restripe entire parking lot using reflectorized paint, with white or yellow 4″ wide painted lines for car stalls, handicap areas, fire zones, and traffic flow.			
Regrade cluster perimeters—Crawl-space flooding is occurring at Building No. 10. Similar conditions were noted at Buildings No. 9 and 11. Foundation wall backfill has settled and the situation has been aggravated by stormwater ponding adjacent to the foundation. These conditions are contributing to crawl-space water seepage and high-humidity problems, which are conducive to rot and termite infestation. Spread and compact additional soil to promote positive drainage away from sidewalks.			
Site lighting—Install 3 new high-pressure, sodium fixtured lighting standards near Buildings No. 10 and 11 to illuminate unsafe areas.			

Item	Quantity & Unit	Unit Cost	Repair Estimate
EXTERIOR			
Exterior painting—Paint on hardboard siding and rough-sawn trim is faded, mildew stained, and deteriorated at all units. Such conditions will eventually lead to rot and deterioration of wood surfaces. Scrape worn painted surfaces, and brush-apply 2 coats of exterior latex paint on the hardboard siding, trim, window frames, and exterior doors. Apply sealant to all open joints.			
Misc. exterior carpentry repairs—Numerous years of deferred maintenance have led to the deterioration of miscellaneous wood trim components at cluster exteriors. Secure loose and cupped rough-sawn battens and loose and hanging soffit panels, and replace rotted cave and fascia trim. Also replace miscellaneous rotted exterior door jambs, sheathing, deteriorated trim sections, etc.			
Asphalt shingle roofing—Remove existing asphalt shingles down to plywood sheathing. Replace damaged sheathing as necessary. Install new #235 asphalt shingle roofs, complete with flashings, at each building.			
MECHANICAL/ELECTRICAL/PLUMBING			
Electric Domestic Hot Water Heaters—Existing domestic hot water heaters have reached their expected useful lives. Budget to replace with new electric domestic hot water heaters, complete with new temperature and pressure safety release valve piped to the floor.			
Bathroom vents—Bathroom vents exhaust in the attic spaces of the units, as in the cases of Units No. 405 and 609, creating warm, humid conditions that have contributed to minor rot and decay of the roof sheathing. Extend bathroom vent ducts though the roofs and terminate with proper flashing and caps.			

Item	Quantity & Unit	Unit Cost	Repair Estimate
INTERIOR			
Carpet—Many units contain dated carpeting that is in need of replacement. Remove existing carpeting and padding, and install new carpet.			
Kitchen vinyl floor covering—Worn, dated vinyl kitchen flooring was reported at most units in the development. Remove existing vinyl flooring, which is said to be faded and lifting at seams, and replace.			
Bathroom vinyl flooring—Worn, dated vinyl flooring was observed at representative bathrooms. Remove discolored and lifting vinyl bathroom flooring and replace with new.			
		Total:	

Ongoing Physical Needs Schedule	**Total GSF:**	**55,821**
[Property Name]	**No. of Bldgs:**	**2**
[Property Address 1]	**Reserve Term:**	**12 years**
[Property Address 2]	**Property Age:**	**11 years**
[Date]		

Sec	Item Description	EUL	Quantity	Unit of Measure	Unit Cost	Total Cost
5.2	Asphalt overlay					
5.2	Building pavement (sealing over term)					
	Building-mounted HID lighting					
	Roof covering, built-up system					
	Exterior walls, painting and coating					
	Rooftop package unit, per ton					
	DHW heaters <150 gal					
	Elevator, cab interiors and doors					
	Total					
	Cost per square foot					
	Average per square foot per year					

Year 1	Year 2	Year 3	Year 4	Year 5	Year 6	Year 7	Year 8	Year 9	Year 10	Year 11	Year 12	Total

INDEX

C

D

E

G

H

ABOUT THE AUTHORS

Precept is today's most important and influential electronic commercial mortgage exchange. Backed by many of Wall Street's leading firms, and working in partnership with Standard & Poor's, it stands at the forefront of commercial mortgage origination, underwriting, placement, and securitization.